T0302148

Accountability, International Business Operations, and the Law

A consensus has emerged that corporations have societal and environmental responsibilities when operating transnationally. However, how exactly corporations can be held legally accountable for their transgressions, if at all, is less clear.

This volume inquires how regulatory tools stemming from international law, public law, and private law may or may not be used for transnational corporate accountability purposes. Attention is devoted to applicable standards of liability, institutional and jurisdictional issues, and practical challenges, with a focus on ways to improve the existing legal status quo. In addition, there is consideration of the extent to which non-legal regulatory instruments may complement or provide more viable alternatives to these legal mechanisms. The book combines legal-doctrinal approaches with comparative, interdisciplinary, and policy insights with the dual aim of furthering the legal scholarly debate on these issues and enabling higher quality decision-making by policymakers seeking to implement regulatory measures that enhance corporate accountability in this context. Through its study of contemporary developments in legislation and case law, it provides a timely and important contribution to the scholarly and sociopolitical debate in the fast-evolving field of international corporate social responsibility and accountability.

Liesbeth Enneking is Endowed Professor on the Legal Aspects of International Corporate Social Responsibility at Erasmus School of Law, Erasmus University Rotterdam.

Ivo Giesen is Professor of Private Law, member of Utrecht Centre for Accountability and Liability Law (UCALL) and Head of Utrecht School of Law, Utrecht University.

Anne-Jetske Schaap is PhD candidate at UCALL and the Criminal Law department of Utrecht School of Law, Utrecht University.

Cedric Ryngaert is Professor of Public International Law and member of UCALL, Utrecht School of Law, Utrecht University.

François Kristen is Professor of Criminal Law and Criminal Procedure and program leader of UCALL, Utrecht School of Law, Utrecht University.

Lucas Roorda is policy advisor at the Netherlands Institute for Human Rights and PhD candidate at UCALL and the International and European Law department of Utrecht School of Law, Utrecht University.

Globalization: Law and Policy

Globalization: Law and Policy builds an integrated body of scholarship that critically addresses key issues and theoretical debates in comparative and transnational law and the principles governance and policy on which they are developed. Volumes in the series focus on the consequential effects of globalization, including emerging frameworks and processes for the internationalization, legal harmonization, juridification, and democratization of law among increasingly connected political, economic, religious, cultural, ethnic, and other functionally differentiated governance communities. Legal systems, their harmonization and incorporation in other governance orders, and their relationship to globalization are taking on new importance within a coordinated network of domestic legal orders, the legal orders of groups of states, and the governance frameworks of non-state actors. These legal orders engage a number of important actors, sources, principles, and tribunals-including multinational corporations as governance entities, contract and surveillance as forms of governance that substitute for traditional law, sovereign wealth funds and other new forms of state activity, hybrid supra national entities like the World Bank and the International Monetary Fund, and international tribunals with autonomous jurisdiction, including the International Criminal Court, the World Trade Organization, and regional human rights courts. The effects have been profound, especially with respect to the role of states, and especially of developed states as their long time position in global affairs undergoes significant transformation. Comparative and transnational law serve as natural nexus points for vigorous and sometimes interdisciplinary approaches to the study of state and non-state law systems, along with their linkages and interactions. The series is intended as a resource for scholars, students, policy makers, and civil society actors, and includes a balance of theoretical and policy studies in single-authored volumes and collections of original essays.

Larry Catá Backer is the W. Richard and Mary Eshelman Faculty Scholar, Professor of Law and International Affairs at the Pennsylvania State University. Previously he served as Executive Director of the Comparative and International Law Center at the University of Tulsa. He has published widely on comparative and transnational law.

Also in the series

Legal and Rhetorical Foundations of Economic Globalization
An Atlas of Ritual Sacrifice in Late-Capitalism
Keren Wang

Accountability, International Business Operations, and the Law
Providing Justice for Corporate Human Rights Violations in Global Value Chains
Liesbeth Enneking, Ivo Giesen, Anne-Jetske Schaap, Cedric Ryngaert, François Kristen, and Lucas Roorda (eds.)

For more information about this series, please visit: www.routledge.com/Globalization-Law-and-Policy/book-series/GLOBLP

Accountability, International Business Operations, and the Law

Providing Justice for Corporate Human Rights Violations in Global Value Chains

Edited by Liesbeth Enneking, Ivo Giesen, Anne-Jetske Schaap, Cedric Ryngaert, François Kristen, and Lucas Roorda

LONDON AND NEW YORK

First published 2020
by Routledge
2 Park Square, Milton Park, Abingdon, Oxon OX14 4RN

and by Routledge
605 Third Avenue, New York, NY 10017

First issued in paperback 2021

Routledge is an imprint of the Taylor & Francis Group, an informa business

© 2020 selection and editorial matter, Liesbeth Enneking, Ivo Giesen, Anne-Jetske Schaap, Cedric Ryngaert, François Kristen, and Lucas Roorda; individual chapters, the contributors

The right of Liesbeth Enneking, Ivo Giesen, Anne-Jetske Schaap, Cedric Ryngaert, François Kristen, and Lucas Roorda to be identified as the authors of the editorial material, and of the authors for their individual chapters, has been asserted in accordance with sections 77 and 78 of the Copyright, Designs and Patents Act 1988.

All rights reserved. No part of this book may be reprinted or reproduced or utilised in any form or by any electronic, mechanical, or other means, now known or hereafter invented, including photocopying and recording, or in any information storage or retrieval system, without permission in writing from the publishers.

Trademark notice: Product or corporate names may be trademarks or registered trademarks, and are used only for identification and explanation without intent to infringe.

Publisher's Note
The publisher has gone to great lengths to ensure the quality of this reprint but points out that some imperfections in the original copies may be apparent.

British Library Cataloguing-in-Publication Data
A catalogue record for this book is available from the British Library

Library of Congress Cataloging-in-Publication Data
Names: Enneking, Liesbeth F. H., 1979–, editor. | Giesen, Ivo, 1972–, editor. | Schaap, A. L. M. (Anne-Jetske L.M.), editor. | Ryngaert, Cedric, editor. | Kristen, F. G. H., editor. | Roorda, Lucas, 1988– editor.
Title: Accountability, international business operations and the law : providing justice for corporate human rights violations in global value chains / edited by L. F. H. Enneking, Ivo Giesen, A. L. M. Schaap, Cedric Ryngaert, François Kristen, and Lucas Roorda.
Description: Abingdon, Oxon ; New York, NY : Routledge, 2020. | Series: Globalization law and policy | Includes bibliographical references and index.
Identifiers: LCCN 2019042121 (print) | LCCN 2019042122 (ebook) | ISBN 9780815356837 (hardback) | ISBN 9781351127165 (ebook)
Subjects: LCSH: Social responsibility of business—Law and legislation. | Corporate governance—Law and legislation. | Business logistics.
Classification: LCC K1329.5 .A23 2020 (print) | LCC K1329.5 (ebook) | DDC 342.08/5—dc23
LC record available at https://lccn.loc.gov/2019042121
LC ebook record available at https://lccn.loc.gov/2019042122

ISBN 13: 978-1-03-208320-9 (pbk)
ISBN 13: 978-0-8153-5683-7 (hbk)

Typeset in Galliard
by Apex CoVantage, LLC

Contents

Tables

Commonly used acronyms

BIT	Bilateral investment treaty
CSR	Corporate social responsibility
EC	European Commission
ECHR	European Convention on Human Rights
ECtHR	European Court of Human Rights
EU	European Union
ICC	International Criminal Court
ICCPR	International Covenant on Civil and Political Rights
ICESCR	International Covenant on Economic, Social and Cultural Rights
ICJ	International Court of Justice
ILO	International Labour Organization
LL	Limited liability
LLC	Large listed company
MNE	Multinational enterprise
NGO	Non-governmental organization
OECD	Organization for Economic Co-operation and Development
OHCHR	Office of the UN High Commissioner for Human Rights
SCP	Separate corporate personality
UK	United Kingdom
UN	United Nations
UNGPs	UN Guiding Principles
UNHCR	UN Human Rights Council
US	United States

Biographies of authors and editors

Nicolas Bueno is Postdoctoral Researcher and Senior Lecturer at the University of Zurich. He conducted a postdoctoral research at the Université de Louvain (2016) and at the London School of Economics Centre for the Study of Human Rights (2017). His postdoctoral research, funded by the Swiss National Research Foundation, focuses on business and human rights and the challenge of implementation in a global competitive economy. He is the author of the article 'Introduction to the Human Economy' (International Association of Labour Law Journals Award 2017) in which he presents a new economic model that goes beyond requiring corporations to account.

Karin Buhmann is Professor in Business & Human Rights at Copenhagen Business School (CBS). Buhmann has an advanced post-doc degree (dr.scient. adm) on a dissertation on Business & Human Rights, a PhD in law, and a master's degree in international humanitarian and human rights law. Her research and teaching focus on business and human rights; regulatory strategies and forms of regulation for CSR; with a strong focus on the interaction between public and private hard, soft, and smart-mix regulation; and implementation in national and transnational contexts. Since 2012, Buhmann serves as one of five part-time members of the Danish National Contact Point (NCP) under OECD's Guidelines for Multinational Enterprises. In 2014, she initiated The BHRight Initiative, an interdisciplinary academic network on research and teaching on business and human rights. Buhmann has published widely in international journals, edited volumes, and monographs. In 2017, she published two monographs based on empirical analysis of the evolution of the business and human rights regime: one on collaborative regulation in the evolution of transnational sustainability norms, and another on the emergence on the business and human rights regime.

Larry Catá Backer is W Richard and Mary Eshelman Faculty Scholar and Professor of Law & International Affairs at the Pennsylvania State University. His research focuses on governance-related issues of globalization and constitutional theories of public and private governance. Current research focuses on transnational problem-solving through law, broadly defined, especially touching on issues of corporate social responsibility and human rights within global supply chains, the relationship between State-based regulation and transnational systems of "soft" regulation, State participation in private markets and the emerging problems of polycentricity where multiple systems apply to a single issue or event, and problems of translation between Western and Marxist Leninist (especially Chinese) constitutional systems. He teaches courses in corporate law, transnational law, and international organizations. He has published extensively on themes related to the topic of this volume. Shorter essays on various aspects of globalization and governance appear on his essay site, 'Law at the End of the Day', http://lcbackerblog.blogspot.com.

Marjolein Cupido holds an LLM in criminal law (*summa cum laude*) from Leiden University where she also participated in the Talent Program, an extra-curricular program on legal research. In 2015, Dr. Cupido defended her doctoral dissertation, 'Facts Matter: A Study into the Casuistry of Substantive International Criminal Law', at Vrije Universiteit Amsterdam. Parts of her dissertation have been published in the *Journal of International Criminal Justice*, the *Leiden Journal of International Law*, and the *Melbourne Journal of International Law*. Dr Cupido is currently working as assistant professor at the department of Criminal Law and Criminology of VU University Amsterdam. She is also a fellow at the Center for International Criminal Justice. In 2016, Dr Cupido was appointed Deputy Judge in the criminal law section of the District Court of Rotterdam. She also has experience at the International Criminal Court, where she worked as visiting professional for the defense of Mr. Jean-Pierre Bemba in the Bemba et al. case.

Daniëlla Dam-de Jong is Associate Professor at the Grotius Centre for International Legal Studies at Leiden University. She has defended her PhD at the same university on a thesis entitled "International Law and Governance of Natural Resources in Conflict and Post-Conflict Situations", for which she received a research prize by the Foundation Praemium Erasmianum and an honorary mention by the Max van der Stoel Human Rights Award. The dissertation has been published as a monograph by Cambridge University (2015). Daniëlla has studied law at the Free University Amsterdam, specializing in public international and European law. In addition, she has studied French language and culture at the University of Lausanne and the Free University Amsterdam. Daniëlla is a member of the International Law Association study group on UN Sanctions and International Law. Her research interests are related to questions in the fields of sustainable development and peace and security.

Paul Dowling is Associate Solicitor at Leigh Day law firm in London. He specializes in international human rights and environmental litigation. Since joining Leigh Day, Paul's notable cases have included: Acting on behalf of Iraqi civilians in relation to allegations of torture and abuse by British soldiers, representing former members of the armed forces in a claim against the Ministry of Defence concerning a "friendly fire" incident in Iraq, representing a group of Colombian farmers who claim to have had their lands devastated by the construction of an oil pipeline, and acting for a group of Kenyan tea pickers in relation to human rights violations during the 2007 post-election violence in Kenya. Paul has a particular interest in the impacts of large-scale extractive industry projects on local communities, and in 2015 drafted an amicus curiae brief in a constitutional rights protection case relating to the ill health of an indigenous Colombian boy allegedly caused by pollution from an open-pit coal mine. Paul contributed to Leigh Day's written submission to the Joint Committee on Human Rights Inquiry on Business and Human Rights in August 2016.

Jessy Emaus was an assistant professor at the Molengraaff Institute for Private Law and a researcher at the Utrecht Centre for Accountability and Liability Law (UCALL) and the Utrecht Centre for Regulation and Enforcement in Europe (RENFORCE). She obtained her doctorate with a dissertation on the enforcement of ECHR rights by means of liability law. Her dissertation focused on how Dutch liability and damages law can contribute to the enforcement of ECHR rights, assuming as a starting point that liability and damages law should be constitutionalized. In January 2020, Emaus will make the switch from academia to the judiciary and become a judge in training at the Gelderland District Court.

Liesbeth Enneking holds a special chair on the Legal Aspects of International Corporate Social Responsibility at Erasmus School of Law (Erasmus University, Rotterdam). She obtained a doctorate at Utrecht University in 2012 for a PhD on the role of tort law in promoting international corporate social responsibility. Over the past 12 years, she has published and presented widely on topics related to corporate social responsibility, fair trade, and business and human rights. She conducted research projects for organizations such as the European Commission, the Netherlands Organization for Scientific Research, the insurance company AXA, and the Royal Netherlands Academy of Arts and Sciences, and participates in a number of multidisciplinary research projects. She was one of the lead authors of the 2015/2016 study for the Dutch Ministries of Foreign Affairs and Security & Justice on duties of care of Dutch internationally operating business enterprises in the context of international corporate social responsibility.

Björn Fasterling joined EDHEC Business School as a law professor in 2003. Currently he serves there as Head of Faculty for Law. He teaches business and human rights, compliance management, and contract law. His research and publications focus on ethics and compliance management in companies, and more recently on business and human rights. Prior to joining EDHEC, Björn Fasterling worked as a German lawyer in the Berlin office of the law firm WilmerHale and practiced in the fields of international commercial transactions, including litigation. He holds a Dr.iur (*summa cum laude*) from the University of Osnabrück.

Ivo Giesen finds (legal) solutions to today's societal problems using the law (torts, civil procedure) in a creative manner while taking in inspiration from elsewhere (empirical legal studies, law, and psychology, etc.) to cross traditional barriers, if needed. From February 2013 until March 2017, he was program director of UCALL, the Utrecht Centre for Accountability and Liability Law, a multidimensional research team focusing on the shifting boundaries of liability rules, both within the domains of public law as well as private law. Between April 2014 and June 2019, he was Research Director and member of the board of Utrecht School of Law. In June 2019, he was appointed Dean of the Law Department of Utrecht University.

Mark J Hornman (LLM Radboud University Nijmegen) is Assistant Professor in Criminal Law at VU University Amsterdam. Prior to joining VU University, he was a lecturer and PhD researcher at Utrecht University where he received his PhD on the criminal liability of corporations and corporate executives in 2016. During his appointment at Utrecht University, he was a research associate at the Utrecht Centre for Accountability and Liability Law (UCALL).

Wim Huisman (1970) is Professor of Criminology and the head of the School of Criminology of the Vrije Universiteit (VU) since 2008. The research focus of Wim Huisman is on the field of white-collar crime, corporate crime, and organized crime. Recently funded research projects focus on criminal careers of white-collar offenders, corporate complicity to gross human rights violations, causes of corruption, corporate environmental crime, and the prevention of food fraud. Wim Huisman is a founder and board member of the European Working Group on Organizational Crime (EUROC) of the European Society of Criminology and he is Chief-Editor of the journal *Crime, Law & Social Change*. Currently, Huisman is Chair of the Netherlands Society of Criminology. Wim Huisman has been a visiting professor at Griffith University, Brisbane, Australia; Northeastern University, Boston, USA; and Mekelle University, Ethiopia.

François Kristen is Professor in Criminal Law and Criminal Procedure at the Willem Pompe Institute for Criminal Law & Criminology of Utrecht School of Law, and the program director of the Utrecht Centre for Accountability and Liability Law. He obtained a PhD at Tilburg University in 2004, with a thesis on the European prohibition on insider trading. His main research topics are substantive criminal law, criminal procedure, European criminal law, and financial criminal law. He is also an expert on the role that Dutch criminal law may play in promoting responsible business conduct abroad. He was one of the lead authors of the 2015/2016 study for the Dutch Ministries of Foreign Affairs and Security & Justice on duties of care of Dutch internationally operating business enterprises in the context of international corporate social responsibility.

Lucas Roorda is a PhD candidate at Utrecht University, and a policy advisor at the Netherlands Human Rights Institute. He holds a bachelor's degree from Utrecht University (2009, *cum laude*) and an LLM from Utrecht University (2012, *cum laude*), and is currently finishing his thesis on jurisdiction as a barrier to remedy in business and human rights litigation in the European Union, under the supervision of Prof Cedric Ryngaert and Prof Liesbeth Enneking.

Lucas has written and edited several publications on transnational litigation against corporate actors, and the human rights responsibilities of businesses including private military and security companies. At the Netherlands Human Rights Institute, he currently works on business and human rights issues, access to justice, and the right to housing.

Cedric Ryngaert (PhD Leuven 2007) is Chair of Public International Law at Utrecht University (Netherlands). Prof Ryngaert is the principal investigator of two projects on unilateral jurisdiction and global values, one funded by a European Research Council starting grant and one by the Dutch Organization for Scientific Research (VIDI scheme). The project focuses specifically on the legal limits and opportunities of unilateral action to further global justice and examines what role territoriality as a principle of jurisdictional order still has to play. Earlier, Prof Ryngaert was Associate Professor of International Law at Leuven University, project leader of an international research community on non-State actors funded by the Flemish Organization for Scientific Research, and was involved in two EU COST actions. He has published widely on topics related to jurisdiction in international law and non-State actor responsibilities. In 2012, he obtained the Prix Henri Rolin, a five-yearly prize for international law and international relations. He was co-rapporteur of the International Law Association's Committee on Non-State Actors between 2007 and 2014. Currently he is an editor of the *Netherlands International Law Review* and the *Utrecht Law Review*.

Anne-Jetske Schaap is a PhD candidate at Utrecht University (Utrecht Centre for Accountability and Liability Law), conducting research on corporate criminal liability and duties of care. In April 2016, she graduated from the Legal Research Master (*cum laude*) at Utrecht University with a specialization in criminal law. She has written her thesis on Corporate Criminal Liability for Modern Slavery, which was published as a monograph in 2017. Anne-Jetske Schaap has also studied law at Cambridge University and the University of Valencia, specializing in criminal law and public international law. In 2013, she completed her LL.B. (*cum laude*) at Utrecht University, participating in the honors law program. Anne-Jetske Schaap is currently an editor of the *Utrecht Law Review*.

Martijn Scheltema is Professor at Erasmus University Rotterdam (The Netherlands). He researches effectiveness of multi-stakeholder initiatives (including their ADR capabilities) in the international arena in connection with business and human rights and the environment. He is partner of Pels Rijcken & Droogleever Fortuijn. He has been involved in several international human rights landmark cases with the Dutch Supreme Court. He is the only Dutch lawyer ranked for business and human rights in the Chambers Global Guide. He chairs the business and human rights practice group of his firm. Further related positions include: Chair of the independent binding dispute resolution mechanism of the Dutch International Responsible Business Conduct

Agreement in the Textile sector (concluded between industry, government and NGOs); chair of the Corporate Social Responsibility Committee of the International Bar Association (involved in business human rights); co-chair of the OECD academic network for Responsible Business Conduct; member of the steering committee of the MSI Integrity Academic network; member of the American Bar Association Business Human Rights Project; founding board member of ACCESS (www.accessfacility.org). His academic work includes over 100 academic publications.

Katerina Yiannibas is Associate Professor at the University of Deusto in San Sebastian, Spain and Lecturer in Law at Columbia Law School in New York, USA. Researcher at the Globernance Institute for Democratic Governance, where her primary area of research is international conflict resolution; in particular non-judicial mechanisms, arbitration, mediation, conciliation, and negotiation. She is a member of the Working Group of the International Arbitration of Business and Human Rights project. She is also the director of the European Dialogues and project manager of a Globernance-lead research consortium, "Business & Human Rights Challenges for Cross Border Litigation in the European Union", which was awarded funding by the European Commission Civil Justice Programme. Furthermore, she is a member of the New York State Bar and a certified mediator. Yiannibas holds a bachelor of arts *summa cum laude* from Duke University and a *juris doctor* from Columbia Law School.

Jennifer Zerk is a freelance writer, researcher, teacher and consultant specializing in law and corporate social responsibility. She holds a LLM from the University of London, a PhD from the University of Cambridge and is an associate fellow in the International Law Programme at Chatham House. Her book, *Multinationals and Corporate Social Responsibility* is now widely regarded as a standard international law text on business and human rights. She has advised on a number of significant law reform and policy initiatives in the business and human rights field including, most recently, as lead legal consultant on the Accountability and Remedy Project of the Office of the UN High Commissioner for Human Rights.

Part 1

General perspectives

1 Introduction

Ivo Giesen, Liesbeth Enneking, François Kristen, Lucas Roorda, Cedric Ryngaert, and Anne-Jetske Schaap

1.1 Introduction

Sneakers, fuel, coffee, smartphones. Many of (the commodities for) our daily products are being produced abroad. Sometimes this takes place under conditions that would be considered unacceptable in the countries where the products involved are put on the market. This raises not only ethical and political questions, but also legal ones. Most of these currently revolve around the legal responsibilities of the companies involved with respect to the detrimental human rights or environmental impacts of business activities in their global value chains. What is the scope of the social responsibility of Western society-based internationally operating business enterprises that have their products manufactured in developing host countries, often at low cost, and put them on the market here? Are they under an obligation to prevent their own activities, or those of their local subsidiaries or suppliers, from having an adverse impact on the human rights of local employees, neighbors, or communities, or on the local environment? And if such adverse impacts do occur, under what circumstances can these internationally operating business enterprises be held liable for this before courts in their Western society home States?[1]

The adverse effects of transnational corporations' business activities, especially on human rights – including labor rights – and the environment in the host country of investment, have been well documented. A consensus has emerged that corporations have societal and environmental responsibilities when operating transnationally. A key development in this respect has been the appointment in 2005 of Prof John Ruggie as Special Representative to the UN Secretary-General on human rights and transnational corporations and other business enterprises.[2] This resulted in the publication of the "Protect, Respect and Remedy" Policy Framework on Business & Human Rights (hereinafter, Policy Framework) in 2008.[3] This policy framework was further operationalized in the 2011 UNGPs.[4] The UNGPs were unanimously endorsed by the UNHRC[5] and have received support from a broad range of stakeholders, including States, international organizations, NGOs, unions, branch organizations, and individual business enterprises.[6]

Together, these two documents constitute an authoritative international soft law instrument, which propagates the message that both States and business enterprises have a role to play in the prevention and remedy of business-related human rights abuse. The Policy Framework rests on three pillars: 1) the State duty to protect against business-related human rights abuse; 2) the corporate responsibility to prevent, mitigate and/or redress the negative effects of operations pursued by or for them on third parties' human rights; and 3) the need for an effective remedy for victims of business-related human rights abuse. The UNGPs contain standards of conduct for States and business enterprises with regard to what is expected of them in each of the three pillars when it comes to the prevention and remediation of business-related human rights abuse. Even though the documents in themselves are non-binding, their wide acceptance justifies the conclusion that a certain degree of international consensus exists on the standards of conduct laid down therein. Moreover, their subsequent uptake in other international and national legal instruments relating to international responsible business conduct (IRBC), some of which are of a more binding nature, has ensured that they are of great significance not only from a normative but also from a legal perspective.[7]

One of the key points of the UNGPs is that business enterprises have an independent responsibility to check whether their operations entail the risk of human rights abuse, to prevent or mitigate these risks as far as possible, and to remedy possible adverse impacts. This responsibility to respect applies regardless of the location of these operations and regardless of the local legal context. It may also include possible adverse human rights impacts that are directly linked to the business enterprise's operations, products, or services through its business relationships. The UNGPs stipulate that business enterprises should have policy measures and procedures in place that are appropriate to their size and operational context in order to meet their responsibility to respect. These include, in any case: 1) a policy commitment as regards their responsibility to respect human rights; 2) a human rights due diligence procedure; 3) procedures to remedy any adverse human rights impacts the business operations caused or to which they contributed. The due diligence procedure is first of all meant to identify, prevent, and restrict, as well as – where necessary – to remedy the adverse effects of the business operations on third parties' human rights. In addition, it should address the public accountability of business enterprises as regards the policies they pursue to restrict adverse human rights effects.[8]

Still, how exactly corporations can be held legally accountable for their transgressions, if at all, remains less clear.[9] The present volume inquires how several distinct regulatory tools stemming from public international law, domestic public law, and/or domestic private law may or may not be used for transnational corporate accountability purposes. Attention is devoted to applicable standards of liability (tort law), institutional, and jurisdictional issues, as well as practical challenges, with a focus on ways to improve the existing legal *status quo*. In addition, there is consideration of the extent to which non-legal regulatory instruments may complement or provide (perhaps more viable) alternatives to these legal mechanisms. This volume emerges from some of the papers that were presented at an international conference on Accountability and International Business Operations, organized at Utrecht University (the Netherlands) on 18–20 May 2017.[10]

1.2 State of the art in the field

The state-of-the-art in the field that this conference and volume departs from can be categorized, in broad terms, as follows. Evidently, the field of business and human rights has seen an increase of academic publications in the last few years, especially after the adoption of the UNGPs put the question on the map of international law. But, at the same time, it is also still very much a field in the early stages of development, if compared to other fields of study. Early publications, such as those of Muchlinski,[11] Joseph,[12] and Zerk,[13] focused on the challenge of regulating business actors generally through international law. These have been followed by more recent general volumes following the renewed interest in the topic,[14] as well as a range of contemporary titles addressing more specific issues such as access to remedies for indigenous peoples,[15] substantive obligations for businesses,[16] prosecution of corporations for genocide,[17] and the upcoming treaty on business and human rights.[18] Most of these contributions, however, focus on issues that concern the adjustment of business behavior toward more human rights-friendly operations and/or focus on the international law dimension of the topic. The current volume, by contrast, aims to contribute to the discussion by focusing on accountability and liability questions that permeate different fields of law, as well as different national legal systems, as will be further explained.

From the more recent literature, only three volumes deal with accountability more conceptually.[19] This book differs from these publications in various respects. Whereas Bernaz takes a more historical perspective and mainly addresses the issue from an international law and policy perspective, this volume tackles more contemporary legal barriers to accountability and liability, and covers both international and domestic trends in doing so. It differs from erni and Van Ho's book in that it is more specifically geared toward *ex post* accountability questions, whereas erni and Van Ho include contributions that address wider issues such as *ex ante* responsibilities of businesses.[20] Furthermore, whereas Khoury and White take a more historical and political economy-oriented approach to the topic, the current volume draws heavily on more recent developments in a very rapidly moving field, including recent legislative initiatives relating to business and human rights issues at the domestic level.

1.3 Goals and ambitions of this volume

As was the case for the conference on Accountability and International Business Operations that was mentioned in section 1.1, this volume seeks to combine legal-doctrinal approaches with comparative, interdisciplinary, and policy insights. It does so in order to attain a dual goal:

(1) To further the legal scholarly debate on these issues, and
(2) To enable higher-quality decision-making by policymakers seeking to implement regulatory measures that enhance corporate accountability.

The common denominator of all chapters in this volume is to provide a timely and important contribution to the scholarly and sociopolitical debate in the field of international CSR and accountability. The papers, taken together, inquire what legal mechanisms could be relied on to create accountability for corporate abuses of public goods and values, and to do so, they bring together (legal) scholars from various backgrounds, in particular from the fields of private law, public law, and international law.

More specifically, this volume, through the different chapters therein, has several ambitions. It sets forth to:

(1) Examine the possibilities to hold transnational corporations (or, more broadly, internationally operating business enterprises) to account under existing legal regimes, and to do so from a *multi-disciplinary* (international law, public law, private law) *multi-level* (international, domestic, corporate) and *multi-State* (comparative) perspective;
(2) Uncover the ways in which mechanisms from different disciplines, levels and States may *interact with* and/or *complement* one another;
(3) Adopt a *holistic approach* as regards corporate violations of standards relating to human rights or the environment that enables cross-learning from issues in these fields;
(4) Provide an assessment of the legal significance and sociopolitical impact of the latest developments in legislation and case law relating to corporate accountability for violations of human rights and environmental standards;
(5) Highlight how the workings of the law may potentially have major *transformative effects* on the conduct of transnational corporations; and finally,
(6) Investigate the feasibility of *legal reform* in those areas where existing law does not offer adequate accountability mechanisms.

This last endeavor is undertaken with a focus on the identification of:

(a) The *application in new ways of existing accountability mechanisms* by legal practitioners (e.g., courts and other law-applying agencies, attorneys, legal counsel, NGOs), and
(b) The *introduction of new accountability mechanisms* by policymakers seeking to implement regulatory measures aimed at enhancing corporate accountability.

Whether all these ambitions are (or maybe, can) in fact realized will be analyzed in the concluding chapter of this volume (Chapter 14), as will be explained later in the text.

1.4 Set-up of this volume

In order to reach the goals set out in section 1.3, this volume is separated into five parts: a general part that offers overarching views on the topic (Part 1), followed by three discipline-specific parts (Parts 2, 3, and 4, respectively) that correspond to the three legal fields that are most relevant to legal accountability in the context of international CSR (i.e., international law, [domestic] public law, and [domestic] private law), and a concluding section (Part 5) with a discussion of the most viable ways forward when it comes to holding international business actors to account for violations of human rights and environmental standards abroad. A more detailed overview[21] of the content of those five separate parts is given in the next sections.

1.4.1 Part 1: general perspectives

In Chapter 2, Björn Fasterling puts the focus on "who" (as in, which corporations or corporate actors) might be (held) responsible under the UNGPs. He argues that corporate responsibility under the UNGPs should be understood as an activity-based concept, according to which business models are to be made compatible with respect for human rights respect. In this light, not the legal entities, but rather business strategy, organizational processes, and managerial routines become constitutive elements of business enterprise. Such business enterprise responsibility also implies individual and collective responsibilities of certain people, who will be referred to as the "function-holders" of an enterprise, to act according to these routines and to take human rights into account when they make decisions. Against the backdrop of the French due diligence law, the *Loi relative au devoir de vigilance des sociétés mères et des entreprises donneuses d'ordre*, this chapter will highlight salient differences between the UNGPs' (extra-legal) corporate responsibility to respect human rights and legal due diligence standards. This demonstration aims at revealing the breadth of challenges the law faces when it seeks transform the UNGPs' due diligence concept into a legal norm. It will show to which extent the French law, albeit clearly being inspired by the UNGPs, has poorly captured essential elements of the UNGPs' corporate responsibility.

The core theme of Chapter 3 by Karin Buhmann is the potential role of National Contact Points (NCPs) as accountability institutions. NCPs are State-based, non-judicial remedy institutions in States that adhere to OECD's Guidelines for Multinational Enterprises. The UN highlighted NCPs as an important modality for providing accountability in The Protect, Respect and Remedy Framework (2008). Since the UNGPs do not have remedy institutions of their own, NCPs provide an important accountability modality for transnational economic activity and its societal impact. Each State has discretion in defining the institutional setup for its NCP. This results in a broad variety of, among others, compositions of NCPs, their organization, and of degrees of independence from the government. Studies have indicated that the diversity of institutional setups of NCPs may affect their legitimacy with stakeholders, affecting the trust in NCPs as remedy institutions able to deliver accountability. However, it is also necessary to consider stakeholders' expectations in regards to remedy, and the procedural as well as substantive aspects of remedy. Analyzing the institutional setup of NCPs against procedural and substantive aspects of "remedy", specific cases, and statistics on home and host State-related specific instances, the chapter provides a critical analysis of the issues set out and recommendations for enhancing the remedial accountability provided by NCPs.

In Chapter 4, Larry Backer sets out to "unpack" accountability when it comes to MEs and the role of the State and the international community. The emerging hard and soft law frameworks for regulating the human rights, labor, and environmental responsibilities of economic enterprises (whether public or private) are to some extent operationalized through mechanisms of accountability. Thus, accountability occupies a central place within the complex of regulatory trends that are shaping the organization of economic (and, to some extent, social, political, and cultural) life within a globalized order. The purpose of this chapter is to unpack the concept of accountability as it is deployed in governance, and then to repack it in a way that makes the concept more useful. The thesis of the chapter is that accountability must be understood as a shorthand for a set of multiple reciprocal relations, manifested in actions responding to expectations that are grounded in normative standards actualized in the context within which the actors are connected, and directed toward general (communal) and specific (individual) ends. A working system of accountability centered on corporate violations of human rights and sustainability requires mutual and simultaneous accounting by all stakeholders to (1) bring each other to account, (2) bring oneself to account, and (3) be brought to account.

1.4.2 Part 2: accountability through international law mechanisms

The fact that many corporations these days operate transnationally does not mean that States have disappeared from view. Corporations always perform their operations on the territory of States, and they are incorporated or headquartered in States. States can use these links to regulate business activities across borders. Pooling their sovereign competences, they may also enter into international agreements to regulate such activities. A number of soft law instruments have been adopted to this end, most notably the OECD Guidelines for Multinational Enterprises.[22] Binding international agreements on responsible business practices are lacking, however, with BITs typically paying only scant attention to the obligations of investors as opposed to those of the host State.[23]

Still, in the wake of the widely accepted UNGPs, a proposal was tabled in 2014 for an international legally binding instrument on internationally operating business enterprises with respect to human rights, which is to impose direct obligations on corporations.[24] Such an instrument is global civil society's hope and corporations' obvious bugbear. For it to be more than a pipedream, the added legal value and effectiveness of imposing binding international obligations on corporations needs to be closely scrutinized. At the same time, the question of what type of existing or to newly established supervisory body should be put in charge of monitoring and enforcing such obligations arises. Given that state of play, this second part contains three chapters on the potential of international legal instruments to accommodate and further corporate accountability in the field of human rights.

Chapter 5 by Katerina Yiannibas analyzes the potential of, and the skepticism toward, international arbitration to provide effective remedy for business-related human rights abuses. Despite the vast prevalence of international arbitration for the resolution of cross-border commercial and investment disputes, the arbitration mechanism has received increased public scrutiny. While human rights considerations have already emerged in international arbitration cases, the arbitration mechanism must be adapted if it is to be used in cases concerning substantive human rights claims. This chapter begins by setting out the advantages and disadvantages of international arbitration for the resolution of disputes concerning business-related human rights abuses against the effectiveness criteria set out for non-judicial mechanisms in the UNGPs. The chapter then puts forward the specific ways in which the international arbitration mechanism should evolve in cases where the substantive claims involve human rights; in particular, a set of procedural rules that ensure transparency, *amicus curiae* participation, specialized arbitrators, and human rights experts, site visits, collective redress, monitoring of award compliance, and financial assistance.

In Chapter 6, Jennifer Zerk challenges the idea that the "territorial" system of regulation of multinationals is necessarily flawed. She does so by examining the arrangements that have developed thus far for cross-border cooperation in complex corporate cases. Drawing from work done in the course of the Ruggie mandate (i.e., the UN Protect, Respect and Remedy Framework) and the OHCHR Accountability and Remedy Project, the author considers the possibilities arising from different models of cooperation that can be used in cases involving allegations of business-related human rights abuses, and the conditions needed for success. While it is important to have mutual legal assistance arrangements in place, it is argued in this chapter that there is a need for greater emphasis on the practicalities of "operational" level cooperation, and on opening up more dynamic and programmatic avenues for cross-border communication and liaison, for instance, through regulators' networks.

Next, Daniela Dam-de Jong in Chapter 7 explores the possibilities for interaction between CSR and the standards set by international criminal law for holding corporations or their representatives accountable for their wrongdoings, focusing on the illegal exploitation and trafficking of natural resources by armed groups. There have been developments in the field of international criminal law that bear great promise for holding corporations accountable for their involvement in these practices, such as the publication of a policy paper by the ICC Prosecutor on case selection and prioritization, in which the prosecutor clearly stated her determination "to give particular consideration to prosecuting Rome Statute crimes that are committed by means of, or that result in, inter alia . . . the illegal exploitation of natural resources". This statement has raised expectations in the NGO community that the ICC will be more inclined in the future to address corporate involvement in international crimes. Such developments attest to a determination to place acts of illegal exploitation of natural resources under closer scrutiny. Nevertheless, to what extent would this be viable in practice? So far, contemporary international criminal tribunals have shied away from prosecuting acts of illicit exploitation of natural resources in conflict zones. Also, there are a number of additional hurdles, such as the problem of establishing knowledge and intent on the part of the corporation or its representatives. This chapter analyzes whether and to what extent contemporary standards developed within the framework of CSR would assist in overcoming such obstacles; it argues that an obligation for corporations to conduct due diligence in relation to their suppliers might, under certain conditions, have relevance for international criminal law.

1.4.3 Part 3: accountability through domestic public law mechanisms

States are responsible for the regulation and supervision of the activities of all persons within their territory. The principle of sovereignty allows States to intervene by any means in order to prevent certain acts from happening, to maintain peace and order, to protect human rights as well as other rights and interests, to steer society in a certain direction, and to influence the behavior of persons or organizations. Policy, financial measures (including taxes), and the law are all instruments that states may rely on for such interventions. Corporations that are incorporated or headquartered in a State are subject to these instruments. The law in particular can be used to set standards for the protection and enhancement of human rights and the environment to which corporations, their managers, employees, and subcontractors have to comply.

In case of non-compliance, public law instruments offer a variety of ways to hold those involved responsible; in some instances, those instruments may also be relied on to address corporate misconduct taking place abroad. Reporting obligations, for instance, may play a role in creating transparency on cases of non-compliance, which in turn facilitates monitoring and enforcement through legal instruments as well as through the "courts of public opinion". Administrative or criminal investigations of business operations that are suspected of harming human rights or the environment may result in legal procedures in order to establish the liability of corporations, managers, employees, and subcontractors, and to impose sanctions. In light of the foregoing, this part contains three chapters discussing the potential of domestic public law instruments to regulate global corporate activity and to hold corporations accountable for transnational misbehavior.

In Chapter 8, François Kristen and Jessy Emaus address the question of whether a corporation that is considered "too big to be governed" might also be "too big to be responsible". In today's day and age, a large multinational company's finances may exceed the finances of a (small) country. Such a firm's economic position in principle means "power". In the meantime, the business operations and the societal position of these companies can affect people and planet. In light of this, the aim of this chapter is to find out if "economic power" is an argument to hold large listed companies (LLCs) liable under private law and/or criminal law for violations of local and international norms which protect people and the planet. The central question is twofold: Can "economic power" provide for a legal basis for holding LLCs responsible for fundamental rights protection" And if so, how? And, subsequently, can LLCs be held liable both under private law and criminal law for not taking responsibility for fundamental rights protection? To answer these questions, attention will be paid to the concepts of LLCs and "economic power", to the position that the use of economic power establishes responsibility, to the duty of care as a potential vehicle to transform responsibility into liability, and more concrete civil and criminal liability in these cases, respectively.

Next, Marjolein Cupido, Mark J Hornman and Wim Huisman raise the question in Chapter 9 of how different types of (causal, motivational, and organizational) remoteness should be tackled when holding business leaders accountable for international crimes. This issue arises because corporate involvement in international crimes is mostly indirect. Businessmen seldom physically perpetrate international crimes, but generally fund or benefit from such crimes in more indirect ways, for example by providing goods, logistical support, or information. Moreover, businessmen normally act with business-related purposes and interests, rather than with the intent to commit international crimes. In particular, when corporations have a complex structure consisting of multiple branches and departments, individual businessmen may also not know exactly what happens within the corporation. This makes it difficult to establish that the businessmen intentionally contributed to the commission of international crimes and thus fulfilled the *actus reus* and *mens rea* requirements of these offenses. This chapter addresses if and how these problems related to remoteness can be tackled in order to prevent impunity, and whether the possible solutions are acceptable from a fair labelling perspective.

Subsequently, Anne-Jetske Schaap in Chapter 10 addresses the potential of domestic criminal law to hold internationally operating corporations legally accountable for the adverse effects of their cross-border activities. This is done by focusing on one particular human rights-related issue that has generated a lot of debate among NGOs, policymakers and scholars recently: the issue of modern slavery. In addressing the potential of domestic criminal law in tackling the issue of modern slavery, the focus will be on Dutch law and the law of England and Wales. Accordingly, the question central to this chapter is whether and to what extent corporations have binding duties under Dutch and English/Welsch criminal law not to commit modern slavery in their cross-border activities. This chapter highlights that domestic criminal law can indeed offer an answer to this question in the case of modern slavery, but potentially also with regard to other transgressions. It can put duties on corporations not to commit modern slavery in their cross-border activities, these duties may also take the shape of duties of care, and domestic criminal law may even offer potential in addressing modern slavery in the supply chain. Thus, domestic criminal law can offer an interesting route to hold corporations legally accountable. However, these possibilities must first be taken up in practice, and therein lies an important task among others lawmakers, policy makers, and legal practitioners.

1.4.4 *Part 4: accountability through domestic private law mechanisms*

The regulation of transnational business practices comprises not only measures to prevent future misconduct, but also measures to establish accountability and remedies for past wrongs. This can be done at the initiative of the State, for instance through criminal law procedures, but also at the initiative of those suffering harm as a result of corporate violations of human rights and/or of civil society organizations.

In the absence of effective State regulation at the domestic or international level, victims of corporate human rights and environmental abuses have increasingly turned to civil law procedures in order to denounce abusive corporate behavior and obtain remedies for their harm over the past two decades. Where local court systems fail, these procedures are often filed abroad, usually in the home countries of the corporate actors involved. The mechanism that is currently most utilized for this is tort law. In addition to the many cases that have been pursued before US federal courts on the basis of the Alien Tort Statute, transnational tort claims relating to corporate human rights and environmental abuse have also been pursued in other jurisdictions, like Canada, Australia, the UK, Germany, The Netherlands, and Sweden.[25]

However, these tort-based claims are not the only option via which accountability and remedies for irresponsible business practices may be sought. Private law mechanisms in the fields of contract law, consumer law, business law, and competition law may also provide possibilities to establish legal accountability for human rights or environmental abuse within the supply chain, at the initiative of shareholders, competitors, or consumers. In addition, non-judicial grievance mechanisms may be relied on to settle disputes and find remedies outside of the courtroom, as is exemplified by the aforementioned contribution by Buhmann on the role that National Contact Points may play in this respect (see section 1.4.1). Yet other private (law) mechanisms may be contemplated for future cases. The fourth part of this volume contains three chapters on how transnational corporations are (or can be) held accountable through private law mechanisms, and on the obstacles faced by those seeking to address irresponsible business practices through such mechanisms.[26]

The purpose of Chapter 11 by Paul Dowling is to is to discuss, from a theoretical and practical perspective, some of the difficulties (i.e., conceptual flaws, accountability gaps) arising from the principles of limited liability (LL) and SCP, particularly in the context of corporate groups and MEs. It starts with a critical analysis of the historical development and theoretical foundation of LL and SCP, followed by a consideration of some of the conceptual difficulties associated with the operation of these principles, e.g., the schizophrenic nature of the corporation as both a commodity and a social entity. It then turns to some of the practical implications of these problems, particularly the manner in which LL and SCP can frustrate the pursuit of legal accountability, followed by a discussion of the potential for reform in this area. Having considered these alternatives, this chapter proposes the adoption of a profit risk/created risk approach to liability for dangerous activities, which seeks to redress the existing imbalance in the burden of risk that LL and SCP impose on tort victims in the context of overseas operations of MEs and corporate groups.

Next, Nicolas Bueno introduces and discusses in Chapter 12 the Swiss Federal Initiative on Responsible Business. Unless the Swiss Parliament adopts a new law on corporate due diligence, Swiss citizens will decide in 2020 whether to adopt or reject a partial revision of the Constitution of Switzerland that aims to introduce a provision on responsible business. According to the proposal, companies that are based in Switzerland are required to carry out appropriate human rights and environmental due diligence in Switzerland and abroad. The proposal also entails a provision for companies that makes them liable for the harm caused by companies under their control unless they can prove that they took all due care to avoid the harm. This contribution presents and assesses the content of the Swiss Popular Initiative on Responsible Business in light of the UNGPs and the Organisation for Economic Cooperation and Development Guidelines for Multinational Enterprises. It also compares the Swiss popular initiative with the recently adopted French *loi relative au devoir de vigilance* and other recent legislative developments. It identifies a trend toward more precise liability provisions for corporate human rights abuses in international operations.

Subsequently, Martijn Scheltema, in Chapter 13, reflects on the possibilities that contract law might offer in fostering corporate accountability for human rights issues in global value chains. To date, 84% of the large internationally operating companies avails over some form of a CSR/Business Human Rights (BHR) policy. However, these corporate policies have not proven to be very effective so far. This might be partially explained by a mismatch between law and policy, especially in connection with contractual management of these issues. Most of the BHR/CSR policies do not, or in rather limited manner, address the way in which contractual mechanisms might be helpful in enhancing human rights compliance in supply chains, although they seem to recognize the need for contractual mechanisms as part of the solution (i.e., better BHR/CSR compliance). As it becomes clear that rather ineffective contractual measures have been implemented, NGOs and governments might question the effectiveness of the corporate policies mentioning contractual arrangements and might even expect the non-financial reports to be more specific on the types of contractual measures implemented. Overall, strengthening these instruments seems pivotal to enhance human rights compliance in supply chains. Thus, corporate policies should be elaborated in connection with contractual management of CSR/BHR issues, and several ways to do so are elaborated upon in this chapter.

1.4.5 Part 5: conclusion

In Chapter 14, the editors conclude this volume by trying to envisage "The Way Forward" in regards to accountability, international business operations, and the law. This concluding chapter will, on the basis of the foregoing chapters, draw conclusions as to the most viable ways forward when it comes to holding international business actors to account for violations of human rights and environmental standards abroad. Returning to the six ambitions mentioned in section 1.2, this chapter will highlight existing accountability mechanisms that are applied in new ways by legal practitioners in the field, as well as new accountability mechanisms that are considered as an addition or alternative to those already-existing mechanisms. It will speculate on the extent to which these mechanisms can have transformative effects on the way in which transnational business operations are conducted, and will address potential thresholds and/or side effects. It will also discuss the sociopolitical sensitivities inherent in the introduction of new mechanisms and/or the optimization of existing ones. It will close off with some recommendations for legal scholars in regards to topics that warrant further research, for legal practitioners in regards to legal avenues that warrant further development through case law, and for policymakers in regards to accountability mechanisms that warrant realization and/or optimization.

1.5 Looking forward . . .

As set out in section 1.3, this volume is compiled with the dual aim to further the scholarly legal debate on international business actors and their accountability for human rights violations and environmental transgressions in host countries, in order to reach higher-quality decision-making by policymakers that seek to implement regulatory measures to enhance corporate accountability in this respect. The chapters that will follow will no doubt provide a valuable contribution to the scholarly legal debate on these issues. Whether the second aim of enhancing the decision-making process at the policy level will also be achieved is a question we cannot answer. We do see all sorts of potential in the following chapters to be of significant influence also on the sociopolitical debate on issues relating to the adverse effects of transnational corporations' business activities on human rights and the environment in host countries, but the receptions of the ideas contained therein is beyond our control. We do look forward, however, to see what might happen with the ideas expressed in this volume and which future developments will be indebted to the work compiled in this volume.

Notes

1 See in more detail: Liesbeth Enneking et al., *Zorgplichten van Nederlandse ondernemingen inzake Internationaal Maatschappelijk Verantwoord Ondernemen – Een rechtsvergelijkend en empirisch onderzoek naar de stand van het Nederlandse recht in het licht van de UN Guiding Principles* (Boom Juridisch 2016). Based on a study commissioned by the Dutch Ministries of Foreign Affairs and Security and Justice, <wodc.nl/onderzoeksdatabase/2531-maatschappelijk-verantwoord-ondernemen-in-het-buitenland.aspx> accessed 22 August 2019.

2 OHCHR, 'Human Rights and Transnational Corporations and Other Business Enterprises: Human Rights Resolution 2005/69' (20 April 2005) UN Doc E/CN.4/RES/2005/69.

3 Special Representative of the UN Secretary-General on the Issue of Human Rights and Transnational Corporations and Other Business Enterprises, 'Protect,

Respect and Remedy: A Framework for Business and Human Rights: Report of the Special Representative of the Secretary-General on the Issue of Human Rights and Transnational Corporations and Other Business Enterprises' [2008] UN doc A/HRC/8/5.

4 OHCHR, *Guiding Principles on Business and Human Rights: Implementing the United Nations "Protect, Respect and Remedy" Framework* (UN 2011).

5 UNHRC Res. 17/4, UN Doc. A/HRC/RES/17/4, signed on 16 June 2011.

6 See in more detail, for example: Nadia Bernaz. *Business and Human Rights History, Law and Policy: Bridging the Accountability Gap* (Routledge 2016).

7 See in more detail, for example, the publications mentioned in section 1.2 below (n 11–9).

8 UNGPs (n 4) Guiding Principles 11–24. See also OHCHR, *The Corporate Responsibility to Respect Human Rights: An Interpretive Guide* (UN 2012).

9 On the above, see for example Liesbeth Enneking, *Foreign Direct Liability and Beyond: Exploring the Role of Tort Law in Promoting International Corporate Social Responsibility and Accountability* (Eleven International Publishing 2012).

10 See <http://blog.ucall.nl/index.php/2017/06/accountability-and-international-business-operations-some-conclusions-of-the-2017-ucall-conference/> for more information on this event. The editors of this volume and authors of this introductory chapter were the organizers of the conference.

11 Peter Muchlinski, *Multinational Enterprises and the Law* (Oxford University Press 1995, revised 2007).

12 Sarah Joseph, *Corporations and Transnational Human Rights Litigation* (Hart Publishing 2004).

13 Jennifer Zerk, *Multinationals and Corporate Social Responsibility: Limitations and Opportunities in International Law* (Cambridge University Press 2006).

14 These include, for instance: Robert Bird et al. (eds.), *Law, Business and Human Rights: Bridging the Gap* (Edward Elgar Press 2014); Dorothée Baumann-Pauly and Justine Nolan (eds.), *Business and Human Rights: From Principles to Practice* (Routledge 2016).

15 Cathal Doyle, *Business and Human Rights: Indigenous Peoples' Experiences with Access to Remedy: Case Studies from Africa, Asia and Latin America Asia* (Indigenous Peoples Pact, ALMÁCIGA and IWGIA 2015).

16 Surya Deva and David Bilchitz (eds.), *Human Rights Obligations of Business: Beyond the Corporate Responsibility to Respect?* (Cambridge University Press 2013).

17 Michael Kelly, *Prosecuting Corporations for Genocide* (Oxford University Press 2016).

18 Surya Deva and David Bilchitz (eds.), *Building a Treaty on Business and Human Rights: Context and Contours* (Cambridge University Press 2017); Jernej Letnar Černič and Nicolás Carrillo-Santarelli, *The Future of Business and Human Rights: Theoretical and Practical Considerations for a UN Treaty* (Intersentia 2018).

19 See Nadia Bernaz, *Business and Human Rights: History, Law and Policy: Bridging the Accountability Gap* (Routledge 2016); Jernej Letnar Černič and Tara Van Ho (eds.), *Human Rights and Business: Direct Corporate Accountability for Human Rights* (Wolf Legal Publishers 2015); Stefanie Khoury and David Whyte, *Corporate Human Rights Violations: Global Prospects for Legal Action* (Routledge 2017).

20 See for example Rivera's chapter on the responsibility to respect, and Carrillo's chapter on the existence of direct obligations, in Černič and Van Ho (n 19).

21 The following overviews are highly indebted to and largely based on (sometimes severely abridged) versions of the abstracts of the contributions that the authors themselves have provided to the editors; we haven't changed too much in its wordings, in order to avoid doing injustice of any kind to the focus that the authors themselves have chosen.

22 OECD, *OECD Guidelines for Multinational Enterprises* (OECD Publishing 2011).

23 See however the developments described in, for example: Niccolò Zugliani, 'Human Rights in International Investment Law: The 2016 Morocco-Nigeria Bilateral Investment Treaty', (2019) 68(3) *International & Comparative Law Quarterly* 761; Yulia Levashova, 'The Accountability and Corporate Social Responsibility of Multinational Corporations for Transgressions in Host States through International Investment Law', (2018) 14(2) *Utrecht Law Review* 40.

24 See for the latest developments and further references: Business & Human Rights Resource Centre, 'Binding treaty' <www.business-humanrights.org/en/binding-treaty> accessed 22 August 2019.

25 See in more detail, for example: Enneking et al. (n 1); Enneking (n 9).

26 Such obstacles may include, but are not limited to domestic courts' competence to adjudicate claims, lack of applicable standards, legal representation and funding, evidential matters, follow-up to non-judicial dispute settlements, and enforcement of awards. See in general Enneking (n 9).

Bibliography

Baumann-Pauly D and Nolan J (eds.), *Business and Human Rights: From Principles to Practice* (Routledge 2016).

Bernaz N, *Business and Human Rights: History, Law and Policy: Bridging the Accountability Gap* (Routledge 2016).

Bird R et al. (eds.), *Law, Business and Human Rights: Bridging the Gap* (Edward Elgar Press 2014).

Černič JL and Carrillo-Santarelli N, *The Future of Business and Human Rights: Theoretical and Practical Considerations for a UN Treaty* (Intersentia 2018).

——— and Van Ho T (eds.), *Human Rights and Business: Direct Corporate Accountability for Human Rights* (Wolf Legal Publishers 2015).

Deva S and Bilchitz D (eds.), *Building a Treaty on Business and Human Rights: Context and Contours* (Cambridge University Press 2017).

——— (eds.), *Human Rights Obligations of Business: Beyond the Corporate Responsibility to Respect?* (Cambridge University Press 2013).

Doyle C, *Business and Human Rights: Indigenous Peoples' Experiences with Access to Remedy: Case Studies from Africa, Asia and Latin America Asia* (Indigenous Peoples Pact, ALMÁCIGA and IWGIA 2015).

Enneking L, *Foreign Direct Liability and Beyond: Exploring the Role of Tort Law in Promoting International Corporate Social Responsibility and Accountability* (Eleven International Publishing 2012).

——— et al., *Zorgplichten van Nederlandse ondernemingen inzake Internationaal Maatschappelijk Verantwoord Ondernemen – Een rechtsvergelijkend en empirisch onderzoek naar de stand van het Nederlandse recht in het licht van de UN Guiding Principles* (Boom juridisch 2016).

Joseph S, *Corporations and Transnational Human Rights Litigation* (Hart Publishing 2004).

Kelly M, *Prosecuting Corporations for Genocide* (Oxford University Press 2016).

Khoury S and Whyte D, *Corporate Human Rights Violations: Global Prospects for Legal Action* (Routledge 2017).

Levashova Y, 'The Accountability and Corporate Social Responsibility of Multinational Corporations for Transgressions in Host States through International Investment Law', (2018) 14(2) *Utrecht Law Review* 40.

Muchlinski P, *Multinational Enterprises and the Law* (Oxford University Press 1995, revised 2007).

OECD, *OECD Guidelines for Multinational Enterprises* (OECD Publishing 2011).

Zerk J, *Multinationals and Corporate Social Responsibility: Limitations and Opportunities in International Law* (Cambridge University Press 2006).

Zugliani N, 'Human Rights in International Investment Law: The 2016 Morocco-Nigeria Bilateral Investment Treaty', (2019) 68(3) *International & Comparative Law Quarterly* 761.

2 Whose responsibilities? The responsibility of the "business enterprise" to respect human rights

Björn Fasterling[*]

2.1 Introduction[1]

Until September 2014, the French industrial group Lafarge operated the Jalabiya cement plant in northeastern Syria, close to Raqqa. The company had acquired the plant in 2008, with the investment amounting to reportedly 680 million euros.[2] Following this, Lafarge Cement Syria (LCS) became the owner of the plant. LCS was a 98.7% subsidiary of the listed French société anonyme (SA) Lafarge. Until 2012, the subsidiary's minority share was held by a rich Syrian family that fell in disgrace with the Bachar al Assad regime after it had joined the opposition. On this occasion, the assets of that family were confiscated, as were, apparently, also their shareholding in LCS.[3] In 2015, the Swiss company Holcim acquired Lafarge, with the effect that the parent company of the group and successor of Lafarge is now LafargeHolcim SA. According to the 2016 annual report of LafargeHolcim, the group still holds a 98.7% stake in LCS.[4] However, the group reports that it has not been operating the plant since September 2014, when it was abandoned for security reasons.[5]

When the Syrian civil war broke out in 2011, Lafarge made the decision to continue operations of the plant. According to Bruno Pescheux, the then CEO (*directeur général*) of the Syrian subsidiary, the company thought that once the war was over there would be at least one plant left that could provide cement for the country's reconstruction.[6] However, from 2012 on the security situation at the plant deteriorated. Armed groups demanded money for passage. Pescheux noted that the plant was confronted with a "racketing economy". To deal with this situation, Lafarge hired Firas Tlass, a well-known Syrian businessman, as its "security advisor". Tlass had contacts among all warring parties, as well as with the Syrian government. He was paid a salary of 75,000 euros per month and was endorsed with a budget for negotiating payments to various militia, including the free army of Syria, Kurdish forces, and jihadist groups. It is reported that payments varied between 80,000–100,000 euros monthly. The payments were accounted for with the help of fake expense reports. The group admitted that the terrorist organization Daesh (ISIS) was on the list of the extortionists and accounted for roughly 10% of the payments.[7]

Lafarge had evacuated its expatriate employees, but LCS's local employees kept the plant operational. As these employees lived tens of kilometers away from the plant, commuting to work became a serious security problem for them. In October 2012, nine employees were kidnapped and liberated against payment of a 200,000-dollar ransom. When Daesh took control of nearby Raqqa, the employees were still not evacuated. Instead, armed Kurdish forces were paid to maintain a "cordon sanitaire" to and from the plant. Later, employees even had to stay confined within the plant. When Daesh troops eventually attacked the plant on 20 September 2014, the employees were able to escape on their own devices. However, Lafarge's management put forward that evacuation plans had been ready but were not implemented.

Contacted by LCS's employees, various non-governmental organizations submitted a complaint to the French legal authorities. The French Ministry of Finance did the same in September 2016. At the time of writing this chapter, three examining magistrates (*juges d'instruction*) are investigating the case for suspected terrorist financing and exposure of employees to life-threatening risks.

Whether, and to what extent, Lafarge and its managers are liable under criminal or civil law is a matter for courts to decide. The case also raises questions about extra-legal corporate responsibilities, in particular Lafarge's responsibilities to respect human rights. But who – in such an extra-legal context – is the subject of responsibility; or, who is "Lafarge"? The parent entity, the corporate group as a whole? Or, could we determine the human rights responsibilities of Lafarge independently of legal considerations regarding entities and groups of entities?

First, this contribution will provide an answer to the previous question; in other words, it will deal with the determination of the bearers of the corporate responsibility to respect human rights under the United Nations Guiding Principles for Business and Human Rights (UNGPs).[8] Of course, it is the "business enterprise" that bears responsibilities; however, here, the meaning of the term "business enterprise" in the extra-legal context of the UNGPs and its consequences for determining responsibilities will be spelled out in more detail. In particular, it will be argued that business enterprise responsibility can be understood as an *activity-centered* concept, according to which business models are to be made compatible with respect for human rights and enterprises assume organizational responsibilities to have *effective managerial routines* in place that aim to prevent and mitigate human rights risks. In this light, business strategy, business objectives, perennial organizational structures, managerial processes, and routines become constitutive elements of the business enterprise. Legal entities that are employed by the business, such as a French *société anonyme*, represent but one of the perennial structures that shape the business enterprise. Business enterprise responsibility, or so it will be argued, also implies individual and collective responsibilities of certain people, who will be referred to as the "function-holders" of an enterprise, to act according to these routines and to take human rights into account when they make strategic decisions.

Second, this chapter will demonstrate the challenges to transpose the extra-legal concept of corporate responsibility into responsibility that takes the form of a legal due diligence standard. This will be illustrated against the backdrop of the French "due diligence law", the "*Loi relative au devoir de vigilance des sociétés mères et des entrprises donneuses d'ordre*", adopted by the French parliament on 21 February 2017[9] and promulgated after the French Constitutional Council's decision of 27 March 2017,[10] – a law that was inspired by the UNGPs.[11] Due diligence as a legal standard, like the UNGPs' due diligence, works as a norm aiming at harm prevention. However, unlike the UNGPs' due diligence, a legal due diligence norm can also encompass standards that determine liability on the basis of an *ex post* assessment of the facts.[12] A legal standard, through its liability and prevention dimensions, should ideally provide sufficient incentives for business enterprises to implement effective human rights due diligence that the UNGPs aim at. Here, it will be argued that the French law falls short of such ambitions, primarily because of its exclusive focus on a parent entity's obligations and its reference to general liability law for fault. Alternative avenues of liability law for enforcing due diligence standards will be explored.

2.2 Human rights due diligence under the UNGPs

The second pillar of the UNGPs details how the corporate responsibility to respect human rights is to be fulfilled: business enterprises are not only expected to avoid infringing on the human rights of others, but must also address adverse human rights impacts with which they are involved, which requires "taking adequate measures for their prevention, mitigation and, where appropriate, remediation".[13] The operational program for addressing human rights responsibilities is spelled out in UNGPs 15–19, and comprises making a policy commitment, conducting human rights due diligence, and establishing processes to enable remediation. UNGP 17 stipulates that human rights due diligence consists of (a) assessing actual and potential human rights impacts, (b) integrating and acting upon the findings, (c) tracking responses, and (d) communicating how impacts are addressed.

From a management perspective, UNGP 17 could be reformulated as a five-step approach. On the one hand, each of these steps involves actions by human beings that exercise functions within the business enterprise. On the other hand, they also require information, documentation, and communication routines that relate different people to each other.

First, people in the organization who occupy functions that allow them to detect human rights risks on the ground are to be trained so that they are capable of detecting information that is relevant for gauging such risks. Second, the business enterprise needs to employ (either externally or internally) people who have the expertise to normatively assess those risks, meaning that they are able to assess the severity of human rights risks. Third, the risk assessment must be "integrated" (see also UNGP 19 [a]) throughout the organization. Integration essentially means that those who detect and assess human rights risks must routinely communicate their assessments to those who have authority and means to take appropriate action. The Interpretative Guide to the UNPGs states that integration is the "micro process of taking the findings about a particular potential impact, identifying who in the enterprise needs to be involved in addressing it and securing effective action".[14] That a business enterprise must take appropriate action in the light of the assessed risk can mean various things, and depends on the concrete context of the case. According to UNGP 19, appropriate action is determined based on whether the enterprise caused or contributed to risk or whether risk is directly linked to the business enterprise's operations, and to what extent the business enterprise has leverage in addressing a negative impact.[15] Fourth, someone must evaluate the action taken with respect to its effectiveness of preventing or mitigating human rights risk (which the UNGPs call "tracking"). Finally, a business enterprise must instruct people to account for and communicate its efforts to a broader public.

From this overview, we see that the human rights due diligence standard of the UNGPs is not to be understood as a liability standard that defines a certain standard of care against which a business enterprise's actions are judged in order to attribute *ex post* responsibility. In fact, the UNGPs say nothing about what happens when due diligence is poorly carried out or not implemented at all. Instead, human rights due diligence under the UNGPs consists of a business process that is meant to operate as a prophylactic measure, so that the term "responsibility" is used exclusively in its forward-looking meaning.[16]

Human rights due diligence as set out in the UNGPs may be viewed as a special form of risk management.[17] On the one hand, it is risk management because the process's steps (impact assessment, integration, tracking, and communication) largely match the steps of common risk-management frameworks such as enterprise risk management (ERM) under the Committee of Sponsoring Organizations of the Treadway Commission (COSO) framework or International Standards Organization (ISO) 31000.[18] The ISO 31000 framework defines "risk" as the "effect of uncertainty on objectives", where "uncertainty" is understood as a "state, even partial, of deficiency of information related to a future event, consequence or likelihood".[19] While this risk definition might raise questions,[20] it does make clear that risk management essentially provides a system that establishes a relevant knowledge base for managers who are supposed to make informed decisions in the interest of the organization they are serving.

On the other hand, human rights due diligence under the UNGPs is special because of the nature of the risk that is to be managed. Enterprises are not required to manage their own social risks (for example, those stemming from stakeholder pushback or other business risks),[21] but rather risks for *rights holders*. The UNGPs thus ask nothing less than that business enterprises conduct risk management in the interest of other people, namely rights holders, even when there is no "business case" for doing so.[22] This is a clear departure from conventional corporate risk-management approaches that focus exclusively on corporate exposures. The UNGPs, at least implicitly, stand in opposition to management theories which presuppose that value maximization is the ultimate corporate objective. If business enterprises managed human rights risk from a value-maximization perspective (for example, in order to avoid liability, forestall business interruptions, or prevent reputation issues), they would not collect and process the same type of risk-relevant information and would not take the same type of risk-reduction or risk-prevention measures.[23]

2.3 Bearers of corporate responsibility: the business enterprise and its function holders

The holder of the corporate responsibility to respect human rights under the UNGPs is the "business enterprise". This term is defined neither by the UNGPs nor by its official commentary. It is also not clarified in the preparatory reports preceding the UNGPs.[24] However, what is clear is that the term "business enterprise" covers a wide range of commercially motivated operations that can be carried out not only by incorporated for-profit companies, but also by other types of business enterprises. For example, sole proprietorships could be used for business enterprises (for instance, a small mineral trader that works on his or her own account), as well as various forms of non-dividend-paying social businesses (for example, Yunus Social Business Funds gGmbH), or even not-for-profit associations (such as Fédération Internationale de Football Association) to the extent that the latter engage in commercial activity.[25] Furthermore, Ruggie wrote that in the case of a multinational corporation, the notion of an "enterprise" includes the "entire corporate group, however it is structured".[26]

Taking into account that human rights due diligence under the UNGPs is understood as a business process and not as a legal standard of conduct for purposes of determining liability,[27] it could indeed be more adequate to determine the business enterprise from a business perspective instead of from a legal one.

2.3.1 A business activity-centered perspective on the business enterprise

Dealing with legal interpretations of the business enterprise may have the advantage of setting clear boundaries that separate holders of rights and obligations from one another. However, when confronted with cases in which business activity is carried out through economically integrated activity that links multiple legal entities to each other through capital participations, contracts, or *de facto* cooperation routines, the focus on the legal entity quickly becomes "atomistic" and risks disregarding organizational realities. Consequently, when harm has been caused through the dealings of such economically integrated organizations, the tenets of any legal system's rules on corporate responsibility and corporate liability law, in particular the imputation of behavior of natural persons to corporations and the fault of corporations, are most likely to be challenged. In this respect, the issue of limited liability could also be a barrier to effectuate compensation for victims of human rights abuses. Next to that, one can also consider personal liability of the business enterprise's managers or other employees.[28]

As previously mentioned, corporate responsibility under the UNGPs does not require the identification of a legal person to which liability may be attributed based on an *ex post* judgement of the facts. Thus, for the assessment of who bears responsibility in this context, it is possible to focus exclusively on the concrete business activity and on the management processes, governance structures, and routines of human interaction that sustain it.

For example, the concrete activity of a shoe retailer that owns a famous brand is to sell shoes in various markets. Establishing and maintaining a globally reputed brand enables the shoe retailer to sell more shoes at a higher price. Suppose the retailer decides to outsource production entirely to supplier factories that are highly integrated into the retailer's value chain through long-term contracts, creating *de facto* economic dependencies and allowing the retailer to closely manage product quality. One could discuss at length whether the supplier is in fact part of the same business enterprise as the retailer. One way to delimit the business enterprise would be to apply notions of "ownership", which would separate the supplier from the enterprise as it does not stand in any share ownership relationship with the retailer. A related criteria for a business enterprise's boundaries could be "control", or "managerial command", if we define control as meaning that a manager of the controlling company can effectively intervene in the strategy or even in the operations of the controlled company.[29] However, focusing on control structures does not provide much insight for solving the question, as the example shows: while the retailer may still have managerial command over product quality through contractual clauses and enforcement processes, it may have let go of control over work processes and labor conditions at the supplier's sites.

Moreover, the question of the reach of managerial control may not be crucial for the determination of enterprise responsibility under the UNGPs. We could put forward that the retailer, through its decision to outsource, has relinquished partial control over production processes and labor conditions. However, from a risk perspective, the retailer now faces higher uncertainties with regard to possible human rights violations occurring in the course of the manufacturing process of shoes bearing the retailer's brand. In other words, the retailer, by outsourcing production, has practically increased human rights risks that are linked to its business activities. The UNGPs prescribe in such cases that business enterprises have a social responsibility to mitigate or prevent the increased human rights risk that the outsourcing decision has brought about. The *process* of retaining "independent suppliers" for production of branded products and the interaction with these suppliers clearly falls within the scope of a business enterprise's activities and thus gives rise to responsibilities under the UNGPs.

To better theorize business enterprise responsibility under the UNGPs, the activity-centered concept of the *business model* could become helpful. The "business model" has become a recognized unit of analysis in management practice and theory. While there are many ways to represent business models,[30] the emphasis will essentially be on a *system of activity* that aims at "*value creation*" and "*value capture*". Broadly speaking, value creation refers to actions that increase the worth of something, such as products, services, or shares, while value capture deals with how the architect of a business model is able to extract benefits from the value that has been created.[31] The business model relates to the way a business enterprise places itself in the value chain of its sector and how it organizes relationships with clients, suppliers, and other partners, in most cases with the objective of generating a profit.[32] The ontological nature of the business model is largely left open. Business models could concern clearly delineated "focal firms" that deal with "peripheral firms", but they could also describe activities of less economically integrated commercial networks where various players are engaged in a common project. Under an activity-centered perspective of the business enterprise, it is fully possible that one company or group of companies entertains several business models at the same time. Conversely, it is also imaginable that one single business model is served by several agents cooperating with each other.

The business model concept delineates organizations by the strategies and perennial structures that serve value creation and value capture. When analyzing business models, attention is drawn to the goals and architecture of business activity. In the context of the UNGPs, we would say that value-creating and value-capturing activities must be organized under the condition that human rights risks are identified, prevented, or mitigated.

If this concept is applied to the aforementioned Lafarge case, it may be said that Lafarge had a distinct business model for Syria. This consisted of creating value by providing a local supply of cement to the Syrian government and private customers. When the armed conflict broke out, Lafarge may have considered that cement would be even more valuable for these stakeholders since it would be used to reconstruct infrastructure and buildings devastated by the war. In maintaining the plant's operations, Lafarge may have assumed that it would benefit from a strong bargaining position, which would increase the firm's "value capture" capability as it would be one of the few suppliers, or even the only supplier, left to serve the local demand for cement. However, the continuation of the plant's operation during violent conflict also significantly increased the risk that employees and other people working at the plant would suffer harm. Instead of preventing these risks altogether, for example by evacuating the site before the situation deteriorated, Lafarge engaged in a mitigation strategy. Through its subsidiary, it engaged an outside intermediary to pay passage for people working at the plant. However, this mitigation strategy generated further human rights risks by increasing uncertainties regarding the recipients of Lafarge's passage money, which could have included, and in fact did include, armed groups that perpetrated grave human rights violations. Even though the actions in this case were taken by various agents (representatives of the parent company who took the strategic decision to stay in Syria, local managers of Lafarge's subsidiary in Syria who dealt with operational problems on the ground, and a hired third party that enacted payments to armed groups for passage), we may conclude that Lafarge's business model for Syria was not compatible with a business enterprise's corporate responsibility to respect human rights under the UNGP because it did not include risk-mitigation and risk-prevention measures that were adequate in the light of human rights risks that the business model generated.

2.3.2 *Implications for human rights responsibilities of individuals*

Analyzing corporate responsibility by focusing on business activity and its "architecture" also has implications for how we represent the responsibilities of individuals who relate to each other through the structures, processes, and routines that constitute the business enterprise. People participating in a business enterprise not only have human rights responsibilities like any other human being, but also have human rights responsibilities that are linked to their respective roles in the business enterprise (which we could refer to as "functional human rights responsibilities"). The former refers to a responsibility that anybody has to respect the human rights of others. The latter refers to a distinct set of human rights responsibilities to properly carry out the function that the individual is entrusted with in terms of the business's activities.

Although the UNGPs only talk of responsibility of business enterprises, the corporate responsibility to respect human rights implicitly assigns responsibilities to all persons, and groups of persons, that are conferred with organizational authority and tasks, such as devising corporate strategy, designing structures, maintaining routines, and implementing processes. For example, the board of a parent company is a group of human beings that formulates or approves top-level corporate strategy and may, in that capacity, commit the organization as a whole to respecting human rights. CEOs have human rights responsibilities not only as fellow human beings, but also as important function holders of an organization, when devising or executing strategies. Even the operative employee on the ground may have responsibilities as a function holder, for example to communicate observed human rights problems to the right person in the organization. Managers on all levels have organizational responsibilities to ensure, among other things, that communication channels do not become dysfunctional. As noted previously, this internal communication routine is the essence of "integration" under UNGP 19, which requires an "integration of findings" of the UNGPs' due diligence process. This means that people on the ground who become privy to human rights risks must communicate their observations to the person in the organization who can most appropriately address the situation and deal with the risk.

In the case of Lafarge, we could assume that Lafarge's CEO at the time played an influential role in deciding to remain in Syria and was thus under a responsibility to organize proper due diligence procedures to even-out increased human rights risks caused by that decision. However, the local managers of Lafarge's Syrian subsidiary also had responsibilities to implement due diligence measures and to report problems to the corporate headquarters, who could have, for example, commanded evacuation of the plant when the situation deteriorated. LafargeHolcim's internal report admits that the group's procedures were inadequate with regard to addressing the risk that a local subsidiary, through an intermediary, would end up paying money to terrorist groups in order to keep the business going.[33]

It is unclear as of yet to what level of detail the senior and top management at the French headquarters of Lafarge were aware of the dealings of the local subsidiary's managers. But even so, with or without knowledge of details, we can make out failings of human rights due diligence at an individual level. We may assume, for example, that the local management had a clear idea of whom the intermediary was paying money. They probably did identify risks to the business and may have come to the conclusion that paying off terrorists was a pragmatic way to deal with the situation, and was possibly in the company's – and also in the Syrian government's – interest because the latter needed a cement supply. Human rights risks were very likely not taken into account, and if they were indeed considered, the economic argument for profit outweighed them.

If the top management in the Paris headquarters was aware of details of the situation on the ground in Syria, it did not take appropriate action (under UNGP 19), which would have meant evacuating the plant before terrorist groups could effectively racket the local management, or, at latest, when the plant fell under a zone of intense armed conflict and the security of employees could in no reasonable way be assured. If the parent company's top management was not aware of the dire security situation at the Syrian plant, we can infer that the top management had not established communication routines by which human rights risks could be reported throughout the group. Therefore, in the case of Lafarge, either managers did not "integrate findings" about severe human rights risks, or Lafarge managers were aware of these risks but chose not to intervene in the subsidiary's problematic dealings with Daesh by evacuating the plant, and thus did not take appropriate action. Despite our lack of full information on the case, we can, with some degree of certainty, conclude that it offers an example of individuals having failed their "functional" human rights responsibilities under the UNGPs.

2.4 Transposing the corporate responsibility in the UNGPs into a legal duty? The French due diligence law and theoretical alternative solutions

The challenges for transposing the UNGPs' corporate responsibility to respect human rights into a legal duty can be exemplified against the backdrop of the French due diligence law. Although this law was inspired by the UNGPs, it features some salient conceptual differences when compared to the UNGPs, even aside from the fact that the law covers areas other than human rights and is only applicable to large companies and not, as in the UNGPs, to any business enterprise.[34]

2.4.1 The French law: focus on parent company and reference to classic liability for fault

The French due diligence law obliges large French companies, in consultation with stakeholders, to implement an effective due diligence plan that addresses business-related environmental, health, security, and human rights risks. The scope of the law extends to all French companies that have more than 5,000 employees domestically, or employ 10,000 employees worldwide.[35]

The obligation to implement a due diligence plan comprises a requirement to map and prioritize the previously discussed risks extending to all companies the parent company directly or indirectly controls, as well as all suppliers and subcontractors with whom the company and its subsidiaries have an established business relationship. Furthermore, parent companies must take reasonable measures to prevent or mitigate such risks, establish an internal whistleblowing procedure, evaluate the effectiveness of measures taken, and finally communicate implementation of the due diligence plan in their annual reports.

Non-compliance with the law can be disciplined through court injunctions, as well as liability provisions.[36] With regard to the latter, the law refers to general liability for fault or violations of the law. The question as to who can seek injunctive relief under this law is yet unanswered. Unlike provisions in recent French anti-bribery laws (that also contain risk-mapping obligations for companies), the due diligence law does not establish any particular agency that could hold companies to comply with the law's requirements. Therefore, we may assume that only a person or entity that would have legal standing in a liability case could also issue a formal notice that would instigate a court procedure for injunctive relief.[37]

The French due diligence law is unique as it is the first domestic law to introduce an obligation not only to map human rights (among other) risks relating to a business enterprise's activities, but also to implement due diligence processes with a view to facilitate risk prevention and mitigation in this context. It seems as if the French due diligence obligation for parent companies transposes some of the UNGPs' requirements into law. The first challenge for drafters of the law was to identify a legal entity that has rights and obligations under the law. A group, under French law, has no distinct legal personality. We have seen that determining a person or entity for assuming responsibilities is not necessary under the UNGPs' concept of responsibility. Thus, the due diligence obligations laid down in the French law are focused on French "parent companies". Meanwhile, those obligations are supposed be enforced through court injunctions and a liability regime. However, the text of the law, in combination with the ruling of the Constitutional Council, have made it clear that the law's liability provisions keep the basic principles of personal liability for fault and limited liability intact.[38] This means that the law cannot be construed as implying vicarious liability, or as offering a special case for piercing the corporate veil. Furthermore, the law does not provide for any legal presumptions that could ease the burden of proof for tort victims. In other words, a victim will have to first prove a violation of the law, and thus that the plan and its implementation were sub-standard. This might be difficult, as the law is not clear on the details of what would make a state-of-the-art due diligence plan. The victim would then have to prove that a loss was suffered due to the absence of an effective due diligence plan drawn up and implemented by the parent company.

Targeting the parent company for enforcement of the due diligence obligation in the French due diligence law has the effect that victims must somehow prove that failures in the due diligence process are traceable to a failure of a parent company's actions. This stands in marked contrast to the business enterprise perspective described earlier, where the responsibility to carry out due diligence is activity-based and spread throughout the entire organization. Under the UNGPs' due diligence, at least as it is understood here, it does not matter whether flawed processes or sub-standard behavior occurs at the parent or subsidiary level. Recall, for example, the UNGPs' concept of "integration" that implies enterprise-wide internal communication routines. If one were to legally enforce UNGP 19, the failure of anyone engaged in the enterprise's due diligence process would be relevant.

Focusing on a parent company's actions only, like the French law does, without any legal presumptions that human rights violations linked to a company's business activity indicate ineffective due diligence, the law seriously hampers victims from arguing their claim in court, while at the same time the parent company is offered generous possibilities to defend against the tort claim. As long as the parent company draws up a state-of-the-art risk map and due diligence plan, and is able to show that it implements and regularly follows up on the plan, the defendant is on the safe side. A strict liability regime where due diligence becomes a means of defense would provide more succor to victims. Furthermore, in practice, the displayable existence of formal measures taken by a parent company such as a group code of ethics, whistleblowing channels, risk mapping with a sophisticated system of weighted scores and figures, as well as training measures may become more important than assessment of the extent to which all these measures actually support the prevention and mitigation of human rights risks. However, the existence of a due diligence plan and risk mapping say nothing about how it is effectively integrated throughout the whole organization. This is precisely one of the most crucial aspects of corporate responsibility to respect human rights under the UNGPs.

Due to the way in which it has been drafted, the French due diligence law risks resulting in a costly bureaucratic exercise of compliance that has little effect on the ground.[39] In addition, a court will hardly be able to assess the effectiveness of a parent company's due diligence plan without judging the actions of people working for subsidiaries or other business partners. and without evaluating the effectiveness of communications between all involved. Thus, isolating the action at the level of the parent company is a hindrance for determining due diligence effectiveness. Furthermore, even if a victim claiming damages is able to establish a failure of the parent company to draw up a proper plan, he or she would still have hardly any means to prove a causal link between the absence of a due diligence plan drawn up in a corporate headquarters and the loss suffered in a different part of the world. After all, establishing causality would probably require some kind of measurement of a plan's hypothetical effectiveness. And about that we know – at most – very little. Thus, since a corporate defendant would not have to prove the effectiveness of a due diligence plan, any possible liability claim could conveniently be rebutted by the argument that the company discharged the law's "due diligence" requirements by taking a number of formal due diligence measures that are easy to display and only supposedly effective.

To conclude, by focusing on the parent company only and referring to traditional liability for fault, one could argue that if the French law was supposed to be a first legal transposition of the UNGPs' corporate responsibility standards. then it would have numerous shortcomings. However, the French legislature was very concerned about providing French companies with a competitive disadvantage by introducing stricter provisions. Nevertheless, the current situation might be counterproductive, as French companies will have to invest resources in formal due diligence plans, while it is not at all certain that these plans will provide any effective relief for victims.

2.4.2 *Ideas for alternatives with a focus on liability: enterprise liability and distributed risk-based liability?*

There are a number of challenges with transposing the extra-legal corporate responsibility of the UNGPs into law. First, the UNGPs, despite being a framework that spells out corporate responsibilities in sufficient detail for the purposes of designing managerial processes, may still be too vague for the purposes of creating an enforceable legal obligation.[40] Furthermore, any transposition would need to reconcile the previously described activity-centered "business enterprise" perspective with a legal entity perspective. As already mentioned, the UNGPs do not deal with the question of what is to happen if due diligence is not implemented, since they provide a purely forward-looking normative framework. Therefore, the UNGPs do not need to attribute consequences to one or the other entity. However, setting and enforcing legal standards implies rules in combination with some kind of legal remedial action that are addressed to an entity capable of bearing rights and obligations. A law could confine itself to obliging companies to undertake certain forward-looking risk-management actions, and enforce this obligation through court or administrative injunctions. This would require a regulatory agency that has the power to initiate proceedings leading to such injunctions. Even in this case, a legal entity would need to be identified against which the procedure can be directed, and upon which the injunction can be imposed. The French law did not create any regulatory agency that would enforce the due diligence obligation. Alternatively, or in parallel to such a "regulatory" enforcement, we could imagine liability provisions. After the French Constitutional Council struck out the penal fine, the French law's main enforcement mechanism became liability for fault, which, as discussed previously, is unlikely to provide much help to human rights victims.

The UNGPs express societal expectations toward business enterprises to respect human rights by implementing effective risk-mitigation and risk-prevention processes. If such an expectation were to "harden" into law, legal measures would need to exert sufficient pressure on legal entities and their representatives to contribute to effective human rights due diligence. Short of a regulatory procedure, a civil liability regime could become useful in this respect, but it would need to overcome limits posed by default burden of evidence rules and the principles of corporate liability, in particular limited liability that benefits "non-human" corporate shareholders. Under these principles, it is possible for business enterprises to organize economically integrated activity, capture value, and at the same time optimize legal liability risk by compartmentalizing it among legally separate entities.[41] Within a corporate group, a parent company may even want to limit, to a certain extent, communication with subsidiaries in order to ensure their "legal separateness", and thus avoid the possibility of corporate veil piercing.

The UNGPs' human rights due diligence requirement, by contrast, would necessitate enhanced communication within corporate groups. This also holds true for communication with business partners. For example, a company outsourcing production to independent suppliers will most likely be able to reduce the risk of liability for harm occurring during production, as under most legal systems the company would not be held vicariously liable for the suppliers' actions. However, delegating production of goods to independent suppliers could increase business-related human rights risk. This is the case if the delegation of activity related to a business model goes hand in hand with a loss of knowledge regarding how that activity is carried out, in particular with regard to work conditions. Effective due diligence under the UNGPs would counter such tendencies because it requires that knowledge about human rights problems and taking appropriate measures to deal with them becomes as integrated as any other activity related to a business model, such as ensuring product quality.

There are a number of proposals as to how liability law could more adequately address economically integrated activity. There is no need to recall the academic discussion about lifting the corporate veil and unlimited shareholder liability in the case of corporate torts,[42] and in particular concerning the case of complex corporate groups.[43] Further-reaching proposals deal with new forms of enterprise liability. For example, Blumberg suggested enterprise liability under the condition that there is "a common public persona featuring a common trade name, logo, and marketing plan", financial and administrative interdependence, as well as group identification of employees.[44] Dearborn wrote that enterprise liability could be premised on a "unity of economic direction and flow of interests and profits".[45]

However, even such "enterprise liability" concepts would not fully enforce integrated management of human rights risks, especially when business models are realized through the engagement of many independent actors. An example would be Uber's business model for competing with transport services. We could argue here that even if drivers are not employed by Uber and are considered to be "independent", they still are integral to the realization of Uber's business model to create and capture value in the transport sector. In the vein of Uberization, we could imagine business models organized in such a way that a mere platform with certain functionalities and "rules of play" incentivizes numerous independent agents to cooperate toward value creation, while most value is captured by those who created the platform.[46]

The UNGPs' human rights due diligence concept could deal with these situations, since the platform would have to prevent and mitigate human rights risks that arise through the coordinated activities of users that the platform enables. However, the concepts of "enterprise liability" previously described would not be sufficient to entice such due diligence efforts, since the platform integrates business activity but not organizations. Ratner's idea of holding companies *prima facie* responsible for acts of contractors and subcontractors concerning contracted-for projects[47] could motivate companies to conduct effective due diligence for activities sustaining a business model, but the conditions for rebutting presumptions would have to be fine-tuned. Ratner's suggestion that *prima facie* responsibility could be overcome, if it were shown, respectively, that the corporation did not exercise real control over execution of the contracted-for project, or, conversely, that it had actual dominion over the contractor,[48] would not be relevant for the aforementioned "platform enterprise", or even for business models that operate through economically independent suppliers.

However, the toolbox of imaginable liability law is far from exhausted. We could work not only with the aforementioned enterprise liability concepts and rebuttable legal presumptions in order to help victims, but also, for example, with notions of distributed liability. The law could establish a ranking of liability with the effect that companies held to manage human rights risk insure a tort victim for losses resulting from human rights violations, but they can seek indemnification from a "higher-ranking" liable person – eventually the person or entity to which the tortious action can be attributed. This distributed liability system would shift the risk that damages cannot be collected from the tortfeasor away from the victim to lower-ranking liable entities. These would bear residual liability risk, which could provide just enough incentive for equipping business models with adequate and effective human rights risk-management processes.

2.5 Concluding remarks

The UNGPs, despite not having any legal quality, have been drafted against the backdrop of the development of international human rights law and extraterritorially applicable national provisions that offer legal remedies for victims of human rights abuses. Despite existing governance gaps, John Ruggie and his team observed an "expanding web of potential corporate liability for international crimes".[49] The commentary to the UNGPs suggests that business enterprises should treat "human rights risk" as a "legal compliance" issue.[50] One could say that the UNGPs are written in anticipation of a denser legal coverage of business-related human rights abuses. Now the question arises as to how the UNGPs can shape future legal due diligence standards that pertain to business-related human rights risk. To prepare the answer to the question, this contribution proposed viewing the bearer of responsibility under the UNGPs, namely the "business enterprise", through the lens of managerial concepts, in particular the "business model" and "value creation". It was put forward that the business enterprise is to be understood and delimited by the activities it carries out in order to pursue its strategies. Such an understanding fits well to the way the UNGPs detail corporate responsibility, but it also reveals the breadth of challenges the law would face if it sought to transform the UNGPs' extra-legal due diligence concept into a legal norm. Here, it has been argued that the French law, albeit clearly inspired by the UNGPs, has poorly captured essential elements of UNGP corporate responsibility by focusing exclusively on parent company obligations and referring to traditional liability law for fault. It has been argued that if human rights due diligence

Table 2.1 Comparison of types of responsibility, UNGPs and French due diligence law

	Corporate responsibility	*Legal Liability*	*French due diligence law*
Type of responsibility	• Forward-looking (human rights risk management) • Responsibility to act	• Ex post assessment of failure to conduct due diligence • Assessment of existing measures and past behaviour	• Obligation to create and implement a due diligence plan that concerns the entire group, as well as suppliers with which the group has an established commercial relationship • Possible liability for damages • Court injunction to enforce compliance
Attribution	• To business enterprise: Responsibility for business model design and having communication and actions routines • To individuals and groups of individuals: Collective and individual responsibilities of a business enterprise's function holders to design business models compatible with respecting human rights and to act according to communication and action routines	• Need to identify legal entity (parent company of a corporate group, for example) • Attribution of liability to individuals, if damage has been caused by personal negligent action	• Parent company liability but no vicarious liability or veil piercing • Liability of individuals is not specified
Measure for fulfilling responsibilities or duties	• Ongoing measure of effectiveness	• Control of discharge of specified tasks • Control of effectiveness only incidentally if causation is analyzed (see next section)	• Drawing up a due diligence plan and risk mapping
Link between human rights violation and assessment of responsibility/duty	• Causation of, contribution to, and direct link to human rights risk	• Causation between lack of due diligence and damage	• Causation between lack of due diligence plan and risk mapping and damage (here, the hypothetical effectiveness of due diligence would play a role)

is to be enforced with the help of liability law, certain deviations from the limited liability principle must be undertaken and the burden of proof eased for victims.

Table 2.1 provides a summary of the salient differences between extra-legal due diligence responsibility and legal liability, including the obligations put forward by the French due diligence law.

Notes

* Professor of Law, EDHEC Business School (France). This chapter is an extended version of the speech I held at the Ucall Conference at Utrecht University on 18 May 2017.

1 This introduction provides a summary of the publicly known facts of the Lafarge-Syria case as of October 2017. It is based on the following sources: Jacques Monin and Others, 'Lafarge en Syrie: du ciment à tout prix' (France Inter, 14 October 2017) <www.franceinter.fr/emissions/secrets-d-info/secrets-d-info-14-octobre-2017> accessed 14 October 2017; LafargeHolcim, 'Summary of Syria Review Findings', <www.lafargeholcim.com/summary-syria-investigation-findings> accessed 27 April 2017; LafargeHolcim, Annual Report 2016 published on 3 February 2017, <www.lafargeholcim.com/annual-report-2016> accessed 27 April 2017.

2 LafargeHolcim, Annual Report 2016 (n 1).

3 The details, to which extent the Syrian government entered into the equity capital of LCS are unclear, cf. Monin and Others, 'Lafarge en Syrie: du ciment à tout prix' (n 1).

4 LafargeHolcim, 'Annual Report 2016' (n 1) 263.

5 LafargeHolcim, 'Summary of Syria Review Findings' (n 1).

6 Cited by Monin and Others, 'Lafarge en Syrie: du ciment à tout prix' (n 1). This report also mentions that the factory might have been used by the French State's secret services to gather intelligence about the war. In this contribution, I will not take this suspicion into account, and will assume Lafarge's business considerations were the only motivations to keep the plant up and running.

7 See Monin and Others, 'Lafarge en Syrie: du ciment à tout prix' (n 1).

8 Human Rights Council, 'Guiding Principles on Business and Human Rights: Implementing the United Nations "Protect, Respect and Remedy" Framework', A/HRC/17/31 (21 March 2011) ['Guiding Principles on Business and Human Rights'].

9 Loi relative au devoir de vigilance des sociétés mères et des entreprises donneuses d'ordre, Act no 2017–399 of 27 March 2017.

10 French Constitutional Council, Decision 2017–750 DC [Devoir de vigilance des sociétés mères].

11 Sandra Cossart, Jérôme Chaplier, and Tiphaine Beau de Lomenie, 'The French Law on Duty of Care: A Historic Step Towards Making Globalization Work for All', (2017) 2(2) *Business and Human Rights Journal* 317.

12 John Gerard Ruggie and John F. Sherman III, 'The Concept of Due Diligence in the UN Guiding Principles on Business and Human Rights: Reply to Professors Bonnitcha and McCorquodale', (2017) 28(3) *European Journal of International Law* 921.

13 Human Rights Council, 'Guiding Principles on Business and Human Rights' (n 8), UNGPs 11, 13.

14 United Nations Office of the High Commissioner, The Corporate Responsibility to Respect Human Rights: An Interpretative Guide, [2012] HR/PUB/12/02, 47.

15 See, in particular, ibid.

16 John Gerard Ruggie and John F. Sherman III, 'The Concept of Due Diligence in the UN Guiding Principles on Business and Human Rights: Reply to Professors Bonnitcha and McCorquodale' (n 12). However, Jonathan Bonnitcha and Robert McCorquodale put forward that the "forward-lookin"' nature of human rights due diligence should not be confounded with the responsibility of enterprises to provide a remedy for adverse human rights impacts that it causes or contributes to. See Bonnitcha and McCorquodale, 'The Concept of "Due Diligence" in the UN Guiding Principles on Business and Human Rights', (2017) 28(3) *European Journal of International Law* 899.

17 Björn Fasterling, 'Human Rights Due Diligence as Risk Management', (2017) 2(2) *Business and Human Rights Journal* 225, with references to the Human Rights Council's preparatory work on the UNGPs.

18 There is no agreed-upon definition of ERM. ERM commonly refers to an integrative approach to risk management that is informed by an organization's highest-level goals and strategies. For example, the COSO defines ERM as "a process, effected by an entity's board of directors, management or other personnel, applied in strategy setting and across the enterprise, designed to identify potential events that may affect the entity, and manage risk to be within its risk appetite, to provide reasonable assurance regarding the achievement of entity objectives". See Committee of Sponsoring Organizations of the Treadway Commission September 2004, Enterprise Risk Management: Integrated Framework, Executive Summary [2004] 2; ISO, ISO 31000, Risk Management, [2009]; ISO, Guide ISO 79 [2009].

19 ISO, ISO 31000 (n 18); ISO, Guide ISO 79 (n 18).

20 Cf., for example, Grant Purdy, 'ISO 31000:2009: Setting a New Standard for Risk Management', (2010) 30(6) *Risk Analysis* 881; Terje Aven, Ortwin Renn and Eugene A. Rosa, 'On the Ontological Status of the Concept of Risk', (2011) 49(8–9) *Safety Science* 1074.

21 For examples of human rights-related business risks, see: Rachel Davis and Daniel Franks, 'Costs of Company-Community Conflict in the Extractive Sector' [2014] Corporate Social Responsibility Initiative Report no 66 (Harvard Kennedy School).

22 For this conclusion, see Fasterling, 'Human Rights Due Diligence as Risk Management' (n 17); and, more generally on the limits of the business case for human rights responsibilities of business enterprises, Florian Wettstein, 'Human Rights as a Critique of Instrumental CSR: Corporate Responsibility Beyond the Business Case', (2012) 28(106) *Notizie di Politeia* 18.

23 This has been demonstrated by Fasterling, 'Human Rights Due Diligence as Risk Management' (n 17).

24 Cf. Human Rights Council, 'Human Rights Impact Assessments: Resolving Key Methodological Questions', [2007] A/HRC/4/74 (5 February 2007); Human Rights Council, 'Promotion of all human Rights, Civil, Political, Economic, Social and Cultural Rights, Including the Rights to Development', Report of the Special Representative of the Secretary-General on the Issue of Human Rights and Transnational Corporations and Other Business Enterprises' [2009] A/HRC/11/13(22 April 2009); Human Rights Council, 'Human Rights and Corporate Law: Trends and Observations from a Cross-National Study by the Special Representative', Report of the Special Representative of the Secretary-General on the Issue of Human Rights and Transnational Corporations and Other Business Enterprises, John Ruggie [2011] A/HRC/17/31/Add.2 (23 May 2011).

25 Two Swiss National Contact Point cases dealing with Fédération Internationale de Football Association (FIFA) are instructive on this point. In both cases, the Swiss NCP held that FIFA's status as a multinational enterprise under the OECD Guidelines must be established on a case-by-case analysis based on the concrete

circumstances and the activities involved. See Swiss National Contact Point, Initial Assessment, Specific Instance regarding the Fédération Internationale de Football Association (FIFA) submitted by Americans for Democracy and Human Rights in Bahrain (ADHRB) of 17 August 2016; the Swiss NCP concluded that the Guidelines were not applicable as the case did not concern FIFA's commercial activities. By contrast, in Swiss National Contact Point Initial Assessment, Specific Instance regarding the Fédération Internationale de Football Association (FIFA) submitted by the Building and Wood Workers' International (BWI) of 15 October 2015, the Swiss NCP held that the Guidelines would be applicable as the case dealt with the commercial consequences of choosing Qatar as a host nation for the Football World Cup 2022.

26 John Ruggie, *Just Business: Multinational Corporations and Human Rights* (W.W. Notron & Co. 2013) 97; For an example, see the 'Human Rights Guide' of Total (2016), a French energy and oil enterprise that is structured as a 'centralized system'. The Guide addresses the human rights policies and measures of the entire Group, and not of the parent company only.

27 Ruggie and Sherman III, 'The Concept of Due Diligence in the UN Guiding Principles on Business and Human Rights' (n 16).

28 Cf. Hugh Collins, 'Ascription of Legal Responsibility to Groups in Complex Patterns of Economic Integration', (1990) 53 *The Modern Law Review* 731.

29 This is not the place to recall the multiple ways of defining corporate groups or undertakings under the law. Next to liability law, for example, tax law, competition law, or accounting standards will have varying criteria. The point here is precisely to provide a plausible understanding of the term "business enterprise" as an extra-legal concept.

30 Christoph Zott and Raphael Amit, 'Business Model Design: An Activity System Perspective', (2010) 43(2/3) *Long Range Planning* 216; for a meta-study on business models in management research, see Christoph Zott, Raphael Amit and Lorenzo Massa, 'The Business Model: Recent Developments and Future Research', (2011) 37(4) *Journal of Management* 1019.

31 "Value creation" and "value capture" are two distinct concepts that are used not only by literature on business models in particular, but in strategic management research and theory more generally. On the distinction between value creation and value capture on individual, organizational, and societal levels of analysis, see David P. Lepak, Ken G. Smith and M. Susan Taylor, 'Value Creation and Value Capture: A Multilevel Perspective', (2007) 32(1) *Academy of Management Review* 180.

32 Cf. Mark W. Johnson, Clayton M. Christensen and Henning Kagermann, 'Reinventing Your Business Model', (2008) *Harvard Business Review* 58.

33 LafargeHolcim, 'Summary of Syria Review Findings' (n 1).

34 Cf. Cossart, Chaplier and Beau de Lomenie, 'The French Law on Duty of Care' (n 11).

35 The law generally only applies to French companies. However, possible extraterritorial effects of the law still need to be clarified. Discussion is also conducted on whether all corporate entity forms are covered. See Arnaud Reygrobellet, 'Devoir de vigilance ou risque d'insomnies?' [2017] Revue Lamy droit des affaires, no 128 (1 July 2017); Sophie Schiller, 'Exégèse de la loi relative au devoir de vigilance des sociétés mères et entreprises donneuses d'ordre', (2017) *JCP E* 1193.

36 The law initially provided for fines in the case of non-compliance. These were struck out by the French Constitutional Council (Devoir de vigilance des sociétés mères, n 11) as unconstitutional because the law's obligations were too indeterminate to justify penal sanctions.

37 See ibid.

38 Ibid.

39 For potential adverse effects of legal incentives to adopt sophisticated compliance programmes in general, see Björn Fasterling, 'Criminal Compliance – Les risques d'un droit pénal du risque', (2016) 2 *Revue Internationale de Droit Economique* 217.
40 The French due diligence law that picks up procedural elements of the UNGP (risk identification and mapping, analysis, tracking, and communication), has turned them into legal obligations, though these were considered by the French Constitutional Council to be too vague to justify penal sanctions for non-compliance. See French Constitutional Council, Devoir de vigilance des sociétés mères, n 10.
41 Collins, 'Ascription of Legal Responsibility to Groups in Complex Patterns of Economic Integration' (n 28).
42 Henry Hansmann and Reinier Kraakman, 'Toward Unlimited Shareholder Liability for Corporate Torts', (1991) 100 *Yale Law Journal* 1879; Nina A. Mendelson, 'A Control-Based Approach to Shareholder Liability for Corporate Torts', (2002) 102 *Columbia Law Review* 1203, 1206–7, 1247–58, 1271–303.
43 David W. Leebron, 'Limited Liability, Tort Victims, and Creditors', (1991) 91 *Columbia Law Review* 1565, 1612–2.
44 Philip I. Blumberg, 'The Transformation of Modern Corporation Law: The Law of Corporate Groups', (2005) 37 *Connecticut Law Review* 605.
45 Meredith Dearborn, 'Enterprise Liability: Reviewing and Revitalizing Liability for Corporate Groups', (2009) 97 *California Law Review* 195, 260.
46 Cf. notion of the 'Web Page Enterprise', Gerald F. Davis, 'What Might Replace the Modern Corporation? Uberization and the Web Page Enterprise', (2016) 39 *Seattle University Law Review* 501.
47 See Steven Ratner, 'Corporations and Human Rights: A Theory of Legal Responsibility', (2001) 111 *The Yale Law Journal* 443, 520.
48 Ibid.
49 Special Representative of the UN Secretary-General on the Issue of Human Rights and Transnational Corporations and Other Business Enterprises, 'Protect, Respect and Remedy: A Framework for Business and Human Rights: Report of the Special Representative of the Secretary-General on the Issue of Human Rights and Transnational Corporations and Other Business Enterprises', (2008) UN doc A/HRC/8/5, 20, 74.
50 Human Rights Council, 'Human Rights and Corporate Law' (n 24).

Bibliography

Aven T, Renn O and Rosa EA, 'On the Ontological Status of the Concept of Risk', (2011) 49(8–9) *Safety Science* 1074.

Blumberg PI, 'The Transformation of Modern Corporation Law: The Law of Corporate Groups', (2005) 37 *Connecticut Law Review* 605.

Bonnitcha J and McCorquodale R, 'The Concept of "Due Diligence" in the UN Guiding Principles on Business and Human Rights', (2017) 28(3) *European Journal of International Law* 899.

Collins H, 'Ascription of Legal Responsibility to Groups in Complex Patterns of Economic Integration', (1990) 53 *The Modern Law Review* 731.

Cossart S, Chaplier J and Beau de Lomenie T, 'The French Law on Duty of Care: A Historic Step Towards Making Globalization Work for All', (2017) 2(2) *Business and Human Rights Journal* 317.

Davis GF, 'What Might Replace the Modern Corporation? Uberization and the Web Page Enterprise', (2016) 39 *Seattle University Law Review* 501.

Dearborn M, 'Enterprise Liability: Reviewing and Revitalizing Liability for Corporate Groups', (2009) 97 *California Law Review* 195.

Fasterling B, 'Human Rights Due Diligence as Risk Management', (2017) 2(2) *Business and Human Rights Journal* 225.

———, 'Criminal Compliance – Les risques d'un droit pénal du risque', (2016) 2 *Revue Internationale de Droit Economique* 217.

Hansmann H and Kraakman R, 'Toward Unlimited Shareholder Liability for Corporate Torts', (1991) 100 *Yale Law Journal* 1879.

Johnson MW, Christensen CM and Kagermann H, 'Reinventing Your Business Model', (2008) *Harvard Business Review* 58.

Leebron DW, 'Limited Liability, Tort Victims, and Creditors', (1991) 91 *Columbia Law Review* 1565.

Lepak DP, Smith KG and Taylor MS, 'Value Creation and Value Capture: A Multilevel Perspective', (2007) 32(1) *Academy of Management Review* 180.

Mendelson NA, 'A Control-Based Approach to Shareholder Liability for Corporate Torts', (2002) 102 *Columbia Law Review* 1203.

Purdy G, 'ISO 31000:2009: Setting a New Standard for Risk Management', (2010) 30(6) *Risk Analysis* 881.

Ratner S, 'Corporations and Human Rights: A Theory of Legal Responsibility', (2001) 111 *The Yale Law Journal* 443.

Reygrobellet A, 'Devoir de vigilance ou risque d'insomnies?', (1 July 2017) (128) *Revue Lamy droit des affaires.*

Ruggie JG, *Just Business: Multinational Corporations and Human Rights* (W.W. Notron & Co. 2013).

——— and Sherman JF, 'The Concept of Due Diligence in the UN Guiding Principles on Business and Human Rights: Reply to Professors Bonnitcha and McCorquodale', (2017) 28(3) *European Journal of International Law* 921.

Schiller S, 'Exégèse de la loi relative au devoir de vigilance des sociétés mères et entreprises donneuses d'ordre', (2017) *JCP E* 1193.

Wettstein F, 'Human Rights as a Critique of Instrumental CSR: Corporate Responsibility Beyond the Business Case', (2012) 28(106) *Notizie di Politeia* 18.

Zott C and Amit R, 'Business Model Design: An Activity System Perspective', (2010) 43(2/3) *Long Range Planning* 216.

Zott C, Amit R and Massa L, 'The Business Model: Recent Developments and Future Research', (2011) 37(4) *Journal of Management* 1019.

3 National Contact Points under OECD's Guidelines for Multinational Enterprises

Institutional diversity affecting assessments of the delivery of access to remedy

*Karin Buhmann**

3.1 Introduction

Adopted in 1976 and revised several times, the OECD's Guidelines for Multinational Enterprises (hereinafter OECD Guidelines)[1] set out standards of conduct for companies with transnational operations in regards to their impact on society. A 2000 revision of the OECD Guidelines charged National Contact Points (NCPs) in adhering states with handling complaints of alleged violations of the Guidelines. This effectively made NCPs accountability institutions for the Guidelines. A 2011 revision to bring the Guidelines in line with the UNGPs,[2] including their Third Pillar on Access to Remedy, led to an increase in complaints lodged with NCPs.[3] The OECD Guidelines use the term "specific instances" for complaints of alleged non-observance of the Guidelines that are brought to NCPs. The updated and human rights-inspired procedural section of the Guidelines for NCPs in their function as remedy institutions applies to complaints regarding all issue areas covered by the Guidelines, including human rights, labor, and the environment.

Due to the substantive connection between the UNGPs and the OECD Guidelines, NCPs serve as *de facto* accountability institutions for business conduct in relation to the UNGPs. Indeed the UNGPs and the 2011 revision of the OECD Guidelines were constructed in such a way that NCPs would serve that role.[4] The potential for NCPs, being state-based remedy institutions, to handle adverse human rights impact caused by business had already been noted in the 2008 UN "Protect, Respect and Remedy" Framework (hereinafter "UN Framework")[5] which was adopted by the UNHRC in 2008 and serves as the theoretical underpinnings of the UNGPs. In addition to handling complaints, NCPs are charged with raising awareness of the OECD Guidelines, for example through the provision of information and guidance to help companies observe them. Within an overall principle of "functional equivalence",[6] each state has some discretion as to how to organize its NCP.

As the Guidelines apply to companies operating in or from adhering countries (currently 48, including several outside the OECD),[7] an NCP in the home state of a business enterprise may be charged with actions of a company registered in that state, but operating elsewhere. Because the Guidelines contain provisions for companies to exercise risk-based due diligence in regard to their supply chains, NCPs may also be charged with actions relating to such companies registered and operating in states that do not adhere to the Guidelines if the main (for example, sourcing or investing) company is directly related to the other company through its operations, products, or services.

Like other remedy institutions, NCPs not only serve to provide accountability for specific incidents leading to complaints of harmful impacts, but also as a potential source of learning on what represents unacceptable business conduct. Links to final statements on cases published by NCPs are available through an OECD database, making findings and recommendations generally accessible. As NCPs are empowered to issue recommendations to companies concerned by a complaint, they may also contribute to ongoing case-based insights on what constitutes business conduct in accordance with the Guidelines and, therefore, business conduct causing a range of potential risks that entail harmful impacts on society. An emerging body of academic literature considers NCPs "jurisprudence",[8] but the field remains relatively unexplored. One reason for this may be the fact that NCPs are hybrid institutions, which are state-based but have certain extraterritorial powers, and are non-judicial.

Individual NCPs differ considerably in their organizational structure, funding, and modes of functioning. The latter point has led civil society organizations to challenge the effectiveness of NCPs in regards to the provision of remedy.[9] Coinciding with the annual UN Forum on Business and Human Rights in Geneva in 2017, the organization OECD Watch took the forum's topic of "Access to Remedy" as an opportunity to launch a campaign to enhance the focus on what can make NCPs deliver remedy, in particular through active company participation in the complaints-handling procedure.[10] At the same time, the campaign was founded on the recognition that until "binding rules for responsible business conduct are in place, OECD Watch believes the OECD Guidelines have the potential to remain an important tool to promote accountability and access to remedy".[11]

In combination, this points to a need for enhanced academic studies of how NCPs can work more effectively to provide accountability, both in the reactive sense of accountability for harm done, and the more proactive sense of delivering recommendations for companies to act in accordance with the OECD Guidelines and their informing normative instruments, in particular the UNGPs.

To fully understand the role of NCPs as accountability institutions, and to critically discuss the legal and other literature on business impacts on society with regard to proposing improvements for NCPs' functioning in that role, it is necessary to take into account and address the diversity of NCPs and their national context. To contribute to advancing analysis of NCPs, their role, functioning, and impact, this chapter sets out some of the diversity of NCPs in regard to their organization by placing some of the data on complaints and their distribution into a broader geographical and sector-related context. The chapter opens by looking at the term "remedy" and its dual elements, which encompass procedural and substantive aspects. It then introduces selected elements of the OECD Guidelines and describes NCPs as national soft-law accountability institutions with diverse organizational structures. Next, it considers quantitative information on NCP cases, acceptance rates, and other data against institutional differences and national contexts for the role of NCPs, before finally concluding.

3.2 Remedy

Access to remedy is a core human right, covered by the UDHR (art 10), the ICCPR (art 14), as well as regional and national human rights instruments. The UNGPs and the UN Framework, adopted by the UNHRC in 2008 and 2011, respectively, devote one of the three "pillars" to access to remedy (complementary to the two pillars of the state duty to protect and the corporate responsibility to respect). The UNGPs distinguish between three forms of remedy: judicial remedy (courts), state-based non-judicial remedy (mainly NCPs and some national human rights institutions), and "operational-level" grievance mechanisms organized by companies.

"Remedy" is a comprehensive concept. Merriam-Webster's online dictionary defines remedy as (1) a medicine, application, or treatment that relieves or cures a disease; (2) something that corrects or counteracts; and (3) the legal means to recover a right or to prevent or obtain redress for a wrong.[12] The online Oxford Dictionary defines "remedy" as "A medicine or treatment for a disease or injury".[13] The Oxford Dictionary lists legal remedy ("a means of legal reparation", related to injury) as the latter of two sub-sets, following "a means of counteracting or eliminating something undesirable".[14] It is worth noting that both definitions understand remedy as a medicine or a cure. In other words, the implication is that remedy cures. This is something different from simply having access to lodging a complaint and having a grievance considered. Remedy assumes a qualitative element of redress, apart from the procedural one of access to lodge a complaint. The qualitative aspect of remedy is also underscored by the explanation of the etymological origin of the term in English; "Remedy" is a Middle English word derived from Anglo-Norman French *remedie*, in turn from Latin *remedium*, composed of *re* (meaning "back", and also expressing intensive force) and *mederi* (meaning "heal").[15] As crucial as it is from a human rights law perspective for a remedy institution to be in place and technically accessible, having access to remedy is no guarantee that harm done will be cured. The irremediability of many business-related human rights violations places the assumption behind the concept of procedural justice into perspective: if an arm or a life is lost in an occupational health or safety accident, or a childhood is lost to work, being able to lodge a complaint and have it addressed might offer some consolation, but will not be able to restore the damage done. The difference is reflected in the fact that the concept of organizational justice recognizes divergent perceptions of justice held by various stakeholders.[16]

Although the procedural aspects of the ability to lodge a complaint of perceived harm and have it considered may in itself contribute to a sense of justice, remedy as cure presumes that harm done is undone in a qualitative sense, for example via a reparation that restores the victim to the situation before the harm occurred. Yet in the human rights field, harm done can rarely be fully repaired in the sense of being redone (which is a key reason why the UN Framework and UNGPs emphasize the need to prevent business-related human rights harm from occurring). This raises important questions on what constitutes a proper remedy, and these are only beginning to be addressed. This issue can be highly context-specific, as indicated by some examples set out in the following, which demonstrate that local customs and values must be considered for the remedy process to not itself, unintentionally, risk causing harm.

Under the "third pillar" of Access to Remedy, the UN Framework and UNGPs recognize three types of remedy mechanisms: judicial remedy mechanisms (courts), state-based non-judicial remedy mechanisms (e.g., NCPs), and operational-level grievance mechanisms. The latter include a company's setup to receive and handle complaints, ideally before the conflict escalates but also to provide reparations when harm has been perceived to have occurred.[17] An operational-level grievance mechanism designed by Barrick Gold (Barrick), the majority owner from 2006–2015 of the Porgera Joint Venture (PGV) mine in Papua New Guinea, to provide remedies to survivors of alleged sexual assaults by PGV employees, illustrates the complexity. The case also illustrates that monetary compensation is not the right form of remedy by which to address (and try to provide some sort of cure for) human rights abuse in all contexts, and that monetary compensation must be approached and applied in a manner that takes the specific context, culture, and the situation of victims into consideration. The relevance of this in a discussion of NCPs is based on the fact that NCPs are unable to make enforceable decisions on compensation, but may support parties in reaching an agreement that might involve a form or forms of reparation, such as cash compensation. For this reason, the complexities surrounding monetary compensation as "cure" need to be considered by NCPs, as well as by studies of NCPs and their effectiveness in delivering remedy. One study of the PGV remedy mechanism explained it as follows:

> In 2012, Barrick launched a company-created remedy mechanism to offer reparations to women sexually assaulted by its security guards and other company employees. During the two years of operation of [the] remedy mechanism, approximately 120 sexual assault victims signed remedy package agreements, in exchange for waiving their right to sue Barrick. Separately, eleven women who refused to accept the packages and who secured legal representation by a U.S.-based human rights non-governmental organization were offered confidential settlement packages believed to be about ten times the amount of the remedy mechanism packages. In July 2015, Barrick offered each of the 120 women an additional payment, but taken together, the initial packages and additional payment remain significantly less than the international settlement.[18]

Another study[19] explained that because under local custom money is not administered by women, the women who received cash compensation were expected to hand the money over to men in their family. This exposed them to outside awareness of the sexual abuse that they had been exposed to, leading to stigma. Moreover, women who received lower compensation (those who had accepted the original Barrick offer) were additionally stigmatized for not only being sexually abused, but "gaining" less cash compensation from that already stigmatizing abuse compared to some others (who only accepted alternative cash compensation offered based on the advocacy of an international civil society organization). While the study noted that the Barrick remedy mechanism was conceived with sincere and considerable commitment to the UNGPs, it observed the following:

> implementation errors compromised the [remedy mechanism's] actual performance. Claimants were thus exposed to a process which failed adequately to protect them and which they did not understand. In the end, successful claimants received remedies that were equitable, even generous, under international law. Nevertheless, many were left disaffected, stigmatized and abused. Responsibility for these results is not the [remedy mechanism's] alone. It should be shared by international stakeholders whose errors of judgment and unwillingness to engage in good faith exacted a great toll on claimants.[20]

Conversely, a specific instance handled by the Dutch NCP and finalized in 2017, concerning former employees of the Uganda-based Bralima subsidiary of the brewery Heineken, led to an agreement between the company and the complainants regarding monetary compensation concerning action on the DRC.[21]

> The complaint was lodged by former employees of Bralima who represented a group of approximately 168 persons formerly employed by Bralima (95% owned by Heineken) in Bukavu, the DRC. The complainants alleged that Bralima took advantage of a period of economic and political turmoil in the DRC to dismiss a large number of employees in a brief period of time, without providing basic guarantees required by Congolese and international law. The former employees alleged that 168 employees were dismissed between sixteen and twelve years prior to the lodging of the complaint in 2015, and that some employees were forced into early retirement in 2000. According to the complaint they were not paid adequate compensation, were deprived of social welfare, were not given due notice, were not informed of the reasons for their dismissal or allowed to challenge their dismissal; and as a direct consequence of their early retirement, their state pension was drastically reduced. Also according to the complaint, for some employees dismissed en masse in 2000 the compensation was not calculated in accordance with Congolese law, and the mass layoff was not authorised by a competent authority, but by a DRC rebel movement. The complainants were seeking financial compensation. Following a mediation dialogue facilitated by the Dutch NCP, the complainants and the company reached agreement on a compensation. In addition to the compensation, Heineken committed to

drawing up a policy and guidelines on how to conduct business and operate in conflict-affected areas.

The issue of monetary compensation had already been addressed when the workers were dismissed. A loss of income has concrete monetary implications for those who suffer the loss of a job, whereas a life or arm lost to an occupational health and safety accident cannot be restored through monetary compensation. Monetary compensation can be seen as a direct reflection of the income gap caused by dismissal. Jobs can be changed, but limbs do no regrow and childhoods lost to child labor cannot be relived.

NCPs are set up in order not only to provide access to remedy in the sense of those who perceive their rights as subject to abuse being able to lodge a complaint and have it considered, but also to assist victims in obtaining a "cure". The technical aspect of access to a remedy institution is addressed by the obligation of states adhering to the OECD Guidelines to establish NCPs. The substantive aspect of providing a "cure" is addressed through the role of NCPs to support a mediated solution via which the parties can agree on a form of reparation. As demonstrated by the Heineken/Bralima case, this aspect should not be overlooked, especially as the effort toward a mediated solution is an early step in the grievance-handling process.

Following this introduction to NCPs as remedy mechanisms, focusing on the procedural as well as substantive aspects, the subsequent section looks at the constitutive document – the OECD Guidelines – and the significance of this soft-law instrument in setting out normative guidance for companies, as well as the substantive and procedural basis for the NCPs.

3.3 OECD's Guidelines: international soft law with important implications

From the outset, the OECD Guidelines were a novelty in terms of an international law instrument to govern business conduct with a particular focus on the impact that business has on society. The Guidelines were adopted just a few years after the UN, the world's largest international organization with objectives of promoting human rights and socioeconomic growth, had launched its first, but never completed, effort to develop normative directives for businesses in order to curtail their adverse societal impacts (the UN draft Code of Conduct for Transnational Corporations).[22] The OECD Guidelines preceded the ILO's Tripartite Declaration of Principles concerning Multinational Enterprises and Social Policy[23] by a year.

Technically, the Guidelines are an Annex to the OECD Declaration on International Investment and Multinational Enterprises (hereinafter "the Investment Declaration").[24] The Guidelines are non-binding and have a soft-law character. Somewhat unusually for an international law instrument, the OECD Guidelines address themselves to companies, albeit through states: the OECD Guidelines are recommendations from governments to companies operating in or *from* adhering states. Under the Investment Declaration, which, like the OECD Guidelines, was first adopted in 1976, adhering governments commit to providing an open and transparent environment for international investment and to encourage the positive contributions that multinational enterprises can make to economic and social progress.

While the original text of the OECD Guidelines was not as comprehensive as the more recent versions, it was significant as a step by an international organization to expand its normative guidance from addressing states to also addressing businesses. Subsequent revisions have expanded the focus and provided more detailed guidance, reflecting the evolution of societal concerns with business impact on society, as well as other normative developments.

In addition to expanding the Guidelines' treatment of human rights from a single reference to a full chapter, the 2011 revision included the adoption of the risk-based due diligence approach (focusing on preventing and managing harm caused by the company to society, rather than risks caused by society to the company), as well as the concepts of "leverage" and responsibility due to direct linkage to business relations in terms of their operations, products, or services. All had been introduced as part of normative standards guiding business conduct by the UN Framework and were elaborated with the UNGPs. Furthermore, the OECD Guidelines' Procedural Guidance was revised to include effectiveness criteria for grievance mechanisms set out by the UNGPs (GP 31). These effectiveness criteria, according to which the grievance mechanism must be legitimate, accessible, predictable, equitable, transparent, and rights-compatible, as well as a source of continuous learning, were incorporated into the Procedural Guidance on the functional equivalence of NCPs, as well as guidance for the handling of specific instances.

Due to the scarcity of enforcement institutions under international law, NCPs fill an accountability gap. The ability of NCPs in this regard is potentially wide-ranging due to their powers to handle complaints concerning actions occurring outside the home state, and their ability to affect a company's economic situation as recognized by the UN Framework's reference to the idea of the social license to operate,[25] the loss of which may have significant economic implications for a company.[26] Thus, NCPs create accountability through economic measures or the market as well.

3.4 National Contact Points: national soft-law accountability institutions with extraterritorial reach

In accordance with a legally binding OECD Council Decision on International Investment and Multinational Enterprises,[27] states that adhere to the OECD Guidelines commit to establishing an NCP.

Furthering the effectiveness of the OECD Guidelines[28] entails a range of roles for NCPs: NCPs should undertake promotional activities, handle enquiries, and contribute to the resolution of issues that arise from the alleged non-observance of the OECD Guidelines.[29] NCPs provide a platform for helping parties resolve cases concerning alleged non-observance of the OECD Guidelines when complaints arise. NCPs can receive complaints from any individual or organization regarding a company, operating in or from the country of the NCP, which is alleged to not have observed the OECD Guidelines.

NCPs handle specific instances in three steps set out in the procedural guidance part of the OECD Guidelines. First, the NCP conducts an initial assessment to evaluate whether the issue or issues raised merit further examination, and either accepts the case or publishes a statement explaining why it has not accepted the case. Second, if the NCP accepts the case, it offers its "good offices"[30] to both parties with a view to resolving the issues. This means that the NCP offers to engage in dialogue, mediation, or conciliation services to assist the parties in reaching an understanding of the issue(s) and possibly entering into an agreement. Such an agreement may include redress such as compensation or non-monetary restitution to help offset the harm incurred by the affected stakeholders, and steps to be undertaken by the company to avoid similar issues from arising in the future. Finally, at the end of the process, the NCP publishes a statement regarding the issues raised in the case, the support offered by the NCP, and the outcomes. Within the procedural guidance part of the Guidelines, NCPs have some leeway to introduce variations.[31]

NCPs currently fill a gap that neither national law, nor international law, nor private CSR schemes cover. Not only are NCPs able to offer mediation to help parties develop joint solutions, which in principle may contain substantive remedy for harmful impacts and prevent future violations of human rights, as was the case in the specific instance involving Heineken and former employees of its subsidiary Bralima (see section 3.2). NCPs are also able to deliver public accountability as a result of final statements setting forth the NCP's findings in regard to allegations of adverse business impacts on society. Moreover, NCPs have powers to deal with alleged violations that occur in countries that do not have an NCP, provided there is a connection between the alleged violation and the state in which the NCP is located (typically because that state is the home state of the company concerned). This provides NCPs with extraterritorial powers that national courts usually do not enjoy. With a few exceptions, mainly emerging from the Inter-American Court of Human Rights,[32] international courts do not provide remedy for business-related adverse societal impacts. The jurisdiction of the ICC is limited to natural persons, and therefore does not include legal persons such as companies.[33] Even if the jurisdiction of the ICC is expanded to include legal persons, the ICC confirms another trend: treaties tend to provide only minimum standards. The ICC is empowered to deal with only the most severe human rights violations, because the acts covered by the ICC's jurisdiction according to the Rome Statute are limited to genocide, crimes against humanity, war crimes, and the crime of aggression. As a result, many business actions that result in adverse societal impacts would not be included even if the ICC's jurisdiction were to be expanded. For example, excessive working hours, lax occupational health and safety standards, or child labor would not be covered, unless they could be demonstrated in context to constitute the types of gross human rights violations covered by the ICC statute.

While NCPs are not able to issue legally enforceable judgments, they can play a role in regards to other forms of reparation or satisfaction that may be offered by a company, such as an official declaration of responsibility, an apology, restitution, and/or guarantees of non-repetition. These have been recognized as significant elements of successful remedies for human rights abuse.[34] In view of the limited legal accountability modalities for transnational business activity and its impact on society, the role that NCPs have as state-based non-judicial remedy institutions is unique and significant. However, studies indicate that at least some NCPs do not fully deploy or live up to the possibilities that they have to provide remedy, whether simply in terms of providing access for those who perceive their rights to be abused to having a complaint considered, or in terms of the reparation or other steps following findings that rights have been abused. This relates to a range of institutional issues, which include the rejection of complaints, the use or non-use of the possibility to assess the substance of a complaint when no mediated solution is reached, and the mutual complementarity or correspondence of NCP statements.

The non-binding nature of NCP statements has been argued to weaken the institution in regards to accountability.[35] Analyses by civil society groups have suggested that the remedial capacity of NCPs remains limited from the perspective of victims. Data on NCP-specific instances indicate that such cases are unevenly spread, and that NCPs' deployment of reaction modalities also differ.[36] While the UK NCP has issued some "landmark" statements on human rights and has therefore been seen to lead the application of the OECD Guidelines in this regard in some academic studies,[37] civil society studies have also issued severe criticisms of that NCP, for example for rejecting a large number of human rights-related complaints due to what is seen as unreasonably high thresholds for evidence.[38] Although it does not distinguish between complaints rejected due to inadequate documentation for alleged abuse or whether the complaint is outside the scope of NCPs, another study has suggested that the average rate of rejection of complaints by all NCPs is at around 50% of received complaints.[39] While some observers have argued that NCPs should increase their focus on proactive action to promote knowledge of the Guidelines, and in that way contribute to preventing harm, they recognize that this may require additional funds in order for NCPs not to reduce their reactive accountability activities.[40]

The OECD Guidelines stipulate that NCPs' final statement on the outcome of the complaint procedure must be made public, whether or not the parties reach an agreement. Thus, final statements, in principle, offer an indication of types of action that are in accordance (or not) with the Guidelines. Moreover, they may contain recommendations to the parties. Certain NCPs take this opportunity to make quite detailed recommendations for the company or companies concerned,[41] and some make determinations of whether a company's conduct was in conformity with the OECD Guidelines. NCPs may follow up with the parties on their response to these recommendations. NCP statements may therefore cause reputational damage to the firm in question, in turn causing economic impacts through loss of customers or decreased investment (in particular, some institutional investors are susceptible to criticisms regarding invested companies' impact on society). Furthermore, some governments consider NCP statements with regard to economic decisions, for instance in the context of public procurement decisions or when providing public support to companies in the form of economic diplomacy or export credits. In 2014, Canada changed its CSR strategy for the extractive sector abroad to include provisions of withdrawal of Government of Canada trade advocacy services if companies refuse to engage in the NCP dialogue facilitation process.[42] The German government has announced similar policies as part of its national action plan on business and human rights.[43]

3.5 Organizational differences

Across countries adhering to the OECD Guidelines, NCPs are organized in a variety of ways that affect their functionality. Some are independent organizations; others are hosted within and/or organized as part of specific government agencies, such as ministries of commerce, labor, or foreign affairs. Some are essentially comprised of a secretariat with one or a few civil servant staff members that handle the entire process of the specific instance; others have more complex structures comprised of an expert committee or supervisory body representing various stakeholders and convening on a part-time basis, supported by a secretariat staffed by civil servants. Recognizing that the structures of NCPs vary considerably, the OECD distinguishes between six forms of NCP organization: *monoagency NCPs* composed of one or more representatives of a single ministry; *monoagency "plus" NCPs* have a secretariat located in one ministry, while other ministries or stakeholders are involved in the work of the NCP on an advisory basis; *interagency NCPs* are composed of representatives of two or more ministries; *tripartite NCPs* are composed of representatives of one or more ministries, business associations, and trade unions; *quadripartite NCPs* are comprised of representatives of one or more ministries, business associations, trade unions, and NGOs; and *independent agency NCPs* generally consist of independent experts connected to a ministry and usually benefiting from secretariat staff within the ministry.[44] Broken down to individual countries,[45] it is clear that there are no uniform patterns on organization in regards to regions within the OECD or other countries adhering to the OECD Guidelines. A 2007 survey conducted by OECD Watch in fact argued that due to different administrative and legal traditions there is not a single one-size-fits-all model for an effective and functional NCP.[46]

However, based on developments in the past 10 years, a tendency may be emerging that when NCPs are reorganized, the multi-partite character and/or independence is enhanced. It is likely that the more independent and/or multipartite, the higher the likelihood that the NCP, the process, and the outcome will be perceived of by stakeholders to be legitimate. The less independent the institutional setup, the bigger the possibility that an NCP may be perceived by victims in host states as too closely linked to the national context of the home state of the transnational enterprise involved.

Moreover, while some NCPs have generous funding, others are more limited regarding funds. For example, the process applied by the Dutch NCP in regard to the Heineken/Bralima case required substantial funds to enable the NCP and complainants to travel and meet. In the process of handling the complaint, meetings between the parties were held on "neutral" ground away from the Netherlands and DRC at the Dutch embassies in Kampala, Uganda, and Paris, France. Heineken and Bralima also met with the complainants in Bukavu.[47] Without funds to allow such activities, it can be difficult for NCPs to connect with complainants in third countries in which the impact has occurred.

The Procedural Guidance of the Guidelines provide some general points on the process, as well as on coordination by NCPs when a specific instance concerns issues in several adhering countries. However, the Guidance is not as detailed as procedures for legal proceedings. This partly serves to enable flexibility within the overall procedural requirements for functional equivalence.

Studies have expressed concern regarding NCP staff or support staff who conduct substantial parts of the assessment of complaints, as they are generalist civil servants rather than experts on human rights or other substantive issues covered by the Guidelines.[48] It is not an impossible situation that NCPs in different countries reach varying conclusions in cases involving one single company, for example, when complaints lodged with various NCPs address different home country organizations, such as institutional investors. Even when such diversity may be technically acceptable due to the home country organizations concerned,[49] such situations may cause confusion and challenge trust in NCPs to deliver accountability for transnational business activity and its adverse impacts.

3.6 What do numbers say on NCPs and accountability?

3.6.1 Data on specific instances: issues, sectors, stakeholders, country differences

Information on NCP-specific instances is accessible from three main sources, one of which is intergovernmental (OECD), and two of which are civil society-based (OECD Watch and the Trade Union Advisory Committee to the OECD [TUAC]). Together, these offer quite detailed information and search options on qualitative data (such as the status of a complaint, the issue it concerns, the content of NCP final statements, etc.). They also offer some basic information that can be compiled into quantitative datasets. The OECD's online resources on the Guidelines offer a list of NCPs with organizational and contact information, and a database of specific instances with some qualitative search options.[50] The TUAC database lists specific instances lodged by the labor movement.[51] OECD Watch, a civil society organization whose mission is "to improve corporate accountability mechanisms in order to achieve sustainable development and enhance the social and environmental performance of corporations worldwide",[52] runs a database on specific instances with a range of search options that differ from those of the OECD Database. As part of their studies, OECD Watch has compiled several quantitative datasets, for example on patterns of issues related to complaints, home, and host states of respondent companies, and the progress/status of complaints.

Since 2000, NCPs have received more than 400 specific instances relating to company operations in over 100 countries and territories. The majority have dealt with employment and worker issues (54%), followed by human rights (28%) and environment (20%), and finally corruption and bribery (less than 10%).[53] Since the 2011 revision when the human rights chapter was added to the OECD Guidelines, specific instances dealing with human rights have been the most frequent. Since 2000, 33% of all specific instances relate to issues arising from multinational enterprises operating in the manufacturing sector. In recent years, specific instances concerning the financial sector have been on the rise, accounting for over 20% of all new cases between 2014 and 2016. Trade unions, NGOs and individuals account for 90% of specific instances submitted to NCPs since 2000. Specific instances have also been submitted by companies and government officials. In regard to outcomes, between 2011 and 2016, 47% of all cases accepted for further examination by NCPs resulted in some form of agreement between the parties, while 37% resulted in an internal policy change by the company in question.[54]

The extraterritorial reach of NCPs is apparent in the types of sectors addressed and countries in which alleged breaches of the Guidelines occurred. Between 2001 and 2015, among filed complaints 57 concerned the mining sector, 33 oil and gas, 29 financial institutions, 23 agriculture companies, and 13 garment companies.[55] During the same period (and including complaints that were eventually rejected), out of complaints concerning alleged abuse in OECD countries 10 complaints concerned the US, 11 the UK, 10 Turkey, 7 New Zealand, 7 Denmark, 6 Germany, 5 Spain, and 5 Canada (and numbers between 4 and 0 in other OECD member states). During the same period, out of complaints concerning alleged abuse in non-OECD states, 25 (the record number of complaints for alleged abuse in one country) concerned the DRC, 11 Uzbekistan, 10 Georgia, 10 India, 9 Azerbaijan, 9 Argentina, 9 Brazil, 7 the Philippines, 7 Bahrain, 6 Uganda, 5 Cameroon, 5 Cambodia, 4 Papua New Guinea, and 4 Ecuador (with complaint numbers between 3 and 1 applying to a range of other non-OECD countries in Asia, Latin America, and Africa).[56] Assessing the information on sectors and countries against the diversity of industries headquartered in various states and against the typical topics of complaints helps to explain part of the distribution of cases between NCPs. For example, in Europe, countries along the North Sea (the UK, the Netherlands, Norway, France, and Denmark) were OECD states with major (if limited numbers of) oil and gas companies, whereas textile companies were more prevalent in Southern, Central, and Eastern Europe during 2001 and 2015. Canada alone is home to around 50% of the world's exploration and mining companies.[57] These companies typically have some of their production in, or source some materials from, regions that are predominantly made up of non-OECD states that do not adhere to the OECD Guidelines. Such host states therefore do not have their own NCPs. Yet, whereas many multinational enterprises are registered in the US, more than half of complaints lodged with the US NCP concerned trade union issues within the US.[58] For France, less than half of all cases concerned France as a host country;[59] and for Norway, only two of a total 14 concerned issues in that country.[60] This diversity does not necessarily explain patterns of specific instance topics, but it does show that it is difficult to compare NCPs against each other or to measure cases and outcomes quantitatively without taking differences in sectors, production, and supply patterns into account. This also applies to assessments of the number of NCP complaints received and actual specific instances accepted and handled, see Table 3.1.

Table 3.1 Specific instances 2000–25 November 2017[61]

NCP State	*Received complaints (2000–25 November 2017)*	*Country for alleged abuse of Guidelines (incl later rejected complaints)*	*Handling NCP for c omplaints on human rights + due diligence (2000–25 Nov. 2017)*
United States	48	10	
United Kingdom	45	11	9
Netherlands	28		4
Germany	26	6	2
Brazil	24		2
France	23		2
Canada	19	5	1
Belgium	18		1
Switzerland	16		2
Denmark	16	7	2
Norway	14		6
Chile	11		
Australia	9		
Italy	9		
Korea	9		
Japan	7		1
Sweden	5	2	1
Austria	5		1
Czech Rep.	5		
Mexico	5		
New Zealand	5		
Spain	5	5	
Finland	4		1
Peru	4		
New Zealand		7	
Turkey		10	
Luxembourg		1	
Hungary		1	
Estonia		1	
Israel		4	
Australia		3	
DRC		25	
Uzbekistan		11	
Georgia		10	
India		10	
Azerbaijan		9	
Argentina		9	

NCP State	*Received complaints (2000–25 November 2017)*	*Country for alleged abuse of Guidelines (incl later rejected complaints)*	*Handling NCP for c omplaints on human rights + due diligence (2000–25 Nov. 2017)*
Brazil		9	
Philippines		7	
Bahrain		7	
Uganda		6	
Zambia		6	
Cameroon		5	
Cambodia		5	
Indonesia		5	
Papua New Guinea		4	
Equador		4	
Kosovo		1	

(data source: OECD Database of specific instance and Daniel, Caitlin, Joseph Wilde, KMG Genovese, Virginia Sandjojo (2015) *Remedy remains rare: an analysis of 15 years of NCP cases and their contributions to improve access to remedy for victims of corporate misconduct*, Amsterdam: OECD Watch.)

Some NCPs receive or handle a considerably larger number of complaints than others. As of late 2017, accounting for 48 and 45 specific instances, respectively, the UK and the US headed the list of specific instances concluded or in progress since 2001 relating to all issue areas covered by the Guidelines. These countries were followed by the Netherlands (28), Germany (26), Brazil (24), France (23), Canada (19), Belgium (18), Switzerland (16), Denmark (16), Norway (14), and Chile (11). Australia, Italy, and Korea each accounted for nine cases, whereas Japan accounted for seven; Sweden, Austria, the Czech Republic, Mexico, New Zealand, and Spain each accounted for five; and Finland and Peru accounted for four each.[62] However, the numbers cover all cases, including those that were concluded after a mediation process, those that were assessed by NCPs leading to the final statement setting out its findings and recommendations, and those that have been rejected. Hence, the list includes complaints rejected for being outside the scope of the Guidelines or because they should have been lodged with another remedy institution, and those rejected due to insufficient substantiation. According to an analysis in 2015 by OECD Watch, 121 complaints out of around 300 had been rejected.[63] An example illustrates the challenge in simply assessing rejection rates based on numbers without considering the substantive reasons: A search of complaints that are "concluded or in progress" for the Danish NCP generates 15 hits in the OECD database, but only a detailed reading of the summary of cases shows that, among these, six were rejected as being outside the scope of the Guidelines. Reports from the Danish NCP after its restructuring in 2012 suggest that the high rejection rate may be due to the restructuring causing heightened media attention on the NCP, which may have generated complaints based on misconceptions among the general public on the role of the NCP vis-à-vis other national complaints institutions, such as consumer protection agencies and agencies charged with medical-related complaints.[64]

Not all NCPs investigate complaints if mediation fails or if a party does not wish to engage in mediation. As a consequence, those NCPs (such as the NCPs of Australia and the US) also do not issue an assessment of whether the company concerned has breached the OECD Guidelines.[65] By contrast, other NCPs (including those of Norway, the UK, and Denmark) conduct thorough examinations of the case if no consensual agreement is reached by the parties or a party refuses to engage in mediation.[66]

3.6.2 Analysis

An analysis conducted for the current chapter found that among 52 concluded specific instances involving human rights,[67] 35 concerned an aspect of risk-based due diligence, either in terms of direct usage of the term or in terms of action that forms part of risk-based due diligence – for example, impact assessment. Only in two specific instances[68] did the outcome explicitly include a form of reparation of the damage caused by inadequate risk-based due diligence. However, in varying manners, the outcomes of most of the 35 specific instances involved some form of either company-based recognition of inadequate exercise of risk-based due diligence, or recommendations by the NCP regarding future conduct in order for the company to act in accordance with the Guidelines, and in doing so prevent similar actions as those that generated the specific instance. Some explicitly referred to efforts to agree on reparation that had not been successfully concluded during the handling of the specific instance.[69] Among specific instances involving human rights without a due diligence aspect, a small number also involved a form of redress, such as an apology.[70]

The analysis also showed a striking geographical pattern in regard to NCPs receiving complaints that either alleged abuse of human rights and non-compliance with the Guidelines' provisions on risk-based due diligence, or addressed these topics in the complaints-handling or final statement. With the exception of two specific instances handled by the NCP of Brazil and one handled by the NCP of Canada,[71] the remaining 31 out of 35 cases were handled by NCPs in North-Western Europe (UK 9; Norway 6; Netherlands 4; Denmark, France, Germany, and Switzerland 2 each; Austria, Belgium, Finland, and Sweden 1 each). In other words, none of these cases were handled by NCPs in the many OECD states in Southern, Central, or Eastern Europe or in the US, Australia, or New Zealand, nor (with the exception of Brazil) by adhering countries outside the OECD. A 2007 survey conducted by OECD Watch suggested that in Southern and Eastern Europe and the Baltic States, where NCPs had then recently been established, the OECD Guidelines were not well known and few complaints had been lodged.[72] However, 10 years on, the number of cases in these countries continues to be low, despite the existence of multinational operations in or from them.

In regards to rejected complaints, a study by OECD Watch found that during the entire first 15 years of the NCPs' complaints-handling existence, from 2001–2015, the average rate of rejection was 43%. During the three years of 2012–2015 it was 52%.[73] The actual number of complaints that technically fall within the competences of NCPs is lower, because complaints rejected include cases that simply do not fall within the competences of NCPs. Yet there are records that NCPs also reject complaints because the complaint is not found to be adequately substantiated, or because the issue is or can be handled by another NCP.[74] Information from OECD Watch suggests that, for complaints rejected from 2001–2015, 43 – or almost half of all 91 rejected complaints – were rejected due to insufficient substantiation, and only 11 because they were outside the scope of the Guidelines.[75]

3.7 Conclusion

This chapter has considered institutional issues affecting the functioning of NCPs in regards to assessing their role and effectiveness in delivering accountability for business-related harmful impacts to society in contravention of the OECD Guidelines. When assessing the effectiveness of NCPs, their powers must be considered. While NCPs are non-judicial remedy institutions, they offer a formal, state-based remedy where national judicial remedies often do not reach due to jurisdictional and territorial limitations. This makes them unique remedial institutions with the potential to offer accountability for occurrences of business-related abuse of human rights, as well as a series of other societal impacts of a transnational character. Being non-judicial institutions, NCPs should be assessed in regards to what they can do, not what they cannot. NCPs cannot make determinations on compensation, but they can make recommendations in their final statements, and they can facilitate agreements between parties, which may include reparations that can take a variety of forms or agreements for future action to avoid infringements of the Guidelines. This can contribute to substantive remedy, which may sometimes offer a cure but does not necessarily do so. NCPs' acceptance and handling of the case can offer a form of procedural remedy.

NCPs are organized according to a variety of structures, which range from mono-agency, through various forms of multi-partite, to independent. The 48 countries within and outside the OECD that adhere to the OECD Guidelines must have their NCPs monitor very diverse industry sectors operating in a range of different host countries. Operating within the principle of functional equivalence, some NCPs apply special measures, such as additional procedural steps or statutory limitations. While the number of specific instances has risen since the 2011 revision of the OECD Guidelines, the increase is not evenly dispersed across NCPs. Some NCPs receive complaints on an almost regular basis, whereas others hardly receive any. Rates of rejection of complaints also vary between NCPs. This suggests that the operation of NCPs in practice is marked by differences, despite the ideal of functional equivalence.

Such a diversity of institutional features within NCPs and in their national contexts of operations means that making assessments of the effectiveness of NCPs in regard to the procedural and substantive remedy that they offer, based on available quantitative and qualitative data from the three databases run by OECD, OECD Watch, and TUAC, is a complex task. At best, such assessments can be considered works in progress that can contribute to highlighting what may be strengths and weaknesses in specific contexts, but should not be the basis for sweeping statements.

To shed more light on the actual implications of independence and multi-partite representation, future research might consider the correlation between NCP structure, the number of complaints received, and the outcomes in regard to the parties' willingness to engage in a mediated process; the result of the mediation; the extent of the assessment and findings, as well as recommendations in the NCP's final statement; and responses/reactions by concerned actors to the final statement (including update of recommendations by the concerned company and the sector in general in the country of the concerned company). Moreover, to fully understand the implication of the organizational structures and other differences between NCPs, research is needed on companies' compliance with final statements and mediated agreements, and the factors that drive such compliance or non-compliance.

If NCPs are not called into action in regards to transnational business activities that cause adverse societal impact within the range of issues covered by the OECD Guidelines (including human rights, labor and industrial relations, environment, bribery, and corruption), victims of such impacts may be left without a remedy, or at least without recourse to a remedy institution that is unique in terms of enjoying powers to assess business action outside of the home state. Similarly, if NCPs do not make recommendations as empowered by the OECD Guidelines, learning with respect to actions that are in accordance (or not) with the OECD Guidelines may be reduced. As specific instances are made public, this means not only that relevant insights for the company concerned by a complaint are reduced, but that such insights that may be useful for other companies, for example in the same sector or area, will also not be forthcoming. Rejection of complaints due, for example, to strict requirements of documentation, or proof or statutory limitations, may also impede the role of NCPs as accountability institutions and the facilitation of relevant learning.

In order to strengthen the contributions of NCPs as accountability institutions for business-related abuse of human rights, labor, the environment, or other societal concerns, additional in-depth studies are needed not only on causes for rejection of complaints that fall within the scope of the OECD Guidelines, but also on what makes the NCP process effective in ensuring substantive remedy through agreement between parties, and in generating longer-term change in corporate conduct through recommendations. Moreover, further research could perform a comparative analysis of NCPs from the perspectives of procedural and organizational justice. An understanding of the types of NCP procedures that offer the highest extent of justice from both perspectives can serve as inspiration for reforms of existing NCPs and the establishment of new NCPs.

Notes

* Professor of Business and Human Rights, Copenhagen Business School. Dr.scient. adm. (CSR) & PhD (law). The author is also a member of the Danish OECD National

Contact Point (NCP). This chapter has been written solely in her academic capacity and does not represent views of the Danish NCP. The author wishes to thank the editors and two reviewers for their useful comments.

1 OECD, *OECD Guidelines for Multinational Enterprises* (OECD Publishing 2011).

2 Guiding Principles on Business and Human Rights: Implementing the United Nations "Protect, Respect and Remedy", Annex to UNHRC, Report of the Special Representative of the Secretary-General on the issue of human rights and transnational corporations and other business enterprises, John Ruggie (21 March 2011) UN Doc A/HRC/17/31.

3 Caitlin Daniel et al., *Remedy Remains Rare: An Analysis of 15 Years of NCP Cases and Their Contribution to Improve Access to Remedy for Victims of Corporate Misconduct* (OECD Watch 2015).

4 Karin Buhmann, 'Business and Human Rights: Understanding the UN Guiding Principles from the Perspective of Transnational Business Governance Interactions', (2015) 6(1) *Transnational Legal Theory* 399.

5 UNHRC, *Protect, Respect and Remedy: A Framework for Business and Human Rights: Report of the Special Representative of the Secretary-General on the Issue of Human Rights and Transnational Corporations and Other Business Enterprises, John Ruggie* (7 April 2008) UN Doc A/HRC/8/5 (UN Framework), para 46.

6 OECD Guidelines (n 1), Procedural Guidance, I.A.

7 OECD, List of National Contact Points <http://mneguidelines.oecd.org/ncps/> accessed 24 September 2019.

8 Eg, Basak Baglayan Ceyhan, 'Corporations and Human Rights: Searching for International Norms for Corporate Conduct in Domestic Case Law' (PhD dissertation, Luxembourg University 2017) <http://hdl.handle.net/10993/32713> accessed 24 September 2019; Larry Catá Backer, 'Rights and Accountability in Development (RAID) vs Das Air and Global Witness v. Afrimex: Small Steps towards an Autonomous Transnational Legal System for the Regulation of Multinational Corporations', (2009) 10(1) *Melbourne Journal of International Law* 258; John Ruggie and Tamaryn Nelson, 'Human Rights and the OECD Guidelines for Multinational Enterprises: Normative innovations and implementation challenges' (3 May 2015) Harvard Kennedy School/Corporate Social Responsibility Initiative Working Paper No 66 <https://papers.ssrn.com/sol3/papers.cfm?abstract_id=2601922> accessed 24 September 2019; Karin Buhmann, 'Analyzing OECD National Contact Point statements for guidance on human rights due diligence: method, findings and outlook,' (2018) 36(4) *Nordic Journal of Human Rights* 390.

9 Eg, Daniel et al. (n 3); Amnesty International, 'Obstacle Course: How the UK's National Contact Point Handles Human Rights Complaints under the OECD Guidelines for Multinational Enterprises' (February 2016) <www.amnesty.org.uk/files/uk_ncp_complaints_handling_full_report_lores_0.pdf> accessed 24 September 2019.

10 OECD Watch, 'Our Campaign Demands for Policymakers' (November 2017) <www.oecdwatch.org/remedy-campaign/learn-more-about-our-demands> accessed 24 September 2019.

11 OECD Watch, 'Mission Statement' <www.oecdwatch.org/about-us/mission-statement> accessed 24 September 2019.

12 Merriam-Webster Online Dictionary <www.merriam-webster.com/dictionary/remedy> accessed 24 September 2019.

13 Oxford Online Dictionary <https://en.oxforddictionaries.com/definition/remedy> accessed 24 September 2019.

14 Ibid.

15 Ibid.

16 Matthew Murphy and Jordi Vives, 'Perceptions of Justice and the Human Rights Protect, Respect, and Remedy Framework', (2013) 116(4) *Journal of Business Ethics* 781.

17 UN Framework (n 5) paras 93–95; UNGPs (n 2) 22, 25, 29. The UNGPs use the term "grievance mechanism" to indicate any routinized, State- or non-State-based, judicial or non-judicial process through which grievances concerning business-related human rights abuse can be raised and remedy can be sought (UNGP [n 2] 25, commentary).

18 Columbia Law School Human Rights Clinic and Harvard Law School International Human Rights Clinic, 'Righting Wrongs? Barrick Gold's Remedy Mechanism for Sexual Violence in Papua New Guinea: Key Concerns and Lessons Learned' (November 2015) <http://hrp.law.harvard.edu/wp-content/uploads/2015/11/FINALBARRICK.pdf> accessed 24 September 2019.

19 Yousuf Aftab, 'Pillar III on the Ground: An Independent Assessment of the Porgera Remedy Framework' (Enodo Rights 2016) <www.barrick.com/files/porgera/Enodo-Rights-Porgera-Remedy-Framework-Independent-Assessment.pdf> accessed 24 September 2019.

20 Ibid.

21 Ministry of Foreign Affairs, 'Final Statement Former Employees of Bralima vs. Bralima and Heineken' (18 August 2017) <www.oecdguidelines.nl/latest/news/2017/08/18/final-statement-notification-former-employees-bralima-vs.-bralima-heineken> accessed 24 September 2019.

22 United Nations Commission on Transnational Corporations, 'Draft United Nations Code of Conduct on Transnational Corporations' (1983) UN ESCOR Spec Sess, Supp No 7, Annex 11, UN Doc E/1983/17/Rev.1; United Nations Commission on Transnational Corporations, 'Development and International Economic Cooperation: Transnational Corporations' (1990) UN ESCOR, 2nd Sess, UN Doc E/1990/94.

23 ILO, 'Tripartite Declaration of Principles Concerning Multinational Enterprises and Social Policy (MNE Declaration)' (5th edn, 17 March 2017) <www.ilo.org/empent/Publications/WCMS_094386/lang-en/index.htm> accessed 24 September 2019.

24 OECD, 'Declaration on International Investment and Multinational Enterprises' (25 May 2011) <www.oecd.org/daf/inv/investment-policy/oecddeclarationoninternationalinvestmentandmultinationalenterprises.htm> accessed 24 September 2019.

25 Karin Buhmann, 'Public Regulators and CSR: The "Social Licence to Operate" in Recent United Nations Instruments on Business and Human Rights and the Juridification of CSR', (2016) 136(4) *Journal of Business Ethics* 699.

26 John Ruggie, *Just Business* (Norton Publishers 2013) 137–9.

27 The OECD Guidelines for Multinational Enterprises: Decision of the Council (27 June 2000) OECD/LEGAL/0307.

28 OECD Guidelines (n 1) Procedural Guidance, I.A.

29 Ibid. II, I.1, Procedural Guidance, I, C.

30 Ibid.

31 For example, the statute for the Danish NCP includes an additional step, which requires the NCP to encourage the parties to reach a settlement between themselves before it offers its good offices. If the parties do reach such a settlement, details on the case and the settlement are not disclosed unless the parties do so themselves, or allow the NCP to do so. (Act on the Danish NCP [*Lov om Mæglings- og Klageinstitutionen for Ansvarlig Virksomhedsadfærd*] Act No 546, 18 Jun 2012 s 7, para 1). The statute also enables the NCP to take up a case on its own initiative; that is, without a complaint (ibid. section 2).

32 Eg, *Kaliña and Lokono Peoples v Suriname* (ser C) No 309 (Inter-Am Ct HR, 25 November 2015).

33 A French proposal to include legal persons in the jurisdiction of the Court was not included in the 1998 Rome Statute of the International Criminal Court.
34 UNHRC, 'International Expert Workshop (Toronto): "Business Impacts and Non-Judicial Access to Remedy: Emerging Global Experience', Addendum to Report of the Working Group on the Issue of Human Rights and Transnational Corporations and Other Business Enterprises (28 April 2014) UN Doc A/HRC/26/25/Add 3, 11; UN General Assembly, Basic Principles and Guidelines on the Right to Remedy and Reparation for Victims of Gross Violations of International Human Rights Law and Serious Violations of International Humanitarian law (21 March 2006) UN Doc A/RES/60/147.
35 European Center for Constitutional and Human Rights, 'Newsletter' No 28 (May 2013).
36 Daniel et al. (n 3).
37 Backer (n 8); Ruggie and Nelson (n 8).
38 Amnesty International (n 9); House of Lords and House of Commons Joint Committee on Human Rights, 'Human Rights and Business 2017: Promoting Responsibility and Ensuring Accountability', HL Paper 153 HC 443 (5 April 2017) 63.
39 Daniel et al. (n 3) 13.
40 House of Lords and House of Commons Joint Committee on Human Rights (n 38) 65.
41 See also OECD, *Responsible Business Conduct for Institutional Investors: Key Considerations for Due Diligence under the OECD Guidelines for Multinational Enterprises* (OECD 2017) 46; Buhmann (n 8)' [(OECD 2017) 46; Buhmann (n 8).
42 Government of Canada, 'Canada's Renewed CSR Strategy: Doing Business the Canadian Way: A Strategy to Advance CSR in Canada's Extractive Sector Abroad' (14 November 2014) <www.canada.ca/en/news/archive/2014/11/canada-renewed-csr-strategy-doing-business-canadian-way-strategy-advance-csr-canada-extractive-sector-abroad.html> accessed 24 September 2019.
43 Government of Germany, *National Action Plan: Implementation of the UN Guiding Principles on Business and Human Rights 2016–2020* (2016), s 1.3. (State Support) 25 <https://business-humanrights.org/sites/default/files/documents/NAP%20Business%20Human%20Rights_English%281%29.pdf> accessed 24 September 2019.
44 OECD, *Annual Report of the OECD Guidelines for Multinational Enterprises 2015* (OECD 2016), 39–40.
45 Ibid.
46OECD Watch, 'Model National Contact Point' (September 2007) <www.oecdwatch.org/publications-en/Publication_2223> accessed 24 September 2019.
47 See National Contact Point OECD Guidelines (Netherlands), 'Final Statement Specific Instance Former Employees Bralima vs. Bralima and Heineken' (18 August 2017) <www.oecdguidelines.nl/documents/publication/2017/08/18/final-statement-notification-bralima-vs-heineken> accessed 24 September 2019.
48 House of Lords and House of Commons Joint Committee on Human Rights (n 38) 63.
49 This was evidenced by the variation in NCP final statements in three cases concerning the POSCO company lodged with the NCPs of Korea, Norway, and the Netherlands. The statement issued by the Korean NCP in 2015 diverged from previous statements made by other NCPs. See discussion in Ceyhan (n 8) 228–9.
50 OECD, 'Case Database, Search for '#all', <http://mneguidelines.oecd.org/database/searchresults/?q=%23all> accessed 24 September 2019.
51 TUAC, 'Cases' <www.tuacoecdmneguidelines.org/Cases2.asp> accessed 24 September 2019.
52 OECD Watch (n 11).
53 OECD, 'Cases Handled by the National Contact Points for the OECD Guidelines for Multinational Enterprises' <https://mneguidelines.oecd.org/Flyer-OECD-National-Contact-Points.pdf> accessed 24 September 2019; for an OECD database of specific

instances, see <http://mneguidelines.oecd.org/database/> accessed 24 September 2019.

54 Ibid.

55 Daniel et al. (n 3) 12.

56 Ibid. 14–15.

57 Government of Canada, 'Canada: A Strong Player in the Global Mining Industry' <www.international.gc.ca/trade-agreements-accords-commerciaux/topics-domaines/other-autre/csr-strat-rse.aspx?lang=eng> accessed 24 September 2019.

58 In 15 out of 26 concluded cases, and 20 out of all 35 cases (including those in progress), on labor and industrial relations with the US NCP 2000–2017, the host country was the US. OECD Watch, 'NCP Case Database', search for (NCP:(United States)) and (Theme:(Employment and industrial relations)) and (Host:(United States)) and (Status:(Concluded)) <http://mneguidelines.oecd.org/database/searchresults/?q=(NCP:(United%20States))%20AND%20(Theme:(Employment%20and%20industrial%20relations))%20AND%20(Host:(United%20States))%20AND%20(Status:(Concluded))> accessed 24 September 2019.

59 iIbid., search for (NCP:(France)) <http://mneguidelines.oecd.org/database/searchresults/?q=(NCP:(France))> accessed 24 September 2019.

60 Ibid., search for (NCP:(Norway)) and (Host:(Norway)), <http://mneguidelines.oecd.org/database/searchresults/?q=(NCP:(Norway))%20AND%20(Host:(Norway))> accessed 24 September 2019.

61 Data source: OECD Database of Specific Instances, see <http://mneguidelines.oecd.org/database/> accessed 24 September 2019; Daniel, Caitlin, Joseph Wilde, KMG Genovese, Virginia Sandjojo (2015) Remedy remains rare: an analysis of 15 years of NCP cases and their contributions to improve access to remedy for victims of corporate misconduct, Amsterdam: OECD Watch.

62 OECD, Case Database, search for '#all' <http://mneguidelines.oecd.org/database/searchresults/?q=%23all> accessed 24 September 2019.

63 OECD Watch, Case database, search for status 'rejected' <www.oecdwatch.org/cases/advanced-search/status/casesearchview?type=Status&search=en_Rejected&b_start:int=90> accessed 24 September 2019.

64 Danish NCP, 'Annual Report' (2012–2013; 2014) <https://virksomhedsadfaerd.dk/publikationer> accessed 24 September 2019.

65 OECD Watch, *Assessment of NCP Performance in the 2013–2014 Implementation Cycle* (OECD Watch 2014).

66 For a detailed discussion, see Juan Carlos Ochoa, 'The Roles and Powers of the OECD National Contact Points Regarding Complaints on an Alleged Breach of the OECD Guidelines for Multinational Enterprises by a Transnational Corporation', (2015) 84(1) *Nordic Journal of International Law* 89.

67 OECD, 'Case Database, Search for (Theme:(Human rights)) and (Status:(Concluded))' <http://mneguidelines.oecd.org/database/searchresults/?hf=10&b=0&q=(Theme%3A(Human+rights))+AND+(Status%3A(Concluded))&s=desc(mne_datereceived)> accessed 24 September 2019.

68 Kinross Brasil Mineracao and Paracatu neighbouring associations, concluded by the Brasil NCP on 22 September 2016; specific instance notified by the trade unions Pragatisheel Cement Shramik Sangh and IndustriALL Global Union regarding the activities of ACC Limited and Ambuja Cement Limited, controlled by Holcim Group, operating in India, concluded by the NCP of Switzerland on 18 December 2014.

69 Specific instance notified by the NGOs the International Federation for Human Rights, the Action contre l'Impunité pour les Droits de l'Homme, and Rights & Accountability in Development regarding the activities of the Forrest Group in the DRC, concluded by the Belgium NCP on 12 February 2013.

70 Human rights issues involving an Australian multinational insurance company operating in New Zealand, concluded by the New Zealand NCP in December 2016.
71 Specific instance notified by the Canada Tibet Committee, on behalf of a group of affected communities, regarding the activities of China Gold International Resources Corp Ltd operating at the Gyama Valley, Tibet Autonomous Region, concluded by the Canada NCP on 8 April 2015.
72 OECD Watch (n 46).
73 Daniel et al., *Remedy Remains Rare* (n 3) 13.
74 See section 3.6.1. Data on specific instances: Issues, sectors, stakeholders, country differences. See also, eg, annual reports from the Danish NCP that also contain examples of rejection of complaints on this basis.
75 Moreover, during 2001–2015, 15 complaints were rejected due to parallel proceedings, 12 because a mediated agreement was found unlikely, and 10 due to the lack of an investment nexus (a requirement that was abolished with the 2011 revision of the OECD Guidelines). See Daniel et al. (n 3) 13.

Bibliography

Aftab Y, 'Pillar III on the Ground: An Independent Assessment of the Porgera Remedy Framework' (Enodo Rights 2016) <www.barrick.com/files/porgera/Enodo-Rights-Porgera-Remedy-Framework-Independent-Assessment.pdf>

Backer LC, 'Rights and Accountability in Development (RAID) vs Das Air and Global Witness v. Afrimex: Small Steps towards an Autonomous Transnational Legal System for the Regulation of Multinational Corporations', (2009) 10(1) *Melbourne Journal of International Law* 258.

Buhmann K, 'Business and Human Rights: Understanding the UN Guiding Principles from the Perspective of Transnational Business Governance Interactions', (2015) 6(1) *Transnational Legal Theory* 399.

———, 'Public Regulators and CSR: The "Social Licence to Operate" in Recent United Nations Instruments on Business and Human Rights and the Juridification of CSR', (2016) 136(4) *Journal of Business Ethics* 699.

Ceyhan BB, 'Corporations and Human Rights: Searching for International Norms for Corporate Conduct in Domestic Case Law' (PhD dissertation, Luxembourg University 2017) <http://hdl.handle.net/10993/32713>

Daniel C et al., *Remedy Remains Rare: An Analysis of 15 Years of NCP Cases and Their Contribution to Improve Access to Remedy for Victims of Corporate Misconduct* (OECD Watch 2015).

Murphy M and Vives J, 'Perceptions of Justice and the Human Rights Protect, Respect, and Remedy Framework', (2013) 116(4) *Journal of Business Ethics* 781.

Ochoa JC, 'The Roles and Powers of the OECD National Contact Points Regarding Complaints on an Alleged Breach of the OECD Guidelines for Multinational Enterprises by a Transnational Corporation', (2015) 84(1) *Nordic Journal of International Law* 89.

Ruggie J, *Just Business* (Norton Publishers 2013) 137–9.

——— and Nelson T, 'Human Rights and the OECD Guidelines for Multinational Enterprises: Normative Innovations and Implementation Challenges' (3 May 2015) Harvard Kennedy School/Corporate Social Responsibility Initiative Working Paper No 66 <https://papers.ssrn.com/sol3/papers.cfm?abstract_id=2601922>

4 Unpacking accountability in business and human rights

The multinational enterprise, the State, and the international community

Larry Catá Backer

4.1 Accountability

Etymology sometimes carries with it the culturally powerful norms that give a word a complex set of social meanings beyond its quotidian use.[1] Such is the case with the words "account" and "accountability". Consider an "account" and the verb "to account"; accounting carries with it the sense of a thing (the noun) and of an act (the verb). It is the *body of a statement* answering for conduct; it is a disclosure, a confession, a memorial of past actions rendered in accordance with a generally accepted framework for rendering such account. It serves as the basis for monitoring, compliance, contrition, and reckoning under the standards of conduct to which the accounting relates. At the same time, *it is the act of rendering account itself*; it is the *act* of explanation, confession, and recalling past actions; it is the act of reckoning. The concept then ties together a series of complex ideas: it serves as a nexus point for concepts of transparency, monitoring and reporting, and normative standards that trigger and structure those. At the same time, it suggests confession and contrition, and bears within it the underlying sense of a set of standards against which both report and reporting are undertaken, and the rules that vest some with the responsibility to engage in such acts.[2]

Thus, accountability is the condition of being accountable, of bearing an obligation to account; that is, of the duty, expectation, act, and form of rendering acts up for judgment. Accountability is the condition of being required to explain and the act of explanation itself. But it is a social act that produces judgment and is rendered in the context of expectations from which judgment can be made and consequences exacted. The implication is that such accounts and accounting, and such amenability to account, are social acts. This is emphasized by the history of its construction – its ancient derivations "from Latin *computare* 'to count, sum up, reckon together', from com 'with, together' (see *com-*) + *putare* 'to reckon', originally 'to prune', from PIE [proto-Indo-European] root *pau- (2) 'to cut, strike, stamp'".[3] Thus, to speak of accountability in the common parlance is to suggest a set of actions and objects bound up in an obligation to undertake both the acts and to deliver the object; that is, a set of disclosures from which judgments may be made in the context of the reciprocal obligations that bind those who account and those to whom the accounting is owed. Those clusters of acts and objects are the means through which *one brings another to account*, but just as importantly, they serve as the means through which *one is brought to account*, and the forms through which *one brings oneself to account*. These three means are united in their fidelity to the forms of accountability, even as each points to quite distinct forms of rendering account.

Accountability has always played a major role in the management of enterprises. Enterprises have long been required to render account to their stakeholders. Business partners account to each other, the managers of business account to their principals. The scope and form of accounting has changed substantially over the years. For business enterprises, the scope of accounts and accounting have been guided by a sometimes-tense relationship between two core principles. The first principle is the obligation of enterprises to maximize the welfare of their owners; the second principle is the obligation to conform to law. Inherent within both of these is the obligation to conform to social and contextual expectations, if only because the failure to so conform could produce business risk (for example, it could negatively impact enterprise performance, which in this century has been the source of the so-called business case for human rights),[4] and might produce legal risk as well (sometimes through legal changes in the wake of social scandal, as in the UK's Modern Slavery Act of 2015). Business enterprise is certainly accountable, yet for much of the contemporary history of the enterprise the accounting of business has focused directly on its financial condition, guided by generally accepted accounting principles (GAAP) and its variations, the normative framework developed by the profession that has grown up around the duty to account, and on judging its consequences,[5] as well as on those conditions that might impact financial performance built into the disclosure regimes of many legal structures for the management of markets for securities.[6]

However, just as globalization substantially changed the relationship of the law of enterprise organization and its governance,[7] globalization has also transformed the character of accountability itself. From the rendering of accounts in specific instances, accountability has become, in some sense, a central concept in governance legitimacy.[8] Accountability has also become both the expression of governance and the act through which governance is conducted. Objectives-based regulation, regulatory governance,[9] and the rise of data-algorithmic systems of compliance by enterprises[10] and States,[11] reward, and punishment have all substantially broadened the scope of accounting as well as the range of those who must account, and the scope of the actions with respect to which an accounting is now expected. With respect to economic activities in general, and enterprises more specifically, the transformation of the scope and utility of accountability has also shifted from a singular emphasis on the financial effects of activity to those that touch on a set of emerging social, philanthropic, sustainability, and human rights items. That shift also underlines a number of other transformations from the centrality of the State in governance through law to a more diffused regulatory system,[12] and from the focus on law making and enforcement to systems of regulation based on disclosure and compliance.[13] In a networked weaving of governance systems that no longer has the government of the State at its center, accountability becomes the means for producing order without a center.[14]

Thus, accountability occupies a central place within the complex of regulatory trends that are shaping the organization of economic (and, to some extent, social, political, and cultural) life within a globalized order.[15] Accountability frames the relationship between actors, both established and emerging, and gives them substance within regulatory environments.[16] This is especially important in the context of the human rights responsibilities of enterprises and the concurrent human rights duties of States relating to their respective economic (and regulatory) activities.[17] Yet, the effective imposition of accounting regimes in governance requires a more nuanced understanding of the structures of the character and ecologies of accounting.

Therefore, the purpose of this chapter is to unpack the concept of accountability as it is deployed in governance, and then repack it in a way that makes the concept more useful. The thesis of the chapter is as follows: accountability must be understood as a shorthand for a set of multiple reciprocal relations that are manifested in actions responding to expectations grounded in normative standards actualized in the context within which the actors are connected, and directed toward general (communal) and specific (individual) ends. A working system of accountability centered on corporate violations of human rights and sustainability requires mutual and simultaneous accounting by all stakeholders to (1) bring each other to account, (2) bring oneself to account, and (3) be brought to account.

The second part of this chapter examines the strands of premises that constitute the complex of concepts for which I have used the shorthand term "accountability". I examine a core set of orienting principles central to the concept of accountability as a governance norm and as the instrument of that norm. To that end, I consider the behavioral core of accountability as (a) the act of answering to, explaining of in relation to an expectation; (b) to a specific and functionally segmented objective; (c) manifested as conduct, norms, methods, consequences; (d) directed to oneself to others; and (e) to the specific ends of making right, disciplining behavior to ensuring order. These elements suggest the relational structures of accountability: one brings another to account, is brought to account, or brings oneself to account. Relational behaviors then suggest a scope of accountability. This "to what ends" of accountability describes a functionally based set of constraints that give accountability its direction and coherence. These rational and functionally constrained actions then suggest the ways that rendering accounts can be manifested. This is determined by context and embedded in formal institutional structures of State and society. That brings accountability to its end point – those to whom accounting is rendered. The beneficiaries of accountability (to whom accountability duties flow) can determine the specific character of accounting.

Next, the third part of the chapter re-bundles accountability. The multi-level multidimensionality of accountability as a dynamic and relational concept is considered as a function of objectives, methods, and subjects. The multi-level, multidimensionality of accountability as a dynamic and relational concept is then considered as a function of objectives, methods, and subjects. The first section looks to its objectives (why account?). Objectives include norm generation, good governance, institutional legitimacy, and remedial mechanisms. The second section considers the systemic elements of accountability systems. Its methods of accountability (institutional and formal or informal) and its governance sources (law or norms) shape the expression of accountability and define its context. The third section then considers the subjects of accountability systems (who accounts?; who is accountable?): States, enterprises, international organizations, and civil society/NGOs.

4.2 Unpacking accounting and accountability

What does it mean to "unpack" accounting and accountability as core concepts of (self-) governance? At its most general level, "unpacking" involves opening a concept and examining its contents or component elements.[18] It is both the act of removal from a container (here, the concept of accounting or accountability) and the act of examining those contents (here, the analysis of the choice of content that makes up the concept) to make meaning clearer. One unpacks a concept not merely to make its meaning clearer, but also to understand the choices of meaning packed into the concept examined. This examination, in turn, serves as a predicate for its effective imposition as well as for a more nuanced understanding of the structures of the character of accounting and accountability; these, in turn, serve to better situate both concepts within ecologies of regulatory governance.[19]

So what might be packed into the container that is the behavior core of accounting; that is, what are the expectations for those who must perform acts of accountability? The unpacking here is fairly straightforward. Each element – the essence of simplicity – is itself merely a doorway to more subtle concepts. Together these elements build the structures around which the act of accounting can be undertaken. It is from these actions (from accounting as a verb) that the content of the account (to accounting as a noun) can be derived. And yet that action is itself directed by the content that action produces – *Ouroboros*,[20] the classical incarnation of a self-reflexive system informed by its internal environment which it itself creates.[21]

4.2.1 To account is to act

The act of accounting can be a single one or a series of actions. It can constitute nothing more than a reflection or something as complex as a constant set of actions that are components of complex institutionalized actions. *To act to account is to answer to an expectation*, to explain, in relation to that expectation or a set of expectations. Of course, these acts and the responses are contextual, with the context defined by the expectation (although the expectation is also defined by the context to some extent). While everything is contextual, the context in the act of accounting to an expectation itself segments the accounting along functional lines. One does not always account for everything; one accounts as a response to expectations that are themselves the expression of a need along functional lines. Traditional corporate financial statements provide an excellent expression of these core notions of reflexive functional segmentation.[22]

4.2.2 *The act of accounting to respond to an expectation is manifested as conduct, norms, methods, and consequences*

The essence of human rights due diligence, as a core means of accounting for the human rights responsibilities of corporations, embodies this complex cocktail – requiring conduct (policy formation, and inward and outward reporting), norms (the International Bill of Human Rights), methods (the systemic due diligence at the heart of human rights due diligence), and consequences (remediation, prevention, mitigation).[23] The act of accounting and its expression are a means to an end; the satisfaction of expectation, which is itself a predicate for and basis of responses on the part of those to whom an accounting is rendered.

4.2.3 *That act of accounting is rendered to oneself and to others*

One brings to account. One is brought to account. One brings oneself to account. One must render account to oneself before one is capable of rendering account to others. This is central to the integrity of capital aggregating market-based systems of economic activity. Accounting to oneself serves as a baseline for systemic integrity.[24] However, it is also understood as the foundation for accounting to others.[25] That interplay between self-assessment and accounting to others is a central element of coherence elements of human rights due diligence.[26]

4.2.4 *To account is to direct acts toward consequential aims*

The aims of the accounting also refines the "for what" aspects of accounting. Thus, while the nature of the accounting tends in the first instance to set out the general direction and structures of the accounting (for example, financial accounting focuses on financial performance), the person or institution to which one accounts changes the expectations at the center of the act of accounting.[27] One is accountable to whoever one has harmed, of course; that is the essence of contemporary human rights-based accountability frameworks for business[28] Here, harm refines the "for what" aspects of accounting. But one can affect others, or oneself, without harm, and may account for those as well. This also produces a distinct approach to the refinement of the "for what" ends of accounting. For enterprises responsible for the harm caused by violation of human rights, environmental and labor standards, the standards themselves define the objects of accountability as well as its scope.[29]

More importantly, the aims of rendering account, the final point of the act and its manifestation trigger response by the person or institution to whom or which accounts are rendered. In politics, elected officials render account that then permit those to whom accounting is made to retain them in office or choose another, or seek to remove them from office.[30] In the business and human rights context, rendering account produces both a responsibility to mitigate and remedy, but also empowers those to whom account is rendered to protect their rights. It also produces a power in consumers to choose to exercise market power elsewhere. Self-accounting permits an enterprise to manage its own internal operations; it permits financial intermediaries to exercise their authority with respect to their own dealings with the entity rendering account.[31]

4.2.5 *As such, the manifestation of the act of accounting is itself related to the nature of the act itself*

The object of accounting further refines the scope (the "for what") for which accounting is undertaken. Likewise, the breadth and form of conduct (accountable manifestations) are (1) determined by context and (2) embedded in formal institutional structures of State and society. These are directed to the beneficiaries of accountability (the "to whom"), it itself changes the character of accounting (act, for what, manifestation). Corporations account to their shareholders through the preparation and delivery of financial statements and other disclosures produced in accordance with legal obligations and the requirements of internal rules.

However, corporations account to themselves reports that are produced from systems of data analytics (qualitative and quantitative) built into the operating structures of business. The forms of internal and external accounting are different;[32] this is a source of some controversy among those who see in transparency as a vital element of accountability.[33] The form of accounting is closely related to the context in which the act of accounting occurs, but it is also to be distinguished from the consequences of accounting. To render account – that is, to produce an explanation related to expectations of those to which the rendering is due – does not inevitably point to the consequences of that rendering. Those consequences are also contextual and tied to the character of the obligation to account, and to the responsibilities of those to whom such accounting is rendered. A consequence of accounting as a legal duty might be the need to compensate, or it may affect the judgment and choices of those to whom accounts are rendered. Accounting as a social duty might give rise to consequences to remediate or to mitigate harm. Accounting to oneself might be a necessary element in the decisions about courses of action and allocation of resources. All three consequences lie at the heart of the UN Guiding Principle's human rights due diligence[34] – the possibility of legal liability (complicity and corruption, for example), the responsibility to mitigate or remediate harms, and the use of accounting to change business behavior and inform decision-making.

Just as important, the concept of accounting (and thus of the state of accountability) runs in both directions. The acts of *rendering account are relational*: one brings to account, one is brought to account, and one brings oneself to account. One who brings oneself or others to account is also accountable to others. Within the context of the human rights effects of economic activity, this cross-hatching of accounting forms an essential part of the governance web. Every entity and person who accounts is also accountable. The cross-hatching of rights to demand an account and the obligation to render account produces the textures of mutual accountability.[35] Cross-hatching also speaks to the anarchic character of rendering account. Multiple obligations to account to a variety of actors who themselves must account to themselves and others produce a texture that may not be entirely coherent when viewed as a whole. Even the individual actor, who is accountable and seeks accounting from others, produces an incoherence in accountability[36] ("multiple accountabilities disorder") that mirrors in some respects what John Ruggie identified in the business and human rights context as legal and policy incoherence.[37] Drake[38] identified the issue as one of polycentrism and what she called the "accountability trilemma".

> The problem of polycentrism (having many "centres" of accountability that have conflicting demands) poses a challenge due to failures to identify a standard metric of value to measure progress or to focus disagreement. . . . More accountability in one direction can mean less in another.[39]

It is possible to understand the core concepts and relationships that together, through dynamic processes of application in context, constitute the action as well as the manifestation of accounting. Accounting is the aggregation of (1) *acts*: answering to, explaining in relation to an expectation; (2) *for ends*: functionally segmented; (3) *manifested as*: conduct, norms, methods, consequences; (4) *directed toward* oneself or others; and (5) *for consequential aims*: to make right, to discipline behavior, and to ensure order. These strands of accounting serve as the critical components of accountability within the context of the human rights effects of economic activity undertaken by enterprises: acts, ends, manifestations directed toward the self or others, and their specific aims. These are the essential elements of accountability that are embedded in the regulatory frameworks emerging in this century and to which enterprise corporate governance (and State management of governance through law and policy) adhere.

4.3 Rendering account: objectives, methods, sources, and objects

Unpacking accountability exposes the web of premises around which accountability is understood. That unpacking is useful not merely in its own right, but as a means of better understanding the way that all the pieces fit together to produce the act and product of rendering account. That fitting together is the object of this part of the chapter. Section 4.3.1 starts with the fundamental question: to what ends does one render account? Put another way, it is necessary to consider the objectives that invest certain relations with the duty to account, that renders a person or institution accountable, both to oneself (again the font of the legitimacy of the cluster of concepts we understand as accounting) and to others. This is particularly important in the context of constructing systems of accountability for the behaviors of enterprises with respect to human rights, environmental, or labor effects of their actions. The answer might be usefully considered as the amalgam of a number of sub-objectives: norm generation, good governance, institutional legitimacy, and remediation. This consideration of objectives then serves as context for a brief examination of the methodologies around which accountability is built (section 4.3.2), its sources (section 4.3.3), and the individuals and entities that are the subjects and objects of the accounting (section 4.3.4).

4.3.1 Objectives

The objectives of rendering account comprise a tightly interwoven set of expectations that build on each other in contextually significant ways. They run as much from those rendering account as from those for whose benefit an accounting is made. Because those who owe accounting may simultaneously comprise parts of other groups to which accounting is owed, the objectives and expectations around the act of accounting and its process shapes both. For ease of discussion, these expectations are divided into four broad categories: norm generation, good governance, legitimacy, and remedy.

1. Norm generation

Accounting and accountability seems an odd place to situate norm generation. The argument is usually inverted so that norm generation produces both a duty to account and describes the range of individuals and entities that are accountable. Accounting is a disciplinary act, the means by which norms are operationalized, yet every application of a norm also refines its character.[40] However, it is just as likely that accountability itself serves to generate norms; it is the means through which the principles inherent in norms are given shape by means of the structures of their application by creating the customs and expectations[41] that are themselves the norms "made flesh".[42]

In the area of business and human rights, the project of norm generation has produced a generalized certainty and substantial ambiguity in its application. It is in this tension between a general sense of normative principles – grounded in human rights and sustainability principles – and their articulation in normative rules that the manifestations of accounting may sometimes drive the manifestation of norms between principle and application. It is at this point of convergence of norm, of actor and justice, that accountability serves as both language and ordering principle. In this case, to account is to manifest norms, to make the abstract concrete specific to the context in which the rendering is expected.

Accountability standards for business were grounded on the satisfaction of shareholders and the welfare of the institution.[43] At the beginning of the contemporary era, in the mid-19th century, and for several generations thereafter, to render account meant compliance with legal standards (Securities Exchange Act of 1934) and societal expectations built around the financial performance of the enterprise through the language of accounting (the connection between the duty to render account and the agents and mediators of that compliance – the accountants – who shaped the language and thus the norms of accountability should not be lost here).[44] For enterprises, rendering account meant providing a picture of the financial condition of the enterprise, to apply those principles as embedded within the forms of the accounting, the Generally Applied Accounting Principles (GAAP).[45]

Non-financial accountability came later. From out of the small opening of corporate charity, accountability has now broadened to embrace non-financial norms, grouped around three sets of normative principles structures: human rights, sustainability, and labor rights. These norm principles were traditionally applied *to* corporations *through* States *by or with* non-State actors (NGOs and IOs). These norm principles were not situated within the structures of the responsibility to account but within core *public law* principles of government and core principles of social organization. To render account was a vector that ran out from authoritative norm-generating bodies to those with the obligation to render account. By the turn of the present century, however, those organizations that generated norms also assumed an obligation to render account themselves. Neutrally applied norms would make distinction among the forms of entities engaging in economic activity. And so norms began to cover norm makers; they applied to States through other actors situated in law and politics, and they applied to NGOs and IOs through other actors, etc.

The object of rendering account is to apply norms to enterprise activity through the exercise of accounting for such behavior to a group of stakeholders to whom a duty (including a duty to render account) is owed. That duty may be grounded in national law or, increasingly, in the expectations of stakeholders. In rendering account, the enterprise must convert principles[46] into expectations that are themselves capable of being the subject of an accounting. One cannot account for conformity for principle without converting that principle into an expectation that is concrete enough to be identified in context, and, for the purposes of rendering account, of identification and (sometimes, with trepidation[47]) measurement.[48] Thus, rendering account invokes an act that is itself pregnant with normative possibility. Thus, the act of rendering account and the development of the expectation to be satisfied by such accounting are intimately interconnected.

2. *Good governance*

Rendering account as acts that also shape the expectations for which the rendering is made shape the norms that comprise the framework within which expectations are understood. However, those expectations are themselves framed by a methodology of organizing activity that is itself a subject with respect to which an accounting must be rendered. "Accountability is the cornerstone of good governance."[49] Here, one encounters the compulsion of rendering account, although the obligation is that of the State, to satisfy the expectation of its people, but with respect to the State's obligation to hold its own individuals and entities (including economic entities) to account.

Therefore, good governance focuses on the integrity of social, political, and economic organizations; a fundamental *prerequisite to capacity to comply* with those principles and norms that form the substance of accountability for economic enterprises under human rights and sustainability standards. That capacity includes the institutional capacity to be reasonably informed about the operation of the entity and to use that information to ensure corporate compliance with its responsibilities, legal or otherwise. This is both a fundamental of modern US corporate law,[50] and a fundamental tenet of the sovereign lending policy of international financial institutions.[51] Normative accountability is aspirational in the absence of the capacity of the accountable entity to structure a mechanism for oversight and then use it to seek to meet those obligations with respect to which they must render account.

If good governance centers partly on the *capacity to account*, then the expectations of actors to which an accounting is rendered must also center on an accounting of the capacity of the actor to account, as well as substantive normative accounting. For enterprises, I refer here to the traditional focus on internal controls and external reporting.[52] These also apply to State-owned enterprises.[53] They revolve around corruption, the efficiencies and direction of monitoring and reporting, technical capacity and proficiency, and policy coherence. Corruption goes directly to capacity, even as it serves as a normative objective of the accounting whose systemic integrity it can undermine.

The essence of good governance is the foundation for human rights due diligence in the UNGP.[54] It is also the foundation for regulatory governance. The UK Modern Slavery Act (2015), the EU Non-Financial Reporting Directive,[55] and the French Supply Chain Due Diligence Law[56] are all prominent examples. Each of these pieces of legislation represents the product of political accounting, with reference to international objectives that produced rules expanding the scope of accountability, as well as its normative content, of enterprises for the economic activities. Accountability itself can generate accountability.

Lastly, there is a contextual element to capacity expectations in the responsibility to account. These can be understood in three aspects of capacity: input, throughput, and output. *Input accounting capacity* centers on the sources of action and norms rules embraced by each of the actors. It touches on the formation of policies or principles on which action will be based. Both the UNGPs[57] and the OECD Guidelines[58] underscore the importance of coherence and capacity in the development and implementation of the normative structures around which accounts are rendered, yet the problem of alignment remains very real. Whatever the level of accounting, in the presence of multiple and potentially inconsistent standards of account, accounting itself might become a strategic element in accounting avoidance.[59] *Throughput accounting capacity* focuses on engagement in crafting structures forms of response (norm, rule, process, action, etc.). This tends to be the area where there is the most attention. The capacity to actually account, through forms, methods, structures, and products, is the showiest part of the performance of accounting, and yet it is merely a bridge from input to output. That position makes it both the critical portion of accounting capacity and sometimes its weakest link. The weakness comes from the ability of those who render account to strategically link useful norms in constructing accounting systems that may undermine other norms and process.

> After green washing and blue washing – using a UN logo to signpost sustainability without doing much – the term SDG washing points to businesses that use the Sustainable Development Goals to market their positive contribution to some SDGs while ignoring their negative impact on others.[60]

Lastly, *output accounting capacity* centers on effectiveness in operation. It is the accounting of accounting. This brings us back to good governance. The effectiveness of remedy, the robust response to the accounting, is the measure of the capacity to account effectively. One measures accounting by its effects with reference to its norms and processes.

3. *Institutional legitimacy*

Closely related to the expectation of good governance is the expectation of institutional legitimacy. The capacity to account, the essence of the good governance objectives enhanced by the act of accounting itself, points to the larger issues of systemic integrity within which accounting as an act and object is deeply embedded. Accountability is not possible in the absence of systemic capacity; it is also worth less under conditions of systemic illegitimacy. Just as there is a strong connection between capacity and accounting, there is an equally strong connection between accounting and legitimacy. Without institutional legitimacy, accounting is not possible; in the absence of accounting, institutional legitimacy fails. It is in that context that one may speak of the nature of accounting as the manifestation of the community between those who account and those to whom an accounting is rendered, its democratic character, and the centrality of transparency as a key objective of legitimacy-enhancing accountability.

Transparency is a legitimacy-enhancing technique[61] that speaks to the legitimacy inherent in the democratic principle,[62] whether in the form of Western-style democratic accountability or the Marxist-Leninist accountability inherent in the Mass Line. That, in a sense, is the expectation of accounting: it incorporates the expectation *of community*, capacity, and the underlying norms with respect to which the substance of account is generated. The objective of accounting – of rendering account – cements the relationship between the entity with the duty to account and the recipient of the accounting. That responsibility to account serves as the manifestation of the connection, of the bond between the entity (State, enterprise, civil society, etc.) and those to whom the obligation is owed. The obligation to account is owed precisely because of the bond. It is the nature of that bond that varies with the context of the relationship, whether it is political, economic, societal, or religious. In each case, the entity renders account, or is made to account, or accounts are extracted (written into the lives and conditions of those to whom an account ought to be rendered) in a way that is consistent with the nature of the organization and of the character of the bond. Political organs account differently than economic, religious, or societal organizations. The response by their respective stakeholders varies as well, from the ballot, to the market, to the abandonment of societal or religious organs in favor of others (or, in some cases, the wresting of control of the direction of those entities).

That legitimacy-enhancing character of transparency is driven not by the inherent power of the democratic principle, but by the value of transparency in strengthening the inherent power of the democratic principle.[63] The connection among accounting, its democratic character (as built on the relational bonds between those who have a responsibility to account and those to whom an accounting ought to be made), and transparency *do not suggest their identity but rather their complementarity*. This complementarity is built into the structures of disclosure regimes that combine the responsibility to account with the obligation to develop both accounting capacity and the methodologies of transparency to ensure accounting legitimacy.[64]

One can get a sense of that connection by considering the normative functions of transparency within accountability regimes.[65]

> The triangular relationship between governmentalization (of both public and private institutional actors with managerial power), the mass of the population (which is its object and now its foundation), and the "statistics" (that both define and serve to manage the mass of the population) is the essence of the problem of transparency. . . . As technique, transparency is the aggregate of methods of producing information for use in managing and policing power relationships. As norms, transparency expresses the normal and acceptable – right conduct, right rule and right relations – it embodies the ends for which it also provides the means.[66]

To render account, to be accountable, is the way that transparency is expressed as a technique, even as it serves as evidence of the capacity of the entity to account. At the same time, it serves as a space in which the normative content of such an accounting may be managed. *As informational transparency*, the control of data manifested as the power to decide what is harvested and what is disclosed can entirely change the substance and direction of accounting. With respect to *process or engagement transparency*, the issues are slightly different. Here, the issue of legitimacy revolves around the nature of engagement (formal or effective), the timing of consultation, and the weight given to input. It also centers on information asymmetries that can substantially erode the value of consultation or engagement.

The recent battles over control of US census data – that is, the power to ask people surveyed whether or not they are US citizens – speaks to that power. Both those who account[67] and those to whom accounting is rendered[68] fought over the propriety of including that data, each resorting in the normative expectations (against what standards are accounts rendered).[69] Transparency, legitimacy, capacity, and good governance connect to the underlying normative framework within which an accounting is to be made to shade its scope, purpose, direction, and form. More importantly, perhaps, it also shapes the way one accounts for the accounting one may be responsible for making.

4. *Objectives: remediation*

Remediation is the last of the objectives (expectations) for those to whom an accounting is necessary. It is its principle consequences in terms of the actions of the accountable party, although it is also connected to the range of responses that may be taken by those to whom an accounting is made. The expectation (objective) of remediation flows inward where one accounts to oneself; it flows outward where one accounts to others.

Remedies can be understood in two distinct ways. The first refers to the mechanism that may be provided to remedy harm by the accounting party or by others (for example, the State through its courts). The second refers to the remedy itself, the action undertaken to remedy the harm. Two other actions that flow from the remedial consequence are connected to post. The first is prospective – the use of accounting to avoid harm in the future by changing behavior in light of the accounting.[70] The second is the duty to change behavior by mitigating harm where action has already been undertaken,[71] "[i]n order to prevent and mitigate adverse human rights impacts, business enterprises should integrate the findings from their impact assessments across relevant internal functions and processes and take appropriate action".[72]

However, remedy within the context of accounting produces its own set of tensions. The first is the problem of layering. Internal accounting and external accounting resonate around each other, but because they are directed to quite distinct recipients in contextually different settings, they do not reflect the same focus or scope. Enterprises, like governments, are entitled to keep their secrets; the discussion always centers on where the line can be drawn to distinguish between legitimacy-enhancing transparency and the protection of the integrity and operation of the entity obligated to render account. Moreover, multi-normativity, the existence of multiple sources of norms that are specific to different functions, may create incentives to account internally in ways that are quite distinct from external accounting.[73]

The second tension touches on the problem of polycentricity. Layering produces a tendency toward multiple remediation regimes being simultaneously applied. Where multiple remedial regimes are compatible, the problem effectively disappears; where they do not, the accounting itself may be reduced in value. Yet it has become clear that the value of remedy may be incompatible across actors situated in various places in accountability continuum states, enterprises NGOs, IOs, etc. These actors disagree not merely with respect to the remedy, but to the systems within which remedy is to be obtained. These issues revolve around the question of effective remedy.[74]

The third tension touches on the question of whose remedy. Traditionally, those who control the remedial system also tend to control the scope and application of remedy. That right is inherent in the police power at the heart of political authority. But is it also at the heart of the economic authority of enterprises (State-owned or non-State-owned) where they are tasked with the enforcement of norms, rendering account directly to affected individuals, and providing an effective remedy? It is not clear, nor is it inherent in the concept of accountability, that the remedy provider should also control the scope and delivery of remedy. But should the remedy recipient be permitted to accept a remedy that larger global communities find unacceptable?

> Conceptual constraint centers on an unwillingness to avoid the imperial project of transposing Western assumptions about rights and of the relationship between states and their people to the rest of the world – and to do so without effective consultation with those affected. This is an important conceptual omission and points to an arrogance of transposing Western conceptions of 'the good' to those who suffer either from false consciousness or conceptual underdevelopment . . . To speak the sort of language of human rights that has become a staple of transnational elite conversation is to ignore the potentially profound differences in approach – though not of objectives – between Western oriented political theology and those of other systems.[75]

The problems of arrogance and privilege – and power – infect the structures of accountability in the context of its remedial and mitigation consequences as much as it affects, more generally, the conversation about the building of robust global standards.

4.3.2 Methods

The expectations of accounting – and of accountability understood as the expression of the relationship between those who account and those to whom an account is owed – revolve around issues of norm generation, good governance legitimacy, and remedy. However, these conceptual elements remain remotely abstract, a comfort to those with little direct relation to the task of actualizing abstraction in concrete form, especially with respect to the consequences of accounting. That task falls to method. The methodologies of rendering account are central to the application of the norms and expectations from which the responsibility arises. These tend to be closely aligned with the context and condition of the entity that must account. That is a core notion built into instruments like the UNGPs.

Method acquires an additional dimension when it moves from the entity rendering account to the beneficiaries of the accounting. It is to this aspect of accountability that method acquires a slightly different dimension. While the conceptual character of accountability shapes its methods, the ideological and operational cultures of accounting methods shape those concepts in turn. As such, accounting methodology becomes an important element in the construction and operation of robust systems of account. In this context, there is a variation that matches that of the operationalization of the act of accounting itself.

Overarching challenges include coherence and jurisdiction. The issue of enforcement always lurks in the background; made more difficult by the possibility of a substantive clash of norms where the methodologies of the jurisdiction imposing consequences vary from those in which enforcement is sought. That produces a consequence that is well known to global litigators: the enforceability within and across systems.

The methodical frameworks of accounting range from formal to informal[76] and may include judicial, political, administrative, professional, and social accountability arrangements. Institutional and formal systems within which accounting is expressed include the judicial authority of domestic legal orders.[77] One renders account to the highest form of political authority within a territory through the processes embedded within the judicial apparatus and expressed through the cultures of judging, which vary considerably from place to place.[78] The variety of forms of arbitration undertaken through institutionalized third parties to a similar effect are less formal, although cultural and historical context makes it difficult to generalize.[79]

Accountability can also lend itself to the most informal and non-binding methods, some of which have begun to play a more important role. Principal among these are the non-binding special instance proceedings undertaken under the OECD Guidelines for Multinational Enterprises[80] through the National Contact Points. Yet enterprise-based accountability and remedial mechanisms have also begun to play a prominent, though controversial, role.[81] Hybrid and ad hoc arrangements are also emerging, including those that might center indigenous rights[82] or consider the use of indigenous law and courts,[83] or regional human rights courts.[84]

4.3.3 Sources

An issue closely tied to the norm-generating expectation of accounting are its sources. These tie together issues of legitimacy and capacity around the problem of sourcing authority norms in institutions that themselves must be called to account. To that end, the issue of sources is also an issue of community; it requires, at a minimum, that all stakeholders within the relationship of accountability agree on the authoritativeness of sources against which accountability may be assessed. Yet this remains one of the more contentious areas of disagreement among influential drivers of accountability in business and human rights.[85]

At its most general, it seeks to develop an approach by which, in a contextually relevant way, all actors may agree about the institutional sources of rules, even if they find it difficult to agree on the range of applicable rules, much less their interpretation. Yet the current disorder in governance makes that difficult. Within this dynamic context, some have argued strongly for sourcing from public and private sources,[86] while others have sought to look more broadly at international sources that are now nationalized within specific contexts of States sharing particular characteristics.[87] The problem is nicely illustrated by the UNGPs themselves: the Pillar I duties of States are limited legal obligations undertaken by

States under international law and domesticated into national legal systems. The Pillar II responsibilities of enterprises are specified in a more coherent manner.[88]

Thus, the issues here are well known and there is a substantial literature, although it does not necessarily tie the issues of accountability to the substantive issues of sourcing laws. The starting point is obviously the choice of law issue; if State law or administrative regulation applies or guides, then the question is selection of the proper domestic legal order. If treaties apply, those State laws may be internationalized if applied by remedial organizations under, for example, a BIT. The problem is compounded where States regulate indirectly through increasingly popular disclosure laws that avoid directly regulating behavior and instead mandate disclosure around behaviors the State would have the enterprise embrace.[89] The problem is magnified if multiple legal sources are identified as impacting accountability, but the systems and their norms cannot be harmonized. Whatever choice is made, accountability loses its power except within the quite specific contexts in which it might be made to apply. Reference has already been made to the application of international law, the serendipity of which remains one of the most challenging issues for global standards grounded in a legal approach to business and human rights responsibility. The problem is compounded when international law and international norms intermesh. In that case, there is a double problem: the legal one and the policy issue around the extent to which international norms may be applied by the State or may be permitted to apply when invoked by an actor operating in national territory.

This mélange[90] can sometimes produce governance from a combination of national and international, public and private law, norms, and practices from which a standard can be articulated against which accountability can be undertaken. It also produces the dissonance that has both moved certain actors toward the comfort of legal coherence through a comprehensive treaty on business and human rights, even as others move decisively toward embracing one of a number of legal pluralism variations.[91] Into the resulting governance gaps that are produced in the transnational spaces that national rules cannot reach is an equally complex set of enterprise self-regulation[92] and third-party standards[93] that sometimes supplement and sometimes substitute for more formal sources. Yet all of these are interdependent,[94] and all increase the contextual variations possible within systems of accountability.

4.3.4 Who accounts?

The discussion now brings us back to the beginning. Having outlined the complexities that must be resolved before a coherent system of accountability is fashioned, and aggregating these individual acts of accountability within coherent systems of self-reflexive accountability with a systemic character,[95] one is brought back to the principal actors who are brought to account, who account to others and to themselves. Each defines both a coherent internally autonomous system within which self-accountability is essential, but also each constitutes an actor who affects others outside of themselves to which accounting may be necessary, especially with respect to the human rights, labor, and sustainability effects of their actions. In this group, one can include the State, the enterprise, international organizations, and civil society. This chapter closes with a very brief examination of the challenges to bringing each to account in the context of multi-vector accountability.

Bringing the State to account is likely both the most straightforward and the most difficult for accountability. The basis of that accounting may be extracted from the State's international obligations and constitutional traditions. However, these obligations and traditions are only as effective as the traditions of implementations and habits of accountability that have been built into the organization of the polity. These may be embedded in law and implemented through government. Or, they may be entirely a function of the exercise of political power (such as democratic accountability). Complicating this accounting is the distinction between the State and the instrumentalities of the State that may be engaged in economic (commercial) activities through SWFs and SOEs. Yet the State also serves as an agent of accounting, determining the scope of responsibility to account, specifying the forms of legal actions permitted in its courts, or succumbing to international pressure. The aftermath of the collapse of the Rana Plaza factory building provides insight into all of these roles.[96]

Bringing the enterprise to account raised some quite distinct issues. It sits at the crossroad of accountability, both accountable and the beneficiary of accountability in others. The enterprise may be brought to account by States and may account with reference to international bodies and third-party standard certification organs.[97] Yet it may demand account of States and others as well, in webs of mutual responsibilities, to respect human rights. The enterprise can also serve as its own agent for accounting, serving in a capacity similar to that of States with respect to the production chains over which they assert a measure of managerial control. It is, then, both an agent of accounting and itself responsible for accounting to others. It may also be subject to accounting from private bodies with which it engages in commercial activities, lenders, and securities holders. The enterprise brings itself to account in one of two principal ways. On the one hand, it is the manager of its own internal controls and internal remediation. On the other hand, it is the object of structures of accounting imposed by or through international organizations from which it draws its objectives and methods.

International organizations tend to be understood as being beyond accountability, although that may be changing as bodies like the UN engage more directly in activity with human rights effects.[98] For the most part, however, international organizations remain a vast emptiness. They weave increasingly baroque standards of norms and methods centered on accountability and yet only account – if they account at all – to themselves, in the form of their bureaucracies and the States that form part of their internal governance. Yet, for the international organization, accounting for the human rights effects of activity may be undertaken indirectly and by proxy. For the international organization, for example, the enterprise might be understood as an agent of accounting, the means through which the expectations of the governance community can be realized. That could suggest a focus on technical assistance, on monitoring and ranking, and on the avenues through which the enterprise bring itself to account. An area that still needs greater development is the turning of these methods and expectations onto the internal operations of the international organization itself, and then outward to its activities with others. That is at best a highly aspirational open element in the systemization of human rights-based accountability.

Lastly, civil society itself has moved from an agent in the process of the rendering of accounts by others to the object of accounting itself. That change in role, as its own role in the systematization of flows of accounting has become more important, was highlighted by the 2017 scandal over the bad behavior of employees and managers of Oxfam in places where it was operating.[99] The failures of accountability were made more acute because Oxfam had been a member of *Accountable Now*, a cross-sector platform for internationally operating civil society organizations.[100] States have begun to move decisively into the field of civil society accountability, but in ways that appear to inhibit the ability of civil society to act without impediment.[101] That itself is worthy of an accounting that is unlikely to occur. However, the civil society enterprise is also an agent of accounting through its monitoring, norm development activities, and as an agent in remediation (judicial and non-judicial).[102]

Together, the State, the enterprise, the international organization, and civil society constitute the constellation of actors whose actions define the system of accountability for the human rights, sustainability, and labor effects of economic activity. Those effects are negligible when undertaken by individual actors, but when aggregated by actors in constant states of accounting to themselves, to each other and to the beneficiaries of accounting beyond the institutions they represent, they contribute to the transformation of accounting from a simple measure of responsibility to a powerful disciplinary system of norms. While much needs to be done to refine the understanding of these actors and the construction of the self-reflective system that is centered on the machinery of accountability, its framework is now clearer and its importance manifest.

4.4 Conclusion: where does that leave the project of accountability?

Accountability is situated within its own complex ecology. At the institutional level it involves obligations to be accountable to others, demand accountability from others, and be accountable to oneself. Accountability itself touches on all aspects of institutional operations, from norms to implementation, behaviors, duties, and responsibilities. Unpacking the concept of rendering account, then, provides a useful framework for discussing the issue of accountability. This has particular relevance for the accountability of States, enterprises, civil society, and individuals for conduct with adverse human rights, sustainability, and labor effects.

Accountability for corporate violations of human rights, labor and environmental standards must be understood as a shorthand for a set of multiple reciprocal relations. The legitimacy of this accountability is grounded on the vitality of structures of self-accountability and fidelity to internal organization and governance. It is also grounded in the accountability of States and non-governmental institutions for the appropriate framework for human rights, labor, and environmental governance standards. Finally, it appears to have been legitimated in relation to and embedded within the accountable behaviors of States and non-governmental and international organizations.

Notes

1 Jan M. Broekmann and Larry C. Backer, *Lawyers Making Meaning: The Semiotics of Law in Legal Education II* (Springer 2013).

2 Kenneth Anderson, '"Accountability" as "Legitimacy": Global Governance, Global Civil Society and the United Nations', (2011) 36(3) *Brooklyn Journal of International Law* 841.

3 Online Etymology Dictionary, 'Account (n.)' <www.etymonline.com/word/account> accessed 28 August 2019.

4 Elizabeth C. Kurucz et al., 'The Business Case for Corporate Social Responsibility', in Andrew Crane et al. (eds.), *The Oxford Handbook of Corporate Social Responsibility* (Oxford University Press 2008).

5 "The items that are formally incorporated in financial statements are financial representations (depictions in words and numbers) of certain resources of an entity, claims to those resources, and the effects of transactions and other events and circumstances that result in changes in those resources and claims". Financial Accounting Standards Board, Statement on Financial Accounting Concepts No. 6 (2008, as amended) <www.fasb.org/jsp/FASB/Document_C/DocumentPage?cid=1218220132831&acceptedDisclaimer=true> accessed 5 September 2019, para. 6.

6 E.g, the US Securities Act of 1933.

7 Larry C. Backer, 'Multinational Corporations, Transnational Law: The United Nation's Norms on the Responsibilities of Transnational Corporations as a Harbinger of Corporate Social Responsibility as International Law', (2005) 37 *Columbia Human Rights Law Review* 287.

8 Ngaire Woods, *The Globalizers: The IMF, the World Bank and Their Borrowers* (Cornell University Press 2006); Jonathan Koppell, *World Rule: Accountability, Legitimacy, and the Design of Global Governance* (University of Chicago Press 2010), Chapter 2.

9 Larry C. Backer, 'Theorizing Regulatory Governance Within Its Ecology: The Structure of Management in an Age of Globalization', (2018) 24(5) *Contemporary Politics* 607.

10 Frank Pasquale, *The Black Box Society: The Secret Algorithms That Control Money and Information* (Harvard University Press 2015).

11 Mara Hvistendahl, 'Inside China's Vast New Experiment in Social Credit Ranking', *Wired* (2017) <www.wired.com/story/age-of-social-credit/> accessed 29 August 2019.

12 Roderick A.W. Rhodes, 'The New Governance: Governing without Government', (1996) 44(4) *Political Studies* 652; Larry C. Backer, 'Governance without Government: An Overview', in Günther Handl et al. (eds.), *Beyond Territoriality: Transnational Legal Authority in an Age of Globalization* (Martinus Nijhoff Publishers 2012).

13 Neil Hodge, 'Human Rights and Corporate Wrongs', *Risk Management* (2016) <www.rmmagazine.com/2016/08/01/human-rights-and-corporate-wrongs/> accessed 29 August 2019.

14 Randall D Germain, 'Between Anarchy and Hierarchy: Governance Lessons from Global Economic Institution', in Joan DeBardeleben and Achim Hurrelmann (eds.), *Democratic Dilemmas of Multilevel Governance: Legitimacy, Representation and Accountability in the European Union* (Springer 2007); Larry C. Backer, 'Are Supply Chains Transnational Legal Orders? What We Can Learn from the Rana Plaza Factory Building Collapse', (2016) 1 *UCI Journal of International, Transnational, and Comparative Law* 11.
15 Julia Black, 'Constructing and Contesting Legitimacy and Accountability in Polycentric Regulatory Regimes', (2008) 2(2) *Regulation and Governance* 137.
16 Bert-Jaap Koops et al., 'Bridging the Accountability Gap: Rights for New Entities in the Information Society?', (2010) 11(2) *Minnesota Journal of Law, Science & Technology* 497.
17 Surya Deva, *Regulating Corporate Human Rights Violations: Humanizing Business* (Routledge 2012).
18 James Mahoney, 'Nominal, Ordinal, and Narrative Appraisal in Macrocausal Analysis', (1999) 104(4) *American Journal of Sociology* 1154.
19 Backer (n 9).
20 Plato, Timeaus (Benjamin Jowett, trans., Pantianos Classics 1871 (360 B.C.)) "Of design he was created thus, his own waste providing his own food, and all that he did or suffered taking place in and by himself. For the Creator conceived that a being which was self-sufficient would be far more excellent than one which lacked anything". ibid., 33c.
21 Backer (n 9).
22 See Financial Accounting Standards Board (n 5): "The objective of general purpose financial reporting is to provide financial information about the reporting entity that is useful to existing and potential investors, lenders, and other creditors in making decisions about providing resources to the entity". ibid., OB2. These are 'the primary users to whom general purpose financial reports are directed'. (ibid., OB 5).
23 OHCHR, *Guiding Principles on Business and Human Rights: Implementing the United Nations "Protect, Respect and Remedy" Framework* (UN 2011) ['UNGPs']; John Ruggie, *Just Business: Multinational Corporations and Human Rights* (W.W. Norton & Company 2013).
24 G20/OECD Principles of Corporate Governance (OECD Publishing 2015), 50 (explaining that an enterprise board "should retain final responsibility for oversight of the company's risk management system and for ensuring the integrity of the reporting systems").
25 Ibid. 37 ("A strong disclosure regime that promotes real transparency is a pivotal feature of market-based monitoring of companies and is central to shareholders' ability to exercise their shareholder rights on an informed basis.".); UNGPs (n 23) Guiding Principle 21.
26 UNGPs (n 23) Commentary to Guiding Principle 19 ("The horizontal integration across the business enterprise of specific findings from assessing human rights impacts can only be effective if its human rights policy commitment has been embedded into all relevant business functions. This is required to ensure that the assessment findings are properly understood, given due weight, and acted upon".).
27 See Financial Accounting Standards Board (n 5) chapter 1, OB8: "Individual primary users have different, and possibly conflicting, information needs and desires".
28 E.g., UNGPs (n 23) Guiding Principle 11.
29 E.g., UNGPs (n 23) Guiding Principle 12 ("The responsibility of business enterprises to respect human rights refers to internationally recognized human rights – understood, at a minimum, as those expressed in the International Bill of Human Rights and the principles concerning fundamental rights set out in

the International Labour Organization's Declaration on Fundamental Principles and Rights at Work".).

30 Anna Drake, *Locating Accountability: Conceptual and Categorical Challenges in the Literature* (ENTWINED, IISD 2012) 8.

31 Larry C. Backer, 'The Corporate Social Responsibilities of Financial Institutions for the Conduct of Their Borrowers: The View From International Law and Standards', (2017) 21(4) *Lewis & Clark Law Review* 881.

32 UNGPs (n 23) Guiding Principle 21.

33 Jonathan Fox, 'The Uncertain Relationship between Transparency and Accountability', (2007) 17(4/5) *Development in Practice* 663; Becky Carter, 'Transparency and Accountability' (Applied Knowledge Services: Helpdesk Research Report 2014).

34 Ruggie (n 23).

35 OECD, 'Mutual Accountability and the Role of the Africa Partnership Forum: Discussion Paper for the Abuja Meeting, April 9–10, 2005', Draft 140305 (2005). 1.

36 Jonathan Koppell, 'Pathologies of Accountability: ICANN and the Challenge of "Multiple Accountabilities Disorder"', (2005) 65(1) *Public Administration Review* 94, 94–5.

37 Prepared Remarks by SRSG John G. Ruggie: Public Hearings on Business and Human Rights Sub-Committee on Human Rights: European Parliament: Brussels, 16 April 2009 <www.business-humanrights.org/sites/default/files/reports-and-materials/Ruggie-remarks-to-European-Parliament-16-Apr-2009.pdf> accessed 29 August 2019.

38 Drake (n 30) 23–5.

39 Ibid. 23, 24.

40 Gunther Teubner, 'Breaking Frames: Economic Globalization and the Emergence of *Lex Mercatoria*', (2002) 5(2) *European Journal of Social Theory* 199.

41 UNHRC, *Protect, Respect and Remedy: A Framework for Business and Human Rights: Report of the Special Representative of the Secretary-General on the Issue of Human Rights and Transnational Corporations and Other Business Enterprises, John Ruggie* (7 April 2008) UN Doc A/HRC/8/5.

42 John 1:14.

43 Dodge v. Ford Motor Co. 204 Mich. 459, 170 N.W. 668 (Mich 1919); Backer (n 7).

44 Tanya Barman, 'New – and Important – Role for Professional Accountants in Assessing Human Rights Risk', (IFAC 2006) <www.ifac.org/global-knowledge-gateway/ethics/discussion/new-and-important-role-professional-accountants-assessing> accessed 29 August 2019.

45 As set by the Financial Accounting Standards Board (n 5).

46 Other than specific requirements of law, of which there are few, such as UNGPs (n 23); OECD, *OECD Guidelines for Multinational Enterprises* (OECD Publishing 2011) ['OECD Guidelines'].

47 See, eg, Sally Engle Merry, 'The Seductions of Quantification: Measuring Human Rights, Gender Violence, and Sex Trafficking' (University of Chicago Press 2016).

48 Todd Landman and Edzia Carvalho, *Measuring Human Rights* (Routledge 2010), 31–44.

49 Mary McNeil and Carmen Malena, 'Social Accountability in Africa: An Introduction', in Mary McNeil and Carmen Malena (eds.), *Demanding Good Governance: Lessons from Social Accountability Initiatives in Africa* (The World Bank 2010) 1.

50 In re Caremark International Inc. Derivative Litigation 698 A.2d 959 (Del. Ch. 1996); Stone v. Ritter, 911 A.2d 362 (Del. 2006) (duty of care and good faith).

51 The World Bank, *Governance and Development* (The World Bank 1992).

52 OECD Guidelines (n 46).
53 OECD, *Corporate Governance: Accountability, and Transparency: A Guide for State Ownership* (OECD Publishing 2010).
54 UNGPs (n 23) Guiding Principles 17–21.
55 Directive 2014/95/EU of the European Parliament and of the Council of 22 October 2014 amending Directive 2013/34/EU as regards disclosure of non-financial and diversity information by certain large undertakings and groups [2014] OJ L 330/1.
56 Loi relative au devoir de vigilance des sociétés mères et des entreprises donneuses d'ordre (21 février 2017).
57 UNGPs (n 23).
58 OECD Guidelines (n 46).
59 Paulo S. Pinheiro, 'Sixty Years after the Universal Declaration: Navigating the Contradictions', (2008) 5(9) *Sur. Revista Internacional de Direitos Humanos* 70.
60 Roel Nieuwenkamp, 'Ever Heard of SDG Washing? The Urgency of Sustainable Development Goals Due Diligence', (2017) <https://medium.com/@OECD/ever-heard-of-sdg-washing-the-urgency-of-sustainable-development-goals-due-diligence-be172fc52fcc> accessed 29 August 2019.
61 Anne Peters, 'Towards Transparency as a Global Norm', in Andrea Bianchi and Anne Peters, *Transparency in International Law* (Cambridge University Press 2013).
62 Cf. Elena Sciso (ed.), *Accountability, Transparency and Democracy in the Functioning of Bretton Woods Institutions* (Springer 2017).
63 B. Peter Rosendorff et al., 'Democracy and Transparency', (2011) 73(4) *The Journal of Politics* 1191.
64 International Corporate Accountability Roundtable, 'Knowing and Showing': Using U.S. Securities Laws to Compel Human Rights Disclosure: A Report by the International Corporate Accountability Roundtable Endorsed by Professor Cynthia Williams 2013 (arguing that responsibility to account for human rights is relevant to corporate securities reporting, that this gives rise to a methodology for assessing relevant information, and that methodological assessment is the foundation for a disclosure system that itself identifies objects of risk mitigation).
65 Generally, Andrea Bianchi and Anne Peters, *Transparency in International Law* (Cambridge University Press 2013).
66 Larry C. Backer, 'Transparency and Business in International Law: Governance between Norm and Technique', in A. Bianchi and A. Peters (eds.), *Transparency in International Law* (Cambridge University Press 2013), 477–8.
67 Hansi Lo Wang, 'House to Hold Hearing on Controversial Census Citizenship Question' (2018) <www.npr.org/sections/thetwo-way/2018/04/11/601685600/house-to-hold-hearing-on-controversial-census-citizenship-question> accessed 30 August 2019.
68 Jillian Kestler-D'Amours, 'Opposition Grows to Putting Citizenship Question on US Census', *Al Jazeera* (2018) <www.aljazeera.com/news/2018/04/opposition-grows-putting-citizenship-question-census-180408093329133.html> accessed 30 August 2019.
69 Michael Scherer, 'Potential Citizenship Question in 2020 Census Could Shift Power to Rural America', *The Washington Post* (2018) <www.washingtonpost.com/politics/potential-citizenship-question-in-2020-census-could-shift-power-to-rural-america/2018/01/23/c4e6d2c6-f57c-11e7-beb6-c8d48830c54d_story.html?utm_term=.75a336612bf7> accessed 29 August 2019; John Wagner, 'Holder-Led Group Sues over Census Citizenship Question', *The Washington Post* (2018) <www.washingtonpost.com/news/post-politics/wp/2018/04/11/holder-led-group-sues-over-census-citizenship-question/?utm_term=.fdb3f847a2fa> accessed 30 August 2019 ("The federal lawsuit, to be filed Wednesday on

behalf of seven residents of Maryland and Arizona, contends that the question is at odds with the constitutional requirement that the census count every person residing in the United States, including noncitizens".).

70 The essence of UNGPs (n 23): "Avoid causing or contributing to adverse human rights impacts through their own activities, and address such impacts when they occur". UNGPs (n 23) General Principle 13(1).

71 UNGPs (n 23) General Principles 7, 13, 15, 17, 19, and 24.

72 Ibid. General Principle 19.

73 Audrey A. Gramling et al., 'The Role of the Internal Audit Function in Corporate Governance: A Synthesis of the Extant Internal Auditing Literature and Directions for Future Research', (2004) 23 *Journal of Accounting Literature* 194.

74 UNGA, *Report of the Working Group on the Issue of Human Rights and Transnational Corporations and Other Business Enterprises United Nations* (18 July 2017) UN Doc A/72/162, examined in Larry C. Backer, 'Reflections on the 2017 "Report of the Working Group on the Issue of Human Rights and Transnational Corporations and Other Business Enterprises" (A/72/162; 18 July 2017)', Coalition for Peace & Ethics Working Paper 10/1 <www.thecpe.org/wp-content/uploads/2013/05/The-Remedial-Pillar-of-the-UN-Guiding-Principles-has-been-a-perennial-focus-of-the-U.pdf> accessed 30 August 2019.

75 Larry C. Backer, 'Conceptual, Structural, and Operationalization Constraints on the Right to Remedy Under the Guiding Principles: Remarks Delivered at the Parallel Events Session of the 3rd UN Forum on Business and Human Rights, Geneva Switzerland, 1 December 2014' <www.backerinlaw.com/Site/podcasts/speeches-and-remarks/conceptual-structural-and-operationalization-constraints-on-the-right-to-remedy-under-the-guiding-principles-remarks-delivered-at-the-parallel-events-session-of-the-3rd-u-n-forum-on-business-and-h/> accessed 30 August 2019.

76 OHCHR, *Who Will Be Accountable? Human Rights and the Post-2015 Development Agenda* (UN 2013) 32–47.

77 Shengnan Qiu and Gillian MacNaughton, 'Mechanisms of Accountability for the Realization of the Right to Health in China', (2017) 19(1) *Health and Human Rights* 279.

78 OHCHR (n 76), 39–42.

79 Qiu and MacNaughton (n 77).

80 OECD Guidelines (n 46).

81 UNGPs (n 23).

82 Johannes Rohr and José Aylwin, *Business and Human Rights: Interpreting the UN Guiding Principles for Indigenous Peoples* (IWGIA 2014).

83 Brendan Tobin, *Indigenous Peoples, Customary Law and Human Rights: Why Living Law Matters* (Routledge 2014).

84 James Cavallaro and Stephanie E. Brewer, 'Reevaluating Regional Human Rights Litigation in the Twenty-First Century: The Case of the Inter-American Court', (2008) 102(4) *American Journal of International Law* 768.

85 Larry C. Backer, 'Moving Forward the UN Guiding Principles for Business and Human Rights: Between Enterprise Social Norm, State Domestic Legal Orders, and the Treaty Law That Might Bind Them All', (2015) 38(2) *Fordham International Law Journal* 457.

86 Ruggie (n 23).

87 Eg, Surya Deva (ed.), *Socio-Economic Rights in Emerging Free Markets: Comparative Insights from India and China* (Routledge 2016).

88 UNGPs (n 23) General Principles 1, 13.

89 Eg, UK Modern Slavery Act (2015).

90 Peer Zumbansen and Gralf-Peter Callies, *Rough Consensus and Running Code: A Theory of Transnational Private Law* (Hart Publishing 2010).
91 Margaret Davies, 'Legal Pluralism', in Peter Cane and Herbert M Kritzer (eds.), *The Oxford Handbook of Empirical Legal Research* (Oxford University Press 2010).
92 Gunther Teubner, 'Self-Constitutionalizing TNCs? On the Linkage of 'Private' and 'Public' Corporate Codes of Conduct', (2011) 18(2) *Indiana Journal of Global Legal Studies* 617.
93 Errol Meidiger, 'The Administrative Law of Global Public-Private Regulation: The Case of Forestry', (2006) 17(1) *European Journal of International Law* 47.
94 Calliess and Zumbansen (n 90).
95 Niklas Luhmann, *Social Systems* (Stanford University Press 1995).
96 Javed Siddiqui and Shahzad Uddin, 'Human Rights Disasters, Corporate Accountability and the State: Lessons Learned from Rana Plaza', (2016) 29(4) *Accounting, Auditing & Accountability Journal* 679.
97 Meidiger (n 93).
98 Krista Larson and Paisley Dodds, 'UN Peacekeepers in Congo Hold Record for Rape, Sex Abuse' (2017) <www.apnews.com/69e56ab46cab400f9f4b3753bd79c930> accessed 30 August 2019.
99 Catherine Porter, 'Haiti Suspends Oxfam Great Britain after Sex Scandal', *The New York Times* (2018) <www.nytimes.com/2018/02/22/world/americas/haiti-suspends-oxfam.html> accessed 30 August 2019.
100 Accountable Now, 'Accountability Reports' <https://accountablenow.org/accountability-in-practice/accountability-reports/> accessed 30 August 2019.
101 Tom Philips, 'China Passes Law Imposing Security Controls on Foreign NGOs', *The Guardian* (2016) <www.theguardian.com/world/2016/apr/28/china-passes-law-imposing-security-controls-on-foreign-ngos> accessed 30 August 2019.
102 Larry C. Backer, 'Economic Globalization and the Rise of Efficient Systems of Global Private Law Making: Wal-Mart as Global Legislator', (2007) 39(4) *University of Connecticut Law Review* 1739.

Bibliography

Anderson K, '"Accountability" as "Legitimacy": Global Governance, Global Civil Society and the United Nations', (2011) 36(3) *Brooklyn Journal of International Law* 841.

Backer LC, 'Are Supply Chains Transnational Legal Orders? What We Can Learn from the Rana Plaza Factory Building Collapse', (2016) 1 *UCI Journal of International, Transnational, and Comparative Law* 11.

———, 'The Corporate Social Responsibilities of Financial Institutions for the Conduct of Their Borrowers: The View from International Law and Standards', (2017) 21(4) *Lewis & Clark Law Review* 881.

———, 'Economic Globalization and the Rise of Efficient Systems of Global Private Law Making: Wal-Mart as Global Legislator', (2007) 39(4) *University of Connecticut Law Review* 1739.

———, 'Moving Forward the UN Guiding Principles for Business and Human Rights: Between Enterprise Social Norm, State Domestic Legal Orders, and the Treaty Law That Might Bind Them All', (2015) 38(2) *Fordham International Law Journal* 457.

———, 'Multinational Corporations, Transnational Law: The United Nation's Norms on the Responsibilities of Transnational Corporations as a Harbinger of Corporate

Social Responsibility as International Law', (2005) 37 *Columbia Human Rights Law Review* 287.

———, 'Theorizing Regulatory Governance Within Its Ecology: The Structure of Management in an Age of Globalization', (2018) 24(5) *Contemporary Politics* 607.

———, 'Transparency and Business in International Law: Governance between Norm and Technique', in A Bianchi and A Peters (eds.), *Transparency in International Law* (Cambridge University Press 2013).

Bianchi A and Peters A, *Transparency in International Law* (Cambridge University Press 2013).

Black J, 'Constructing and Contesting Legitimacy and Accountability in Polycentric Regulatory Regimes', (2008) 2(2) *Regulation and Governance* 137.

Broekmann JM and Backer LC, *Lawyers Making Meaning: The Semiotics of Law in Legal Education II* (Springer 2013).

Carter B, *Transparency and Accountability* (Applied Knowledge Services: Helpdesk Research Report 2014).

Cavallaro J and Brewer SE, 'Reevaluating Regional Human Rights Litigation in the Twenty-First Century: The Case of the Inter-American Court', (2008) 102(4) *American Journal of International Law* 768.

Davies M, 'Legal Pluralism', in Peter Cane and Herbert M Kritzer (eds.), *The Oxford Handbook of Empirical Legal Research* (Oxford University Press 2010).

Deva S, *Regulating Corporate Human Rights Violations: Humanizing Business* (Routledge 2012).

——— (ed.), *Socio-Economic Rights in Emerging Free Markets: Comparative Insights from India and China* (Routledge 2016).

Drake A, *Locating Accountability: Conceptual and Categorical Challenges in the Literature* (ENTWINED, IISD 2012).

Fox J, 'The Uncertain Relationship between Transparency and Accountability', (2007) 17(4/5) *Development in Practice* 663.

Germain RD, 'Between Anarchy and Hierarchy: Governance Lessons from Global Economic Institution', in J DeBardeleben and A Hurrelmann (eds.), *Democratic Dilemmas of Multilevel Governance: Legitimacy, Representation and Accountability in the European Union* (Springer 2007).

Gramling AA et al., 'The Role of the Internal Audit Function in Corporate Governance: A Synthesis of the Extant Internal Auditing Literature and Directions for Future Research', (2004) 23 *Journal of Accounting Literature* 194.

Koops B-J et al., 'Bridging the Accountability Gap: Rights for New Entities in the Information Society?', (2010) 11(2) *Minnesota Journal of Law, Science & Technology* 497.

Koppell J, 'Pathologies of Accountability: ICANN and the Challenge of "Multiple Accountabilities Disorder"', (2005) 65(1) *Public Administration Review* 94.

Kurucz EC et al., 'The Business Case for Corporate Social Responsibility', in A Crane et al. (eds.), *The Oxford Handbook of Corporate Social Responsibility* (Oxford University Press 2008).

Landman T and Carvalho E, *Measuring Human Rights* (Routledge 2010).

Luhmann N, *Social Systems* (Stanford University Press 1995).

Mahoney J, 'Nominal, Ordinal, and Narrative Appraisal in Macrocausal Analysis', (1999) 104(4) *American Journal of Sociology* 1154.

McNeil M and Malena C, 'Social Accountability in Africa: An Introduction', in Mary McNeil and Carmen Malena (eds.), *Demanding Good Governance: Lessons from Social Accountability Initiatives in Africa* (The World Bank 2010).

Meidiger E, 'The Administrative Law of Global Public-Private Regulation: The Case of Forestry', (2006) 17(1) *European Journal of International Law* 47.

Merry SE, *The Seductions of Quantification: Measuring Human Rights, Gender Violence, and Sex Trafficking* (University of Chicago Press 2016).

Pasquale F, *The Black Box Society: The Secret Algorithms That Control Money and Information* (Harvard University Press 2015).

Peters A, 'Towards Transparency as a Global Norm', in A Bianchi and A Peters (eds.), *Transparency in International Law* (Cambridge University Press 2013).

Pinheiro PS, 'Sixty Years after the Universal Declaration: Navigating the Contradictions', (2008) 5(9) *Sur. Revista Internacional de Direitos Humanos* 70.

Qiu S and MacNaughton G, 'Mechanisms of Accountability for the Realization of the Right to Health in China', (2017) 19(1) *Health and Human Rights* 279.

Rhodes RAW, 'The New Governance: Governing without Government', (1996) 44(4) *Political Studies* 652; Larry C Backer, 'Governance without Government: An Overview', in G Handl et al. (eds.), *Beyond Territoriality: Transnational Legal Authority in an Age of Globalization* (Martinus Nijhoff Publishers 2012).

Rohr J and Aylwin J, *Business and Human Rights: Interpreting the UN Guiding Principles for Indigenous Peoples* (IWGIA 2014).

Rosendorff BP et al., 'Democracy and Transparency', (2011) 73(4) *The Journal of Politics* 1191.

Sciso E (ed.), *Accountability, Transparency and Democracy in the Functioning of Bretton Woods Institutions* (Springer 2017).

Siddiqui J and Uddin S, 'Human Rights Disasters, Corporate Accountability and the State: Lessons Learned from Rana Plaza', (2016) 29(4) *Accounting, Auditing & Accountability Journal* 679.

Teubner G, 'Breaking Frames: Economic Globalization and the Emergence of *Lex Mercatoria*', (2002) 5(2) *European Journal of Social Theory* 199.

———, 'Self-Constitutionalizing TNCs? On the Linkage of "Private" and "Public" Corporate Codes of Conduct', (2011) 18(2) *Indiana Journal of Global Legal Studies* 617.

Tobin B, *Indigenous Peoples, Customary Law and Human Rights: Why Living Law Matters* (Routledge 2014).

Woods N, *The Globalizers: The IMF, the World Bank and Their Borrowers* (Cornell University Press 2006); Jonathan Koppell, *World Rule: Accountability, Legitimacy, and the Design of Global Governance* (University of Chicago Press 2010).

Zumbansen P and Callies G-P, *Rough Consensus and Running Code: A Theory of Transnational Private Law* (Hart Publishing 2010).

Part 2

Accountability through international law mechanisms

5 The effectiveness of international arbitration to provide remedy for business-related human rights abuses

*Katerina Yiannibas**

5.1 Introduction

Access to justice and to an effective remedy is a fundamental component of the promotion and protection of human rights. Yet access to justice and forms of remedy are not singular phenomena reduced to one modality. For victims of business-related human rights abuses there are a number of mechanisms, both judicial and non-judicial, available to provide access to remedy. Notwithstanding the legal nature of the parties or the dispute, there is no one-size-fits-all solution. This in turn means that parties have options, allowing them to draw distinctions between various choices of conflict resolution mechanisms to select the mechanism best suited to the particular needs and challenges presented by the nature of the parties and the subject matter of the dispute. The key is that access to remedy should be both uncomplicated and unhindered by legal and practical barriers.

The UNGPs ultimately relegate the duty of ensuring access to effective remedy to States.[1] As part of the State duty to protect against business-related human rights abuse, the UNGPs provide that States should take appropriate steps to ensure the effectiveness of domestic judicial mechanisms as well as non-judicial mechanisms, both State-based and non-State-based.[2] The inclusion of non-judicial mechanisms in a comprehensive system for remedy is particularly relevant when considering that domestic jurisdictions are often unavailable or difficult to access for victims of business-related human rights abuses.[3] International arbitration, while not named explicitly in the UNGPs, is a prolific dispute-resolution mechanism in a cross-border context.[4] However, the default international arbitration mechanism has been contemplated largely for the resolution of commercial and investment disputes and lacks certain procedural safeguards that are important when the substantive claims of a dispute concern human rights. As a result, international arbitration has garnered considerable scrutiny from both civil society and policy makers. There is a case to be made for and against international arbitration for the resolution of disputes concerning business-related human rights abuses. This chapter considers both the advantages and disadvantages of international arbitration from a business and human rights perspective vis-à-vis the effectiveness criteria in the UNGPs and puts forward recommended measures for international arbitration reform if and when disputes concern business-related human rights abuses.

5.2 Effectiveness of the international arbitration mechanism: advantages and disadvantages

Arbitration is a non-judicial mechanism that provides a final and binding resolution by one or more party-appointed arbitrators.[5] In a cross-border context, arbitration has proliferated as a mechanism for the resolution of international commercial and investment disputes. This is due in large part to certain elements of international arbitration that are advantageous in cross-border cases in comparison to the formalities of national jurisdictions; in particular, neutrality of the forum, party autonomy, procedural flexibility, and near universal enforceability of arbitral awards, at least in principle. Despite the mechanism's inherent flexibility, the default international arbitration mechanism has largely been contemplated to meet the needs of cross-border commerce, where the premium is on the efficiency and the finality of dispute resolution.

On the choice between arbitration or litigation, Justice Learned Hand of the US Supreme Court, in the 1944 landmark decision *American Almond v Consolidated Pecan*, reasoned that:

> Arbitration may or may not be a desirable substitute for trials in courts; as to that the parties must decide in each instance. But when they have adopted it, they must be content with its informalities; they may not hedge it about with those procedural limitations, which it is precisely its purpose to avoid. They must content themselves with looser approximations to the enforcement of their rights than those that the law accords.[6]

As Justice Hand pointed out, arbitration is not a privatized version of litigation; by its nature, it is a flexible mechanism not overly restricted with procedural limitations. The issue is whether this flexibility can be used to make the arbitration mechanism effective for the resolution of business-related human rights abuses.

As human rights claims emerge in international arbitration, the conduct of contemporary international arbitration also evidences a number of concerns that have garnered scrutiny from both civil society and policy makers, including the arbitrability of human rights claims, the refusal of enforcement on grounds of public policy, confidentiality of the arbitral proceedings, and the award, costs, and equality of arms, witness protection, issues particular to marginalized and/or vulnerable populations, the selection and accountability of arbitrators, and the absence of an appellate procedure. To ensure the effectiveness of non-judicial mechanisms, Guiding Principle 31 identifies a set number of criteria: legitimacy, accessibility, predictability, equitability, transparency, rights-compatibility, and a source of continuous learning. The advantages and disadvantages of international arbitration in a business and human rights context will be examined in turn based on these effectiveness criteria for non-judicial mechanisms.

5.2.1 The legitimacy criterion and international arbitration

According to the UNGPs' effectiveness criteria for non-judicial mechanisms, a mechanism's legitimacy should enable trust from the stakeholder groups for whose use it is intended.[7] As concerning the issue of enabling trust, one of the advantages of international arbitration for the resolution of cross-border disputes regarding business-related human rights abuses is the mechanism's neutrality. The parties to the arbitration select the seat of the proceedings and therefore have the autonomy to select a neutral forum. Accordingly, arbitral proceedings can take place anywhere in the world,[8] independent of the parties' nationalities and without regard to establishing a nexus to the substantive matter of the dispute. In this way, arbitration provides access to an international enforcement mechanism, without the exhaustion of domestic remedies – which is generally an admissibility requirement in international human rights procedures.[9]

One of the legitimacy concerns over international arbitration for the resolution of business-related human rights abuses is the use of a private adjudicative procedure to resolve disputes involving aspects of public law and policy, particularly human rights. Whether a particular human rights claim is subject to decision by arbitration is an issue relegated to the applicable domestic law; the law of the seat of the arbitration or the law(s) of the State(s) in which recognition and enforcement is sought. Under art V of the UN Convention on the Recognition and Enforcement of Foreign Arbitral Awards, the recognition and enforcement of an arbitral award may be refused if the competent authority in the State in which recognition and enforcement is sought finds that "the subject matter of the difference is not capable of settlement by arbitration under the law of that country; or the recognition or enforcement of the award would be contrary to the public policy of that country".[10] There is no international standard of arbitrability, or of the cited public policy exception for that matter, and what is or is not subject to arbitration differs between jurisdictions. Moreover, the jurisdiction of an arbitral tribunal is limited by the scope of the arbitration agreement.[11] Limited jurisdiction as defined by a particular arbitration agreement may also limit the substantive scope of arbitrability in any given case.

Another issue regarding the legitimacy of international arbitration concerns the selection and accountability of arbitrators. One of the main features of international arbitration is the ability of the parties to select their adjudicators case by case. This allows parties to choose arbitrators that have established expertise in the subject matter of the case, for example in human rights. Moreover, there is no international qualification or accreditation for arbitrators. Appointments are made in large part from reputation. However, this allows a regime in which, for example, counsel can act as arbitrator in other cases. Therefore, the dual arbitrator/counsel role raises issues of independence and impartiality. The concern is that the decision of an arbitrator in one case, for example, consciously or not, might advance the interests of a client in a case he or she is handling in another case as counsel.[12] Such conflicts of interest do not advance a coherent or predictable system of law.

5.2.2 *The accessibility and equitability criteria and international arbitration*

One of the measures identified under the UNGPs' effectiveness criteria concerning the accessibility of a non-judicial mechanism pertains to whether the mechanism provides adequate assistance for those who may face particular barriers to access.[13] Considering that victims of business-related human rights abuses often face jurisdictional challenges in accessing domestic courts,[14] international arbitration in comparison has the advantage of being more directly accessible since it is based on party consent. In theory, mutual consent, to the extent permitted by mandatory law, is a much more effective and efficient solution to overcome jurisdictional barriers to access to remedy.

There are various possibilities to establish party consent to arbitrate. Parties can consent to arbitrate *ex ante* or *ex post* via contract. In a business and human rights context, *ad hoc* consent may be more efficient, but may not be used in practice. Alternatively, there might be an instrument for open offer to consent. Such an instrument would involve a State-based tool that would structure a system in which there is a standing option to arbitrate from business to some recipients. In this case, recipients would need to be defined by class, project, or some relationship to the business. Another option could be a standing instrument, similar to the UN Global Compact model, which businesses sign up to join. Third-party beneficiary principles could establish a space for consent to arbitration where the ultimate beneficiaries are identified in a contract; however, it would be highly unlikely for a company to offer open consent to an unidentified group of persons, particularly without privity.

Evidence shows that non-State actors who access arbitration are typically investors and not other persons or non-commercial actors, revealing that the mechanism is mostly used by large or extra-large multinational enterprises.[15] This raises concern for the equality of arms between the parties, and the related issue of costs.

Costs are practical barrier to access to both judicial and non-judicial remedies. Costs can be an even greater issue when contemplating the equitability of a mechanism in a business and human rights context because of the inequality of arms between a business and a victim, or a class of victims, to retain counsel and experts and to collect evidence, not to mention other costs associated with the conduct of proceedings. The costs of international arbitration can be offset to some extent with the mechanism's inherent flexibility. Party autonomy over conduct of the proceedings allows parties to limit costs by design. For example, parties can choose to constitute arbitral tribunals with fewer members, limit the amount of pages of written pleadings, limit the number of days of hearings, and use evidentiary sampling. To this end, a number of leading international arbitral institutions have developed a set of fast-track arbitration rules to expedite procedures and lower costs.[16] These cost-saving options would have to be considered on a case-by-case basis. Depending on the alleged human rights abuse, there may be a need to submit substantial evidence or more detailed pleadings.

While there have been cases where arbitrators have been willing to waive all fees,[17] legal aid for international arbitration is not common practice.[18] The Permanent Court of Arbitration (PCA) established a Financial Assistance Fund with the objective of helping developing States with the costs of PCA-administered international dispute resolution, but the Fund is currently only available to qualifying States or State-controlled entities.[19] The establishment of need-based legal funds could be work undertaken by arbitral institutions.

Equitability under the UNGPs' effectiveness criteria also refers to a process that is based on fair, informed, and respectful terms. In the business and human rights context, special attention should be given to witness protection and the case of human rights defenders. Amnesty International reported that 281 human rights defenders were killed in 2016, up from 156 in 2015.[20] While this challenge is not relegated to one single mechanism, it is an issue that would require address so that the remedy does not further the abuse.

5.2.3 The predictability criterion and international arbitration

The UNGPs' effectiveness criteria set out that a mechanism is predictable if it provides a clear and known procedure with an indicative timeframe for each stage, clarity on the types of process and outcome available, and means of monitoring implementation.[21] Due to the procedural flexibility of international arbitration, each case is unique and driven in large part by party autonomy. Accordingly, the system overall does not lend a single, known process. This in turn detracts from predictability but gives the parties more control to tailor the dispute resolution process to their particular needs. However, if there is an inequality of arms issue between the parties – a prevalent issue in a business and human rights context – care should be given to promote the adoption and application of a fair set of default arbitration rules that take into account the particularities of human rights disputes, rather than relegate these particularities to negotiation.

One of the oft-cited advantages of international arbitration concerning predictability of the mechanism is the international enforcement of foreign arbitral awards. This is attributed to the adoption of the UN Convention on the Recognition and Enforcement of Foreign Arbitral Awards in 1958 (hereinafter "New York Convention").[22] The New York Convention obliges the Contracting States to recognize and enforce foreign or non-domestic awards in the same way as domestic awards, as well as requiring national courts to give full effect to arbitration agreements by requiring courts to enforce arbitration agreements and deny parties access to court in contravention of their agreement. The result is that foreign arbitral awards are more widely and directly enforceable across the globe compared to foreign judgments. Under the New York Convention there are limited grounds for the refusal of recognition and enforcement of foreign arbitral awards.[23] Despite the limited grounds of refusal to recognize or enforce an award under the New York Convention, awards are also vulnerable to annulment. The domestic arbitration law of the seat of arbitration governs the grounds for annulment of a foreign arbitral award, the content of which can vary between jurisdictions. As concerning oversight of award compliance, this is not a default feature of international arbitration. This could be subject to party agreement but would need to include extension of the jurisdiction of the arbitral tribunal beyond the arbitral proceedings to include a specified period of award compliance.

5.2.4 *The transparency criterion and international arbitration: a source of continuous learning*

As stated by the late Hans Smit, a prominent international arbitrator and arbitration professor, "confidentiality is a way of covering up mistakes".[24] International arbitration has been scrutinized for its confidentiality,[25] particularly when one of the parties is a State or State-controlled entity and/or the substantive claims concern matters inherent to the public interest. However, arbitration is not by its nature confidential. Confidentiality depends rather on party agreement or as provided by applicable rules, and to some degree the discretionary power of the arbitral tribunal. Parties can in fact agree to have fully transparent proceedings, as evidenced in the *Abyei Arbitration* between the government of Sudan and the Sudan People's Liberation Army.[26]

Recent trends, particularly in treaty-based investor–State arbitration, reveal strides toward more transparency. On 1 April 2014, the UN Commission on International Trade Law Rules on Transparency in Treaty-Based Investor-State Arbitration (hereinafter "UNCITRAL Transparency Rules") came into effect. To enable the UNCITRAL Transparency Rules to apply to the existing investment agreements signed before 1 April 2014, the UN Convention on Transparency in Treaty-Based Investor-State Arbitration (hereinafter "Mauritius Convention") was adopted on 10 December 2014 and entered into force 18 October 2017. The UNICTRAL Transparency Rules and the Mauritius Convention provide the legal basis to open arbitral hearings to the public, to allow interested parties to make submissions to the tribunal, and to make arbitration documents publicly available (the notice of arbitration; the response to the notice of arbitration; the statement of claim; the statement of defense; any further written statements or written submissions by a disputing party; a table listing all exhibits to those documents, if it had been prepared for the proceedings; any written submissions by the non-disputing treaty party/parties and by third parties; transcripts of hearings, where available; and orders, decisions, and awards of the arbitral tribunal).[27] Transparency adds legitimacy to international arbitration because it allows for more examination and accountability, which in turn serves as a check on arbitrators' reputations and provides a source of continuous learning for the progressive development of law. In practice, this leads to the development of arbitral jurisprudence, which is necessary to promote a coherent body of international arbitration law and more substantiated evidence of *lex mercatoria.*

5.2.5 *The rights-compatibility criterion and international arbitration*

Rights-compatibility of a non-judicial mechanism, as construed by the UNGPs, ensures that outcomes and remedies accord with internationally recognized human rights.[28] Party autonomy is a salient feature of international arbitration, including the choice of applicable substantive law. Accordingly, a mandatory application of human rights law, international and/or domestic, would be at odds with the principle of party autonomy in international arbitration. Nonetheless, human rights standards could be applied in international arbitration to the extent that international or domestic human rights standards are included in the parties' applicable law clause. In the absence of party agreement, under the International Centre for Settlement of Investment Disputes (ICSID) Convention, for example, an arbitral tribunal

> shall decide a dispute in accordance with such rules of law as may be agreed by the parties. In the absence of such agreement, the Tribunal shall apply the law of the Contracting State party to the dispute (including its rules on the conflict of laws) *and such rules of international law as may be applicable*' (art 42[1]).[29]

In practice, there is conflicting jurisprudence concerning the application of human rights standards by arbitral tribunals. On the one hand, the tribunal in *Biloune v Ghana Investments Centre*[30] dismissed human rights arguments, stating that its competence is limited only to the commercial merits in the dispute and that ruling on human rights violations is outside the scope of its jurisdiction. On the other hand, tribunals in *Urbaser v Argentina*[31] and *Tulip Real Estate v Turkey*[32] decided that rules of international law, of which human rights are also a part, could not be ignored when adjudicating a claim arising out of a BIT. In the decision for annulment in *Tulip Real Estate v Turkey*, the arbitral tribunal relied on a study by the International Law Commission on the fragmentation of international law: "But if . . . all international law exists in systemic relationship with other law, no such application can take place without situating the relevant jurisdiction-endowing instrument in its normative environment".[33] Ultimately, such determinations should not be handled on a case-by-case basis, as it leads to incoherence within international law and, overall, lends a lack of legal security to disputing parties. The goal should be one of systemic coherence, which could be better addressed by the express inclusion of human rights provisions in international trade and investment agreements.

There is a further issue of rights compatibility concerning the composition of arbitral tribunals themselves and the lack of regional, generational, and gender diversity. In recognition of the lack of gender diversity in international arbitration tribunals, the arbitration community drew up a pledge for equal representation in arbitration with the goal of achieving full gender parity.[34] Statistics reveal a significant underrepresentation of women in international arbitration. In 2016, the International Chamber of Commerce Court of Arbitration established a policy to publish limited information relating to arbitrators sitting in International Chamber of Commerce cases. In 2016, women arbitrators represented 14.8% of all arbitrators appointed by International Chamber of Commerce arbitration parties, co-arbitrators, or directly by the International Chamber of Commerce.[35] While party autonomy in the selection of arbitrators is a key feature of arbitration, more can be done to provide more representative lists.

5.3 Recommended measures for international arbitration reform in matters concerning business-related human rights abuses

Alongside both judicial and non-judicial mechanisms, international arbitration for the resolution of business-related human rights abuses should be further developed in light of specific human rights considerations. In order for international arbitration to better provide effective remedy for victims of business-related human rights abuses, reforms need to be adopted that provide procedural safeguards, as well promote the direct application of human rights. At the least, international arbitration institutions should work to adopt a specialized set of procedural rules and financial assistance for matters concerning business-related human rights abuses. At best, States should work to develop and promote the direct application of substantive human rights standards, both domestically and internationally. To various degrees, all require a mandate from States. The recommended measures in this section do not strive to transform arbitration into litigation, only to add some procedural safeguards to make it a more effective remedy for the resolution of cases concerning human rights claims.

5.3.1 Rules for arbitration of disputes concerning business-related human rights abuses[36]

Discussion for the adoption of a specialized tribunal and rules for arbitration of disputes concerning business-related human rights abuses has been proposed by the Working Group on International Arbitration of Business and Human Rights.[37] The core of the proposal is the drafting of arbitration rules that focus on the special requirements of human rights disputes.

The adoption of specialized arbitration rules, adjusted to the needs of a particular subject matter or parties, is not uncommon in international arbitration. On the contrary, the international arbitral community has often developed rules, and even entire institutions, to better address cross-border challenges: intellectual property,[38] sport,[39] foreign investment,[40] maritime disputes,[41] and the noble goal of lasting peace between States.[42] Consider, for example, that the PCA at the Hague has twice set the precedent for a specific set of specialized arbitration rules in consideration of a strong public interest: the Optional Rules for Arbitration of Disputes Relating to the Environment and/or Natural Resources (2001) (hereinafter "PCA Environmental Rules") and the Optional Rules for Arbitration of Disputes Relating to Outer Space Activities (2011) (hereinafter "PCA Outer Space Activities Rules").[43] A key feature of both the PCA Environmental Rules and the Outer Space Activities Rules is that they provide for the establishment of a specialized list of arbitrators considered to have expertise in the subject matters of the dispute,[44] as well as scientific and technical experts.

While such examples for procedural reform can be extrapolated from the aforementioned PCA Optional Rules, if arbitration rules for business-related human rights are developed, they can, and should, go even further. The content of such rules should contemplate procedural safeguards relevant to particular human rights considerations. In particular, a potential set of arbitration rules for matters concerning business-related human rights abuses (hereinafter "BHR Arbitration Rules") should promote transparency, *amicus curiae* participation, specialized panels of arbitrators and experts in human rights, site visits, collective redress, and oversight of award compliance and implementation.

With respect to transparency, a proposed set of arbitration rules in matters of business-related human rights abuses should stipulate the publicity of the notice and commencement of arbitration, publicity of the final award, open hearings, and public access to documents: the notice of arbitration, the response to the notice of arbitration, the statement of claim, the statement of defense, any other written statements or submissions by a disputing party, a table listing all exhibits to those documents, any written submissions by non-disputing parties or third parties, transcript of hearings, orders of the arbitral tribunal, expert reports, and witness statements (subject to exceptions for confidential or protected information).[45]

Amicus curiae, or friends of the court, are third parties or non-disputing parties, and their submissions should be carefully considered and promoted in any proposed BHR Arbitration Rules. The inclusion of provisions concerning *amicus curiae* submissions are important considering the difficulty of assembling a complete roster of experts in each type of case. This issue is tied closely to the issue of transparency, since *amici* will need to depend on access to pleadings to form their submissions. *Amici* submissions have been used to provide useful factual or legal information to the arbitral tribunal regarding a matter within the scope of the dispute, though provisions should also require the *amicus* to disclose their interest in the dispute and any direct or indirect connection, financial or otherwise, with the disputing parties.[46]

The development of a specialized list of arbitrators and human rights experts would be another important component of proposed rules. The potential for a case to be resolved by the most knowledgeable experts in the subject matter(s) of a dispute is an important feature of the arbitration mechanism. Secretariats of international arbitral institutions do in fact compile lists of arbitrators and often act as appointing authorities. The PCA has twice before compiled lists of specialized arbitrators pursuant to optional rules for matters relating to the environment and/or natural resources, as well as for outer space activities. Such work could therefore be undertaken to identify arbitrators with established expertise in business and human rights. As with arbitral selection generally, party autonomy is the bedrock of the arbitration mechanism and there is no obligation to select recommended arbitrators, but it is undoubtedly a service to disputing parties.

The inclusion of a provision regulating site visits would also be useful to further complete a set of BHR Arbitration Rules. Site inspections or visits allow for collection of evidence that can be helpful to an arbitral tribunal. Such visits usually occur based on party agreement[47] and allow an arbitral tribunal or representatives to gather information from a place connected with the subject matter in dispute. Site visits are not novel, and are already part of international arbitral practice.[48]

Considering that business-related human rights abuses can often involve a large class of victims, a set of BHR Arbitration Rules might consider providing a framework for collective redress. While consent to collective redress in international arbitration is determined by the arbitration agreement, and not from arbitration rules, proposed BHR Arbitration Rules could set out and further clarify a mass claims procedure.[49]

Rather than establish an appellate procedure, in order to maintain the efficiency of the arbitration mechanism, potential BHR Arbitration Rules might rather stipulate oversight of award compliance and implementation. Consider the limited jurisdiction of arbitral tribunals: in order for there to be an award compliance or implementation feature, the arbitration agreement would have to be adapted to extend the competence of the arbitral tribunal to cover the period of enforcement and implementation of the arbitral award. Accordingly, BHR Arbitration Rules should contemplate and include a series of model clauses to facilitate drafting. Alternatively, the Rules can provide for a reporting requirement to an administering arbitral institution.

5.3.2 *Financial assistance*

Costs associated with access to justice should not result in a threshold denial of justice. Beyond the cost-cutting measures through party agreement – such as constituting arbitral tribunals with less members, limiting the amount of pages of written pleadings, limiting the number of days of hearings, and using evidentiary sampling – there are a number of measures that could be developed to make international arbitration more accessible for victims of business-related human rights. For example, international arbitration institutions could develop financial assistance funds. In the case of the PCA, rather than creating a new fund for cases involving substantive human rights claims, the PCA Member States could consider reforming the existing Financial Assistance Fund to provide assistance to non-State parties. Moreover, international arbitration institutions might consider developing legal aid programs, or at least a *pro bono* list of skilled and knowledgeable arbitrators, counsel, and experts.

5.4 Conclusion

Arbitration and litigation are distinct mechanisms, the former far more flexible than the latter. However, this does not imply that some procedural safeguards cannot or should not be introduced to better adapt the arbitration mechanism to the needs of the parties or the subject matter of the case. It is indeed procedural flexibility, a core feature of arbitration, which renders the mechanism advantageous for the resolution of cross-border disputes. Therefore, the question is not one of limitations on arbitration, but rather one of enhancement. States have a responsibility to provide and to promote effective and appropriate judicial *and* non-judicial mechanisms, including international arbitration.

The international arbitration mechanism provides a number of advantages in a cross-border context for dispute resolution, namely direct access to a neutral and flexible international forum that provides nearly universal enforceability of final awards. However, if international arbitration is to be used in matters where the substantive claims involve human rights, certain procedural safeguards must be provided for. In particular, transparency of the proceedings and the award, *amicus curiae* participation, specialized panels of arbitrators and human rights experts, site visits and collective redress where relevant, oversight of award compliance, and financial assistance. Procedural reform to render both judicial and non-judicial mechanisms more effective is of great importance. The more comprehensive task before States, which, while independent of the model for international dispute resolution is heavily connected to its effectiveness, is to promote a coherent normative environment that fosters both economic development and social justice.

Notes

* The research in this chapter falls under the framework of the Ministry of Economy, Industry, and Competiveness of Spain and the European Regional Development Fund R&D + i project, *Mecanismos de reclamacion de DDHH a nivel corporativo* (Ref: DER 2017-87712-R).

1 Guiding Principles on Business and Human Rights: Implementing the United Nations "Protect, Respect and Remedy", Annex to UNHRC, Report of the Special Representative of the Secretary-General on the issue of human rights and transnational corporations and other business enterprises, John Ruggie (21 March 2011) UN Doc A/HRC/17/31, Guiding Principle 25.

2 UNGPs (n 1) 26–8.

3 See generally, Juan José Álvarez Rubio and Katerina Yiannibas (eds.), *Human Rights in Business: Removal of Barriers to Access to Justice in the European Union* (Routledge 2017); see also Gwynne Skinner, Robert McCorquodale, Olivier de Schutter and Andie Lambe, *The Third Pillar: Access to Judicial Remedies for Human Rights Violations by Transnational Business* (ICAR, CORE, ECCJ 2013).

4 Christopher R. Drahozal, 'Empirical Findings on International Arbitration: An Overview', in Thomas Schultz and Federico Ortino (eds.), *Oxford Handbook on International Arbitration* (Oxford University Press 2018); see, eg, UN Conference on Trade and Development (UNCTAD), 'World Investment Report 2017: Investment and the Digital Economy' (UN 2017) 109–10 <http://unctad.org/en/PublicationsLibrary/wir2017_en.pdf> accessed 24 September 2019.

5 For a more comprehensive discussion of the international arbitration mechanism, see generally, Gary Born, *International Arbitration: Law and Practice* (2nd edn, Wolters Kluwer 2015).

6 *American Almond Prod Co v Consolidated Pecan S Co*, 144 F.2d 448, 451 (US 2d Cir 1944).

7 UNGPs (n 1) Guiding Principle 31(a): 'Legitimate: enabling trust from the stakeholder groups for whose use they are intended, and being accountable for the fair conduct of grievance processes.'

8 There is an emergent practice to conduct arbitration online. Both the Russian Arbitration Association and the China International Economic and Trade Arbitration Commission have developed online arbitration rules. See generally UN Commission on International Trade Law (UNCITRAL), 'Online Dispute Resolution:

On-line Resources' <www.uncitral.org/uncitral/publications/online_resources_ODR.html> 24th September 2019.

9 See generally, Cesare P.R. Romano, 'The Rule of Prior Exhaustion of Domestic Remedies: Theory and Practice in International Human Rights Procedures', in Nerina Boschiero et al. (eds.), *International Courts and the Development of International Law* (Springer 2013).

10 Convention on the Recognition and Enforcement of Foreign Arbitral Awards 330 UNTS 3, art V(2)(a)(b).

11 Ibid. art V(1)(c).

12 Nathalie Bernasconi-Osterwalder, Lise Johnson and Fiona Marshall, 'Arbitrator Independence and Impartiality: Examining the Dual Role of Arbitrator and Counsel', IV Annual Forum for Developing Country Investment Negotiators Background Papers (27–29 October 2010) 3 <www.iisd.org/sites/default/files/publications/dci_2010_arbitrator_independence.pdf> accessed 24 September 2019.

13 UNGPs (n 1) Guiding Principle 31(b).

14 See, eg, Daniel Augenstein and Nicola Jägers, 'Judicial Remedies: The Issue of Jurisdiction', in Juan José Álvarez Rubio and Katerina Yiannibas (eds.), *Human Rights in Business: Removal of Barriers to Access to Justice in the European Union* (Routledge 2017) 110.

15 Daniel Behn, 'Legitimacy, Evolution and Growth in Investment Treaty Arbitration: Empirically Evaluating the State-of-the-Art', (2015) 46 *Georgetown Journal of International Law* 363, 386.

16 International Chamber of Commerce (2017), Swiss Chambers Arbitration Institution (2004), Hong Kong International Arbitration Centre (2008), Stockholm Chamber of Commerce (2010), the Singapore International Arbitration Centre (2010), AAA International Centre for Dispute Resolution (2014).

17 Katerina Yiannibas, 'Case Study on the Potential of the Arbitration Mechanism: Permanent Court of Arbitration', in Juan José Álvarez Rubio and Katerina Yiannibas (eds.), *Human Rights in Business: Removal of Barriers to Access to Justice in the European Union* (Routledge 2017) 110.

18 The Court of Arbitration for Sport has developed Guidelines on Legal Aid before the Court of Arbitration for Sport (in force as from 1 September 2013; amended on 1 January 2016) <www.tas-cas.org/en/arbitration/legal-aid.html> accessed 24 September 2019. Art 5 of the Guidelines provides: "Legal aid is granted, based on a reasoned request and accompanied by supporting documents, to any natural person provided that his income and assets are not sufficient to allow him to cover the costs of proceedings, without drawing on that part of his assets necessary to support him and his family. Legal aid will be refused if it is obvious that the applicant's claim or grounds of defence have no legal basis. Furthermore, legal aid will be refused if it is obvious that the claim or grounds of defence are frivolous or vexatious".

19 PCA, Financial Assistance Fund for Settlement of International Disputes: Terms of Reference and Guidelines (as approved by the Administrative Council on 11 December 1995) <https://pca-cpa.org/wp-content/uploads/sites/175/2016/02/Financial-Assistance-Fund-for-Settlement-of-International-Disputes.pdf> accessed 24 September 2019, arts 4–5.

20 Amnesty International, 'Attacks on Human Rights Activists Reach Crisis Point Globally' (16 May 2017) <www.amnesty.org/en/latest/news/2017/05/attacks-on-rights-activists-reach-crisis-point-globally/> accessed 24 September 2019.

21 UNGPs (n 1) Guiding Principle 31(c).

22 The New York Convention on the on the Recognition and Enforcement of Foreign Arbitral Awards (330 UNTS 38) replaced the Geneva Protocol on Arbitration Clauses of 1923 (League of Nations Treaty Series 678) and the Geneva

Convention on the Execution of Foreign Arbitral Awards of 1927 (League of Nations Treaty Series 301). The New York Convention entered into force 7 June 1959. As of October 2017, there are 157 Contracting States.

23 Convention on the on the Recognition and Enforcement of Foreign Arbitral Awards (n 22) art V: 1. Recognition and enforcement of the award may be refused, at the request of the party against whom it is invoked, only if that party furnishes to the competent authority, where the recognition and enforcement is sought, proof that:

a) The parties to the agreement referred to in art II were, under the law applicable to them, under some incapacity, or the said agreement is not valid under the law to which the parties have subjected it or, failing any indication thereon, under the law of the country where the award was made; or
b) The party against whom the award is invoked was not given proper notice of the appointment of the arbitrator or of the arbitration proceedings or was otherwise unable to present his case; or
c) The award deals with a difference not contemplated by or not falling within the terms of the submission to arbitration, or it contains decisions on matters beyond the scope of the submission to arbitration, provided that, if the decisions on matters submitted to arbitration can be separated from those not so submitted, that part of the award which contains decisions on matters submitted to arbitration may be recognized and enforced; or
d) The composition of the arbitral authority or the arbitral procedure was not in accordance with the agreement of the parties, or, failing such agreement, was not in accordance with the law of the country where the arbitration took place; or
e) The award has not yet become binding on the parties, or has been set aside or suspended by a competent authority of the country in which, or under the law of which, that award was made.

2. Recognition and enforcement of an arbitral award may also be refused if the competent authority in the country where recognition and enforcement is sought finds that:

a) The subject matter of the difference is not capable of settlement by arbitration under the law of that country; or
b) The recognition or enforcement of the award would be contrary to the public policy of that country.

24 Katerina Yiannibas, Notes of Lecture on International Commercial Arbitration by Professor Hans Smit at Columbia University School of Law, 11 September 2007, on file with the author.

25 See Horatia Muir Watt, 'The Contested Legitimacy of Investment Arbitration and the Human Rights Ordeal' (2012) 4 <https://hal-sciencespo.archives-ouvertes.fr/hal-00972976/document> accessed 12 November 2018; International Institute for International Development and Center for International Environmental Law, 'Ensuring Transparency in Investor-State Dispute Resolution under the UNCITRAL Arbitration Rules' (2011) <www.iisd.org/sites/default/files/publications/ensuring_transparency.pdf> accessed 24 September 2019. See generally, Avinash Poorooye and Ronán Feehily, 'Confidentiality and Transparency in International Commercial Arbitration: Finding the Right Balance', (2017) 22 *Harvard Negotiation Law Review* 275; Catherine A. Rogers, 'Transparency in International Commercial Arbitration', (2006) 54 *University of Kansas Law Review* 1301.

26 PCA, 'The Government of Sudan/the Sudan People's Liberation Movement/Army (Abyei Arbitration)' <https://pca-cpa.org/en/cases/92/> accessed 24 September 2019.

27 See UNICITRAL, Rules on Transparency in Treaty-based Investor-State Arbitration (UN 2014) (UNICITRAL Transparency Rules) <www.uncitral.org/pdf/english/texts/arbitration/rules-on-transparency/Rules-on-Transparency-E.pdf> accessed 24 September 2019.

28 UNGPs (n 1) Guiding Principle 31(f).

29 Convention on the Settlement of Investment Disputes Between States and Nationals of Other States 575 UNTS 159, art 42(1).

30 *Biloune and Marine Drive Complex Ltd v Ghana Investments Centre and the Government of Ghana*, Ad Hoc Tribunal (UNCITRAL Rules,) 30 June 1990 (Schwebel, Wallace Jr, Leigh, Arbs).

31 *Urbaser SA and Consorcio de Aguas Bilbao Bizkaia, Bilbao Biskaia Ur Partzuergoa v the Argentine Republic*, ICSID Case No ARB/07/26, 8 December 2016 (Bucher, Martínez-Fraga, McLachlan Arbs).

32 *Tulip Real Estate and Development Netherlands BV v Republic of Turkey*, ICSID Case No ARB/11/28, Decision on Annulment, 30 December 2015 (Tomka, Booth, Schreuer, Arbs) (para 87: 'The relevant rules of international law cover all sources of international law').

33 Ibid. para 89, citing International Law Commission, Report of a study group on Fragmentation of International Law: Difficulties Arising from the Diversification and Expansion of International Law (13 April 2006) UN Doc A/CN.4/L.682, paras 410–80.

34 'Equal Representation in Arbitration Pledge' <www.arbitrationpledge.com/> accessed 24 September 2019. There are 2,131 individual and organization signatories as of November 2017.

35 International Chamber of Commerce, 'ICC Court Sees Marked Progress on Gender Diversity (31 May 2017) <https://iccwbo.org/media-wall/news-speeches/icc-court-sees-marked-progress-gender-diversity/> accessed 24 September 2019 (the 2016 figure went up 4.4 per cent from 2015 statistics).

36 This section is based on Katerina Yiannibas, 'The Adaptability of International Arbitration: Reforming the Arbitration Mechanism to Provide Effective Remedy for Business-Related Human Rights Abuses', (2018) 36(3) *Netherlands Quarterly of Human Rights* 214.

37 In February 2017, the Working Group on International Arbitration of Business and Human Rights proposed the creation of an International Arbitration Tribunal on Business and Human Rights, contemplating also the adoption of specialized rules. See Claes Cronstedt, Jan Eijsbouts and Robert C. Thompson, 'International Business and Human Rights Arbitration' (13 February 2017) <www.l4bb.org/news/TribunalV6.pdf> accessed 24 September 2019. The Working Group consists of Claes Cronstedt, Jan Eijsbouts, Steven Ratner, Martijn Scheltema, Robert Thompson, and Katerina Yiannibas. The Drafting Team consists of Bruno Simma (chair), Anne van Aaken, Diane Desierto, Martin Doe-Rodriguez, Jan Eijsbouts, Cesar Rodriguez-Garavito, Ursula Kribaum, Abiola Makinwa, Richard Meeran, Serigio Puig, Steven Ratner, Martjin Scheltema, and Suzanne Spears.

38 World Intellectual Property Organization, 'WIPO Arbitration Rules (1994, 2014). The 2014 Arbitration Rules are available at <www.wipo.int/amc/en/arbitration/rules/index.html> accessed 24 September 2019.

39 Court of Arbitration for Sport, Code of Procedural Rules for sports-related disputes (2004, 2012, 2013, 2016, 2017) <www.tas-cas.org/en/arbitration/code-procedural-rules.html> accessed 24 September 2019.

40 International Centre for the Settlement of Investment Disputes, ICSID Convention (1966) and Rules (1968, 1984, 2003, 2006) <https://icsid.worldbank.org/en/> accessed 24 September 2019.

41 For a list of maritime arbitration associations and their respective arbitration rules, see, eg, International Congress of Maritime Arbitrators, 'Maritime Arbitration Associations' <https://icmaweb.com/maritime-arbitration-associations> accessed 24 September 2019.
42 PCA Founding Conventions (1899, 1907) and Internal Rules (2012) <https://pca-cpa.org/en/documents/pca-conventions-and-rules/> accessed 24 September 2019. The PCA Arbitration Rules 2012 are a consolidation of four prior sets of PCA procedural rules: the Optional Rules for Arbitrating Disputes between Two States (1992); the Optional Rules for Arbitrating Disputes between Two Parties of Which Only One is a State (1993); the Optional Rules for Arbitration Between International Organizations and States (1996); and the Optional Rules for Arbitration Between International Organizations and Private Parties (1996).
43 In both cases, the Member States of the PCA decided that the subject matters had a strong public interest.
44 PCA Environmental Rules, art 8(3); PCA Outer Space Activities Rules, art 10(4).
45 To advance coherence between international arbitration instruments, transparency provisions can be modeled on the UNICTRAL Transparency Rules (n 27), art 2–3.
46 See, eg, UNCITRAL Transparency Rules (n 27) arts 4–5.
47 Gary Born, *International Commercial Arbitration: Commentary and Materials* (2nd edn, Kluwer Law International 2001).
48 See, e.g., ICSID Arbitration Rules 2006 (n 40) art 34(2)(b); PCA Arbitration Rules 2012 (n 42) art 27(3).
49 Collective redress is already emerging in both institutional and *ad hoc* arbitration, and there is a need to clarify procedural aspects in these cases. See generally, Jan K. Dunin-Wasowicz, 'Collective Redress in International Arbitration: An American Idea, a European Concept?', (2011) 22(2) *The American Review of International Arbitration* 285. See also, European Union Agency for Fundamental Rights, Opinion 1/2017, 10 April 2017, 7 (EU institutions are called upon to "provide stronger incentives to Member States to provide for effective collective redress in cases of business-related human rights abuse").

Bibliography

Álvarez Rubio JJ and Yiannibas K (eds.), *Human Rights in Business: Removal of Barriers to Access to Justice in the European Union* (Routledge 2017).

Augenstein D and Jägers N, 'Judicial Remedies: The Issue of Jurisdiction', in Juan José Álvarez Rubio and Katerina Yiannibas (eds.), *Human Rights in Business: Removal of Barriers to Access to Justice in the European Union* (Routledge 2017).

Behn D, 'Legitimacy, Evolution and Growth in Investment Treaty Arbitration: Empirically Evaluating the State-of-the-Art', (2015) 46 *Georgetown Journal of International Law* 363.

Bernasconi-Osterwalder N, Johnson L and Marshall F, 'Arbitrator Independence and Impartiality: Examining the Dual Role of Arbitrator and Counsel', IV Annual Forum for Developing Country Investment Negotiators Background Papers (27–29 October 2010) <www.iisd.org/sites/default/files/publications/dci_2010_arbitrator_independence.pdf>

Born G, *International Arbitration: Law and Practice* (2nd edn, Wolters Kluwer 2015).

———, *International Commercial Arbitration: Commentary and Materials* (2nd edn, Kluwer Law International 2001).

Drahozal CR, 'Empirical Findings on International Arbitration: An Overview', in Thomas Schultz and Federico Ortino (eds.), *Oxford Handbook on International Arbitration* (Oxford University Press 2018).

Dunin-Wasowicz JK, 'Collective Redress in International Arbitration: An American Idea, a European Concept?', (2011) 22(2) *The American Review of International Arbitration* 285.

Muir Watt H, 'The Contested Legitimacy of Investment Arbitration and the Human Rights Ordeal', (2012) 4 <https://hal-sciencespo.archives-ouvertes.fr/hal-00972976/document>

Poorooye A and Feehily R, 'Confidentiality and Transparency in International Commercial Arbitration: Finding the Right Balance', (2017) 22 *Harvard Negotiation Law Review* 275.

Rogers CA, 'Transparency in International Commercial Arbitration', (2006) 54 *University of Kansas Law Review* 1301.

Romano CPR, 'The Rule of Prior Exhaustion of Domestic Remedies: Theory and Practice in International Human Rights Procedures', in Nerina Boschiero et al. (eds.), *International Courts and the Development of International Law* (Springer 2013).

Skinner G, McCorquodale R, de Schutter O and Lambe A, *The Third Pillar: Access to Judicial Remedies for Human Rights Violations by Transnational Business* (ICAR, CORE, ECCJ 2013).

Yiannibas K, 'Case Study on the Potential of the Arbitration Mechanism: Permanent Court of Arbitration', in Juan José Álvarez Rubio and Katerina Yiannibas (eds.), *Human Rights in Business: Removal of Barriers to Access to Justice in the European Union* (Routledge 2017).

———, 'The Adaptability of International Arbitration: Reforming the Arbitration Mechanism to Provide Effective Remedy for Business-Related Human Rights Abuses', (2018) 36(3) *Netherlands Quarterly of Human Rights* 214.

6 Justice without borders

Models of cross-border legal cooperation and what they can teach us

*Jennifer Zerk**

6.1 Introduction

There has been much debate lately about the extent to which the "territorial" system of regulation of multinational enterprises offers adequate protections to those whose human rights have been adversely impacted by their business activities. The territorial system of regulation is the logical consequence of the international law principle of territorial sovereignty, under which each State has exclusive jurisdiction to regulate the activities of individuals, corporations, and other entities within the limits of its own territory.[1]

With these regulatory rights come regulatory responsibilities. As the UNGPs make clear, "States must protect against human rights abuse within their territory and/or jurisdiction by third parties, including business enterprises. This requires taking appropriate steps to prevent, investigate, punish and redress such abuse through effective policies, legislation, regulations and adjudication".[2]

The principle of territorial sovereignty is unproblematic in cases where all of the relevant actors, actions, impacts, and evidence are located in one jurisdiction. However, in many contexts involving adverse human rights impacts of multinational enterprises, this is not the case. In such situations, a number of difficult additional questions often arise. Which of the various interested States should be responsible for ensuring that there is redress for injuries or harm? Are there cases in which a State other than the "territorial State'"[3] should take the lead? If so, what are these cases and how can concerns about interferences by one State in the domestic affairs of another be overcome? How can States work together, in specific cases, to ensure that adverse human rights impacts are properly redressed and remedied?

This chapter is concerned primarily with the last of these questions. Following a discussion of why effective cross-border legal cooperation regimes are necessary for access to remedy (regardless of whether the "home State" or the "host State" takes the lead), this chapter identifies the main models of cross-border legal cooperation that have emerged thus far. It then moves on to consider a series of issues relevant to the implementation of cross-border cooperative arrangements related to business and human rights cases, highlighting areas in which attention to practical and operational matters, including awareness of the human element, can help to improve the effectiveness of these regimes in practice.

6.2 Why cross-border legal cooperation is an important part of access to remedy in business and human rights cases

In many cases involving allegations of business involvement of human rights abuses, there is more than one State with a legal, political, economic, or regulatory interest in the matter. This is particularly likely to be the case where the business enterprise concerned is made up of control relationships (for example, relationships between parent and subsidiary companies) or contractual relationships (for example, distribution arrangements and supply chains) that operate across national borders. Guiding Principle 1 reaffirms the position under international human rights law that the State with primary responsibility in such cases is the State in which the harm occurs. But what is the position if that State (often referred to in this context as the "host State") is unwilling or unable to take the necessary investigative, adjudicative, and remedial action? There are many reasons why this might be the case. The company whose activities appear to have the closest physical relationship to the damage (for example, the local subsidiary) may not have sufficient resources to meet a claim, or may no longer exist. The harm may have occurred in an area affected by conflict, where there are no institutions or judicial mechanisms that would offer a realistic prospect of effective remedy. The proper functioning of the relevant domestic judicial mechanisms could be impaired by corruption or a lack of capacity or resources. In such a situation, it is likely that the host State would be in breach of its international law obligations to ensure a prompt, adequate, and effective remedy for human rights abuses. However, this will not, of itself, deliver an effective remedy for the harm the victim has individually suffered. In such cases (which are not at all uncommon), victims of business-related human rights abuses may look to other jurisdictions for help. Victims and their legal representatives may seek to commence proceedings in the States in which parent companies of the relevant multinational enterprises are domiciled (often referred to as the "home State" of the business enterprise).[4] However, claimants in these kinds of cross-border civil cases against parent companies face enormous legal, financial, and practical barriers, and effective legal remedies are rarely, if ever, achieved.[5]

Criminal cases do not fare much better. It is rare, in practice, that prosecutors are persuaded to take on cases involving extraterritorial human rights abuses. As the OHCHR puts it,

> [i]nvestigations and prosecutions of business enterprises can be resource-intensive and time-consuming, especially where there is a cross-border element or where complex corporate structures are involved. In the face of multiple, sometimes conflicting, demands on limited resources, prosecutors may be reluctant to prioritize a legally challenging, novel or complex case.[6]

This has led to claims by many commentators and campaigners that multinationals are operating "beyond the law", and that business and human rights cases involving multinational enterprises are "falling through the cracks" of the international legal system. A number of proposals have been put forward to encourage home States of multinationals to take a greater role in delivering justice in cross-border cases. These include proposals aimed at removing the legal distinction between parent companies and subsidiaries (thus making it easier for victims of business-related human rights abuses to make a legal case against a parent company for abuses perpetrated by subsidiaries),[7] proposals for strict liability of parent companies (which would reverse the burden of proof so that a parent company would have to show why it should *not* be held responsible for its subsidiary's activities in the circumstances),[8] and imposing statutory duties on parent companies to supervise their subsidiaries effectively.[9]

More work is needed to fully understand the feasibility and implications of these various reform proposals in different jurisdictions and operating contexts, and to build political support for them.[10] In the meantime, it is important to recognize that there are significant practical, as well as legal, obstacles to address in cross-border cases. Although the proposals outlined previously could be helpful in removing some of the *legal* obstacles to remedy against complex business organizations in human rights-related cases, significant *practical* obstacles remain with respect to gathering information and testimony from witnesses in different jurisdictions.

Given their significance for access to remedy in cross-border business and human rights cases, it is surprising that cross-border legal cooperation regimes have received so little attention in this context to date.[11] Where the need for better cross-border cooperation has been discussed, it tends to have been in the context of cases against parent companies concerning the acts of subsidiaries or contractors abroad. This is because, in a case commenced in a home State of a parent company ("State A") arising from harm suffered in State B, it may be necessary, in order to prove the claim, to access information held in State B, such as medical records or documentation relating to inspections or investigations by foreign regulatory agencies.

However, the need for cross-border legal cooperation may be just as great in cases that are litigated in *host States*. For example, in a case where the host State ("State B") has taken jurisdiction, but where the culpability of a foreign parent company is at issue, it may be necessary to access information in State A in the possession of that parent company, such as information about the design of a plant or policies with respect to the hiring of personnel.

In some cases (for example, cases arising out of complex supply or distribution chains), the adverse human rights impacts arising from a single set of circumstances may be felt in more than one State. There are also likely to be cases where adverse human rights impacts in one State may be the end result of a combination of corporate actions or decisions in more than one other State. Regardless of which State ("home State" or "host State") takes jurisdiction over a matter (and on what basis), some degree of cross-border legal cooperation is frequently required to ensure that those seeking to enforce the law have access to the extraterritorial information and evidence they may need to pursue their case.

As will be seen from the discussion in the next sections, cross-border arrangements already exist between many States to facilitate the to and fro of information and legal assistance in a wide range of cases. While these arrangements have not yet been widely used in cases where companies are accused of being responsible for, or complicit in, serious human rights abuses, they have proved vital in the fight against some specific categories of cross-border harm which have close links to human rights, including efforts to combat human trafficking, environmental protection and anti-corruption.[12]

6.3 Five models of international cooperation

States have developed a range of solutions to the challenges of investigating and enforcing legal standards where the relevant actors, evidence, or harms (or a combination of all three) are located in more than one State. Obviously, State-to-State agreements, such as mutual legal assistance treaties, are important in this regard. However, States have also developed systems for direct contact between law enforcement and regulatory agencies of different jurisdictions, as well as regimes that can be directly accessed by individuals seeking to enforce their legal rights. As will be seen, the effects of these arrangements can be far-reaching. As well as helping to reduce barriers to remedy in individual cases, they can contribute to consensus-building around legal standards, the dissemination of know-how with respect to best regulatory practice, and the realization of improvements in the effectiveness of domestic regulatory bodies.

6.3.1 Mutual legal assistance

Criminal cases

In the criminal law setting, mutual legal assistance is a method of cooperation between States whereby courts and prosecutors can obtain assistance from their counterparts in other States to investigate possible criminal offenses.

Mutual legal assistance arrangements can be formalized by way of bilateral or multilateral treaties. These treaties can take different forms: they may be general treaties on judicial cooperation applicable to a range of law enforcement contexts;[13] they may create bespoke regimes for specific types of evidence-gathering and cross-border investigative cooperation;[14] or they may be aimed at matters of international concern (for example, drug trafficking, human trafficking, bribery and corruption, or organized crime), which include provisions on mutual legal assistance between State parties as part of a wider package of law-enforcement measures.[15]

The kinds of assistance frequently provided for in international treaties include obtaining written testimony and documentary evidence for use in court proceedings, service of court documents (for example, summonses), making arrangements for witnesses to appear and give testimony at judicial proceedings (including persons who are in custody), providing access to judicial records, and searching for and seizing evidence on behalf of foreign law enforcement authorities.

Treaties aimed at combating bribery, terrorism or organized crime are likely also to contain provisions aimed at assisting with the tracing, freezing, and confiscating of proceeds of crime. For instance, the UN Convention Against Transnational Organized Crime[16] requires that States parties "afford one another the widest measure of mutual legal assistance in investigations, prosecutions and judicial proceedings in relation to the offences covered by this Convention",[17] and goes on to stipulate that assistance may be requested for purposes including "taking evidence or statements from persons"; "effecting service of judicial documents"; "executing searches and seizures"; "freezing assets"; "examining objects and sites"; "providing information, evidentiary items and expert evaluations"; "providing originals or certified copies of relevant documents and records, including government, bank, financial, corporate or business records"; "identifying or tracing proceeds of crime, property, instrumentalities or other things for evidentiary purposes"; and "facilitating the voluntary appearance of persons in the requesting State Party".[18] Similar provisions can also be found in the UN Convention Against Corruption.[19] The more recent international agreements, such as the agreement between the EU and Japan,[20] provide for cooperation through modern technologies, notably the use of video conferencing facilities to obtain oral evidence in judicial proceedings from witnesses located in other States.

Civil ("private law") cases

States have also entered into international treaties and other legal arrangements governing legal cooperation in civil and commercial cases. Within the EU, cross-border service of documentation in civil cases is governed by a Council Regulation.[21] Under this Regulation, each EU Member State designates a central body to be responsible for transmitting and receiving court documents in cross-border cases. Once service has been carried out, this is confirmed back to the transmitting agency by way of a certificate. However, in an important innovation, claimants and their representatives in the EU can also send documents directly to the relevant judicial officer in another EU Member State for service on another person (that is, without having to go through any consular or diplomatic channels and without the need to involve the central transmitting body in the claimants' own jurisdiction).

It is also possible for claimants and their legal representatives to arrange for the collection of evidence in other States, provided the necessary State-to-State arrangements have been put in place. Under the Hague Convention on the Taking of Evidence Abroad in Civil or Commercial Matters,[22] requests to obtain evidence in another State that is needed for the purposes of judicial proceedings are conveyed by "Letters of Request" from one central authority to another, specifying the nature of the proceedings for which the evidence is required and the evidence that needs to be obtained (or any other judicial act that must be performed). The Letters of Request can also specify the questions that must be put, and the documents or property to be inspected. However, under Article 9, the judicial authority executing the request applies its own law as to the methods and procedures to be used. The Convention lays out the circumstances in which requests for the taking of evidence can be refused. There are also provisions relating to the taking of evidence, without compulsion, by diplomatic officers and consular agents.

Within the EU, these arrangements have been further enhanced by provisions that permit, in certain circumstances, the presence of the parties to litigation (or their legal representatives) at the foreign evidence collection procedures.[23] In exceptional circumstances, it may be possible for the competent court of the requesting State to take evidence directly (in which the court of the requesting State, rather than that of the requested State, takes the lead in the evidence collection). EU law imposes statutory time limits on responses to evidence-gathering requests. In addition, the intra-EU mutual legal assistance arrangements in civil and commercial cases provide for the use of teleconferencing and videoconferencing technology, provided that this use is consistent with the laws of the requested State.[24]

6.3.2 Joint investigation teams

Joint investigation teams (JITs) are a method of legal cooperation between States whereby special-purpose criminal investigation teams are set up, by agreement with the States concerned, to investigate specific crimes with cross-border elements. Their key feature is that they combine operatives from different interested States (and representing different State agencies) into a single investigative team with its own chain of command and reporting arrangements. They are a relatively recent innovation, but are gaining in frequency and popularity.

The legal basis for JITs in the EU dates back to 2000, and the adoption by EU Member States of the Convention on Mutual Assistance in Criminal Matters between the Member States of the European Union.[25] Article 13 of that Convention provided that

> competent authorities of two of more Member States may set up a JIT for a specific purpose and a limited period . . . to carry out criminal investigations in one of more of the Member States setting up a team.

Under this Convention, the establishment of JITs is recommended where "a Member State's investigations into criminal offences require difficult and demanding investigations having links with other States" or "a number of Member States are conducting investigations into criminal offences in which the circumstances of the case necessitate coordinated, concerted action in the Member States involved".[26] General conditions for the operation of a JIT in EU Member States are set out in the EU Framework Decision.[27] The team's structure and composition, and the respective roles and responsibilities of team members, are set out in a special agreement between the agencies concerned.[28] Team members carry out their investigative responsibilities under the direction of a team leader,[29] and in accordance with a pre-agreed "Operational Action Plan". The Operational Action Plan sets out the parameters of activities of "seconded" team members (that is, investigators brought in from other jurisdictions), including matters such as whether they will be entitled to be present at interviews of witnesses, at searches of properties, and at press briefings, and the conditions under which they will be allowed to carry weapons.[30]

Use of JITs has gradually increased over the past 15 years or so. An OHCHR discussion paper prepared for the Accountability and Remedy Project[31] notes that "[w]hile most of these have been bilateral (the most frequent pairing being France and Spain), multilateral arrangements (involving three or more States) are now becoming more common".[32]

Uptake by non-EU member states is also increasing. The JIT to investigate the crash of Flight MH17 in the Ukraine (involving Netherlands, Belgium, Australia, Ukraine, and Malaysia) is a good example of cooperation between criminal investigators between EU and non-EU Member States.[33] Greater exposure to this method of international cooperation is likely to help fulfill the ambition of many States for more widespread use of JITs, including outside the EU, in tackling serious cross-border crimes such as drug trafficking, corruption, and organized crime. For example, Article 19 of the UN Convention Against Organized Crime calls on State parties to consider establishing bilateral and multilateral arrangements to facilitate and support joint investigations or, in the absence of such arrangements, to allow them to go forward on an ad hoc basis. The agreement between the EU and the US on legal cooperation,[34] signed in the wake of the 9/11 terrorist attacks on the US, commits the parties to "take such measures as may be necessary to enable JITs to be established and operated in the respective territories of the US and each Member State for the purpose of facilitating criminal investigations or prosecution" involving the US and one or more EU Member States.[35]

From a law enforcement point of view, the main advantage of JITs (over the more traditional mutual legal assistance method of cooperation) is their flexibility. They enable information relating to an investigation to be shared quickly and easily among operatives (and hence between different State agencies) and thus avoid, to a large extent, the legal complexities and procedural delays often associated with mutual legal assistance and other cooperative criminal investigation regimes.[36] An OHCHR discussion paper, prepared for the purposes of the OHCHR Accountability and Remedy Project,[37] explains the advantages of the JIT model as follows:

> Under the JIT model, investigators have, by comparison, a more simplified and arguably more efficient method of cooperating and exchanging information relating to an investigation. Although there is likely to be some political oversight with respect to the establishment of the JIT, once the JIT is operational, team members are able to share information relatively freely and directly with each other, subject to the terms of the JIT agreement. In addition (again, subject to the terms of the JIT agreement) seconded members

of JITs may be present when key investigative actions are taken (e.g. witness interviews, searches of premises, etc). They may also make requests directly to their own competent authorities to take specific investigative steps in their own jurisdiction in furtherance of the investigation, the outcomes of which can be shared directly with other members of the JIT.

In addition to the potential efficiency improvement and cost savings, the JIT model provides a flexible framework under which the competent authorities from different jurisdictions can explore and develop ways of responding to specific legal and practical challenges in advance. Problems such as differences in definitions of offences, differences in sanctions, differences in rules on collection and admissibility of evidence, differences in disclosure rules and questions relating to the distribution of confiscated assets . . . can be anticipated, considered and dealt with in advance by agreement, rather than reactively on an ad hoc basis as the investigation develops.[38]

6.3.3 Ad hoc cooperation

A recent study by the UN Working Group[39] provides several examples of cases in which investigators from different jurisdictions have cooperated closely and successfully to investigate and prosecute companies alleged to have been involved in serious criminal wrongdoing. The case of *Kronos Sanitärservice GMBH and NV Carastel Motorway Services* was an example of successful cooperation between law enforcement authorities in Belgium and France to investigate, prosecute, and ultimately convict companies and related individuals for human trafficking offenses.[40]

In the anti-corruption field, prosecutors from different jurisdictions have not only provided each other with legal and practical assistance at the investigation stage, but have also cooperated with respect to enforcement and sanctioning. In some cases, this cooperation has been sufficiently close that the relevant authorities have managed to reach bilateral (and on occasion multilateral, multi-agency) agreements with respect to the apportionment of resultant financial penalties between their respective governments. The UN Working Group study cites the example of the investigation into bribery allegations against Odebrecht SA and Braskem SA with respect to their activities in Latin America and Asian countries.[41] This investigation, involving parallel investigations and prosecutions in Brazil, Switzerland, and the US, resulted in guilty pleas by the two companies concerned and financial penalties of approximately US$3.5 billion, which were then distributed between the governments of these three States.[42]

The legal basis for cooperation in individual cases will vary from case to case, and may draw from a combination of models and approaches. In some cases, the cooperation proceeds under the usual arrangements with respect to mutual legal assistance, which may be supplemented by more detailed interagency agreements (for example, by way of memoranda of understanding) on operational and enforcement matters, subject always to the legal mandates of the agencies concerned. In addition, international regimes put in place to respond to cross-border challenges, such as human trafficking and bribery, provide important political and legal backing to such cooperative efforts. Both the UN Convention on Transnational Organized Crime[43] and its 2000 Protocol on Human Trafficking[44] recognize the importance of close cooperation by law enforcement authorities to enhance the effectiveness of domestic legal regimes in cross-border cases, employing a mix of aspirational language[45] as well as more detailed provisions on matters such as confiscation of assets,[46] information sharing,[47] training,[48] and border measures.[49]

6.3.4 Regimes for cross-border access to regulatory information

Information held by regulatory bodies that may be relevant to a civil claim (for example, in a product liability case, scientific research carried out by a regulatory agency in a home State, and the product safety standards developed as a result) may be directly accessible to a claimant through Freedom of Information regimes.[50] However, these regimes can be disadvantageous to claimants in cross-border cases in several ways. First, they usually only provide for applications for information held by public authorities;[51] business enterprises are generally out of their reach, unless their activities are somehow "public" in nature – for example, utilities or other public services.[52] Second, they often contain many exceptions (under which access can be denied if it is deemed to be contrary to the public interest, or for reasons of "commercial confidentiality").[53] Third, while transparency procedures are often open to foreign applicants,[54] this has not always been the case.

Over the past few decades, a number of international and regional regimes have emerged with the aim of improving public access to regulatory information. The foremost example in the environmental sphere is the Convention on Access to Information, Public Participation in Decision Making and Access to Justice in Environmental Matters[55] (commonly known as the "Aarhus Convention"). This Convention calls on State parties to "guarantee the rights of access to information, public participation in decision making, and access to justice in environmental matters in accordance with the provisions of this Convention".[56] Importantly for those needing to access environmental information from other States, the Convention imposes an obligation of non-discrimination. In the words of Article 3(9),

> the public shall have access to information, have the possibility to participate in decision-making and have access to justice in environmental matters without discrimination as to citizenship, nationality or domicile and, in the case of a legal person, without discrimination as to where it has its registered seat or an effective centre of its activities.

Despite innovations such as these, claimants and their legal representatives continue to face difficulties in accessing information and help from regulatory agencies in cross-border cases in practice. Because of the potential evidential value of regulatory information in some business and human rights cases, the final report of the OHCHR to the UNHRC on Phase 1 of the Accountability and Remedy Project[57] identifies improving transparency and exchange of regulatory information, particularly in a cross-border context, as a potentially useful action point for the future. Specifically, the report suggests that each State

> actively engages in bilateral, regional and multilateral initiatives aimed at improving the ease with which and speed at which information can be exchanged between claimants and their legal representatives and the relevant State agencies of other States in cross-border cases.[58]

6.3.5 *Law enforcement networks and related multilateral initiatives*

The proliferation of international and regional law enforcement and regulators' networks over the past two decades is an indication of the growing awareness of the inter-relatedness of domestic regulatory systems and the importance of good working relationships between law enforcement officials from different States. As the UN Working Group observes,

> [j]oining networks is a useful way of building trust with foreign counterparts. International and regional associations of prosecutors often organize conferences to share best practices and promote cross-border relationships. Those associations also have other resources, such as training documents and online communication tools, to foster cooperation.[59]

Law enforcement and regulator networks vary greatly in terms of their structure and membership requirements, as well as their geographic and substantive scope, depending on their aims and the extent to which they have needed to respond to political and legal change. Some, such as the International Association of Prosecutors,[60] are focused on criminal law cooperation in general. Others, such as the International Association of Labour Inspection,[61] are more specialized. Some exist as self-administered membership bodies; some operate under the auspices of other organizations with wider mandates, such as Interpol[62] or Europol.[63]

As well as providing a forum to develop relationships and discuss regulatory best practices, some of these networks (and those active in the financial and securities sectors in particular) have pioneered approaches designed to develop greater convergence between different jurisdictions with respect to regulatory standards and methods. For instance, the Committee of European Securities Regulators[64] works to improve coordination between the securities regulators of EU Member States to monitor implementation of EU securities law, and to act as an advisory body to the EC on securities regulation issues. The International Organisation of Securities Commissions (IOSCO) has established an Assessment Committee to be responsible for the monitoring of implementation of IOSCO principles, recommendations, and policies across its membership.[65] The Financial Action Task Force on Money Laundering, a G7 initiative that dates back to 1989, has developed a sophisticated system of compliance monitoring that takes account of both technical compliance with recommendations and practical impacts.[66]

Calls for greater cooperation between domestic regulatory and law-enforcement agencies to raise standards, share resources, and generally improve institutional and regulatory effectiveness are now a common feature of international instruments on the prevention and enforcement of serious crimes with a cross-border element.[67] In its 2016 report to the UNHRC on accountability and access to remedy in business and human rights cases, the OHCHR encourages each State to see that

> [e]nforcement agencies and judicial bodies support and encourage the involvement of their personnel in relevant bilateral and multilateral initiatives and networks aimed at (a) facilitating contact and exchange of know-how between counterparts in other States; and (b) promoting awareness of different opportunities and options for international cooperation and the provision of legal assistance in cross-border cases.[68]

6.4 Getting practical: some notes on implementation

6.4.1 Laws, procedures, and space to innovate

Cross-border legal cooperation regimes frequently need legal backing to get started. This is most commonly done by way of an international instrument, which is then implemented through domestic legislation to the extent necessary to make its provisions legally effective at domestic level. Mutual legal assistance regimes will often include provisions on the types of assistance that can be sought, any pre-conditions to the provision of such assistance, institutional and procedural matters (such as the designation of central authorities to be responsible for the handling of requests), specifications as to the formats in which requests must be given, and, in some cases, time scales for dealing with requests.

Provisions on JITs, by comparison, tend to be somewhat looser, and allow considerable scope for interpretation by States in how they are implemented. However, in the EU, where this method of legal cooperation is used most and where practice is most advanced, JITs are underpinned by fairly detailed regulations as to administrative and operational matters, which are further supplemented by manuals and guidance.

However, the presence of a detailed legal regime is not necessarily the most important component of successful cross-border legal cooperation. While such regimes are undoubtedly useful as a way of laying down a framework for legal cooperation and clarifying expectations between the State parties, they are not necessarily a prerequisite. Domestic law-enforcement agencies can and do request and provide each other with legal cooperation in the absence of formal mutual legal assistance obligations (specifically by way of treaty) between the States concerned, for example on an ad hoc or case-specific basis. It is also worth noting that some of the mechanisms discussed concerning regulatory cooperation have been constituted and have continued to operate without formal treaty backing. The Financial Action Task Force, for example, began its life as a result of a 1989 resolution by G7 ministers in response to concerns about the global drug trade and the misuse of banks and financial institutions around the world to launder illicit funds. Since then, it has expanded its activities to cover terrorist financing and other forms of abuse of the banking sector that require a multinational response. IOSCO, also discussed earlier, is an international association of securities regulators that grew out of a regional association of 11 securities regulators based in North and South America.

The nature and scope of legal backing needed by different legal cooperation mechanisms will obviously be influenced by the type of cooperation envisaged, and the needs and ambitions of the States involved. Relevant to these decisions will be the extent to which the mechanism will need the flexibility to devise its own procedures, and develop its operations to respond to new challenges, set against the need for clarity and consensus at State level surrounding the mechanism's mandate and modes of operation.

In some settings, flexibility will also be required to ensure that the legal cooperation mechanism is sufficiently adaptable to different legal structures, cultures, legal and operational rules, and standards in different jurisdictions. In the EU, the flexibility of the JIT concept (under which the relevant law-enforcement bodies anticipate and take account of differences in approach between EU Member States with respect to issues such as admissibility of evidence, disclosure, and data protection in their case-specific agreements and action plans) have been key to their success. As a result, investigators and prosecutors have been able to utilize this mechanism in a wide range of cross-border criminal investigations.[69]

6.4.2 *The importance of good working relationships and ready access to information about conditions and requirements in other jurisdictions*

A further extra-legal aspect to legal cooperation mechanisms that is easy to overlook is the importance of good working relationships between the relevant people – members of the judiciary, prosecutors, police, and other law enforcement personnel – and their counterparts in other States. In practice, having ready access to names and contact details, and familiarity with the procedures, priorities, and constraints affecting a counterpart's activities and operations, can make all the difference in the speed and efficiency with which a cross-border problem can be addressed. On the other hand, a lack of knowledge and contacts can hamper effective cooperation and undermine the ability of legal cooperation regimes to live up to their promise in practice.[70]

It is for this reason that the OHCHR's 2016 report to the UNHRC on accountability and access to remedy in business and human rights cases[71] draws particular attention to coordination and communication aspects in its discussion of the management of cross-border cases. For instance, in its discussion of public law cases, the OHCHR suggests that States give consideration to becoming

> actively involved with relevant bilateral and multilateral initiatives aimed at improving the ease with which and speed at which (a) requests for mutual legal assistance can be made and responded to; and (b) information can be exchanged between enforcement agencies and/or judicial bodies in cross-border cases, including through information repositories that provide clarity on points of contact, core process requirements and systems for updates on outstanding requests.[72]

6.4.3 *The importance of proactive outreach and technical support for practitioners*

Providing legislative backing for cross-border legal cooperation arrangements may be necessary, though not sufficient, for those arrangements to succeed. The point is illustrated by early experiences with JITs in the EU. Immediately following the EU Convention that gave legal support for JITs,[73] and the subsequent Council Framework Decision,[74] take-up was slow. The EU body responsible for coordinating JIT arrangements, Eurojust, considered that the reasons for this were most likely to be lack of awareness and familiarity with this particular mode of cooperation, due to its relative novelty at that stage. Observers suggested that concerns about the additional risk, inconvenience, complexity, and costs of constituting a JIT[75] (as well as, perhaps, a lack of attention to operational needs and the experiences of practitioners at the time of the development of the EU regime)[76] may also have played a part.[77]

However, the steady increase in the number of newly initiated JITs since 2007 shows how, with dedicated and proactive support, reluctance and skepticism about new legal cooperation mechanisms and ways of working can be gradually overcome.[78] In the EU, the main provider of this support is Eurojust. Eurojust was formally constituted pursuant to the 2002 Council Framework Decision[79] as part of a package of measures to stimulate greater use of JITs among EU Member States. In addition to its awareness-raising and education role, Eurojust makes technical support available in the form of assistance with the drafting of legal documentation, offers advice on various legal and strategic matters (for example, background legal frameworks, procedural issues, and whether a specific case under investigation of domestic authorities would benefit from the establishment of a JIT), and publishes a range of manuals and other resources for practitioners. In addition, Eurojust can provide limited financial assistance to some JITs to cover specific items such as accommodation, transport, equipment hire, communications, translation, and interpretation.[80]

This level of intervention and support may not be necessary for, or appropriate to, all contexts. However, this example illustrates the importance of working proactively and constructively with practitioners to ensure that the opportunities created by legal cooperation mechanisms on paper can be taken advantage of in practice.

6.4.4 *Creating opportunities for familiarization with different legal systems*

As noted previously, the diversity of legal traditions and structures around the world means that mutual legal assistance regimes need a certain amount of built-in flexibility to be workable. For this reason, cross-border legal cooperation regimes rarely insist on precise legal equivalence between the requesting State and requested State as a condition of cooperation.[81] Instead, States' parties may agree to provide legal assistance regardless of whether the conduct being investigated is punishable in both States.[82] Nevertheless, even if lack of legal equivalence is not a legal impediment to cooperation, it can still be a practical one. The UN Office on Drugs and Crime describes the problem as follows:

> Counsel grow accustomed to the legal regime within which they work on a daily basis, and it can sometimes be difficult to overcome the biases that become almost second nature when there has been limited exposure to other legal systems. Lawyers are usually trained in one of the major legal traditions of the world and, even today, it is relatively rare to see a lawyer who has been trained and practises in more than one of the major traditions. . . . Government lawyers also view themselves as being the guardians of their nation's laws and can view the unfamiliar as being the unobtainable, particularly as it relates to the possible dilution of laws that are designed to govern and protect the country's citizenry. Legal systems are heavily entrenched in a society, and particularly among members of the legal profession and judiciary. 'Upholding' the law has sometimes meant being inflexible in its application, perhaps nowhere more so than when members of one legal tradition ask members of another legal tradition to adopt their ways with respect to international cooperation. Such a reaction can sometimes have negative consequences when it comes to international cooperation.[83]

In other words, lack of understanding of how other legal systems work, and the structural and policy underpinnings for different approaches, can cause requests to be misinterpreted or de-prioritized and, in some cases, not actioned at all. A combination of education and awareness-raising seems the most promising route to overcoming these kinds of barriers. Creating opportunities for direct contact and exchanges of knowledge and views between practitioners from different jurisdictions is an important part of this. The OHCHR, in its 2016 final report to the UNHRC on accountability and access to remedy in business and human rights cases[84] highlights the importance of "facilitating contact and exchange of know-how between counterparts in other States"[85] as part of a series of practical suggestions to States as to how they can improve the effectiveness of domestic institutions in cross-border business and human rights cases. When it comes to creating opportunities for exposure to different legal systems, international professional networks such as the International Bar Association and the International Association of Prosecutors clearly play a vital role.

6.4.5 *Creating opportunities for peer learning and exchanges of views*

Peer review systems are increasing in number and are presently emerging as important mechanisms for building consensus as to good regulatory practice, as well as for providing opportunities for exposure to different legal regimes.

Examples of peer review systems can be found in international legal harmonization regimes. An important and influential example is the peer review system that has been built into the monitoring arrangements for the OECD Convention on Combating Bribery of Foreign Public Officials in International Business Transactions.[86] This system involves periodic evaluations by experts appointed from two other "examining" Member States (chosen on a rotation basis). The review process itself has two parts; the first involves a review of the States parties' relevant legislation, regulations, and policy directives to assess their compliance with the Convention, and the second focuses on practical implementation and enforcement.

Examples of this basic two-stage methodology can be found elsewhere, including as part of regulatory cooperation initiatives. The Financial Action Task Force, for instance, operates to a similar framework in its own peer review processes (known as "mutual evaluations").

6.4.6 *Addressing the problem of resource shortages through capacity-building, sharing of know-how, and the provision of technical assistance*

Lack of resources is a serious impediment to the proper and efficient functioning of legal cooperation regimes in many jurisdictions. Although the problem is an intractable one, it is at least acknowledged in many international legal cooperation regimes, and especially those between States at different stages of development. The UN Convention Against Corruption,[87] for instance, calls on State parties to

> according to their capacity, consider affording one another the widest measure of technical assistance, especially for the benefit of developing countries, in their respective plans and programmes to combat corruption, including material support and training . . . and training and assistance and the mutual exchange of relevant experience and specialized knowledge, which will facilitate international cooperation between States Parties in the areas of extradition and mutual legal assistance.[88]

6.5 Conclusion

In business and human rights cases, there is often more than one State with a potential regulatory, political, or economic interest in the matter. The debate about the role of these different States in ensuring access to remedy for victims of business-related human rights abuses looks set to carry on for the time being. There is a range of views among business and human rights practitioners about where efforts should be best directed. Should the focus be on developing more opportunities (indeed legal obligations) for home States to determine and deliver remedies in these cases? Or, would it be better to step up efforts to ensure that victims can access remedies closer to home?

In reality, progress is needed on both fronts. But whatever the outcome of this wider debate – and regardless of which forums are chosen in individual cases – domestic courts will continue to rely on a variety of methods of cross-border cooperation in business and human rights cases. As States work toward the possibility of a future international treaty on business and human rights it will be important to take account of the cross-border legal cooperation arrangements that already exist. This is true for two reasons: first, because of the possibility that there may be legal architecture that is already available for use in business and human rights cases that could be adapted and improved upon, rather than replaced; and second, because of what these regimes can teach us about the practical, organizational, strategic, technological, and human components (as well as the legal components) that can make the difference between a regime that fulfills its potential as a vehicle for dynamic and effective cross-border legal cooperation, and one that sits on a shelf.

The organizational- and operational-level interventions that may be needed to boost the effectiveness of cross-border legal cooperation in business and human rights cases will vary from setting to setting. In some cases this may be achieved through education and awareness-raising, or simply creating opportunities for practitioners from different jurisdictions to get to know each other. In other cases, technological innovations, such as new internet-based tools, may help to streamline the relevant procedures and improve the secure and speedy flow of information back and forth. For some cross-border arrangements (and particularly those between States at different stages of development) there is likely to be a need for capacity-building and technical assistance to strengthen institutions and remove legal and practical barriers to cooperation. Other contexts may require something more ambitious and permanent, such as a dedicated institution to provide advice and technical assistance to practitioners. While these practical details may seem small in themselves, they are an important part of strengthening the capacity of domestic courts and law-enforcement agencies to respond to business and human rights issues in cross-border cases, and ultimately improving the prospect of effective remedies for victims.

Notes

* The author is grateful to the OHCHR for its permission to refer to work undertaken in the course of the OHCHR Accountability and Remedy Project, in which the author was involved as a legal consultant. However, while this chapter draws on a range of different research sources and activities, the views expressed in this chapter are the personal views of the author and cannot be taken to reflect the views of the OHCHR or any other organization or institution.

1 Jennifer Zerk, *Multinationals and Corporate Social Responsibility: Limitations and Opportunities in International Law* (Cambridge University Press 2006).
2 Guiding Principles on Business and Human Rights: Implementing the United Nations "Protect, Respect and Remedy", UN Guiding Principles on Business and Human Rights, Annex to UNHRC, Report of the Special Representative of the Secretary-General on the issue of human rights and transnational corporations and other business enterprises, John Ruggie (21 March 2011) UN Doc Resolution A/HRC/17/31, Guiding Principle 1.
3 In this chapter, the "territorial State" means the State in which the harm has occurred.
4 For short case summaries of a small sample of cases, see Jennifer Zerk, 'Corporate Liability for Gross Human Rights Abuses: Towards a Fairer and More Effective System of Domestic Law Remedies' (February 2014) 17-23 <www.ohchr.org/Documents/Issues/Business/DomesticLawRemedies/StudyDomesticeLawRemedies.pdf> accessed 24 September 2019.
5 Ibid.
6 OHCHR, Explanatory notes on guidance to improve accountability and access to remedy for victims of business-related human rights abuse – Addendum to report of the United Nations High Commissioner for Human Rights (12 May 2016) UN Doc A/HRC/32/19/Add.1, para 24.
7 Gwynne Skinner, Robert McCorquodale, Olivier de Schutter and Andie Lambe, *The Third Pillar: Access to Judicial Remedies for Human Rights Violations by Transnational Business* (ICAR, CORE, ECCJ, 2013); Olivier de Schutter, 'Towards a Treaty on Business and Human Rights', in Frederic Bernard and Fatimata Niang (eds.), *Commerce et Droits Humains* (University of Geneva, Global Studies Institute, 2016).
8 Amnesty International and Business and Human Rights Resource Centre, 'Creating a Paradigm Shift: Legal Solutions to Improve Access to Remedy for Corporate Human Rights Abuse' (4 September 2017) <www.amnesty.org/en/documents/pol30/7037/2017/en/> accessed 24 September 2019; de Schutter (n 7) 95–7.
9 Traidcraft, 'Above the Law?: Time to Hold Irresponsible Companies to Account' (November 2015) 11 <https://corporate-responsibility.org/wp-content/uploads/2015/12/Above-the-Law-FINAL-EMBARGOED.pdf> accessed 24 September 2019; de Schutter (n 7) 97–100; see also Amnesty International and Business and Human Rights Resource Centre (n 8).
10 Zerk (n 4) 108–11.
11 However, for recent discussion see de Schutter (n 7) 121–8; OHCHR, Improving Accountability and Access to Remedy for Victims of Business-Related Human Rights Abuse (10 May 2017) UN Doc A/HRC/32/19, paras 24–28. On cooperation in the field of public (that is, criminal and administrative) law, see UN Working Group on Business and Human Rights, Best practices and how to improve on the effectiveness of cross-border cooperation between States with respect to law enforcement on the issue of business and human rights: Study of the Working Group on the issue of human rights and transnational corporations and other business enterprises (25 April 2017) UN Doc A/HRC/35/33.
12 UN Working Group on Business and Human Rights (n 11) paras 27–85.
13 See, eg, the European Convention on Mutual Assistance in Criminal Matters [1959] ETS 030. Arrangements between EU Member States are governed by the Council Act of 29 May 2000 establishing, in accordance with Article 34 of the Treaty on European Union, the Convention on Mutual Assistance in Criminal Matters between the Member States of the European Union [2000] OJ C 197/1.
14 In the EU, see, eg, the European Investigation Order (EIO) regime established pursuant to the Directive 2014/41/EU of the European Parliament and of the Council of 3 April 2014 regarding the European Investigation Order in criminal matters [2014] OJ L 130/1.

15 See United Nations Convention on Transnational Organized Crime, Annex I to UN General Assembly resolution 55/25 (8 January 2001) UN Doc A/RES/55/25, art 18; Protocol to Prevent, Suppress and Punish Trafficking in Persons, Especially Women and Children, supplementing the United Nations Convention against Transnational Organized Crime, Annex II to UN General Assembly resolution 55/25 (8 January 2001) UN Doc A/RES/55/25, art 10; United Nations Convention Against Corruption, Annex to UN General Assembly resolution 58/4 (31 October 2003) UN Doc A/RES/58/4, art 46.
16 United Nations Convention on Transnational Organized Crime (n 15).
17 Ibid. art 18(1).
18 Ibid. art 18(3).
19 United Nations Convention Against Corruption (n 15) art 46.
20 Agreement between the EU and Japan on mutual legal assistance in criminal matters [2010] OJ L 39/20.
21 Council regulation (EC) No 1348/2000 of 29 May 2000 on the service in the Member States of judicial and extrajudicial documents in civil or commercial matters [2000] OJ L 160/37.
22 Convention on the Taking of Evidence Abroad in Civil or Commercial Matters, 847 UNTS 231.
23 Council Regulation (EC) No 1206/2001 of 28 May 2001 on cooperation between the courts of the Member States in the taking of evidence in civil or commercial matters [2001] OJ L 174/1.
24 Ibid. art 10(4).
25 European Convention on Mutual Assistance in Criminal Matters (n 13). Note that a further legal basis was provided by way of a 2002 EU Council Decision. See Council Framework Decision of 13 June 2002 on joint investigation teams [2002] OJ L 162/1.
26 European Convention on Mutual Assistance in Criminal Matters (n 13) art 13.
27 See Council Framework Decision of 13 June 2002 on joint investigation teams (n 25) art 1.
28 For an example of a model JIT agreement see Council Resolution on a Model Agreement for setting up a Joint Investigation Team (JIT) [2017] OJ C 18/1.
29 The EU's manual on JITs recommends that the team leader should be a member of the judiciary in those jurisdictions, and in those cases, where investigations are typically directed by an investigating magistrate or prosecutor, and the appropriate law enforcement agencies (for example, the police) in other cases. See Council of the European Union, Joint Investigations Team Manual (4 November 2011) Doc 15790/1/11 9 <http://library.college.police.uk/docs/joint-investigations-team-manual-2011.pdf> accessed 24 September 2019.
30 For further information, see ibid. See also OHCHR, Business and Human Rights: Enhancing Accountability and Access to Remedy: International operational-level cooperation with respect to criminal investigations: a short study of the work of Joint Investigation Teams (JITs) in the European Union (27 July 2015) <www.ohchr.org/Documents/Issues/Business/DomesticLawRemedies/Project6_a_study_JIs_in_EU.pdf> accessed 24 September 2019.
31 OHCHR, OHCHR Accountability and Remedy Project: Improving accountability and access to remedy in cases of business involvement in human rights abuses <www.ohchr.org/EN/Issues/Business/Pages/OHCHRaccountabilityandremedyproject.aspx> accessed 24 September 2019.
32 OHCHR (n 30) 9 (footnotes omitted).
33 For further information, see Openbaar ministerie, 'MH17 Crash: Criminal Investigation MH 17' <www.om.nl/onderwerpen/mh17-crash/> accessed 24 September 2019.

34 Agreement on Mutual Legal Assistance Between the United States of American and the European Union (25 June 2003), Treaties and other international acts series 10–201.1, art 5.
35 Ibid.
36 In the EU, see, eg, Directive 2014/41/EU (n 14).
37 OHCHR (n 30).
38 OHCHR (n 30) 11 (footnotes omitted). See further Conny Rijken and Gert Vermeulen, 'The Legal and Practical Implementation of JITs: The Bumpy Road from EU to Member State Level', in Conny Rijken and Gert Vermeulen (eds.), *Joint Investigation Teams in the European Union: from Theory to Practice* (TMC Asser Press 2006).
39 UN Working Group on Business and Human Rights (n 11).
40 Ibid. para 39.
41 Ibid. para 82.
42 For further examples of cross-border bribery cases in which there was substantial cooperation between different States with respect to investigation, prosecution, and sanctioning of the relevant companies, see Jennifer Zerk, 'Extraterritorial Jurisdiction: Lessons for the Business and Human Rights Sphere from Six Regulatory Areas: A Report for the Harvard Corporate Social Responsibility Initiative to Help Inform the Mandate of the UNSG's Special Representative on Business and Human Rights', Working Paper No. 59/2010, 44–46 <www://sites.hks.harvard.edu/m-rcbg/CSRI/publications/workingpaper_59_zerk.pdf> accessed 24 September 2019.
43 United Nations Convention on Transnational Organized Crime (n 15).
44 Protocol to Prevent, Suppress and Punish Trafficking in Persons, Especially Women and Children, supplementing the United Nations Convention against Transnational Organized Crime (n 15).
45 United Nations Convention on Transnational Organized Crime (n 15) art 27.
46 Ibid. arts 13–14.
47 Ibid. art 26.
48 Protocol to Prevent, Suppress and Punish Trafficking in Persons, Especially Women and Children, supplementing the United Nations Convention against Transnational Organized Crime (n 15) art 10.
49 Ibid. art 11.
50 Becky Allen and Jennifer Zerk, 'Information Is Power', (2005) 148 *Environment Information Bulletin* 14.
51 See, for instance, United Kingdom Freedom of Information Act 2000, s 1.
52 Directive 2003/4/EC of the European Parliament and of the Council of 28 January 2003 on public access to environmental information and repealing Council Directive 90/313/EEC [2003] OJ L 41/26, art 2(2); Allen and Zerk (n 50).
53 Directive 2003/4/EC (n 52) art 4.
54 Zerk (n 1) 177–8.
55 United Nations Economic Commission for Europe, Convention on Access to Information, Public Participation in Decision-making and Access to Justice in Environmental Matters (25 June 1998).
56 Ibid. art 1.
57 Phase 1 of the Accountability and Remedy Project was concerned with judicial mechanisms and was carried out pursuant to the mandate set out in UNHRC, Human rights and transnational corporations and other business enterprises (27 June 2014) UN Doc A/HRC/RES/26/22, para 7. The OHCHR then received a follow-up request from the UNHRC to "identify and analyse lessons learned, best practices, challenges and possibilities to improve the effectiveness of *State-based non-judicial mechanisms* that are relevant for the respect by business

enterprises for human rights, including in a cross-border context", see UNHRC, Business and Human Rights: Improving Accountability and Access to Remedy (15 July 2016) UN Doc A/HRC/RES/32/10 (emphasis added). At the time of writing, this second phase of work focusing on State-based *non-judicial* remedies (Phase 2) was already underway.

58 OHCHR (n 11) para 18.1.
59 UN Working Group on Business and Human Rights (n 11) para 14.
60 International Association of Prosecutors <www.iap-association.org/> accessed 24 September 2019.
61 International Association of Labour Inspection <www.iali-aiit.org/> accessed 24 September 2019.
62 For example, the Interpol Pollution Crime Working Group <www.interpol.int/Crime-areas/Environmental-crime/Committee-and-Working-Groups/Pollution-Crime-Working-Group> accessed 24 September 2019. See also UN Working Group on Business and Human Rights (n 11) para 48.
63 See, for instance, the Camden Asset Recovery Inter-Agency Network, hosted by Europol. See also UN Working Group on Business and Human Rights (n 11) para 76.
64 Commission Decision of 6 June 2001 establishing the European Securities Committee [2001] OJ L 191/45.
65 See International Organisation of Securities Commissions <www.iosco.org/about/?subsection=display_committee&cmtid=19> accessed 24 September 2019.
66 Financial Action Task Force, Annual Report 2015–2016, 31 <www.fatf-gafi.org/media/fatf/documents/reports/FATF-annual-report-2015–2016.pdf> accessed 24 September 2019.
67 See, eg, United Nations Convention on Transnational Organized Crime (n 15) art 27; ILO, Protocol of 2014 to the Forced Labour Convention, 1930 (11 June 2014) para 14.
68 OHCHR (n 11) para 9.6.
69 OHCHR (n 30) 16.
70 OHCHR (n 6) paras 36–38. See also UN Working Group on Business and Human Rights (n 11), esp para 13,
71 OHCHR (n 6).
72 Ibid. 15 (para 9.5).
73 European Convention on Mutual Assistance in Criminal Matters (n 13).
74 Council Framework Decision (n 25).
75 As opposed to, say, a parallel or "mirror" investigation.
76 Ludo Block, 'Joint Investigation Teams: The Panacea for Fighting Organised Crime?' (25 August 2011) 28 <https://papers.ssrn.com/sol3/papers.cfm?abstract_id=1981641> accessed 24 September 2019.
77 OHCHR (n 30) 13.
78 Ibid. 9.
79 Council Framework Decision of 13 June 2002 on joint investigation teams (n 25).
80 OHCHR (n 30) 6.
81 Regimes on extradition are exceptions to this, in which "double criminality" is virtually always a requirement.
82 See, for instance, European Convention on Mutual Assistance in Criminal Matters (n 13) arts 1 and 2.
83 UN Office on Drugs and Crime, Manual on Legal Assistance and Extradition (UN 2012) 8 <www.unodc.org/documents/organized-crime/Publications/Mutual_Legal_Assistance_Ebook_E.pdf> accessed 24 September 2019.
84 OHCHR (n 6).
85 Ibid. 15 (para 9.6), 20 (para 17.5).

86 OECD Convention on Combating Bribery of Foreign Public Officials in International Business Transactions (17 December 1997) DAFFE/IME/BR(97)20, art 12.
87 United Nations Convention Against Corruption (n 15).
88 Ibid. art 60.

Bibliography

Allen B and Zerk J, 'Information Is Power', (2005) 148 *Environment Information Bulletin* 14.

Block L, 'Joint Investigation Teams: The Panacea for Fighting Organised Crime?' (25 August 2011) <https://papers.ssrn.com/sol3/papers.cfm?abstract_id=1981641>

de Schutter O, 'Towards a Treaty on Business and Human Rights', in Frederic Bernard and Fatimata Niang (eds.), *Commerce et Droits Humains* (University of Geneva, Global Studies Institute 2016).

Rijken C and Vermeulen G, 'The Legal and Practical Implementation of JITs: The Bumpy Road from EU to Member State Level', in Conny Rijken and Gert Vermeulen (eds.), *Joint Investigation Teams in the European Union: From Theory to Practice* (TMC Asser Press 2006).

Skinner G, McCorquodale R, de Schutter O and Lambe A, *The Third Pillar: Access to Judicial Remedies for Human Rights Violations by Transnational Business* (ICAR, CORE, ECCJ, 2013).

Zerk J, 'Extraterritorial Jurisdiction: Lessons for the Business and Human Rights Sphere from Six Regulatory Areas: A Report for the Harvard Corporate Social Responsibility Initiative to Help Inform the Mandate of the UNSG's Special Representative on Business and Human Rights', Working Paper No. 59/2010, <www://sites.hks.harvard.edu/m-rcbg/CSRI/publications/workingpaper_59_zerk.pdf>

———, *Multinationals and Corporate Social Responsibility: Limitations and Opportunities in International Law* (Cambridge University Press 2006).

7 *Ignorantia facti excusat?* The viability of due diligence as a model to establish international criminal accountability for corporate actors purchasing natural resources from conflict zones

*Daniëlla Dam-de Jong**

7.1 Introduction

"Wars need money",[1] and especially since the 1990s, with superpower financing drying up as a result of the end of the Cold War, exploitation of and trade in natural resources have become primary means for parties to an armed conflict to obtain the necessary revenues to finance their armed struggle.[2] Examples include the former armed conflicts in Angola, Sierra Leone, and Côte d'Ivoire, which were financed by the trade in diamonds, or the current armed conflict in the DRC, which is financed by the trade in precious minerals and gold. Because of the commercial nature of these practices, corporations are by definition involved. Reports drafted by a variety of Panels of Experts established by the UN Security Council in relation to natural-resources-driven armed conflicts show the participation of corporations in such diverse practices as the exploitation of natural resources in rebel-controlled territory, the smuggling of natural resources from conflict zone, and the delivery of weapons to armed groups in exchange for natural resources.[3]

In addition to these direct forms of corporate involvement in the illicit exploitation of and trade in natural resources, many other corporations contribute indirectly, notably by purchasing natural resources from conflict regions.[4] It is on these corporations that the current contribution focuses. Although they are more remote from the realities of the armed conflict, corporations purchasing natural resources from conflict regions indirectly contribute to perpetuating often devastating armed conflicts.[5] After all, the very reason for armed groups to engage in the exploitation of natural resources is because they know they will be able to sell the natural resources and make a profit.

Calls to hold corporations accountable for their contribution to the financing of bloody armed conflicts have grown louder in recent years. In 2003, former ICC prosecutor Luis Moreno-Ocampo pointed to the relationship between the direct perpetrators of international crimes and those who facilitate these crimes, designating the latter as "authors of the crimes, even if they are based in other countries".[6] In addition, current ICC prosecutor Fatou Bensouda, in a 2013 interview, advanced the possibility that corporate officials responsible for the financing of armed conflicts would be charged before the ICC.[7] Furthermore, in a 2016 Policy Paper on Case Selection and Prioritisation, the prosecutor clearly stated her determination "to give particular consideration to prosecuting Rome Statute crimes that are committed by means of, or that result in, *inter alia* . . . the illegal exploitation of natural resources".[8] This statement has raised expectations in the NGO community that the ICC will be more inclined in the future to address corporate involvement in international crimes.[9]

In light of these developments, the current contribution aims to assess the potential of the Rome Statute framework to address corporate involvement in the illegal exploitation of natural resources, focusing specifically on the role of corporate actors in purchasing natural resources from conflict regions. The principal question that this contribution aims to answer is whether, and to what extent, the Rome Statute offers a viable framework to hold corporate actors accountable for purchasing natural resources from conflict regions. For this purpose, the current contribution focuses on the war crime of pillage, since this is the only avenue available to hold corporate officials directly accountable for the purchasing of natural resources from conflict regions. It identifies opportunities, constraints, and challenges offered by the war crime of pillage. The most important challenge that the current contribution identifies is the issue of *mens rea* for corporate actors. The war crime of pillage holds potential if it can be demonstrated that the corporate official acted with full knowledge of the circumstances when he or she purchased the natural resources. However, this is often not in conformity with practical realities. Besides the most apparent cases of direct business dealings between corporations and armed groups, the majority of corporate officials purchasing natural resources from conflict zones do not trade directly with armed groups and/or do not act with the specific intent to commit international crimes or to contribute to their commission. Rather, these corporate officials simply "bury their heads in the sand".[10]

This raises the question of whether a deliberate choice on the part of corporate officials to remain ignorant with respect to the origin of their natural-resource procurements implies that these officials are beyond the reach of international criminal law. A domestic decision by the Swiss prosecutor in 2015 to dismiss proceedings against Argor Heraeus, a major Swiss gold refiner that had refined three tons of gold procured from the African Great Lakes region, is a case in point to illustrate the problem.[11] Argor Heraeus escaped responsibility for refining illegal gold because the prosecutor was unable to gather sufficient evidence pointing to the corporation's positive knowledge concerning the illicit origin of the gold it refined, notwithstanding a wealth of indications pointing in this direction that were simply ignored by officials within the corporation.

However, the facts of this case predate important developments in the framework of CSR. The numerous initiatives that have been developed in recent decades to flesh out CSR, even though primarily as a matter of soft law, have resulted in an increasingly refined standard for corporations against which to assess their behavior, which is one of due diligence. Due diligence is defined in general terms as "an ongoing risk management process . . . in order to identify, prevent, mitigate and account for how [a company] addresses its adverse human rights impacts".[12] This standard has also been embraced in a more hard-law context by the UN Security Council as part of its natural resource-related sanctions regimes,[13] and by national jurisdictions. The current contribution assesses the extent to which the investigative duty that is inherent in the due diligence standard can help to determine knowledge for the purpose of international criminal law.

This contribution proceeds in three steps. Section 7.2 examines the opportunities, constraints, and challenges of the war crime of pillage, with an emphasis on the mental elements of the crime. Section 7.3 focuses on the due diligence standards that have been developed over the past decade, and the question of how they could inform the mental elements of the war crime of pillage. Finally, Section 7.4 scrutinizes the viability of the Rome Statute framework for addressing the role of corporate actors in perpetuating armed conflicts through their purchasing policies.

7.2 Establishing criminal accountability for corporate officials purchasing natural resources from conflict regions

This section explores how the purchasing of natural resources by corporate actors from conflict regions could be brought under the Rome Statute. Section 7.2.1 introduces the war crime of pillage as the most promising avenue to prosecute these practices. Section 7.2.2 discusses the elements of the crime in more detail.

7.2.1 The war crime of pillage and illegal exploitation of natural resources

The Rome Statute does not contain a crime definition that is specifically tailored to the prosecution of acts of illicit exploitation of, or trade in, natural resources. In the absence of such an express definition, the war crime of pillage, included in Article 8(2)(b)(xvi) and 8(2)(e)(v) of the Rome Statute, would be the most appropriate avenue to address the illicit exploitation of natural resources in conflict regions.[14] This is because it is the only crime listed in the Statute that would allow us to recognize illicit exploitation and trafficking as criminal acts in themselves, instead of seeing these acts as means to commit other crimes, such as the war crimes of murder or slavery. In addition, the relevance of the war crime of pillage for the illicit exploitation and trafficking of natural resources has been confirmed by the ICJ, which expressly relied on the underlying prohibition of pillaging in international humanitarian law to hold Uganda responsible for acts of plundering of natural resources in the DRC committed by members of its armed forces.[15] Even though its relevance is therefore clear, there is very little to rely on as precedent for interpretation of the crime in relation to the illicit exploitation and trafficking of natural resources from conflict regions. With the exception of the Nuremberg Tribunal and the subsequent military tribunals, which dealt more generally with the issue of exploitation of occupied territory under the rubric of "plunder",[16] international criminal courts have reserved the crime of pillage for raids of villages and thefts of personal belongings of civilians.[17]

Pillage can be defined as the intentional appropriation of property in an armed conflict for the personal use of the perpetrator and without the consent of the owner.[18] In other words, it concerns theft committed within the context of an armed conflict. As a property crime, it aims to preserve the rights of persons with respect to their belongings, without regard for the nature of the property (physical or intellectual) or the owners (civilians or the State).[19] The notion of "property" would therefore cover all forms of property, including rights with respect to property (such as concessions) and State-owned property.

The inclusion of State-owned property is of the utmost importance for the applicability of the crime to natural resources, since their international legal status is governed by the principle of permanent sovereignty over natural resources. This principle considers natural resources to constitute State property and leaves questions of ownership to national law.[20] This implies that it is ultimately the government, as the representative of the State, which must determine ownership in concrete circumstances. Of course, this raises a number of fundamental questions regarding the application of pillage to internal armed conflict situations. A first relates to the question of whether the government in power is entitled to exercise ownership rights over natural resources on behalf of the State in situations in which its authority as the principal State representative is contested. Could armed groups qualify as State representatives, for example, when they exercise effective control over portions of the territory? And what does this imply for corporations doing business with these armed groups? Even though these questions are important and may prove to be an actual concern impacting the criminality of the exploitation and trafficking of natural resources in particular situations, these situations would be exceptional. This is because international law formulates a presumption in favor of the *de jure* government as representative of the State that is very difficult to rebut.[21] The *de jure* government would remain entitled to dispose of the State's natural resources until the situation becomes ostensibly hopeless. Inversely, other entities claiming to represent the State would not be entitled to dispose of the State's natural resources as long as the conflict remains undecided.[22] Exploitation of natural resources by armed groups would therefore, as a general rule, be illegal, while exploitation by the domestic government would be legal.

This brings us to a second, perhaps even more fundamental, question, which shows the limitations of the war crime of pillage as a means to address the contribution of natural resources to financing armed conflicts. The war crime of pillage clearly creates inequality between the different parties to an internal armed conflict.[23] The war crime of pillage would not be an appropriate avenue to prosecute corporate actors procuring natural resources from the State, even though the proceeds may just as well be used to finance military actions that entail serious human rights violations. This does not mean that corporate actors would necessarily meet impunity when trading with a government that commits gross human rights violations; however, it does imply that these practices should be approached differently from an international criminal law perspective. Instead of prosecuting corporate actors for the economic crime of procuring natural resources, the prosecutor would have to focus on the contribution of these actors to more classic crimes, such as murder, torture, or slavery, that were committed with the proceeds of the natural resources sales.[24]

The following section examines the requirements that have to be met in order to establish criminal accountability for corporate actors purchasing natural resources from conflict zones. In this respect, it is important to note from the outset that the Rome Statute is centered around the notion of individual responsibility for international crimes, thereby ruling out the possibility to try corporations directly.[25] A proposal by France to include a provision on criminal liability for legal persons in the Statute did not make it to the final text.[26] Of course, this is not cast in stone – the Statute could be amended at some point in the future to accommodate corporate criminal liability. However, for the purposes of this contribution it is relevant to note that prosecution for acts of purchasing natural resources from conflict zones would be confined to individuals representing the corporation.

Criminal accountability for the purchasing of natural resources can be approached from two different perspectives.[27] The first is to consider purchasing as a form of pillage itself through the notion of indirect appropriation (receiving stolen goods).[28] This is the approach that was followed in earlier case law by the Nuremberg Tribunal and related courts.[29] The second approach is to consider purchasing of the natural resources as providing a form of assistance, or as a contribution to the crime of pillage as committed by an armed group. This is the avenue that was taken by the Swiss prosecutor in the Argor Hereaus case referred to in the introduction. The current contribution chooses the first perspective, because it is more straightforward and places more direct emphasis on the corporate actor itself. The challenges are *grosso modo* similar for both modes of liability.

7.2.2 Purchasing natural resources as a form of pillage

The Elements of Crimes for the Rome Statute distinguish five elements for the war crime of pillage: (1) the perpetrator appropriated certain property; (2) the perpetrator intended to deprive the owner of the property and to appropriate it for private or personal use; (3) the appropriation was without the consent of the owner; (4) the conduct took place in the context of, and was associated with, an international armed conflict/with an armed conflict not of an international character; and (5) the perpetrator was aware of factual circumstances that established the existence of an armed conflict. These elements are briefly considered in the following sub-sections.

1. Actus reus

The objective elements of the crime of pillage are fairly straightforward in the sense that it concerns the appropriation (or taking) of property without the consent of the owner during an armed conflict. Since it has already been determined that natural resources constitute property, the most important issue in relation to this element relates to the notion of appropriation. Can one contend that the term "appropriation" includes forms of indirect appropriation? As demonstrated by Stewart, post-World War II (WWII) case law supports such a broad understanding of the notion of appropriation.[30] Since the Elements of Crime do not qualify the notion either, it would in principle be possible to construe the notion of appropriation as including the purchasing of natural resources by actors that were not involved in the original exploitation and trafficking.[31] This reading is supported by various domestic criminal systems that incorporate notions of direct and indirect appropriation within the notion of theft.[32]

Naturally, property can only be stolen if the owner did not consent to the appropriation. It is important to note that consent must be freely given. Post-WWII case law indicates that involuntary transfer of ownership does not qualify as consent.[33] This implies that armed groups that have taken effective control over a mine do not qualify as owners and, hence, that corporations cannot rely on concessions granted by them.

Finally, it must be established that the conduct took place in the context of, and was associated with, an armed conflict, whether of an international or internal character. This element is crucial for the purpose of establishing that a war crime has been committed. It requires a nexus between the crime and the armed conflict. More specifically, it requires that "the perpetrator acted in furtherance of or under the guise of the armed conflict".[34] Since the current contribution focuses on the exploitation of natural resources as a means to finance an armed conflict, the nexus element will be readily satisfied in most situations. Nevertheless, it remains important to apply the nexus requirement on a case-by-case basis.

2. *Mens rea*

The Elements of Crime formulate specific subjective elements for the war crime of pillage. These elements should therefore be considered as setting out a *dolus specialis* for the war crime of pillage that supersedes the general rules on *mens rea* formulated in Article 30 of the Rome Statute. In its judgment in the *Katanga* case, Trial Chamber II indicated that "pillaging requires a particular mental element or *dolus specialis.* The latter consists in the fact that the perpetrator intended to 'deprive the owner' of his or her property and to 'appropriate . . . for private or personal use'".[35] In addition, the Chamber specified that "under article 30(3) of the Statute the perpetrator must also have known that the appropriation was without the consent of the owner [and] that the perpetrator was aware of 'factual circumstances that established the existence of an armed conflict'".

It must therefore be proven that the corporate official purchasing the natural resources did so purposely and with knowledge of the circumstances. The Chamber further noted that "the volitional element can be inferred from the specific conduct of the perpetrator of the deprivation."[36] Since the current contribution is concerned with commercial transactions, the intention to appropriate the property is materialized in the transaction.

A complicating factor may be the requirement that the appropriation was committed for private or personal use. In relation to members of armed groups committing pillage, the interpretation of this requirement is not as straightforward as it seems. It could either oppose exploitation for the purpose of personal enrichment of the members of the armed group ("private") to exploitation for the purpose of financing an armed conflict ("public"), or it could call for a distinction between natural resources exploited in the interest of the armed group (the procurement of weapons, food, and clothes for the members of the armed group as a "private" purpose) and exploitation in the interest of the local population (financing a civilian administration as a "public" purpose).[37] However, notwithstanding the problematic effects of this qualification for determining the scope of the war crime of pillage committed by armed groups, one may assume that it will not directly affect the application of the crime in relation to corporate actors, since commercial actors act almost by definition for private or personal purposes.[38]

More importantly, however, the cognitive component of the *mens rea* prescribes that the perpetrator must "*have known* that the appropriation was without the consent of the owner" and that he or she was aware of factual circumstances establishing the existence of an armed conflict.[39] This cognitive element, which in fact requires the prosecutor to establish that the perpetrator was aware that the property was stolen and that it originated from a conflict region, is an essential component of the requisite *mens rea* for the crime. It is precisely this awareness that is often difficult to ascertain in practice, especially when the corporate official dealt with an intermediary rather than with the armed group directly.

This raises the question of the standard for *mens rea* that is encompassed in the Rome Statute. Article 30(3) defines knowledge as "awareness that a circumstance exists or a consequence *will* occur in the ordinary course of events".[40] This has been interpreted to imply positive knowledge that a circumstance exists or virtual certainty that a consequence will occur.[41] In other words, it must be proven that the accused had positive knowledge of the illegal origin of the natural resources or, at a minimum, that he or she was aware that the illegal origin was virtually certain. Strict adherence to the positive knowledge test would make it virtually impossible to prosecute corporate officials purchasing natural resources from conflict regions under the Rome Statute, since it rarely happens that a corporate official knows for certain that the natural resources that he or she procured were obtained from illicit exploitation by an armed group. More likely, he or she will have ignored indications pointing to that direction, unless he or she traded directly with the armed group concerned.

Does this mean that the ICC cannot play a role in addressing these practices? The drafters of the Rome Statute have indeed made an express choice to exclude a "should have known" or *dolus eventualis* standard from the remit of the ICC.[42] However, they have thereby departed from the practice of *ad hoc* criminal tribunals, which do accept a *dolus eventualis* test.[43] In addition, the *dolus eventualis* test is common to several national jurisdictions, which themselves play an important role in the Rome Statute framework based on the principle of complementarity.[44] In light of this other practice, the following section introduces due diligence as an arguably acceptable bridge between simple risk-taking as excluded by the Rome Statute and the stringent requirement of virtual certainty. Section 7.3 argues that a failure by corporate officials to conduct a proper investigation into the origin of the natural resources that they purchased can inform the subjective elements of the crime of pillage. For this purpose, it explores, first, the extent to which international law currently contains an obligation for corporations to assess risks in the supply chain, and what this obligation entails. It subsequently examines the legal status of this due diligence obligation and how it can be used within the context of international criminal law.

7.3 The due diligence model and its potential for international criminal law

The concept of due diligence refers to a standard of care aimed at preventing the occurrence of harm caused either by an actor's own behavior or by third parties on which the actor exerts influence.[45] The concept as such has a longstanding tradition in international law. It occupies an important place in various fields in international law, including international environmental and human rights law.[46] Due diligence obligations are typically obligations of conduct, often phrased as obligations to take all reasonable or appropriate measures.[47] As such, this type of obligation can be defined as a standard of conduct that is required to discharge other – more material – obligations.[48]

This section traces the development of due diligence standards for corporate actors, starting with human rights due diligence as developed within the UN to more specific due diligence requirements relating to the minerals supply chain. It assesses the nature and legal status of the due diligence standards for corporations for the purpose of evaluating the viability of using this model within the context of international criminal law.

7.3.1 The emergence of a standard: human rights due diligence

Specifically for corporations, due diligence standards started to gain traction notably as a result of the adoption of the UNGPs, also referred to as the "Ruggie Principles", named after UN Special Representative on Business and Human Rights John Ruggie.[49] These principles provide a framework for States and corporations to prevent corporate human rights abuses. The concept of due diligence figures prominently in the UNGPs as a means to address negative human rights impacts by corporations. It is first promulgated as a means for States to discharge their obligation under international law to protect human rights, which entails an obligation for States to prevent infringements on human rights by corporations operating within their jurisdiction. In relation to corporations, due diligence is presented as a means for them to prevent negative human rights impacts ensuing from their operations.[50]

More specifically, Guiding Principle 15 formulates a recommendation for corporations to "have in place policies and processes appropriate to their size and circumstances, including . . . [a] human rights due diligence process to identify, prevent, mitigate and account for how they address their impacts on human rights". The key provision is Guiding Principle 17, which defines human rights due diligence in the corporate context as an ongoing process aimed at identifying, preventing, and mitigating human rights impacts, as well as to account for how these impacts are addressed. Most importantly, this requirement relates not only to the corporation's own activities, but also to its business relationships.[51] It therefore entails an obligation for corporate actors to investigate their suppliers and other business partners.

As such, the guidelines provide a framework for action, but they do not provide clear legal standards that can be relied on in a criminal law context. Besides the fact that the guidelines do not formulate obligations under international law in the first place, another impediment is their lack of precision. The guidelines provide much discretion in terms of their operationalization and the scope of the due diligence exercise. This lack of precision makes it extremely difficult to translate the guidelines into legal obligations.

7.3.2 Specific due diligence guidelines for the minerals sector

Inspired by the UNGPs, the concept of human rights due diligence was also included in the 2011 revision of the OECD Guidelines for Multinational Enterprises. The inclusion of human rights due diligence significantly developed the basic due diligence requirements that were part of previous OECD Guidelines.[52] It also spurred the development of more specific guidelines within the OECD, which aim to provide corporations in designated sectors with practical guidelines on how to implement due diligence in their supply chains. For the purposes of the present contribution, the most relevant of these documents is the OECD Due Diligence Guidance for Responsible Supply Chains of Minerals from Conflict-Affected and High-Risk Areas.[53]

This Guidance applies to corporations based in OECD and other adherent countries that operate in or procure minerals from volatile regions worldwide, including, but not limited to, conflict regions. As regards the material scope, it is relevant to note that the Guidance applies exclusively to minerals, thereby excluding other natural resources that finance armed conflicts, such as timber. In practice, the Guidance's primary focus is on tin, tantalum, tungsten, and gold (3TG). These minerals have a high commercial value and a strong connection to the financing of the armed conflict in the DRC. The armed conflict in this State was in fact a primary concern of the drafters. The Guidance was developed in close cooperation with the UN Group of Experts on the DRC, established by the UN Security Council, and the International Conference on the Great Lakes Region, an inter-governmental organization consisting of States in the African Great Lakes region.

The Guidance introduces a five-step, risk-based approach to due diligence, consisting of strengthening company management systems, identifying and assessing supply chain risks, designing and implementing strategies to respond to identified risks, conducting independent audits, and publicly disclosing supply chain due diligence and findings in annual sustainability or corporate responsibility reports.[54] Importantly, these risks include those associated with the commission of war crimes and providing direct or indirect support to armed groups.[55] The objective of the Guidance is therefore to provide corporations with the tools to conduct a proper risk assessment in order to enable them to adequately respond to these risks. Once a risk has been identified, the Guidance requires corporations to suspend contracts with their suppliers until the risk has been removed. These requirements form the core of the due diligence exercise.

For the purposes of the current contribution, the most important feature of the Guidance is the independent investigative duty that it imposes on corporations in relation to their business partners. This duty is integrated in the various steps of the due diligence assessment and works throughout the supply chain. In terms of obligations, the Guidance distinguishes between "upstream" companies (that is, from mine to smelter or refiner), and "downstream" companies (from smelter or refiner to end-use products).[56] The reason for this distinction is related to the different capacities of the corporations within the supply chain to verify the origin of the minerals. For example, upstream companies are "expected to clarify chain of custody and the circumstances of mineral extraction, trade, handling and export and identify and assess risk by evaluating those circumstances against the model supply chain policy on minerals from conflict-affected and high-risk areas", while downstream companies are required to assess the due diligence practices of their smelters or refiners.[57] Importantly, the Guidance identifies "red flags" that trigger application of the Guidance. These refer to locations (the minerals originate from or have been transported via a conflict-affected or high-risk area; the minerals are claimed to originate from a country that has limited known reserves, or from a country that is known as a transit country) and suppliers (the supplier has interests in a company that supplies minerals from, or operates in, a red-flag location; or is known itself to have sourced minerals from a red-flag location within the past 12 months).[58]

In contrast to the UNGPs, the OECD Guidance therefore formulates detailed requirements regarding verification of the origin of the minerals. These requirements translate easily into concrete obligations for corporations procuring minerals from conflict regions. The following section considers the possibilities for transposing these requirements into the *mens rea* assessment under international criminal law.

7.3.3 Application of due diligence to the war crime of pillage

Interpretation of the Rome Statute is primarily governed by Articles 31 and 32 of the 1969 Vienna Convention on the Law of Treaties, except that the principle of legality incorporated in Article 22 of the Rome Statute opposes a liberal interpretation.[59] Therefore, interpretation of the knowledge requirement in Article 30 of the Rome Statute is suggested to proceed in light of the due diligence standards discussed in this section. However, since this interpretation would provide a specific meaning to Article 30 that was not envisaged previously, the principle of legality prescribes that the due diligence standards can only be used as an interpretative tool if it can be established that the corporation was under a legal obligation to conduct due diligence in the first place. The question can therefore be raised as to whether the due diligence requirements amount to legally binding obligations.

Of course, the Due Diligence Guidance itself is a soft-law instrument that does not impose direct obligations on corporations. Nevertheless, the Guidance, and the requirements that it contains, have been embraced by other institutions as well. First, the OECD Guidance in particular, and the due diligence requirements more generally, have been referred to in several resolutions adopted by the UN Security Council.[60] Furthermore, in its Resolution 1952 (2010) relating to the DRC, the Security Council took a bold step in the sense that it established an express link between compliance with the due diligence requirements and the imposition of financial and travel sanctions. It decided that the failure of an individual or entity to exercise due diligence consistent with the five-step approach set out in the resolution was a factor to be taken into account by the Sanctions Committee in its decision to place an individual or entity on the sanctions list.[61] In this way, the Security Council indirectly ensured that the Guidance became mandatory, at least for corporations operating in or sourcing from the DRC. In addition, the Council made it very clear that a failure to conduct due diligence would be considered an indication that the respective individual or entity was in fact violating the sanctions imposed by the Council.

Furthermore, due diligence obligations have increasingly become part of domestic legal systems. First and foremost, important measures have been taken in States from which a significant portion of conflict minerals are exported. The member States of the International Conference on the Great Lakes Region have adopted a regional certification system that incorporates the due diligence requirements of the OECD Guidance.[62] Furthermore, similar measures have been taken by consumer States. Under section 1502 of the US Dodd – Frank Act, corporations listed on the American stock market are obligated to report on the origin of the minerals in their products to the US Securities and Exchange Commission.[63] In addition, the EU has adopted a regulation that requires all major corporations – whether listed or not – importing raw 3TG minerals to conduct due diligence, based on the five-step approach set out in the OECD Guidance.[64] These developments signal the emergence of an obligation for corporations procuring minerals to conduct due diligence. Perhaps, we could even say that this obligation has already been in place for much longer on the national level, since the concept of due diligence is closely related to the duty of care that is part of tort law under most domestic systems.[65]

Therefore, there are persuasive arguments to accept due diligence as a legal obligation, at least under domestic law within various systems. In addition, exclusively in the context of minerals procured from the DRC, the Security Council resolution may have the effect of elevating due diligence to a rule of international law. As far as the OECD Guidance itself is concerned, no such conclusion can be drawn. The Guidance does not aim to impose directly binding obligations on corporations and leaves it up to the member States to decide whether to adopt binding national legislation to this effect.[66]

If we accept that a due diligence assessment could inform the subjective elements of the war crime of pillage, it would operate as both a sword and a shield. The most far-reaching option would be to use the due diligence assessment to determine positive knowledge on the part of the corporate official as to the origin of the minerals. The due diligence assessment would then directly inform the cognitive element of the crime of pillage (awareness of the illicit origin of the minerals and of the factual circumstances establishing the existence of an armed conflict). A failure by corporate officials to conduct a proper due diligence assessment – that is, an assessment that would encompass more than simply asking the supplier whether he or she has complied with relevant regulations – would then be used as evidence to prove that the official had the requisite awareness of the illegal origin of the minerals. This would be based on reasoning that the official, by deliberately not discharging his or her obligation to conduct due diligence, must have known that the minerals were stolen. A less far-reaching option would be to consider the (lack of a) due diligence assessment as a factor in a broader pattern. This is also more in line with UN Security Council sanctions practice, where the sanctions committee was instructed to "consider, *amongst other things*, whether the individual or entity has exercised due diligence".[67] In this setting, due diligence obligations could support other evidence at the disposal of the prosecutor because it places a positive obligation on corporations to acquire knowledge. After all, a deliberate choice by a corporate official to refrain from investigation, despite being confronted with strong indications pointing in the direction of the illicit origin of the natural resources that he or she is buying (such as procurement from red-flag locations or suppliers), can be regarded as indicative of intent. In contrast, if a corporate official can demonstrate having conducted proper due diligence and the prosecutor is unable to show that the official ignored readily available information on the origin of the minerals that were procured, the official should be able to rely on his or her due diligence efforts to refute knowledge.

7.4 Concluding remarks

This contribution set out to assess the viability of the Rome Statute framework to hold corporate officials accountable for purchasing natural resources from conflict regions. It evaluated the war crime of pillage as the principal avenue to address these practices. Conceptually, this crime is appropriate since it criminalizes theft committed within the context of an armed conflict. However, it also requires proof that the accused was actually aware that the property was stolen. This is a difficult test to satisfy within the context of establishing accountability for corporate officials purchasing conflict minerals, since the culprits are often removed from the situation and generally do not trade directly with the armed group that originally pillaged the natural resources.

Therefore, the question was raised as to whether current due diligence obligations developed for corporations sourcing minerals from conflict regions can inform the knowledge requirement under international criminal law. These due diligence obligations seek to eliminate the risk that corporations contribute to financing armed conflicts, and include an independent investigative duty for corporations throughout the supply chain regarding their suppliers. The current contribution argued that these obligations are an acceptable solution to bridge the gap between mere risk taking and full awareness of the circumstances. This would allow the ICC to play a role in addressing the contribution of commercial actors to perpetuating devastating armed conflicts.

Of course, international criminal law is but one of several possibilities to scrutinize these practices. From a regulatory perspective, the due diligence standards are in themselves powerful tools to address the practices. In addition, measures adopted by the UN Security Council play a pivotal role in curbing the trade in conflict resources. However, even when we focus exclusively on the possibilities of international criminal law, it should be kept in mind that the ICC itself is not the only relevant institution. Based on the principle of complementarity and national implementation legislation, most cases will be brought before national courts, many of which embrace broader notions of *mens rea*, including *dolus eventualis.* It may be assumed that an obligation to conduct due diligence can play a greater role in these trials, since a failure to conduct proper due diligence would readily qualify as wilful blindness. This will help to ensure that corporate actors can no longer bury their heads in the sand.

Notes

* Grotius Centre for International Legal Studies – Leiden University. This contribution builds on the author's previous research, notably Daniëlla Dam-de Jong, *International Law and the Governance of Natural Resources in Conflict and Post-Conflict Situations* (Cambridge University Press 2015); and Larissa van den Herik and Daniëlla Dam-de Jong, 'Revitalizing the Antique War Crime of Pillage: The Potential and Pitfalls of Using International Criminal Law to Address Illegal Resource Exploitation', (2011) 3 *Criminal Law Forum* 237.

1 Global Witness, 'The Sinews of War: Eliminating the Trade in Conflict Resources' (November 2006) 2 <www.globalwitness.org/sites/default/files/import/the_sinews_of_war.pdf> accessed 24 September 2019.

2 See, eg, Karen Ballentine and Jake Sherman (eds.), *The Political Economy of Armed Conflict: Beyond Greed, and Grievance* (Lynne Rienner Publishers 2003).

3 See, eg, Final Report of the Monitoring Mechanism on Angola Sanctions, (21 December 2000) UN Doc S/2000/1225, in particular paras 154–61; Report of the Panel of Experts appointed pursuant to Security Council resolution 1306 (2000), para 19, in relation to Sierra Leone, (15 December 2000) UN Doc S/2000/1195; and Final report of the Panel of Experts on the Illegal Exploitation of Natural Resources and Other Forms of Wealth of the Democratic Republic of the Congo, (16 October 2002) UN Doc S/2002/1146, which recommended that the Security Council impose financial sanctions against 29 corporations that were considered to be directly responsible for financing the armed conflict in the DRC, and which named and shamed 85 corporations considered to be violating the OECD Guidelines on Multinational Enterprises.

4 See, eg, Final Report of the UN Panel of Experts on Violations of Security Council Sanctions Against Unita: The "Fowler Report" (10 March 2000) UN Doc S/2000/203, paras 87–93. This report showed the relative ease with which diamonds exploited by the Angolan rebel movement União Nacional Para a Independência Total de Angola (UNITA) could enter the legal diamond market.
5 See, eg, OHCHR, Report of the Mapping Exercise Documenting the Most Serious Violations of Human Rights and International Humanitarian Law Committed within the Territory of the Democratic Republic of the Congo between March 1993 and June 2003, August 2010, para 727.
6 Second Assembly of States Parties to the Rome Statute of the International Criminal Court, Report of the Prosecutor of the ICC, Mr Luis Moreno-Ocampo, 8 September 2003 <www.icc-cpi.int/NR/rdonlyres/C073586C-7D46-4CBE-B901-0672908E8639/143656/LMO_20030908_En.pdf> accessed 24 September 2019.
7 See International Criminal Justice Today, 'International Corporate Liability in Conflict Zones', interview with the ICC Prosecutor Fatou Bensouda (21 March 2013) <www.international-criminal-justice-today.org/events/international-corporate-liability-in-conflict-zones/> accessed 24 September 2019.
8 ICC, 'Office of the Prosecutor: Policy Paper on Case Selection and Prioritisation' (15 September 2016) para 41 <www.icc-cpi.int/itemsdocuments/20160915_otp-policy_case-selection_eng.pdf> accessed 24 September 2019. Of course, this does not necessarily mean that the prosecutor would address the illicit exploitation of natural resources directly. She may also take it into account as a contextual factor when deciding on the prosecution of other crimes, such as enslavement as a crime against humanity in relation to civilians taken captive by rebel groups to work in mines.
9 See Nadia Bernaz, 'An Analysis of the ICC Office of the Prosecutor's Policy Paper on Case Selection and Prioritization from the Perspective of Business and Human Rights', (2017) 15 *Journal of International Criminal Justice* 528.
10 International Criminal Justice Today, 'International Corporate Liability in Conflict Zones', interview with the ICC Prosecutor Fatou Bensouda (n 7).
11 Schweizerisches Bundesanwaltschaft, Dismissal of proceedings against Argor-Heraeus, Case number SV13-MUA (Bern 10 March 2015). For more information and further references, see Business & Human Rights Resource Centre, 'Argor-Heraeus Investigation (re Dem. Rep. of Congo)' <www.business-humanrights.org/en/argor-heraeus-investigation-re-dem-rep-of-congo> accessed 24 September 2019. This gold refiner had refined 3 tons of gold obtained from a UK trading corporation that had close connections with a Congolese armed group.
12 See UNGPs Reporting Framework <www.ungpreporting.org/glossary/human-rights-due-diligence/> accessed 24 September 2019.
13 See, eg, UN Security Council Resolution 1952 (29 November 2010) UN Doc S/Res/1952 on the DRC.
14 For a more thorough analysis, see, eg, James Stewart, *Corporate War Crimes: Prosecuting the Pillage of Natural Resources* (Open Society Justice Initiative Publication 2011); van den Herik and Dam-de Jong (n *) 237–73; and Michael Lundberg, 'The Plunder of Natural Resources During War: A War Crime (?)', (2008) 39(3) *Georgetown Journal of International Law* 495.
15 ICJ, *Armed Activities on the Territory of the Congo (Democratic Republic of the Congo v. Uganda)*, Judgment of 19 December 2005, ICJ Rep 2005, para 245.
16 See *Trial of the Major War Criminals Before the International Military Tribunal*, Volume I, Nuremberg (1947) 239; *Trials of War Criminals Before the Nuremberg Military Tribunals Under Control Council Law No. 10*, Volume IX, 1341 and 1342. The terms plunder, spoliation, and pillage are generally recognized as synonymous. See Stewart (n 14) ch III.
17 For an overview of relevant case law, see van den Herik and Dam-de Jong (n *) 266–71. To this overview can be added ICC, *The Prosecutor v. Germain Katanga*,

Judgment pursuant to article 74 of the Statute, 7 March 2014, ICC-01/04-01/07-3436.

18 This definition is based on the Elements of Crimes that have been drafted specifically for the purposes of interpreting and applying the crime within the context of the Rome Statute. See ICC, Elements of Crimes, (ICC 2011) <www.icc-cpi.int/NR/rdonlyres/336923D8-A6AD-40EC-AD7B-45BF9DE73D56/0/ElementsOfCrimesEng.pdf> accessed 24 September 2019.

19 See van den Herik and Dam-de Jong (n *) 251–2.

20 Pursuant to the principle of permanent sovereignty over natural resources, every State owns the natural resources found within its jurisdiction. See, eg, UNGA resolution 1803 (XVII) of 14 December 1962, 'Permanent sovereignty over natural resources'. On this resolution and the principle of permanent sovereignty over natural resources generally, see Nico Schrijver, *Sovereignty over Natural Resources: Balancing Rights and Duties* (Cambridge University Press 1997).

21 See Hersch Lauterpacht, *Recognition in International Law* (first published 1947, Cambridge University Press 2013) 94; Tom Ruys, 'Of Arms, Funding and "Non-Lethal Assistance": Issues Surrounding Third-State Intervention in the Syrian Civil War', (2014) 13 *Chinese Journal of International Law* 38.

22 For an analysis of this question, see Daniëlla Dam-de Jong, 'Armed Opposition Groups and the Right to Exercise Control over Public Natural Resources: A Legal Analysis of the Cases of Libya and Syria', (2015) 62(1) *Netherlands International Law Review* 3.

23 See van den Herik and Dam-de Jong (n *) 254–5.

24 For relevant examples, see Harmen van der Wilt, 'Corporate Criminal Responsibility for International Crimes: Exploring the Possibilities', (2013) *Chinese Journal of International Law* 43. The Talisman case discussed by van der Wilt illustrates the difficulties of this approach.

25 There is an impressive body of legal literature discussing this limitation and ways to counter it. See, eg, in chronological order, Larissa van den Herik, 'Corporations as Future Subject of the International Criminal Court: An Exploration of the Counterarguments and Consequences', in Larissa van den Herik and Carsten Stahn (eds.), *Future Perspectives on International Criminal Justice* (TMC Asser Press 2010); Norman Farrell, 'Attributing Criminal Liability to Corporate Actors: Some Lessons from the International Tribunals', (2010) 8 *Journal of International Criminal Justice* 873; van der Wilt (n 24); Philipp Ambach, 'International Criminal Responsibility of Transnational Corporate Actors Doing Business in Zones of Armed Conflict', in Freya Baetens (ed.), *Investment Law within International Law: Integrationist Perspectives* (Cambridge University Press 2013); Joanna Kyriakakis, 'Corporations before International Criminal Courts: Implications for the International Criminal Justice Project', (2017) 30 *Leiden Journal of International Law* 221.

26 See van der Wilt (n 24) 46–9.

27 The current contribution focuses on the possibilities that arise directly out of the Rome Statute. However, it should be noted that in domestic proceedings the crime of money laundering would also offer a promising avenue to prosecute the purchasing of illegal natural resources. After all, by purchasing natural resources from armed groups, corporations assist these armed groups in disguising the illicit origin of the natural resources; it is in this way that illegally obtained natural resources enter the legal market. However, money laundering is not an autonomous offense; money can only be "laundered" if it has been obtained through a predicate crime. Prosecutions based on money laundering would therefore have to be linked to an underlying crime, such as pillage. See Jessie Ingle, 'The International Criminal Court and Financial Crime', in Barry Rider (ed.), *Research Handbook on International Financial Crime* (Edward Elgar Publishing 2015).

28 See Stewart (n 14), ch VII.
29 Ibid.
30 Ibid. 35–7.
31 Ibid.
32 Ibid.
33 See, eg, *United States v Krauch et al.* (*I.G. Farben* Case), VIII(10) Trials of War Criminals Before the Nuremberg Military Tribunals Under Control Council Law No. 10 (1948) 1135–6.
34 See International Criminal Tribunal for the Former Yugoslavia, *Prosecutor v Dragoljub Kunarac et al.*, Judgment, 12 June 2002, IT-96-23&IT-96-23/1-A, paras 57–9. For a more extensive analysis, see van den Herik and Dam-de Jong (n *) 255–6.
35 See *Katanga* (n 17) para 913.
36 Ibid.
37 The first interpretation is inspired by the distinction in international humanitarian law between pillage and seizure. See van den Herik and Dam-de Jong (n *) 262. The second interpretation is based on the law of occupation and with the limitations imposed on the right of *usufruct*. See Dam-de Jong (n *) 226–33. Obviously, the first interpretation is very problematic since it would remove exploitation of natural resources for the purpose of financing an armed conflict from the remit of pillage. However, even if the ICC were to adopt the second interpretation, it would require an investigation into the end uses of the proceeds from natural resources exploitation, which is problematic in itself.
38 However, it should be noted that whether corporate actors would be prosecuted as perpetrators (meaning that they have to satisfy the elements of the crime themselves) or as accomplices (meaning that the accomplices can only be held liable if it can be established that the original perpetrators – for instance, members of an armed group – satisfied the elements of crime) makes a difference.
39 *Katanga* (n 17), para 914 (emphasis added).
40 Emphasis added.
41 ICC, *The Prosecutor v. Thomas Lubanga Dyilo*, Judgment pursuant to Article 74 of the Statute, 14 March 2012, ICC-01/04-01/06-2842, para 1012; and William Schabas, *The International Criminal Court: A Commentary on the Rome Statute* (Oxford University Press 2016).
42 Ibid.
43 Elies van Sliedregt, *Individual Criminal Responsibility in International Law* (Oxford University Press 2012).
44 Ibid. 40–5. On the question of whether it is appropriate for national courts to apply domestic standards in trials concerning international crimes, see also Wim Huisman and Elies van Sliedregt, 'Rogue Traders: Dutch Businessmen, International Crimes and Corporate Complicity', (2010) 8 *Journal of International Criminal Justice* 803.
45 For general information on due diligence, see Timo Koivurova, 'Due Diligence' (Max Planck Encyclopedia of Public International Law, online edn, 2010) <http://opil.ouplaw.com/home/EPIL> accessed 24 September 2019. See also the 2014 and 2016 Reports of the Former ILA Study Group on Due Diligence in International Law, <www.ila-hq.org/index.php/study-groups> accessed 24 September 2019.
46 Due diligence obligations are also emerging in other areas, such as in relation to the responsibility of States for armed groups (including terrorist groups) operating from their territory. In this context, the concept can be traced back to the Corfu Channel judgment, in which the ICJ formulated the principle that every State is obligated to not knowingly allow its territory to be used to commit acts against the rights of any other State. See ICJ, *Corfu Channel (United Kingdom of Great Britain and Northern Ireland v. Albania)*, Judgment of 9 April 1949, ICJ Rep 1949, 22.

47 In international environmental law, States have, for example, an obligation to take all reasonable steps to prevent significant transboundary damage. ICJ, *Pulp Mills on the River Uruguay (Argentina v. Uruguay)*, Judgment of 20 April 2010, ICJ Rep 2010, para 101; and Article 3 of the ILC Draft articles on Prevention of Transboundary Harm from Hazardous Activities, with Commentaries (2001) <http://legal.un.org/ilc/texts/instruments/english/commentaries/9_7_2001.pdf> accessed 24 September 2019.

48 See Jonathan Bonnitcha and Robert McCorquodale, 'The Concept of "Due Diligence" in the UN Guiding Principles on Business and Human Rights', (2017) 28(3) *European Journal of International Law* 900.

49 Guiding Principles on Business and Human Rights: Implementing the United Nations "Protect, Respect and Remedy", Annex to UNHRC, Report of the Special Representative of the Secretary-General on the Issue of Human Rights and Transnational Corporations and Other Business Enterprises, John Ruggie (21 March 2011) UN Doc A/HRC/17/31. The guidelines were subsequently endorsed by the UNHRC, see UNHRC, Human Rights and Transnational Corporations and Other Business Enterprises (6 July 2011) UN Doc A/HRC/17/4.

50 See John Ruggie and John Sherman, III, 'The Concept of "Due Diligence" in the UN Guiding Principles on Business and Human Rights: A Reply to Jonathan Bonnitcha and Robert McCorquodale', (2017) 28(3) *European Journal of International Law* 923–4.

51 See also Guiding Principles 18–22.

52 The 2000 version contained a rudimentary provision on supply chain due diligence only, stating merely that "[e]nterprises should encourage, where practicable, business partners, including suppliers and sub-contractors, to apply principles of corporate conduct compatible with the Guidelines". See OECD, *Guidelines for Multinational Enterprises* (OECD Publishing 2000), ch II, para II.10.

53 See OECD, *OECD Due Diligence Guidance for Responsible Supply Chains of Minerals from Conflict-Affected and High-Risk Areas* (3rd edn, OECD Publishing 2016). Similar guidelines have been developed for the agriculture sector (in relation to issues such as land grabbing) and for the footwear and garment sector (in response to the Rana Plaza disaster in 2013). For a detailed assessment of the Guidance, see Mary Footer, 'Human Rights Due Diligence and the Responsible Supply Chain of Minerals from Conflict-Affected Areas: Towards a Normative Framework?', in Jernej Letnar Černič and Tara Van Ho (eds.), *Human Rights and Business: Direct Corporate Accountability for Human Rights* (Wolf Legal Publishers 2015).

54 See OECD Due Diligence Guidance (n 53) para 318.

55 See ibid. 20–4.

56 See ibid. 32–3.

57 See ibid. 41–3.

58 See ibid. 33–4.

59 See ICC, *Situation in the Democratic Republic of the Congo*, Judgment on the Prosecutor's Application for Extraordinary Review of Pre-Trial Chamber I's 31 March 2006 Decision Denying Leave to Appeal, 24 July 2006, ICC-01/04-168, para 5. Article 22(2) of the Rome Statute prescribes that: "The definition of a crime shall be strictly construed and shall not be extended by analogy. In case of ambiguity, the definition shall be interpreted in favour of the person being investigated, prosecuted or convicted".

60 See, eg, UN Security Council resolution 1952 (n 13); UN Security Council resolution 2153 (29 April 2014) UN Doc S/Res/2153 (in relation to Côte d'Ivoire).

61 UN Security Council resolution 1952 (n 13) para 9.

62 ICGLR Regional Certification Mechanism (RCM): Certification Manual (26 September 2014) <www.deutsche-rohstoffagentur.de/EN/Themen/Min_rohstoffe/

CTC/Downloads/ICGLR_def_manual.pdf;jsessionid=CA367A68B23B148B46 6137B4514AB8AF.2_cid292?__blob=publicationFile&v=5> accessed 24 September 2019.

63 Dodd – Frank Wall Street Reform and Consumer Protection Act, 21 July 2010, Bill number HR 4173, Report number H Rept 111–517, S Rept 111–76.

64 Regulation (EU) 2017/821 of the European Parliament and of the Council of 17 May 2017 laying down supply chain due diligence obligations for Union importers of tin, tantalum, and tungsten, their ores, and gold originating from conflict-affected and high-risk areas [2017] OJ L 130/1.

65 See Cees van Dam, 'Human Rights Obligations of Transnational Corporations in Domestic Tort Law', in Černič and Van Ho (n 53). Interestingly, van Dam argues that "the concept of due diligence does not differ substantially from the risk assessment that is required by the standard of care in tort law. Hence, carrying out due diligence is not a *choice* but a *duty* for the corporation and Ruggie's soft law instrument of due diligence does not bring anything new in this respect" (emphasis in original). It is important to note that this is not just a Western interpretation. The Chinese tort liability law of 2009 includes similar obligations. See Tort Liability Law of the People's Republic of China (26 December 2009) <www.wipo.int/edocs/lexdocs/laws/en/cn/cn136en.pdf> accessed 24 September 2019. For a thorough analysis of the potential for domestic criminal courts to hold corporations accountable for violating this duty of care, see Cedric Ryngaert, 'Accountability for Corporate Human Rights Abuses: Lessons from the Possible Exercise of Dutch National Criminal Jurisdiction over Multinational Corporations', (2017) 29(1) *Criminal Law Forum* 1.

66 OECD Due Diligence Guidance (n 53).

67 UN Security Council resolution 1952 (n 13) para 9 (emphasis added).

Bibliography

Ambach P, 'International Criminal Responsibility of Transnational Corporate Actors Doing Business in Zones of Armed Conflict', in Freya Baetens (ed.), *Investment Law within International Law: Integrationist Perspectives* (Cambridge University Press 2013).

Ballentine K and Sherman J (eds.), *The Political Economy of Armed Conflict: Beyond Greed, and Grievance* (Lynne Rienner Publishers 2003).

Bonnitcha J and McCorquodale R, 'The Concept of "Due Diligence" in the UN Guiding Principles on Business and Human Rights', (2017) 28(3) *European Journal of International Law* 900.

Dam-de Jong D, 'Armed Opposition Groups and the Right to Exercise Control over Public Natural Resources: A Legal Analysis of the Cases of Libya and Syria', (2015) 62(1) *Netherlands International Law Review* 3.

———, *International Law and the Governance of Natural Resources in Conflict and Post-Conflict Situations* (Cambridge University Press 2015).

Farrell N, 'Attributing Criminal Liability to Corporate Actors: Some Lessons from the International Tribunals', (2010) 8 *Journal of International Criminal Justice* 873.

Footer M, 'Human Rights Due Diligence and the Responsible Supply Chain of Minerals from Conflict-Affected Areas: Towards a Normative Framework?', in Jernej Letnar Černič and Tara Van Ho (eds.), *Human Rights and Business: Direct Corporate Accountability for Human Rights* (Wolf Legal Publishers 2015).

Huisman W and van Sliedregt E, 'Rogue Traders: Dutch Businessmen, International Crimes and Corporate Complicity', (2010) 8 *Journal of International Criminal Justice* 803.

Ingle J, 'The International Criminal Court and Financial Crime', in Barry Rider (ed.), *Research Handbook on International Financial Crime* (Edward Elgar Publishing 2015).

Kyriakakis J, 'Corporations before International Criminal Courts: Implications for the International Criminal Justice Project', (2017) 30 *Leiden Journal of International Law* 221.

Lauterpacht H, *Recognition in International Law* (first published 1947, Camdridge University Press 2013) 94.

Lundberg M, 'The Plunder of Natural Resources During War: A War Crime (?)', (2008) 39(3) *Georgetown Journal of International Law* 495.

Nadia Bernaz N, 'An Analysis of the ICC Office of the Prosecutor's Policy Paper on Case Selection and Prioritization from the Perspective of Business and Human Rights', (2017) 15 *Journal of International Criminal Justice* 528.

OECD, *OECD Due Diligence Guidance for Responsible Supply Chains of Minerals from Conflict-Affected and High-Risk Areas* (3rd edn, OECD Publishing 2016).

Ruggie J and Sherman J, III, 'The Concept of "Due Diligence" in the UN Guiding Principles on Business and Human Rights: A Reply to Jonathan Bonnitcha and Robert McCorquodale', (2017) 28(3) *European Journal of International Law* 923–4.

Ruys T, 'Of Arms, Funding and "Non-Lethal Assistance": Issues Surrounding Third-State Intervention in the Syrian Civil War', (2014) 13 *Chinese Journal of International Law* 38.

Ryngaert C, 'Accountability for Corporate Human Rights Abuses: Lessons from the Possible Exercise of Dutch National Criminal Jurisdiction over Multinational Corporations', (2017) 29(1) *Criminal Law Forum* 1.

Schabas W, *The International Criminal Court: A Commentary on the Rome Statute* (Oxford University Press 2016).

Schrijver N, *Sovereignty over Natural Resources: Balancing Rights and Duties* (Cambridge University Press 1997).

Stewart J, *Corporate War Crimes: Prosecuting the Pillage of Natural Resources* (Open Society Justice Initiative Publication 2011).

van Dam C, 'Human Rights Obligations of Transnational Corporations in Domestic Tort Law', in Jernej Černič and Tara van Ho (eds.), *Human Rights and Business: Direct Corporate Accountability for Human Rights* (Wolf Legal Publishers 2015).

van den Herik L, 'Corporations as Future Subject of the International Criminal Court: An Exploration of the Counterarguments and Consequences', in Larissa van den Herik and Carsten Stahn (eds.), *Future Perspectives on International Criminal Justice* (TMC Asser Press 2010).

——— and Dam-de Jong D, 'Revitalizing the Antique War Crime of Pillage: The Potential and Pitfalls of Using International Criminal Law to Address Illegal Resource Exploitation', (2011) 3 *Criminal Law Forum* 237.

van der Wilt H, 'Corporate Criminal Responsibility for International Crimes: Exploring the Possibilities', (2013) *Chinese Journal of International Law* 43.

van Sliedregt E, *Individual Criminal Responsibility in International Law* (Oxford University Press 2012).

Part 3

Accountability through domestic public law mechanisms

8 From "too big to be governed" to "not too big to be responsible"?

*François Kristen and Jessy Emaus**

8.1 Introduction

Virunga National Park, situated in the Democratic Republic of the Congo (DRC) is Africa's oldest national park and is home to rare mountain gorillas. In 1994, UNESCO designated the park as a World Heritage Site because of its outstanding diversity of habitats.[1] The park's territory also contains an oil field, but the DRC's government has forbidden drilling activities. Congolese Law No 069-041 forbids oil exploration work in the park because it would violate the protected status of the World Heritage Site. The act also determines that forced entry to the park is a criminal offense.

SOCO International PLC is an international oil and gas exploration and production company established in London. SOCO is listed on the main market of London Stock Exchange,[2] a regulated market as defined in the MiFIR, an EU Regulation on markets in financial instruments.[3] SOCO runs business activities in the UK, the DRC, Vietnam, and Angola, and is one of the UK's 200 largest companies. Despite Congolese Law No 069-041, SOCO obtained a presidential decree to exploit the oil field in Virunga National Park in 2010, and started oil exploration work shortly thereafter.

In 2011, Park Ranger Katembo found SOCO employees in the park preparing to build a test drilling installation. Allegedly, the SOCO staff tried to bribe Katembo, but he refused and, with some effort, forced the SOCO employees to leave. In February 2011, The Virunga National Park Authority filed a complaint with the civil court against SOCO after this incident. Meanwhile, Katembo started to gather documents and covert film reports. In 2013, Katembo was arrested by the DRC's secret service and tortured to show that SOCO should not be hindered in its activities. Katembo's footage was used in the documentary *Drillers in the Mist*, which was made by Global Witness and released in 2014. This documentary has raised public attention for the case.

In October 2013, the World Wildlife Fund (WWF) filed a complaint against SOCO at the UK National Contact Point under the OECD Guidelines for Multinational Enterprises because of SOCO's ignorance of the protected status of Virunga National Park, the intimidation of opponents, and the non-disclosure of information about the potential environmental and health impacts of the oil exploration work. In 2015, the British newspaper *The Telegraph* published an article about the Church of England and other interest groups protesting against SOCO because of reports of bribery and intimidation of park rangers. As a consequence of these and other actions against SOCO, SOCO agreed with WWF to stop its oil exploration work in Virunga National Park. In November 2015, SOCO retreated from the park. In April 2017, Katembo was awarded with the Goldman Environmental Prize, similar to a green Nobel Prize.[4]

8.2 Research questions

The case of SOCO and Virunga National Park is not an isolated one, but can be placed in a broader context of cases in which large listed companies (hereinafter, LLCs; the concept will be defined in Section 8.3) are linked to fundamental rights infringements. These cases raise many questions, both legal and non-legal. The legal questions are very diverse and relate to such areas as private international law, international human rights law, national criminal law, and national private law. This contribution, in light of the foregoing, aims to link fundamental rights law and national liability law and is directed toward finding a potential new underlying argument for accepting legal responsibility of LLCs for fundamental rights infringements. We are searching for this argument in the economic reality of LLCs and their economic sphere of influence[5] in our society. Therefore, the central questions in this contribution read as follows:

> *Can "economic power" provide for a legal basis for holding LLCs responsible for fundamental rights protection, and if so, how?*

And, if the answer to the first question is "yes", the subsequent question is:

> *Can economically powerful LLCs be held liable both under national private law and national criminal law for not taking responsibility for fundamental rights protection?*

These research questions imply at least three limitations. First, we focus on LLCs and exclude other actors that may bear legal responsibilities with regard to fundamental rights protection in the context of economic activities.

A second limitation relates to the norms, rules, and standards that are the subject of our research. We focus on norms, rules, and standards that are usually related to CSR; that is, norms, rules, and standards that balance "economic, social and environmental imperatives" – thus, the triple bottom line, or the 3P (people, planet, and profit).[6] It therefore encompasses human rights as used and defined in the UNGPs.[7]

Lastly, we focus on violations of prohibitions by the LLCs that result in fundamental rights infringements. Although fundamental rights law also identifies obligations to guarantee fundamental rights standards by effort – the so-called positive duties or obligations –[8] it is not a generally accepted concept with respect to private parties like companies in the sense that they are subjected to positive obligations directly. For that reason, we disregard that concept here and only include obligations to respect fundamental right standards.

An overall limitation of our contribution is that, with regard to the law, norms, and rules applicable to companies, we focus on the level of the EU, because those norms and rules are directly or via national implementing measures applicable to companies in all EU Member States. Therefore, our contribution will be of relevance for all EU-based LLCs. With respect to national private law and national criminal law, we use Dutch law as an example.

In Section 8.3, we first define two key concepts in this contribution: LLCs and economic power. It is important to discuss these concepts in detail and contrast them with similar concepts, since the characteristics of the LLCs and the concept of economic power *per se* form a part of our argument to accept that a specific form of power implies a specific responsibility. In Section 8.4, we construct LLCs' responsibility for fundamental rights protection. We link power to responsibility and transform responsibility into liability. In Section 8.5, we explain how responsibility can be transformed into liability through national laws. Finally, we will answer both research questions in Section 8.6.

8.3 Large listed companies, economic power, and the relation between the two concepts

8.3.1 Large listed companies and economic power

The first research question that was presented in Section 8.2 includes both LLCs and economic power. That gives rise to the question of why we have used LLCs separately since the concept of economic power could already include them. As we will explain in Section 8.4, the concept of economic power is related to a societal and legal responsibility for companies to protect fundamental rights. At the same time – and this is the downside of economic power – it can create immunity for liability in any sense. Immunity means particularly that LLCs cannot be held liable for human rights violations by State or non-State actors for legal and practical reasons. The practical reasons encompass, in any case, the potential factual situation that LLCs have such economic power that neither states nor victims of human rights infringements dare to hold them liable; they are too big to be held responsible (compare the adage: "too big to jail"). It is our assumption that small companies do not have such economic power, which makes it reasonable to focus on large companies. Those companies must also have a specific quality, which is expressed by the listing requirement, as will be explained in Section 8.3.2.

At the same time, however, it is conceivable that not all LLCs have such economic power. One can think of a LLC that is overshadowed in a specific market and in society by another LLC operating in the same branch. Or, a LLC that is completely inward-directed. Furthermore, as our research question already indicates, we will propose in this contribution to use economic power as an underpinning for holding LLCs responsible for fundamental rights protection and, subsequently, liability for not taking this responsibility. We want to prevent the sheer size of a company from resulting in this responsibility; it's all about how a LLC *acts* and what it *does* with its economic power (including how it neglects this power). That is why we also define "economic power" and, as a consequence, propose a twofold test.

8.3.2 *Large listed companies*

A distinction should be made regarding the kind of entity involved in (an) economic activity(ies) because not all entities that employ business activities can and will have economic power. For that reason, we have developed the following definition of LLCs:

> *A LLC is a legal entity that runs a business on a large scale and is listed on a financial market as defined in the MiFIR.*

This definition of the LLC has a few characteristics: (i) legal entity, (ii) runs a business, (iii) large scale, and (iv) listed on a specific financial market. We will discuss these characteristics in the next section.

1. A legal requirement: legal entity

The company must be a legal entity; that is, an entity irrespective of its particular legal form. National law determines the legal forms of companies; it may be the British public limited company (PLC, like SOCO), the French Société Anonyme (SA), the German Aktiengesellschaft (AG), or the Dutch Naamloze Vennootschap (NV), each of which has its own legal requirements. As our definition of LLC should be applicable in multiple countries and therefore not be dependent on local legal requirements, we developed a definition that is indifferent to the legal form.[9] The legal form of a legal entity is needed for establishing civil and/or criminal liability according to national laws (as we will explain in Section 8.5).

We have deliberately not used the term "enterprise" because we will use this for our definition of economic power (see Section 8.3.4) and we want to distinguish between the definitions of LLC and economic power in order to prevent both definitions from automatically coinciding and thus being indistinct.

2. A purpose requirement: running a business

A company only qualifies as a LLC when it runs a business, by which we mean that it employs commercial activities aimed at profit. The activities can encompass the extraction, trade, distribution, and/or storage of raw materials and commodities, the manufacturing of products, the development of products and services, the trade and/or distribution and/or storage of goods, the transporting of people and/or animals, the provision of services, etc., all of which have the purpose of earning money. With this purpose requirement, we exclude non-profit activities; this is related to our definition of economic power (see Section 8.3.4).

3. *An amplitude requirement: large-scale operations*

The business that a LLC runs must be on a large scale. We define a large scale by means of the generally accepted criteria that the EC uses. An enterprise is large when:

- Its staff headcount is equal to or greater than 250 employees during the financial year, regardless of revenue, and,
- It has a turnover of more than EUR 50 million and/or a balance sheet total of more than EUR 43 million.[10]

These formal criteria have the advantage of being simple to determine; they concern data that each listed company in the EU must publish in its annual financial report.[11] Furthermore, they do not depend on the legal form. The size requirement assumes that the large size of the company usually also implies economic power as defined in Section 8.3.4. However, as mentioned before, size and power do not necessarily coincide (see Section 8.3.1).

4. *A quality requirement: listed on a financial market*

The company must be listed on a financial market as defined by the MiFIR. This listing requirement relates to a certain quality of a company that enables the company to possess and exercise power. When a company is listed or requests admission to trading for its financial instruments, it is oriented toward investors and the general public. An IPO (initial public offering) by which a company's financial instruments are offered to the general public and a listing is obtained aims to raise capital for the benefit of the company. Therefore, a listed company will invest in branding and visibility. It will continue to do so to obtain a good price for its admitted financial instruments. Stock prices and movements in stock prices are considered to be indicators of a company's wealth. Stock prices are published in real-time or with a short delay on a daily basis. There will be media coverage in case of events that might influence stock prices. Furthermore, a listing on a financial market, particularly a regulated market, means that a company matters; in other words, the company belongs to the "league" of listed companies, has a certain quality, and can afford the listing.

Finally, several duties are imposed on listed companies, particularly a range of reporting duties. Those duties vary from publishing annual financial reports[12] to making inside information public as soon as possible.[13] The EU even obliges its Member States to impose on (very) large listed companies that are public-interest entities[14] the general reporting duty of an annual non-financial statement, which must include information on environmental, social, and employee matters, such as the (foreseeable) impact of the business activities on the environment; information on respect for human rights, like how human rights abuses are prevented;

and information on anti-corruption measures and the company's policies in this respect (including due diligence processes).[15] Companies, like SOCO, that are listed on regulated markets active in extractive industries or logging of primary forest industries should annually disclose their payments to governments in the countries where those activities take place.[16] All these duties have the effect that relevant information for pricing mechanisms at the financial markets flow to those markets in order to create a level playing field for investors and contribute to fair, ethical, efficient, and transparent financial markets. This fosters the smooth functioning of those markets, promotes public confidence in those markets, and enhances investor protection.[17]

We adhere to financial markets as defined by the MiFIR because this is the EU-wide standard. The MiFIR entered into force on 3 January 2018 and sets uniform standards for all EU financial markets. Due to the legal status of a regulation in EU law, its rules are directly applicable in each EU Member State.[18] Accordingly, the MiFIR's definitions and rules are the same in the EU, which favors the use of these definitions and rules.

The MiFIR defines a financial market as a regulated market, multilateral trading facility, organized trading facility, or trading venue, each with references to other provisions of EU law, setting specific requirements (Article 2(1)(13–16) MiFIR). Its wide scope includes the London Stock Exchange, Euronext Paris, Euronext Amsterdam, and the Frankfurt Stock Exchange. The main markets of these stock exchanges list companies that meet the large-scale criteria already mentioned. However, the stock exchanges also exploit markets on which smaller companies are listed, like the market Euronext Growth (a multilateral trading facility) for small caps (small and medium-sized companies).[19] National law that governs the financial markets in its territory provides the rules for admission to trading on those markets.[20] Thus, the listing requirement itself is not defined on the level of the EU, but depends on national law. However, it is also a formal requirement: a LLC is listed when the competent authority for the concerned trading facility has decided to admit the financial instruments issued by the LLC (for instance shares or bonds) to trading on that facility. Consequently, orders in these financial instruments can be placed in the order book and there is a quotation on the market.

We should note that an extension of the listing requirement seems to be reasonable.[21] In some countries, LLCs can have a legal form that does not allow listing at a financial market, because they cannot issue financial instruments that can be admitted to trading. One of the three largest commercial banks in the Netherlands is Rabobank, which is a cooperative rather than a public company. Taking into account its position on the financial markets in the Netherlands and its meaning for the Dutch society, Rabobank meets all other requirements of a LLC as well as the rationale of the listing requirement. It can also be concluded that Rabobank has economic power (compare Section 8.3.4).

5. *Irrespective national or transnational business operations*

Our definition of LLC does not include a requirement with regard to transnational aspects of its commercial activities. Consequently, the definition of a LLC includes a company that operates transnationally as well as a company that only operates within one country. That is different from the commonly used term "multinational enterprise", a characteristic of which is their international business operations.[22] However, LLCs which operate only locally – that is, on the territory of one country – can have economic power within the national borders. Therefore, we are of the opinion that our definition of LLC has added value compared to an ME-like definition. When a LLC does run transnational business operations, it can also qualify as a ME.

8.3.3 Existing legal duties for LLCs

LLCs must comply with a variety of legal duties concerning their business operations. On the international level, there are the duties in non-legally binding instruments like the Ruggie framework, the UNGPs, the OECD Principles of Corporate Governance, and the OECD Guidelines for Multinational Enterprises and the Principles of United Nations Global Compact. For instance, the UNGPs formulate for all business enterprises, including LLCs, the foundational principle that business enterprises should respect human rights (Guiding Principle 11). The rationale of this principle is explained as: "The responsibility to respect human rights is a global standard of expected conduct for all business enterprises wherever they operate."[23] This rationale is exemplified in the context of Guiding Principle 23:

> The responsibility to respect human rights applies in all contexts. It is a uniform standard, reflecting its roots in the universal expectation that enterprises should not harm the dignity of people as they go about their business.[24]

The general duty to respect human rights is also reflected in the first two principles of United Nations Global Compact[25] and the OECD Guidelines for Multinational Enterprises.[26] The UNGPs make the general duty more concrete in the subsequent Guiding Principles 12–24. In this respect, it is noteworthy that Guiding Principle 14 has an underlying notion that the business enterprise's size matters. Guiding Principle 14 reads as follows:

> The responsibility of business enterprises to respect human rights applies to all enterprises regardless of their size, sector, operational context, ownership and structure. Nevertheless, the scale and complexity of the means through which enterprises meet that responsibility may vary according to these factors and with the severity of the enterprise's adverse human rights impacts.

The first sentence of the commentary on that principle reads, "The means through which a business enterprise meets its responsibility to respect human rights will be proportional to, among other factors, its size."[27] The Interpretative Guide explains that size is related to human rights risks. The line or reasoning is as follows. A larger business enterprise will run larger businesses because it will employ more commercial activities, have more employees, have more business relationships, have more and more complex value chains, and have more clients or customers than a small business enterprise. Furthermore, a larger business enterprise will probably have a more complex organizational structure, which may hamper decision-making processes, communication, monitoring mechanisms, and oversight possibilities. All these factors may increase the risk of human rights abuse.[28]

Thus, as a general rule, larger business enterprises carry more responsibility to respect human rights, although it is acknowledged that small business enterprises can be involved in activities that can have a "very high human rights risk profile", like mining and trading minerals or metals in conflict areas.[29] In this sector and operational context, the responsibility to respect human rights is also larger. We can identify a risk-based approach, which is also connected to the severity of the human rights impact. The more severe the consequences, the greater the responsibility to act upon it in terms of the swiftness of the response, the prioritization of the response, the kind of measures to stop the human rights abuses, and the remediation of the consequences.[30]

At the EU level, many different duties have been laid down in legally binding instruments, some of which are directly applicable to LLCs, like the MiFIR (see Section 8.3.2), and most of them are applicable via national implementing measures, such as the EU directives mentioned in Section 8.3.2. These entail duties concerning reporting and transparency, which are mostly applicable to LLCs regardless of the kind of commercial activities they engage in. Beside those duties, there are many more that are sector-specific.

At a national level, LLCs are bound to a variety of duties laid down in national law. Which duties it concerns depends on the national law, the local situation, the LLC's type of commercial activities, and the market where the LLC's products, goods and/or services are offered and/or traded. Many duties in national law concern the implementation of measures of international standards or reflections of those standards[31] or implementing measures of EU legal instruments like directives. Some of those duties, such as the duties that follow from the criminal offense of modern slavery, are applicable to all LLCs in a country;[32] while other duties are only applicable to LLCs active in a certain sector, like commercial banks in the financial sector. This shows that one must be aware of the general and specific norms, rules, and arrangements that can govern the LLC's commercial activities.

All these duties are applicable to LLCs because their commercial activities interfere with, infringe upon, endanger and/or create risks with regard to the interests of people, the planet, and society. The LLCs are responsible for preventing this because they are in the position to do so and they have the power to take measures. This brings us to our concept of economic power.

8.3.4 Economic power

The definition of economic power that we apply in this contribution is based on a definition by Strange (1975).[33] Power, according to Strange (citing Northedge), is:

> the capability of a person or group to make his or its will felt in the decision-making process of another person or group.[34]

This led Strange to the observation that "wealth gives the state an influence base from which to use either rewards or threats to achieve its own objectives or to impose its will on other states."[35] In terms of economic power of large listed companies, this could express that the economic strength of a company, like a state's wealth, entails the conditions necessary to be able to use rewards or threats to achieve objectives or impose its will on, for instance, States.

Based on Strange's definition of economic power, we define economic power as follows:

> *Economic power refers to wealth, which gives an enterprise an influence base from which to use any means to achieve its own objectives or to impose its will on its surroundings.*

This definition includes elements that require further comment. First of all, there is an element of "wealth". Wealth refers to the value of the capital of the enterprise at a point in time. The capital is the enterprise's total assets, which includes both tangible and intangible assets, such as buildings and machinery, natural resources, working capital, financial claims, property rights, copyrights, market position, brand, and reputation.[36]

A second element is "enterprise", which is any company, irrespective of its legal form, that runs a business, so it must concern commercial activities aimed at gaining profit.[37] This element excludes the non-profit sector. By the term "enterprise", we seek a connection with the UNGPs, which use the term "business enterprise". The UNGPs themselves do not define "business enterprise", but the Interpretative Guide to the UNGPs sheds some light on what the term means. It distinguishes enterprises by size (large, medium-sized and small enterprises),[38] it is indifferent toward ownership (publicly listed, private owned, State-owned, or a combination),[39] and it is indifferent toward legal structures (company, group of companies, parent company, subsidiary, cooperative, franchise model, etc.).[40] The business enterprise potentially includes organizations from the non-profit sector that we have excluded.[41]

The third element of "any means to achieve its own objectives" in our definition implies financial, political, and legal means, both in a positive and negative way. Financial means encompasses not only paying money for certain goods and/or rights, but also offering credit facilities or acting as a guarantee in order to enable another person to acquire credit under more favorable conditions. Political means include two types of influencing the decision-making processes of the administration: (1) influencing impressions and decisions at a political level, like local municipalities or the national politics, and (2) influencing the official channels in order to obtain favorable decisions. Legal means is the use of all kind of legal instruments to a certain end, like filing a tort claim against another person (the State, governmental bodies, other enterprises in the same or another business, societal institutions, employees, customers, and citizens), or opposing (the conditions of) a permit in administrative proceedings, or reporting a crime to the police. Which kind of legal means is available will depend on the specific circumstances of the case and the availability according to national law.

Lastly, the element of "surroundings" covers the sphere around the enterprise, which includes the State, other enterprises, societal institutions, customers, and citizens. The surroundings do not need to be physically close.[42] After all, modern communication techniques allow for a span of control that could easily cross borders.

In light of this definition, economic power implies that the economically powerful LLCs assume a particular position in society. That societal position refers to the relationship between the powerful on the one hand and people, planet, and profit on the other. The economically powerful LLCs have an impact on society, people, and planet. The plants of an enterprise provide for employment and economic activities related to the plants, but can also have an ecological footprint and, therefore, consequences for the environment. The decision of where to locate the enterprise's headquarters may even be coined as a political success by local and/or national governmental bodies.[43] The seat of a LLC further determines its legal form and all rights and duties connected to that legal form. The LLC's business activities are governed by rights and duties that follow from the law applicable to the territory in which the business activities are situated. The effectuation of these rights and duties has a cost, and the LLC's economic position determines whether and how it can bear those costs. Accordingly, the LLC also has a legal position that is influenced by its economic power, so the LLC's activities can and will influence or even change the positions, possibilities, and rights of others. However, this will probably not be the main objective of a LLC; its aim of achieving a profit will usually lead the LLC to enhance or improve its own economic position.

A final, crucial element in our research is the *use* of economic power by the LLC. In line with one of the limitations of this research, as explicated in Section 8.2, here we focus on the use of economic power that results in violations of standards by LLCs that imply fundamental rights infringements. These violations can take place precisely because of the existence and use of economic power by the LLCs.

8.4 The triptych of constructing legal responsibility for fundamental rights protection: power – responsibility – liability

The use of economic power establishes responsibility in the sense that economic powerful LLCs, precisely because of their economic power, are expected to act with due care; that is, at least to respect fundamental rights standards. We distinguish between three types of use of economic power.

First of all, there is active use of power, which could include using bribery to obtain a permit. In this case, our definition of economic power means that the LLC's wealth allows it to utilize its financial means for illegal payments to representatives of a governmental body in order to obtain a permit that would probably not have been granted otherwise. Another example is a LLC that threatens to move production facilities and/or its headquarters to another city, region, or country, with a loss of (many) jobs, economic activities, and/or tax income for the concerned area, in order to get something beneficial done by local and/ or national governments. Secondly, there is passive use of power, which is control and apparent approval. In this case, the LLC's wealth gives it such a societal and/or economic position that other market participants will follow the LLC and await its (informal) approval. In this way, the LLC is standard-setting in a certain sector or branch. A third and final use of economic power is adopting an indifferent attitude. This means the LLC, feeling comfortable with the position that it is too big to be held responsible, allows the LLC to continue disrespecting fundamental rights standards. Only the LLC's wealth can allow such an attitude. In the case of SOCO, the indifferent attitude was reflected in the ignorance of the protected status of Virunga National Park; SOCO felt comfortable in its economic position (see Section 8.1).

These three types of use of economic power have a clear impact on governmental bodies, other companies, institutions, and (local) communities, and therefore also affect citizens and/or the environment. In our opinion, it is this impact of economic power that establishes responsibility. In particular, three circumstances can underpin this responsibility. First of all, economic power has *leverage*. When a LLC has economic power it can use it in such a manner that it can take advantage of a kind of "multiplier effect". If a LLC dominates a sector or branch and is therefore standard-setting, other companies will follow the LLC in ignoring fundamental rights standards, for instance by making use of child labor for the production of goods. Or, when a LLC has the economic power and thus the financial means to bribe government officials at different levels in local and national governmental bodies, it will be probably more successful in obtaining what it wants.

Second, economic power brings *increased risks.* This argument can be found in the UNGPs and its Interpretative Guide, which acknowledges that the business activities of a large enterprise will bring more and/or serious human rights risks (see Section 8.3.3). As the Interpretative Guide states – correctly, in our opinion – the increased risks relate to the size of the enterprise, the number of employees and the "more complex systems and procedures" that are inherent in large companies.[44] This line of reasoning can be traced back to the Ruggie framework for business and human rights.[45] In such cases, larger business operations will affect more people and/or more territories, which means there are increased chances of "rotten apples" within the organization, and/or more impediments for effective governance of the organization and/or effective supervision on the daily business operations. Thus, there are more possibilities for infringements of fundamental rights and therefore increased risks regarding the amount, kind, and/or severity of fundamental rights violations.

Third, as has already been implied previously, the effects of the use of economic power can be *severe* in the sense of having serious consequences. The severity of the human rights infringement is considered to be a factor giving rise to specific duties under the UNGPs.[46] Also in Dutch tort law, as will be further explained in the next section, the severity of the effects when risks materialize is relevant for the required standard of care. In line with this, and to paraphrase Kool, responsibility means that the economically powerful LLCs accept that society can call them to account "to accept the consequences of [their] irresponsible behaviour".[47]

Having accepted that power brings responsibility, we need liability to enforce respect for fundamental rights. Only particular behavior is legally relevant; it may involve a crime or a tort. The legal concept of the duty of care, both known in national criminal law and national tort law, can be the vehicle to transform responsibility into liability through a two-step approach. The first step is to accept that responsibility leads to a duty of care; the second, that the violation of a duty of care establishes liability.

8.5 The two-step approach

8.5.1 The necessity to concentrate on national law

The line of reasoning presented in Section 8.4 is neither new nor unusual. It has been accepted on an international level in the Ruggie framework for business and human rights, as well as in the UNGPs. However, the Ruggie framework and the UNGPs are not legally binding.[48] On the contrary, national law provides legally binding examples of this two-step approach. In national tort law, responsibility is translated into a concrete duty of care. Subsequently, the violation of a particular duty of care leads to civil liability. Also, Dutch private law has standards, such as the good employer standard, to address the responsibility of powerful actors. The line of reasoning is visible in criminal law as well. Dutch criminal law entails specific duties of care in criminal offenses, and a general duty of care for the liability of legal persons.

Although other areas of national law could also be relevant to unravel legally relevant responsibilities in the form of duties of care, we have not included them. In particular, company law seems relevant at first sight. However, as is clear from the study by Enneking *et al.*, the rules of Dutch company law are facilitating and set a framework, but include only a few substantive norms.[49] Furthermore, according to the "stakeholder model", the rules focus on the company's interest. In this regard, the interests of shareholders come first, while the interests of employees and other parties who are directly involved under circumstances are relevant as well, but there is no general duty to respect social and environmental interests. In addition, it is not possible for those who suffer from the fundamental rights infringements by the LLCs to rely on the enforcement mechanisms that derive from company law.[50]

8.5.2 Dutch private law

When we take a closer look at Dutch private law, the general tort clause provides for a legal basis to hold corporations civilly liable if their conduct breaches an unwritten standard of due care (Article 6:162[2] Dutch Civil Code, hereinafter DCC).[51] These unwritten standards not only aim to prevent damage to persons or assets, but also aim to prevent damage to other interests. The interests particularly include those protected by fundamental rights provisions. However, as Hartkamp and Sieburgh stressed, it is decisive whether the breach of an interest in light of a particular private law relationship invokes a breach of a duty of care.[52] Economic power can be a relevant factor in defining the standard of due care, as power brings responsibility in the sense that, as discussed in Section 8.4, the economic powerful LLCs, precisely because of their power, are expected to act with due care. The general tort clause provides a basis for reception of domestic and/or international standards that protect people and the planet.

Situations in which fundamental rights are at stake often involve risky activities, such as oil extraction in the case of SOCO and Virunga National Park. In the context of risks inherent to activities, the aforementioned standard of due care is defined using four criteria: the so-called "cellar hatch criteria", named after the *Cellar Hatch* case.[53] These criteria are the probability that the risk will materialize, the seriousness of the expected damage, the character and benefit of the activities in question, and the burden of taking precautionary measures.[54] According to Enneking, in the context of so-called foreign direct liability cases,[55] this test

> boils down to an assessment of whether that parent company has exercised due care toward the foreseeable and legally protected interests of the host country plaintiffs, in light of the potential risks inherent in the multinational corporation's host country activities.[56]

The last criterion can be linked to the use of power by the economic powerful LLCs.[57] Since we utilize the use of power as a starting point for economically powerful LLCs, we can assume that they are in a position to take precautionary measures. In concrete situations, however, the exact expectations depend on the particular circumstances of each situation.

Following another line of reasoning, one could also accept that the cellar hatch criteria are not necessary to define a standard of due care. A standard of due care could be based more directly on the idea that we expect economic powerful LLCs to act responsibly, which particularly means that they respect fundamental rights standards. Such a standard could be accepted, as stated in Section 8.4, due to the leverage of economic power, the increased risks that are attached to economic power, and the seriousness of the consequences or the severity of the effects of the use of economic power.

8.5.3 Dutch criminal law

Dutch criminal law allows for criminal liability of legal persons. Article 51(1) of the Dutch Criminal Code (hereinafter: DCrimC) determines that criminal offenses can be conducted by natural persons and legal persons. "Conducted" encompasses direct perpetration as well as participation in the offense, such as co-perpetration and complicity. Legal persons are the entities as defined in Book 2 DCC, such as the already mentioned Naamloze Vennootschap. This category of addressees is extended to enterprises without legal personality in Article 51(3) DCrimC, such as partnerships.[58]

To establish criminal liability of legal persons, it is necessary to first determine whether the legal person conducted the criminal offense. As a legal person has no body to kick,[59] a judge must assess whether the *actus reus* of the offense that was committed by one or more natural persons can be attributed to the legal person. According to the Dutch legislature, this requires the imputation of the acts of natural persons to the legal person.[60] It has left it to the judiciary to decide under which conditions and/or according to which criteria this imputation should take place.[61] Once the *actus reus* is attributed to the legal person, another process of attribution from natural person(s) to the legal person can be required, namely in case the criminal offense has a *mens rea*-element.[62]

In the landmark decision *Drijfmest,* the Dutch Supreme Court developed a framework with a general standard and subsequent criteria for establishing the *actus reus* of legal persons. According to this decision, the acts (including omissions) of one or more natural persons can be considered as the *actus reus* of the legal person when it is reasonable to impute those acts to the legal person.[63] Therefore, the general standard is reasonable imputation. Whether it is reasonable to impute the natural person's act to the legal person depends on the specific circumstance of the case, which also includes the nature of the prohibited act.[64] The Supreme Court acknowledged that this general standard might lack guidance for legal practice, so it gave subsequent criteria by which judges can decide whether it is reasonable to impute a natural person's act to the legal person. An important factor that a judge can take into account is the question of whether the act took place or was conducted in the sphere of the legal person. If this question can be answered in the affirmative then it is, in principle, reasonable to impute the natural person's act to the legal person.[65] This so-called sphere-criterion is specified by the Supreme Court in order to provide more guidance. A natural person's act can be considered to belong to the sphere of the legal person when one or more of the following non-cumulative and non-exhaustive criteria are met:

1 Was the act committed by a natural person who was an employee of the legal person or worked for the legal person on another basis?
2 Does the natural person's act fit into the normal course of business of the legal person?
3 Was the natural person's act beneficial for the legal person's business?
4 Did the legal person have de facto "power of disposal" over the prohibited act *and* did it accept this act or was it accustomed to accepting the act of similar acts as appeared from the actual course of events? This acceptance includes the situation in which the legal person did not meet the duty of care that could reasonably be expected of the legal person to prevent the prohibited act.[66]

The meaning, inclusiveness, and application of these four criteria have been discussed in the scholarly literature.[67] The point we want to make is that these criteria do not refer to economic power of a legal person, because the criteria are directed inward: by applying the criteria, a judge can look "inside" the legal person, determine which act(s) of one or more natural persons constitute the prohibited behavior, and then decide whether it is reasonable to impute the act(s) to the legal person. Our argument of economic power is outward-looking: What is the position of the economically powerful LLC in relation to its surroundings? Does it have an influence base from which it can use any means to achieve its own objectives or to impose its will on its surroundings? (See Section 8.3.4.)

However, the framework of the Supreme Court for establishing the *actus reus* of a criminal offense for legal persons is an open, adaptive framework. The criteria are non-exhaustive; the framework is flexible, permits adjustment to the kind of legal person,[68] and allows for adding new criteria, provided that the imputation of the natural person's act(s) to the legal person is reasonable. This is the general standard that must be met for establishing criminal liability of an economic powerful LLC. We are of the opinion that the LLC's economic power can make the imputation more reasonable. Economic power brings responsibility to respect fundamental rights, which means a duty to prevent that illegal conduct that amounts to fundamental rights abuse and falls within the scope of a criminal offense occurs within the sphere of the LLC.

It is obvious that the economic power argument is related to the sphere of a legal person. After all, this argument focuses on the enterprise's wealth, which allows it to use any means to achieve its own objectives or to impose its will on its surroundings. It concerns its economic sphere of influence. That said, there are two avenues to fit the economic power argument in the framework for establishing *actus reus* of a legal person. First, the economic power argument can be added to the preceding list of four criteria as a new, fifth criterion. In this case, the line of reasoning is that a LLC had economic power and used it in such a way that a fundamental rights abuse occurred (see Section 8.4). Then the act(s) of the natural person(s) that constitute the crime took place within the sphere of the LLC, so it is reasonable to impute those acts to the economic powerful LLC. It can be considered as the perpetrator and it can be held criminally liable (the latter, if the criminal offense's *mens rea*-element is also met).

Second, the economic power argument can serve as predicate for a duty of care, as meant in the fourth criterion. The line of reasoning is then that the prohibited act(s) of the natural person(s) that constitute the crime can be qualified as accepted by the economically powerful LLC because its economic power establishes a duty of care to prevent the prohibited act(s), which duty can be reasonably expected, because it follows from international standards such as the UNGPs and/or EU law and/or national law (see Section 8.3.3). Furthermore, because of the LLC's economic power the sub-criterion of the power of disposal is also met, its economic power presumes that this LLC is able to influence its surroundings or has any means to achieve its objectives (see Section 8.3.4). As a result, prohibited act(s) of the natural person(s) can be considered to have taken place in the sphere of the economically powerful LLC. It is then, in principle, reasonable to impute this act (or these acts) to the LLC. Thus, the second avenue will also lead to the economic powerful LLC as the perpetrator of the criminal offense. It can be held criminally liable (provided the criminal offense's *mens rea*-element is also fulfilled). Both avenues show that Dutch criminal law allows for the reception of international, European, and/or national standards aimed at protecting people and the planet in the framework for establishing the economic powerful LLC's *actus reus* of a criminal offense, and thus paves the way for criminal liability of economic powerful LLCs in case of fundamental rights abuses.

8.6 Closing remarks

As the Spider-Man comic book said, "With great power comes great responsibility".[69] SpiderMan feels the duty to fight crime and evil because of his specific powers, which he wants to use to save people and society. It is this basic thought that can be transposed to the duty of business enterprises to respect fundamental rights, one of the pivotal Guiding Principles of the UNGPs (see Guiding Principles 11 and 14). This duty was at stake in the SOCO and Virunga National Park case, a relatively random example of a large UK company doing business in extracting oil in the DRC despite the World Heritage Site status of Virunga National Park, and allegedly involved in bribing governmental officials and violent intimidation of park rangers. Reflections on the UNGPs, partly in combination with this case, brought us to the following first central research question: "Can 'economic power' provide a legal basis for holding large listed companies responsible for fundamental rights protection and, if so, how?"

In order to answer this research question, we developed three definitions. First, we delineated the categories of business enterprises to a specific category in order to operationalize the duty to respect fundamental rights in the context of economic power. To that end, we have defined and confined ourselves to large listed companies, or LLCs. These are legal entities that run a business on a large scale and are listed on a financial market as defined in the MiFIR. Such LLCs can have economic power, because both the size requirement and the listing requirement in the LLC's definition are closely connected to our definition of economic power. We have defined economic power as referring to wealth, which gives an enterprise an influence base from which to use any means to achieve its own objectives or to impose its will on its surroundings. However, it conceivable that some LLCs do not have economic power; for that reason, both definitions must be distinguished, although some requirements are connected.

Similar to the Spider-Man adage, we developed the line of reasoning that the use of economic power by economically powerful LLCs establishes responsibility in the sense that these LLCs – precisely because of their economic power – are expected to act with due care; that is, to at least to respect fundamental rights standards. Economic power can be used in three ways: actively, passively, and by adopting an indifferent attitude toward fundamental rights infringements.

In order to enforce respect for fundamental rights, liability of economically powerful LLCs is needed. In our opinion, the legal concept of the duty of care, both known in national criminal law and national tort law, can be the vehicle to transform responsibility into liability, through a two-step approach. The first step is to accept that responsibility leads to a duty of care, and the second is that the violation of a duty of care establishes liability. This two-step approach is our answer to our subsequent research question for this contribution: "Can economically powerful large listed companies be held liable both under national private law and national criminal law for not taking responsibility for fundamental rights protection?" In order to demonstrate how this liability under national private law and national criminal law can be established, we explained, both for Dutch private law and Dutch criminal law, how the economic power argument in case of economic powerful LLCs can be assimilated in existing frameworks and criteria for establishing liability. Two avenues to this end are sketched for both private law and criminal law. Civil liability and criminal liability can thus be the final piece in the power – responsibility – liability triptych.

Notes

* Prof Dr François Kristen is Professor of Criminal Law and Criminal Procedure at Utrecht University School of Law and program leader of the Utrecht Centre for Accountability and Liability Law (Ucall). Dr Jessy Emaus is Assistant Professor of Private Law at Utrecht University School of Law and a researcher at Ucall. Contact: F.G.H.Kristen@uu.nl / J.M.Emaus@uu.nl.

1 See <https://virunga.org/> and < https://whc.unesco.org/en/list/63>.

2 See the information on the website of the London Stock Exchange <www.londonstockexchange.com/exchange/prices-and-markets/stocks/summary/company-summary-chart.html?fourWayKey=GB00B572ZV91GBGBXSSMM> accessed 18 August 2019.

3 See Regulation (EU) No 600/2014 of the European Parliament and the Council of 15 May 2014 on markets in financial instruments and amending Regulation (EU) No 648/2012, [2014] OJ L 173/84, Article 2(1)(13).

4 The description of the SOCO – Virunga National Park case is based on information available on several websites: OECD Watch, 'WWF vs SOCO' <www.oecdwatch.org/cases/Case_307> accessed 18 August 2019; UK National Contact Point for the OECD Guidelines for Multinational Enterprises, 'Final Statement Following Agreement Reached in Complaint from WWF International against SOCO International Plc' (July 2014) <https://assets.publishing.service.gov.uk/government/uploads/system/uploads/attachment_data/file/330392/bis-14-967-uk-ncp-final-statement-following-agreement-reached-in-complaint-from-wwf-international-against-soco-international-plc.pdf> accessed 18 August 2019; Global Witness, 'Virunga: UK Company Bankrolled Soldiers Accused of Bribery and Violence in Quest for Oil in Africa's Oldest National Park' (10 June 2015) <www.globalwitness.org/en/campaigns/democratic-republic-congo/soco-in-virunga/>; Joshua Alter, 'April 2013: A Responsibility to Preserve: Protecting Virunga National Park from Oil Drilling, Poaching and Armed Groups' (16 April 2013) <https://savevirunga.com/2013/04/16/a-responsibility-to-preserve-protecting-virunga-national-park-from-oil-drilling-poaching-and-armed-groups/> accessed 18 August 2019; Martin Fletcher, 'Soco Chief under Fire over Reports Oil Firm "Violently Intimidated Opponents" of Exploration

in Congo' (12 June 2015) <www.telegraph.co.uk/news/worldnews/africaand-indianocean/11668711/Soco-chief-under-fire-over-reports-oil-firm-violently-intimidated-opponents-of-exploration-in-Congo.html> accessed 18 August 2019; 'Profiel Rodrigue Mugaruka Katembo' (24 April 2017) *De Volkskrant*; and the former official park site <https://virunga.org/archives/legal-action-by-iccn-against-soco/> (no longer available).

5 The "economic sphere of influence" is inspired by the sphere of influence concept, which is commonly used in the CSR discourse; see, for instance, John Ruggie, Promotion and Protection of All Human Rights, Civil, Political, Economic, Social and Cultural Rights, Including the Right to Development: Clarifying the Concepts of "Sphere of influence" and "Complicity": Report of the Special Representative of the Secretary-General on the Issue of Human Rights and Transnational Corporations and Other Business Enterprises (15 May 2008) UN Doc A/HRC/8/16, 3–6. However, in this chapter we have narrowed it down to the economic power of a LLC.

6 United Nations Industrial Development Organization, 'What Is CSR?' <www.unido.org/our-focus/advancing-economic-competitiveness/competitive-trade-capacities-and-corporate-responsibility/corporate-social-responsibility-market-integration/what-csr> accessed 18 August 2010.

7 UNHRC, 'Guiding Principles on Business and Human Rights: Implementing the United Nations "Protect, Respect and Remedy" Framework', A/HRC/17/31 (21 March 2011) ['Guiding Principles on Business and Human Rights'], Guiding Principle 11; and OHCHR, The Corporate Responsibility to Respect Human Rights: An Interpretative Guide, [2012] HR/PUB/12/02 ['UNGPs Interpretative Guide'], 9.

8 See, for instance, the landmark decision ECtHR, Case of *Öneryildiz v Turkey*, App no 48939/99 (30 November 2004) and Laurent Lavrysen, *Human Rights in a Positive State: Rethinking the Relationship between Positive and Negative Obligations under the European Convention on Human Rights* (Intersentia 2016).

9 As is common practice with such definitions. See, for instance, the use of the term "business enterprise" in the UNGPs (see Section 8.3.4) and the definition of an "enterprise" in the EU; see Commission Recommendation of 6 May 2003 concerning the definition of micro, small and medium-sized enterprises, [2003] OJ L 124/36, Article 1.

10 Cf. Commission Recommendation (n 9), Article 2(1).

11 Directive 2004/109/EC of the European Parliament and of the Council of 15 December 2004 on the harmonization of transparency requirements in relation to information about issuers whose securities are admitted to trading on a regulated market and amending Directive 2001/34/EC, [2004] OJ L 390/38 ['Transparency Directive 2004'], Article 4, as amended by Directive 2013/50/EU of the European Parliament and of the Council of 22 October amending Directive 2004/109/EC of the European Parliament and of the Council on the harmonization of transparency requirements in relation to information about issuers whose securities are admitted to trading on a regulated market, Directive 2003/71/EC of the European Parliament and of the Council on the prospectus to be published when securities are offered to the public or admitted to trading and Commission Directive 2007/14/EC laying down detailed rules for the implementation of certain provisions of Directive 2004/109/EC, [2013] OJ L 294/13 ['Transparency Directive 2013'], Article 1(3).

12 Transparency Directive 2004 (n 11), Article 4, as amended by Transparency Directive 2013 (n 11), Article 1(3).

13 Regulation (EU) No 596/2014 of the European Parliament and of the Council of 16 April 2014 on market abuse (market abuse regulation) and repealing

Directive 2003/6/EC of the European Parliament and of the Council and Commission Directives 2003/124/EC, 2003/125/EC and 2004/72/EC, [2014] OJ L 173/1 ['MAR'], Article 17.

14 That is, companies with an average number of at least 500 employees during the financial year and listed on a regulated market, as well as banks, insurance companies, and designated public-interests entities; see Directive 2014/95/EU of the European Parliament and of the Council of 22 October 2014 amending Directive 2013/34/EU regarding disclosure of non-financial and diversity information by certain large undertakings and groups, [2014] OJ L 330/1 ['Disclosure of Non-Financial Information Directive'], Article 1(1). There is an extension for parent organizations; see Article 1(3). This threshold is twice as high as our threshold of 250 employees (see Section 8.3.2).

15 Disclosure of Non-Financial Information Directive (n 14), consideration (7) of the preamble and Article 1(1).

16 Transparency Directive 2013 (n 11), Article 1(5).

17 Transparency Directive 2004 (n 11), considerations (1) and (2) of the preamble; Transparency Directive 2013 (n 11), considerations (3), (8) and (29) of the preamble; MAR (n 13), considerations (2)–(4), (8), (23)–(24), (31), (58) and (63) of the preamble; MiFIR (n 3), considerations (1), (3), (5), (8), (14), (23), (46) and (48) of the preamble.

18 According to the TFEU, Article 288, which reads in this respect: "A regulation shall have general application. It shall be binding in its entirety and directly applicable in all Member States".

19 See Euronext, 'Choosing Your Market' <www.euronext.com/en/raise-capital/how-go-public/choosing-market> accessed 18 August 2019.

20 See Directive 2014/65/EU of the European Parliament and of the Council of 15 May 2014 on markets in financial instruments and amending Directive 2002/92/EC and Directive 2011/61/EU, [2014] OJ L 173/349, Article 18(2) for multilateral trading facility and organization trading facility and Article 51(1) for regulated markets.

21 A more technical remark is that a systematic approach must follow the extension of the listing requirement in the MAR, namely that financial instruments for which a request for admission to trading on a financial market has been made are equated with those financial instruments listed at such financial market; see MAR (n 13), Article 2(1)(a) and (b).

22 See this description of MEs in the OECD Guidelines for Multinational Enterprises: "They usually comprise companies or other entities established in more than one country and so linked that they may co-ordinate their operations in various ways". OECD, *OECD Guidelines for Multinational Enterprises* (OECD Publishing 2011), 17.

23 Guiding Principles on Business and Human Rights (n 7), commentary to Guiding Principle 11.

24 UNGPs Interpretative Guide (n 7) 77.

25 Principle 1 reads: "[b]usinesses should support and respect the protection of internationally proclaimed human rights", and Principle 2 reads that businesses "make sure that they are not complicit in human rights abuses"; see United Nations Global Compact, 'The Ten Principles of the UN Global Compact' <www.unglobalcompact.org/what-is-gc/mission/principles> accessed 18 August 2019.

26 Chapter IV, first duty reads: "[r]espect human rights, which means they should avoid infringing on the human rights of others and should address adverse human rights impacts with which they are involved", see OECD, *OECD Guidelines for Multinational Enterprises* (OECD Publishing 2011), 31.

27 Guiding Principles on Business and Human Rights (n 7) 15.

28 UNGPs Interpretative Guide (n 7) 19–20.
29 Ibid. 20.
30 See Guiding Principles on Business and Human Rights (n 7), Guiding Principles 14 and 24, as well as UNGPs Interpretative Guide (n 7) 19–20, 23, 33, 40, 50, 79, 82–4, particularly page 19: "The severity of a potential adverse human rights impact is the most important factor in determining the scale and complexity of the processes the enterprise needs to have in place in order to know and show that it is respecting human rights".
31 Cf. UNGPs Interpretative Guide (n 7) 77: "The responsibility to respect human rights is itself often reflected – at least in part – in laws and regulations".
32 Cf. the contribution by Schaap in this volume.
33 Susan Strange, 'What Is Economic Power and Who Has It?', (1975) *International Journal* 207.
34 Ibid. 210. See also Frederick Samuel Northedge (ed.), *The Use of Force in International Relations* (Faber & Faber 1974) 12.
35 Strange (n 33) 210.
36 Based on Frank J. Fabozzi and Pamela Peterson Drake, *Finance: Capital Markets, Financial Management, and Investment Management* (John Wiley & Sons 2009) 449–50.
37 Compare the contribution by Fasterling in this volume, who defines the "business enterprise" not from a legal perspective, but by means of an activity-centered concept of the business model.
38 A large enterprise has more activities, more employees, more relationships, more clients, probably operates cross-border, and has a more complex organization and governance structure, with more formal internal control and oversight systems, and often with divisions or departments, than a small enterprise, while a small enterprise has more informal processes and management structures and may have fewer than 10 staff, as can be derived from the UNGPs Interpretative Guide (n 7) 19–20, 29, 46–7, 70.
39 UNGPs Interpretative Guide (n 7) 21–2.
40 Ibid. 22, 32.
41 We deviate from the definition of "business enterprise" of the Guiding Principles on Business and Human Rights, which can also include non-profit associations; see the contribution by Fasterling in this volume (Chapter 2).
42 Cf. Ruggie (n 5) 6.
43 See, for instance, the positive reaction of the Dutch Prime Minister Mark Rutte to Unilever's decision to concentrate its headquarters in Rotterdam: Jonathan Guthrie, 'Unilever Has Chosen to Protect Itself from British Capitalism: The Netherlands Is Friendlier to Establish Business That the UK Neglects', *Financial Times* (16 March 2018) <www.ft.com/content/d6807a36-284a-11e8-b27e-cc62a39d57a0> accessed 18 August 2019. However, in October 2018 Unilever revoked its decision, see Leila Abboud et al., 'Unilever Backs Down on Plan to Move Headquarters from UK', *Financial Times* (5 October 2018) <www.ft.com/content/7c1cabf4-c864-11e8-ba8f-ee390057b8c90> accessed 18 August 2019.
44 UNGPs Interpretative Guide (n 7) 19 and, for an explanation, Section 8.3.3.
45 Special Representative of the UN Secretary-General on the Issue of Human Rights and Transnational Corporations and Other Business Enterprises, 'Protect, Respect and Remedy: A Framework for Business and Human Rights: Report of the Special Representative of the Secretary-General on the Issue of Human Rights and Transnational Corporations and Other Business Enterprises' [2008] UN doc A/HRC/8/5, 14 ff.
46 Guiding Principles on Business and Human Rights (n 7), Guiding Principles 14, 17(b), 21, 24; and UNGPs Interpretative Guide (n 7) 8, 19, 50, 83.

47 Renée Kool, '(Crime) Victims' Compensation: The Emergence of Convergence', (2014) *Utrecht Law Review* 14, 16.
48 See, for instance, OHCHR, 'Frequently Asked Questions about the Guiding Principles on Business and Human Rights' [214] UN doc HR/PUB/14/3, 8–9; Liesbeth Enneking et al., *Zorgplichten van Nederlandse ondernemingen inzake internationaal maatschappelijk verantwoord ondernemen. Een rechtsvergelijkend en empirisch onderzoek naar de stand van het Nederlandse recht in het licht van de UN Guiding Principles (with a summary in English)* (Boom uitgevers 2016) 64, 72–3.
49 Enneking et al. (n 48) 607 ff.
50 Ibid.
51 DCC, Article 6:162 reads as follows (emphasis added):

> '1 A person who commits a tort against another which is attributable to him, must repair the damage suffered by the other in consequence thereof.
> 2 Except where there are grounds for justification, the following are deemed tortious: the violation of a right and *an act or omission breaching a duty imposed by* law or *a rule of unwritten law pertaining to proper social conduct.*
> 3 A tortfeasor is responsible for the commission of a tort if it is due to his fault or to a cause for which he is accountable by law or pursuant to generally accepted principles.

See Sterre van der Hell et al., *Warendorf Dutch Civil and Commercial Law Legislation: Section 1 CC Bk 6 General Provisions (art. 162–168)* (Wolters Kluwer 2015).
52 Arthur S. Hartkamp and Carla H. Sieburgh, *Mr. C. Assers Handleiding tot de beoefening van het Nederlands Burgerlijk Recht: 6. Verbintenissenrech: Deel IV. De verbintenis uit de wet* (Wolters Kluwer 2015) 75.
53 Dutch Supreme Court, *Coca-Cola v Duchateau* NJ 1966, 136.
54 Hartkamp and Sieburgh (n 52) 58; see also Ivo Giesen et al., 'How Dutch Tort Law Responds to Risks', in Matthew Dyson (ed.), *Regulating Risk through Private Law* (Intersentia 2018) 176 ff.
55 Defined by Enneking as: tort-based civil liability claims brought against parent companies of multinational corporations before courts in their Western society home countries for harm caused to the people- and planet-related interests of third parties (local employees, neighbors, local communities, etc.) in developing host countries as a result of the local activities of the multinational corporations involved. See Liesbeth Enneking, *Foreign Direct Liability and Beyond: Exploring the Role of Tort Law in Promoting International Corporate Social Responsibility and Accountability* (Eleven International Publishing 2012) 92.
56 Ibid. 233.
57 Cf. Sylvie Bleker-van Eyk, *Multinational Enterprises and Human Rights: A Report by the Dutch Sections of Amnesty International and Pax Christi International, Utrecht* (Amnesty 1998) 63.
58 Basically, only the sole proprietorship is not included. See François Kristen, 'Maatschappelijk verantwoord ondernemen en strafrecht', in Jan Eijsbouts et al. (eds.), *Maatschappelijk verantwoord ondernemen: Handelingen Nederlandse Juristen-Vereniging 2010–1* (Wolter Kluwer 2010) 132–3.
59 Inspired by the adage of Lord Chancellor of England Edward: "it has no soul to be damned, and no body to be kicked", see John C. Coffee, Jr., '"No Soul to Damn: No Body to Kick": An Unscandalized Inquiry into the Problem of Corporate Punishment', (1981) 79 *Michigan Law Review* 386.
60 *Parliamentary Papers II* 1975/76, 13655, No 3, 8, 14; Kristen (n 58) 133. See also the contribution by Schaap in this volume.

61 Supreme Court 21 October 2003, ECLI:NL:HR:2003:AF7938, para. 3.2.3.
62 *Parliamentary Papers II* 1975/76, 13655, No 3, 14, 19; *Parliamentary Papers II* 1975/76, 13655, No 5, 2; Supreme Court 21 October 2003, ECLI:NL:HR:2003:AF7938, para. 3.5; Kristen (n 58) 133, 138–9. See also the contribution by Schaap in this volume.
63 Supreme Court 21 October 2003, ECLI:NL:HR:2003:AF7938, para. 3.3.
64 Ibid., para. 3.4.
65 Ibid.
66 Ibid.
67 See for instance Kristen (n 58) 134–7; Jaap de Hullu, *Materieel strafrecht* (Wolters Kluwer 2018) 173–9; Bram Meyer et al., 'Corporate Criminal Liability for Corruption Offences and the Due Diligence Defence: A Comparison of the Dutch and English Legal Frameworks', (2014) 10 *Utrecht Law Review* 37, 46–9. See also the contribution by Schaap in this volume.
68 Marjan Groenouwe and Esther Baakman, 'Changing Ideas on Corporate Criminal Liability', in Ferry de Jong et al. (eds.), *Overarching Views of Crime and Deviancy* (Eleven International Publishing 2015) 283; de Hullu (n 67) 178.
69 Stan Lee, *Amazing Fantasy* (Marvel 1962). It is said (see Quote Investigator, 'With Great Power Comes Great Responsibility' <https://quoteinvestigator.com/2015/07/23/great-power/#note-11700-1> accessed 18 August 2019) that this quote's origins can be found in a French decree from 8 May 1793 promulgated by the *Convention Nationale* during the French Revolution: "qu'une grande responsabilité est la suite inseparable d'un grand pouvoir", *Collection Générale des Décrets rendu par la Convention Nationale* (Chez Baudouin 1793), 72.

Bibliography

Coffee JC, Jr., '"No Soul to Damn: No Body to Kick": An Unscandalized Inquiry into the Problem of Corporate Punishment', (1981) 79 *Michigan Law Review* 386.

de Hullu J, *Materieel strafrecht* (Wolters Kluwer 2018).

Enneking L, *Foreign Direct Liability and Beyond: Exploring the Role of Tort Law in Promoting International Corporate Social Responsibility and Accountability* (Eleven International Publishing 2012).

——— et al., *Zorgplichten van Nederlandse ondernemingen inzake internationaal maatschappelijk verantwoord ondernemen. Een rechtsvergelijkend en empirisch onderzoek naar de stand van het Nederlandse recht in het licht van de UN Guiding Principles (with a summary in English)* (Boom uitgevers 2016).

Fabozzi FJ and Peterson Drake P, *Finance: Capital Markets, Financial Management, and Investment Management* (John Wiley & Sons 2009).

Giesen I et al., 'How Dutch Tort Law Responds to Risks', in Matthew Dyson (ed.), *Regulating Risk through Private Law* (Intersentia 2018).

Groenouwe M and Baakman E, 'Changing Ideas on Corporate Criminal Liability', in Ferry de Jong et al. (eds.), *Overarching Views of Crime and Deviancy* (Eleven International Publishing 2015).

Hartkamp AS and Sieburgh CH, *Mr. C. Assers Handleiding tot de beoefening van het Nederlands Burgerlijk Recht: 6. Verbintenissenrech: Deel IV. De verbintenis uit de wet* (Wolters Kluwer 2015).

Kool R, '(Crime) Victims' Compensation: The Emergence of Convergence', (2014) *Utrecht Law Review* 14.

Kristen F, 'Maatschappelijk verantwoord ondernemen en strafrecht', in Jan Eijsbouts et al. (eds.), *Maatschappelijk verantwoord ondernemen: Handelingen Nederlandse Juristen-Vereniging 2010–1* (Wolter Kluwer 2010).

Lavrysen L, *Human Rights in a Positive State: Rethinking the Relationship between Positive and Negative Obligations under the European Convention on Human Rights* (Intersentia 2016).
Meyer B et al., 'Corporate Criminal Liability for Corruption Offences and the Due Diligence Defence: A Comparison of the Dutch and English Legal Frameworks', (2014) 10 *Utrecht Law Review* 37.
Northedge FS (ed.), *The Use of Force in International Relations* (Faber & Faber 1974).
Strange S, 'What Is Economic Power and Who Has It?', (1975) *International Journal* 207.
van der Hell S et al., *Warendorf Dutch Civil and Commercial Law Legislation: Section 1 CC Bk 6 General Provisions (art. 162–168)* (Wolters Kluwer 2015).
van Eyk Bleker- S, *Multinational Enterprises and Human Rights: A report by the Dutch Sections of Amnesty International and Pax Christi International, Utrecht* (Amnesty 1998).

9 Holding businessmen criminally liable for international crimes

Lessons from the Netherlands on how to address remote involvement

Marjolein Cupido, Mark J Hornman, and Wim Huisman

9.1 Introduction

The Netherlands is a forerunner in fighting core international crimes, such as genocide, crimes against humanity, and war crimes. In addition to prosecuting political and military figures for their involvement in international crimes,[1] the Dutch Prosecution Service has issued charges against two businessmen – Frans van Anraat and Guus Kouwenhoven – for aiding war crimes in Iraq and Liberia, respectively. After long procedures, both Van Anraat and Kouwenhoven have been successfully convicted for these charges.[2]

The prosecution of businessmen for (participation in) international crimes is often perceived as challenging, since it is complicated by "multiple layers of . . . remoteness".[3] In particular, Burchard has made a distinction between three, often mutually reinforcing,[4] types of remoteness: causal, motivational, and organizational or structural. Causal remoteness relates to the fact that businessmen rarely perpetrate international crimes directly, but generally fund or benefit from such crimes in more indirect ways, for example by providing goods, logistical support, or information.[5] This makes it difficult to establish how businessmen contributed to the commission of international crimes and thus fulfilled the *actus reus* requirements of these offenses. Motivational remoteness alludes to the fact that businessmen normally act with business-related purposes and interests, rather than with the intent to commit international crimes. As a consequence, they might not meet the required *mens rea* standards for establishing criminal liability. Finally, organizational or structural remoteness primarily concerns complications resulting from the fact that businessmen operate in the context of corporations and from a great distance. In particular, when corporations have a complex structure consisting of multiple branches and departments, individual businessmen may not know exactly what happens within the corporation, which complicates establishing their participation in international crimes. Such complications are only further exacerbated by the geographical remoteness of businessmen, who usually facilitate the commission of crimes from a distance.

In this contribution, we analyze whether, and if so how, difficulties concerning the remote involvement of businessmen in international crimes can be addressed.

Thus, our contribution is restricted in two important ways: (i) it focuses on the *individual* liability of businessmen, rather than the corporate responsibility of legal entities, and (ii) it is mainly concerned with establishing *criminal* responsibility for (participation in) international crimes. Issues regarding civil liability, or international due diligence responsibilities for serious human rights violations, are not (elaborately) discussed.

The contribution is structured as follows. First, we explore the different types of remoteness in Section 9.2 and consider whether and how remoteness (potentially) complicates prosecutions of businessmen for (participation in) international crimes. In Section 9.3, we assess how the notion of remoteness plays out in individual cases. In this respect, we primarily draw upon Dutch case law. The Netherlands is one of the few countries that has experience with prosecuting businessmen for international crimes, and its judgments provide useful insights on how to respond to the criminal participation of businessmen. In particular, we use the Van Anraat and Kouwenhoven cases to determine (i) whether remoteness was present in these cases, and, if so, what types; and (ii) how the Dutch courts dealt with these types of remoteness. Considering that the requirements for participation in international crimes will not always be met, in Section 9.4 we appraise whether there are alternative routes by which to effectively address remote corporate involvement in international crimes. For this purpose, we again use Dutch criminal law as an illustration, and discuss a number of separate crimes, including participation in a criminal organization and money laundering. In Section 9.5, we conclude by evaluating whether the alternative routes are satisfactory from the perspective of fair labeling and the expressive function of international crimes prosecutions.

9.2 Three types of remoteness

9.2.1 Causal remoteness

As became clear in the introduction, *causal remoteness* relates to the fact that businessmen often contribute to international crimes in an indirect way by providing goods, logistical support, or information. Thus, their *actus reus* is only loosely connected to the actual commission of international crimes. Kaleck and Saage-Maaß accordingly emphasized that "a line must be drawn between the morally condemnable behaviour of 'doing business with a bad actor' and criminally relevant contributions to another entity's international crimes."[6] However, as Huisman and Van Sliedregt explained, the boundaries between doing business on the one hand, and making a criminal contribution on the other, are fluid, in particular when businessmen provide goods or services that are in themselves not unlawful, such as selling trucks or building roads.[7] While such acts may seem harmless at first sight, they can be put to detrimental use and facilitate heinous criminal offenses. For example, roads and trucks can be used for forced relocations, or for transporting troops to crime sites. The question that consequently arises pertains to the conditions under which providing neutral – yet potentially harmful – services or goods constitutes a form of criminal participation. International and national courts have answered this question in different ways.

At the international level, the possibilities for establishing criminal responsibility for neutral contributions have recently come to the fore in response to a controversial judgment of the Appeals Chamber of the ICTY in the *Perišić* case. In this case, against former general Perišić, who had assisted the general war efforts of the Bosnian-Serb troops by supplying weapons, the Appeals Chamber ruled that the *actus reus* of aiding entails that the accused *specifically directed* his assistance at the commission of crimes. According to the Appeals Chamber, this requirement establishes an essential culpable link between the assistance provided by the aider and the crimes committed by the principal perpetrators,[8] in particular in cases concerning remote involvement.[9] Following the specific direction requirement, the Appeals Chamber acquitted Perišić of aiding war crimes, considering that his supply of weapons – which could be used for lawful and unlawful purposes – was insufficient for concluding that Perišić specifically directed his assistance at the commission of crimes.[10]

The *Perišić* judgment was strongly criticized both in literature and in later case law, and was eventually rejected by the Appeals Chamber of the ICTY in *Prosecutor v. Šainović et al.* and *Prosecutor v. Stanišić & Simatović*.[11] Under current law,[12] it only needs to be established that the aider *knowingly* made a *substantial* contribution to the commission of international crimes.[13] Despite the fact that the Tribunal ultimately rejected the specific direction requirement, the debate in international case law and scholarship on this matter remains significant, since it illustrates the challenges that courts face when evaluating neutral business conduct, and demonstrates the controversies concerning criminal liability for supplying lawful goods and services.

In addition to these international views, the challenges and controversies concerning criminal responsibility for neutral acts have been addressed by national courts. It is noteworthy that the issue of neutral acts has received specific attention in Germany, where scholarship and case law have developed particularly extensive and precise views on this matter. Under German law, neutral acts only qualify as aiding in two situations.[14] First, aiding exists when the accused's conduct explicates a solidarization with the perpetrator (*Solidarisierung mit dem Täter*) and can therefore not be considered "socially adequate" and "neutral". This requires (i) that the aider knew (*dolus indirectus*) that his or her goods or services could and would be used to further the perpetrator's crime, and (ii) that the sole purpose of the perpetrator was to commit a criminal offense. Because the aider in these cases makes the objectives of the perpetrator his or her own, the neutral contribution is no longer socially adequate but constitutes a wilful contribution to the perpetrator's offense, and as such loses its neutral, everyday character (*Alltagscharakter*).[15]

Second, neutral acts can qualify as aiding when the aider did not know that the goods or services he or she supplied would be used to commit a criminal offense, but accepted the fact as a *possibility* (*dolus eventualis*). German law strictly interprets this requirement of acceptance. Liability can only be established when the principal perpetrator was visibly inclined to commit a crime (*erkennbare Tatgeneigtheit*). Because of the perpetrator's clear tendency to commit an offense, which is judged predominantly on objective grounds, the aider can no longer convincingly argue that he or she trusted the perpetrator, took a permitted risk, or in any other way misjudged the situation. In fact, the aider's contributions can, in light of these circumstances, only be interpreted as deliberate assistance to the perpetrator.[16]

As the international and German case law makes clear, courts are well aware that establishing criminal responsibility based on neutral (business) conduct is not self-evident. Since such acts are often only loosely connected to the criminal offense of the principal perpetrator, courts have formulated additional requirements – such as solidarization – to still create a proper basis of criminal liability.

9.2.2 Motivational remoteness

In addition to causality issues, cases against businessmen can create *mens rea* challenges that concern the accused's mental disposition. In most cases, businessmen do not aim to commit international crimes and do not act for political purposes, such as suppression, expulsion, or ethnic cleansing, but instead act to pursue economic goals. Such goals can coincide with political ambitions, as the fulfilment of one can be a prerequisite for the accomplishment of another, but this is not necessarily the case. Depending on which goal businessmen pursue, different challenges arise for establishing their criminal *mens rea*.

First, we should be mindful that the intentions of principal perpetrators can shift or only reveal themselves overtime. As a result, it may be difficult to establish what businessmen foresaw and knew about the criminal intent of the perpetrators. Therefore, in appraising the *mens rea* of businessmen we should be mindful of the specific (political) context in which they act and in which international crimes are committed. On the other hand, we also have to be aware of the possibility that businessmen pretend to be ignorant of the criminal intent of their business partners, a technique used to diffuse their initial intentions. Such neutralization techniques increase problems of establishing *mens rea*.[17] After all, corporate and political interests are not always mutually exclusive and can coincide, thus giving corporations an indirect interest in the commission of international crimes, especially in economies where public procurements heavily depend on personal favors of those in power.

Second, it is unlikely that businessmen jeopardize carefully established business relations at the slightest alarm. However, the continuance of business relations under dubious circumstances should not be automatically interpreted as a sign of solidarization. It may just as well result from businessmen's ignorance, indifference, or belief in their ability to change the perpetrator's course of action or to mitigate the consequences of the perpetrator's conduct.

Third, we should appreciate that going against the interests of the political leadership can qualify as "economic suicide",[18] especially when corporate success depends on the whim of certain powerful political figures. In determining whether to support a political leader with a questionable track record, businessmen will therefore consider the potentially high costs of withdrawing their business from a country. This may, for example, explain the continued operation of Royal Dutch Shell in South Africa under the apartheid regime.[19] Even though many oil companies had economic interest in South Africa at the time, Shell was the only corporation that actually had large-scale facilities on the ground, making its costs of withdrawing much higher in comparison to those of its competitors.[20]

9.2.3 Organizational or structural remoteness

As we clarified in the introduction to this chapter, organizational or structural remoteness primarily relates to the geographical distance between the location where management decisions are made and the place where the crimes are committed and the characteristics of corporations as abstract entities. However, organizational remoteness also affects how individual businessmen become involved in international crimes and the possibilities for establishing their criminal responsibility. For example, it is significant that knowledge within companies is often spread across its members and is only shared on a "need-to-know" basis between departments or with other subsidiary companies belonging to the same corporate group. As a consequence, employees working for one department/company may remain unaware of the activities of other departments or subsidiary companies. Moreover, even within these departments or subsidiary companies, knowledge is often dispersed as a result of specialization and division of labor, so that colleagues might not be aware of each other's actions.[21]

It is also important to realize that while corporations are often perceived as fully rational, efficient, and strong economic actors that operate as well-oiled machines, the reality could not be more different.[22] Corporate information processes are often defective and crucial information is regularly distorted, incomplete, outdated, or even blocked, hindering it from reaching the right persons.[23] Consequently, individual directors and managers may validly claim that they were not (sufficiently) *aware* of the nature and seriousness of the crimes committed within the corporation (lack of *mens rea*).[24] Furthermore, directors and managers may argue that they lacked sufficient control over the corporation, and were therefore unable to prevent and intervene in the commission of crimes (lack of *actus reus*), especially if these crimes were committed by persons working for a subsidiary company.[25] As such, organizational or structural remoteness can shield Western directors and managers from liability for the crimes committed by their partners and associates in foreign countries. In fact, corporations may be organized in such a way that senior managers are kept at a safe distance while others take the blame, thus pushing criminal responsibility down the corporate hierarchy.[26]

9.3 Dutch experience

In this section, we will analyze the Dutch Van Anraat and Kouwenhoven cases in order to determine whether remoteness was present in these cases, and, if so, what types of remoteness and how Dutch courts dealt with it.

9.3.1 The Van Anraat case

Through his trading company, Frans van Anraat supplied large quantities of the chemical gas thiodiglycol (TDG) to the government of Saddam Hussein. Hussein used Van Anraat's TDG to produce chemical weapons that were deployed during the war between Iraq and Iran in 1988. This use of chemical weapons – a war crime under the Geneva Conventions – resulted in a vast number of casualties, in particular in the city of Halabja. Based on his contribution to these atrocities, the District Court of The Hague convicted Van Anraat for complicity in war crimes.[27] On appeal, the Court of Appeal upheld Van Anraat's conviction, finding that "the defendant was very aware of the fact that – 'in the ordinary [course] of events' – the gas[28] was going to be used" to commit war crimes. The Court imposed a prison sentence of 17 years.[29] In 2009, the Supreme Court confirmed the Court of Appeal's ruling.[30] Van Anraat's appeal to the ECtHR was declared inadmissible.[31]

Looking at the *Van Anraat* case in light of the three previously discussed types of remoteness, the most prominent issue that arises concerns the neutral character of Van Anraat's contribution – that is, the issue of causal remoteness. In this respect, it is important that the selling of TDG was not unlawful *per se*, since the chemical could in theory be used for legitimate purposes (dual-use character). However, the Court of Appeal dismissed the possibility of such legitimate application, holding that the "TDG, in the quantities as supplied by the defendant . . . could only serve for the production of mustard gas".[32] The defense argument that Van Anraat assumed that his TDC would be used in the textile industry was dismissed, mainly because there were no appropriate textile facilities in Iraq at that time.

Moreover, in relation to the issue of motivational remoteness, it bears noting that the Court of Appeal established that Van Anraat – who was well aware of the situation in Iraq and had lived there for a long period – acted with knowledge of the "unscrupulous character" of the Iraqi regime, and was aware of how his materials were going to be used. He even made efforts "to conceal the nature and the final destination of the chemicals",[33] thus casting severe doubt on the credibility of the alternative scenario he submitted.

Notably, the findings of the Court of Appeal concerning the issues of causal and motivational remoteness, and the way in which the Court addressed these issues, very much depend on the large quantity of TDG provided by Van Anraat. From this fact, the Court inferred that the TDG could only be used for the purpose of committing crimes, and that Van Anraat knew that his conduct would have criminal consequences, yet still decided to supply the chemicals. Thus, the Van Anraat case appears to be a clear example of "solidarization" (*Solidarisierung*). Van Anraat clearly knew (in the sense of *dolus indirectus* rather than *dolus eventualis*) that his chemicals could and would be used to commit war crimes, and was actually aware (again, in the sense of *dolus indirectus* rather than *dolus eventualis*) that the sole purpose of Saddam Hussein was to use them to that effect.

Finally, in relation to organizational remoteness, it is relevant that Van Anraat – who lived in Iraq during the relevant period – basically directed a one-man business and had direct links to Saddam Hussein. Thus, in terms of proximity,

Van Anraat was relatively close to the crimes and the principal perpetrators.[34] This helped to prove that he knew about the commission of crimes and that he was assisting these crimes by delivering TDG to Saddam Hussein.

9.3.2 *The Kouwenhoven case*

Guus Kouwenhoven – also known as "Mr Gus" – was the shareholder and director of several timber companies in Liberia. Through these companies, Kouwenhoven smuggled weapons into the country that were used by the army of Charles Taylor – the former President of Liberia – to attack civilians during the civil war between 2000 and 2002. In addition, Kouwenhoven made his security personnel available to participate in military operations of Taylor's army. After a long and complex procedure – including appeal, cassation, and retrial[35] – in April 2017, the Court of Appeal of 's-Hertogenbosch convicted Kouwenhoven for aiding war crimes and violating the (inter)national embargo that prohibited the supply of weapons to Liberia.[36] Kouwenhoven was sentenced to 19 years of imprisonment.

When assessing the *Kouwenhoven* case in light of the three previously distinguished types of remoteness, it becomes clear that this case was more challenging than the *Van Anraat* case. In particular, it is noteworthy that the District Court in the first instance held that the delivery of arms by Kouwenhoven was in itself insufficient for establishing that he had aided the war crimes committed by the forces of Charles Taylor. Indeed, the District Court accepted that weapons are highly dangerous goods, which armed conflicts often involve the commission of international crimes, and that war crimes had in fact been committed by Taylors' troops. This was also why the UN had imposed a weapons embargo, which Kouwenhoven violated. Nevertheless, while these factors make the risk of unlawful use of weapons foreseeable, it was insufficient for holding that Kouwenhoven made a causal contribution to (*actus reus*) and was aware of (*mens rea*) the commission of war crimes.[37]

According to Van den Herik, the conclusions of the District Court can be explained in terms of Kouwenhoven's causal remoteness. In particular, Van den Herik submitted that there was no sufficient causal connection between the accused's acts of facilitation and the crimes for which he stood trial, since "it is difficult to connect small arms deliveries to specific crimes".[38] Indeed, the causal connection between Kouwenhoven's assistance and the commission of war crimes is somewhat diffused by the fact that his weapons did not serve an exclusive malicious purpose, but could – in theory – also be used for legitimate reasons.[39] Having said that, lawful use was certainly not realistic in the particular circumstances, considering that there were clear signals that Kouwenhoven's weapons would be used to inflict harm. On this account, the Kouwenhoven case can be perceived as a prime example of so-called "visible inclination" (*erkennbare Tatgeneigtheit*), whereby Kouwenhoven at least accepted the *substantial possibility* (*dolus eventualis*) that the weapons he supplied would be used to commit war crimes.

This reasoning also seems to underlie the judgment of the Court of Appeal of 's-Hertogenbosch. Interestingly, this Court assessed the neutral character of

Kouwenhoven's conduct in light of his *mens rea*, thus making a connection with the accused's (lack of) motivational remoteness. In this respect, it is relevant that Kouwenhoven himself had stated that "African wars do not comply with the Geneva Conventions".[40] The Court of Appeal also determined that Kouwenhoven was aware of Taylor's previous involvement in armed conflicts, and knew that Taylor's forces made no distinction between civilians and combatants. Nevertheless, Kouwenhoven became increasingly associated with the Taylor regime. In particular, he transferred part of the ownership of his companies to Taylor and his inner circle, granted key positions within his companies to senior commanders of Taylor's forces, and made facilities, vehicles, and staff of his company available to store and transport weapons for the forces of Taylor.[41] Ultimately, the ties between the two men were so close that Kouwenhoven effectively shared Taylor's political, financial, and private interests. Therefore, the Kouwenhoven case did not generate particular problems concerning the issue of motivational remoteness.

Moreover – like the Van Anraat case – the Kouwenhoven case is characterized by a lack of organizational or structural remoteness. While Kouwenhoven was an ordinary businessman on paper, in reality he was so close to Taylor and had such good relations with his administration that the lines between Kouwenhoven's company and corporate activities on the one hand, and Taylor's regime and State-sponsored conduct on the other, were blurred. In fact, Kouwenhoven became so involved with Taylor's regime that the continued existence of his company depended solely on his good relations with the regime and the power of Taylor.[42] Not only was the company headed by senior officials who were close to Taylor, the company also became engaged in activities that were not related to the company's main activity – producing timber – but that only served the purpose of advancing Taylor's political agenda. As such, it could be argued that Kouwenhoven's company effectively became a *de facto* extension of the Liberian state and its criminal endeavours. Thus, where corporate involvement is normally only indirect and with senior Western management officials standing at a safe distance, the *Kouwenhoven* case expresses a clear example of direct and personal involvement in those offenses.

9.3.3 Evaluation

The findings discussed demonstrate that issues of remoteness played a relatively minor role in the *Van Anraat* and *Kouwenhoven* cases. The intentions and contributions of both businessmen were clear and rather closely linked to the war crimes committed in Iraq and Liberia, while their companies were quite small and directly connected with criminal regimes. Thus, Dutch courts in the *Van Anraat* and *Kouwenhoven* cases did not face the usual challenges of trying to establish criminal responsibility for indirect corporate involvement in international crimes. In this sense, the *Van Anraat* and *Kouwenhoven* cases are atypical, which arguably explains the successful conviction of both accused. The lack of remoteness of Van Anraat and Kouwenhoven also means that their conviction for aiding war crimes did not automatically entail that Dutch law provided sufficient "tools" for criminalizing indirect corporate involvement. We expect that it will be more difficult to hold businessmen criminally responsible for (participation in) international crimes when they participate in complex organizations and when their *mens rea* and *actus reus* are more loosely connected to the actual commission of crimes. As Huisman and Van Sliedregt pointed out, in these cases the "guilty mind" is often spread over multiple persons,[43] while the influence of senior managers on day-to-day operational activities will usually be indirect, and their knowledge thereof limited.[44] As such, the basis for establishing individual criminal liability for participation in international crimes becomes fragile.[45]

Since the *Kouwenhoven* and *Van Anraat* cases do not address such issues, in the next section we will further assess the question of how to overcome remoteness by looking at the recent Dutch *Rabobank* case. This case differs from the *Kouwenhoven* and *Van Anraat* cases in the sense that it involves the responsibility of not only individual businessmen, but also the corporation as such. In this sense, the *Rabobank* case might go somewhat beyond the scope of this chapter. Nevertheless, discussing this case is useful as it provides relevant insights into whether and how criminal law can address indirect corporate involvement. In particular, the *Rabobank* case demonstrates that it may be beneficial to look beyond the framework of criminal participation to establish the liability of businessmen acting within complex organizations that are far removed from the crime scene, both geographically and structurally.

9.4 Overcoming remoteness by going beyond criminal participation

9.4.1 *The Rabobank case*

In February 2017, the human rights group SMX Collective filed a criminal complaint with the Dutch Prosecution Service against Rabobank – the biggest Dutch bank – and its board of directors.[46] The group is accusing Rabobank and its directors of laundering the criminal profits of Mexican drug cartels. Allegedly, the Rabobank subsidiary in Calexico, USA accepted large sums of cash from Mexican drug cartels and assisted in recycling this money to Mexico, where it was used to commit large-scale and systematic crimes against humanity, including murder and rape.[47] SMX Collective claims that by providing such financial services, Rabobank and its directors participated in the criminal organization of Mexican drug cartels, which is criminalized in Article 140 of the Dutch Penal Code (DPC).[48] In particular, Rabobank and its directors allegedly made an essential contribution to the criminal conduct of these cartels by laundering money on a large scale, thus enabling the cartels to reinvest their profits and use these to commit crimes. According to the complaint, this contribution was intentional in the sense that Rabobank and its directors at least accepted the significant risk that they would contribute to the crimes of Mexican drug cartels.[49] The Dutch Prosecution Office is currently assessing whether SMX's complaint contains sufficient starting points for opening a criminal investigation. In February 2018, the bank had already reached a settlement of almost 369 million dollars with the US authorities.[50]

It is noteworthy that the complaint against Rabobank and its directors is not based on criminal participation; in other words, the complaint does not allege that Rabobank and its directors committed or assisted crimes against humanity. Instead, the complaint relies upon several alternative avenues to prosecute businessmen for their involvement in international crimes, in particular participation in a criminal organization and money laundering. These alternatives may help to overcome issues of remoteness and will therefore be further discussed in the next sub-sections.

9.4.2 Participation in a criminal organization

Under Dutch law, the crime of participation in a criminal organization is regulated in Art 140 of the DPC. It provides an autonomous type of criminal responsibility based on an accused's contribution to an organization that seeks to engage in criminal conduct. Art 140 of the DPC entails four requirements.

First, there needs to be an *organization* – that is, an enduring (non-incidental) and structured collaboration between the accused and at least one other person.[51] It is not required that the organization continuously consists of the same persons;[52] however, occasional types of cooperation in which persons work together only shortly (for example, mob violence) do not suffice.[53] It is accepted that organizations are small and loosely structured.[54] Therefore, circumstances such as the formulation of common rules or goals, the existence of a hierarchy, pressure to enforce conformity, deliberations between members, a division of tasks, and joint planning are relevant for establishing an organization, but are not recognized as necessary requirements.[55]

Second, the organization must have a *criminal purpose*; that is, it must be directed at committing or participating in multiple crimes.[56] It is not required that these crimes are in fact realized,[57] nor that the commission of crimes was the organization's principal purpose.[58] Thus, regular corporations can qualify as criminal organizations when they seek to achieve lawful goals by criminal means.[59]

Third, the accused must have *participated* in the criminal organization. This entails that the accused *belonged* to – that is, was a member of[60] – the organization, and *contributed* to or *supported* acts that benefitted or directly related to the organization's criminal purpose.[61] While the contribution requirement is broad in scope,[62] it must be established that the accused's contribution was aimed at or directly related to the *criminal* purpose of the organization.[63] Interestingly, in a case concerning money laundering, the Supreme Court has accepted that developing or upholding a corporate policy or culture in which crimes can be committed can qualify as contributing to a criminal organization.[64]

Fourth, Art 140 of the DPC stipulates that the accused *intentionally* (*dolus eventualis*) participated in the criminal organization, and had positive *knowledge* (*dolus indirectus*) of the organization's criminal purpose. It is not required that the accused intended to commit specific crimes, or even that he or she knew that the organization sought to commit such crimes.[65]

Together, the four requirements of Art 140 of the DPC create a broad basis of liability. The provision allows for intervening in the early stages of criminal conduct (because it is not required that a crime was actually committed, or even prepared or attempted) without having to establish the accused's participation in, or knowledge of, specific crimes. This makes participation in a criminal organization a potentially useful tool for criminalizing the remote and neutral involvement of businessmen.[66] Indeed, Art 140 of the DPC has already been successfully applied in white-collar crime cases concerning *inter alia* the illegal discharge of chemical waste by a waste-processing company, and the conspiracy to defraud by executives of real estate companies.[67]

Notwithstanding the potential advantages and prospects of using Art 140 of the DPC in cases against businessmen, challenges remain. In particular, it may be difficult to prove that corporations involved in lawful business conduct qualify as *criminal* organizations that seek to commit international crimes. While proving the organization's criminal purpose may be possible in relation to so-called "risky businesses" – such as, weapons trade, or the extraction of natural resources – establishing such a purpose may be more difficult where it concerns business branches that are only remotely linked to criminal conduct, such as the food and finance industry. Moreover, establishing that businessmen were members of a criminal organization will not always be self-evident. Recent case law clarifies that making a contribution to the organization is in itself not sufficient to establish membership.[68] Something more is required to prove that the accused was actually part of the criminal organization, though it remains unclear what, exactly, this "more" entails.

Possibly, these challenges for applying Art 140 of the DPC to businessmen have also had a bearing on the Rabobank complaint. In this respect, it is noteworthy that – rather than arguing that Rabobank constitutes a criminal organization itself – SMX Collective alleges that the bank and its Dutch directors participated in the criminal organization of Mexican drug cartels. By doing so, SMX Collective seems to circumvent the difficulty of proving that Rabobank – a completely lawful enterprise – is itself a criminal organization that operates with the *purpose* of committing crimes. However, it is doubtful whether this approach gives sufficient expression to Rabobank's own responsibilities and distinct criminal role, irrespective of the drug cartels. These responsibilities and this role are arguably better reflected in the recently concluded American investigation into Rabobank's alleged failure to exercise sufficient control over money laundering practices.

Furthermore, the complaint of SMX Collective creates the challenge of establishing that Rabobank and its Dutch directors *participated* in the criminal organization of the drug cartels – that is, that they *contributed* to and were *members* of these cartels. This means that it must be clarified how Rabobank's financial activities are linked to the crimes committed by drug cartels in Mexico and how these activities influenced such crimes.[69] While the complaint touches upon the contribution element – which may indeed be satisfied by Rabobank's financial support to the drug cartels – it does not explain how this contribution proves that Rabobank and its Dutch directors were members of the drug cartels. Thus, it remains doubtful whether and how the bank itself and its directors aligned themselves with the drug cartels, supported their goals, and sought to implement these goals. Consequently, the question arises as to whether it is in fact more likely that Rabobank and its directors were outside participants who (unknowingly) facilitated the crimes committed by a criminal group without being part of it. A possible solution to this issue would be to limit membership of the Mexican drug cartels to the local branch of Rabobank – the Calexico office – instead of expanding it to the bank as a whole and the directors in the Netherlands. However, this approach would raise jurisdictional issues for the Dutch Prosecution Service, since the Netherlands lacks jurisdiction over the Calexico office in the US.

The latter is important, because SMX Collective unequivocally tries to link the responsibility of Rabobank and its directors in the Netherlands to the crimes against humanity committed in Mexico. It is interesting to see how this attempt reinforces issues of remoteness. As previously noted, the notion of participation in a criminal organization constitutes an autonomous offense, separate from the principal crime, which in principle allows for loosening the linkage with international crimes. Yet by seeking to connect the conduct of Rabobank and its directors to the crimes committed in Mexico, the complaint brings the principal crime back into the picture and thus weakens the potential advantage of resorting to participation in a criminal organization. Questions concerning causal, motivational, and organizational or structural remoteness consequently re-emerge and may complicate the prosecution of Rabobank and its directors. The previously discussed option to focus the complaint on Rabobank's financial role would prevent such complications, as it would give better expression to the autonomous character of Art 140 of the DPC, and its position as a separate crime that is only loosely linked to the principal offense. However, the downside of this option is that presenting Rabobank and its directors as mere financial actors does not show the entire picture, since it does not accurately reflect their involvement in human rights violations. This may trigger questions of fair labeling, upon which we will further reflect in the conclusion.

9.4.3 Money laundering

The complaint against Rabobank and its directors is based on the submission that the bank's office in Calexico participated in laundering the profits of Mexican drug cartels by receiving large sums of cash and transferring this money to other bank accounts (so-called "layering"). According to the complaint, this practice of money laundering is well known and frequently used by drug cartels to hide the profits that they make from selling drugs.[70] Therefore, Rabobank arguably *must have known* (in the sense of having constructive knowledge) that the money it received came from criminal activities. Moreover, while Rabobank was warned by the US authorities that its control over money laundering was insufficient, it nevertheless failed to take adequate measures to monitor money laundering activities. In this way, Rabobank allegedly accepted the significant risk that its Calexico office was used for money laundering.

Whether the complaints against Rabobank will indeed trigger criminal prosecutions in the Netherlands remains to be seen. Yet, at first sight, it seems that the complaints are not completely without grounds. Under Dutch law, the scope of the money laundering provisions are wide. Besides benefitting from a crime by obtaining objects or profits while concealing their criminal origin, it also entails the mere possession of such objects without any act of concealment, provided that the accused knew or should have known about the criminal origin (Art 420bis and 420quater of the DPC). Dutch law requires that the objects or profits originate from *a* crime (*afkomstig uit enig misdrijf*). This can be a crime outside the Netherlands, as long as the *actus reus* takes place in the Netherlands.[71] With regard to that *actus reus*, it is noteworthy that Advocate General Vegter has argued that failing to live up to a duty to notify the authorities, as is the case with so-called unusual transactions (see Section 9.4.4), could in itself qualify as an act of money laundering.[72] It is not unlikely that these substantive elements are met in the Rabobank case if it can indeed be established that money obtained by illegal means was knowingly accepted. More generally, it seems that the conduct and intentions of businessmen within financial institutions are often relatively closely linked to money laundering activities. By focusing on the financial role of banks and their directors, and by disconnecting their responsibility from the international crimes committed, money laundering prosecutions may thus provide a useful alternative when criminal participation of businessmen in international crimes is difficult to prove because of problems of causal and motivational remoteness. Having said that, as noted before, disconnecting the role of businessmen from the international crimes committed can trigger new problems related to the notion of fair labelling. Presenting businessmen as "mere" financial profiteers arguably mischaracterizes their critical role in the commission of international crimes and may not do justice to the importance of their conduct. Moreover, the mere circumstance that certain people or subsidiaries within Rabobank were aware of and involved in these activities does not automatically entail that the whole corporate group and its top directors are also liable. A clear distinction must be made between the Calexico office and its employees and leading officials, Rabobank North America, which was supposed to supervise the Calexico office, and the senior companies of the corporate group in the Netherlands and their directors.[73] The first and second have been dealt with by the US authorities, while the complaint lodged by SMX Collective aims to trigger prosecutions against the third and least-involved category. Whether the latter are also liable remains to be seen.

9.4.4 *Facilitating contributions as autonomous offenses*

In addition to the specific crimes included in the Rabobank complaint, there are several other autonomous offenses in the sphere of trade and financial regulations, which potentially provide a useful basis for establishing liability upon businessmen. In this respect, it is important to note that the commission of international crimes generally does not come as a surprise. In many cases, the international community witnesses the deterioration of the political climate and human rights situation to which it responds by issuing economic and diplomatic sanctions, such as embargos and trade restrictions. Violations of EU trade embargos and restrictions, UN Security Council resolutions, and other economic and diplomatic sanctions can constitute autonomous offenses.[74] While the *Rabobank* case does not touch upon this issue, the *Kouwenhoven* case illustrates that these offenses can be a useful alternative when the accused's involvement in or awareness of international crimes cannot be proven.[75] In this case, the Court of Appeal also came to a conviction for violation of the international and domestic weapons embargo against Liberia. Establishing criminal responsibility for these offenses was facilitated by the fact that the offenses do not require proving knowledge of the intentions of the "bad actor". Doing business with that actor is in itself prohibited.

Another category of autonomous offenses that can be used to address issues of remoteness concerns violations of notification requirements. Many of these requirements are directed against financial institutions and serve to prevent or help discover criminal activity. For example, in the Netherlands, financial institutions are obliged to notify the Dutch Finance Intelligence Unit[76] in case of so-called "unusual transactions" (*ongebruikelijke transacties*) in order to prevent money laundering and financing terrorism.[77] Furthermore, corporations can be required to conduct client research and trace the identity of the "ultimate beneficial owner" before concluding a business deal, or to identify so-called "politically exposed persons"[78] among their business associates. The US has similar legislation, which constituted the basis of the American investigation into Rabobank's office in Calexico.[79] All of these offenses[80] can help to prevent businessmen from indirectly contributing to international crimes and other serious human rights violations.

9.5 Concluding reflections

In this chapter, we have addressed how the issue of remoteness complicates establishing criminal responsibility of businessmen for international crimes. After having assessed the different types of remoteness and how these affected the *Van Anraat* and the *Kouwenhoven* cases, we introduced three alternative avenues for evaluating the role of businessmen: participation in a criminal organization, money laundering, and facilitation as an autonomous crime. These alternatives allow for loosening the link between businessmen and international crimes, and can thus be used to address issues of remoteness. However, before embracing the idea that such crimes provide a wholesome alternative for international crime prosecutions, we should be mindful of the previously signaled concerns regarding fair labeling. In particular, we should assess whether the alternative offenses do justice to businessmen's moral reproach and properly reflect their role and responsibility.

The principle of fair labeling basically entails that the basis of criminal responsibility must correspond to the personal guilt and responsibility of the accused. The label attached the accused's conduct and the stigma that is thereby put on him or her have to match his or her moral blame, and should correctly display the wrongfulness and severity of the accused's conduct.[81] This is particularly important in relation to international crimes, where criminal law has an important expressive function and where courts are much concerned with the message they convey to the public.

Considering the expressive function of the law, it is significant that convicting businessmen for crimes such as money laundering or violating notification requirements mainly highlights their economic role and financial responsibilities. As such, it arguably neglects to portray the involvement of businessmen in the related international crimes. This is significant, in particular since it is exactly this link between businessmen and international crimes that has recently been emphasized in scholarship. In particular, in a policy paper on case selection and prioritization from the perspective of business and human rights, the ICC Office of the Prosecutor has raised expectations among those campaigning for increased scrutiny of the human rights impacts of business activity.[82] In addition, business and human rights scholars have suggested using the enforcement pyramid and applying criminal justice to the most serious cases of human rights violations by businesses at the top of the pyramid in order for soft-law tools to be effective in improving human rights performance by businesses at the bottom of the pyramid.[83] In this view, "reducing" the criminal responsibility of businessmen to autonomous offenses that are somewhat detached from the commission of international crimes is a step back. The cases against Van Anraat and Kouwenhoven prove that it is not always necessary to take this step. At the same time, we may need to recognize that establishing businessmen's participation in international crimes is only feasible in specific types of cases concerning relatively clear and direct business involvement whereby issues of remoteness are less prominent. In other cases, the weak causal and motivational link between businessmen and international crimes, and the organizational distance between these crimes and individual businessmen, can hamper establishing criminal liability for (participation in) international crimes. In these cases, autonomous and delinked types of criminal responsibility might be the only successful alternative to ascertain some type of accountability and to prevent complete impunity.

Notes

1 See, eg, the prosecutions that have been launched against Joseph Mpambara (Court of Appeal [CA] The Hague, 17 December 2007, ECLI:NL:GHSGR:2007:BC1757), Yvonne Basebya (District Court [DC] The Hague, 1 March 2013, ECLI:NL:RBDHA:2013:8710), and Eshetu Alemu (DC The Hague, 15 December 2013, ECLI:NL:RBDHA:2017:16383). All verdicts of Dutch Courts referred to in this article can be found <http://uitspraken.rechtspraak.nl/>.

2 CA The Hague, 9 May 2007, ECLI:NL:GHSGR:2007:BA6734; CA The Hague, 10 March 2008, ECLI:NL:GHSGR:2008:BC7373; Supreme Court (SC) 20 April

2010, ECLI:NL:HR: 2010:BK8132, *NJ* 2011, 576 (official Dutch verdict); CA 's-Hertogenbosch 21 April 2017, ECLI:NL:GHSHE:2017:2650. The defense counsel has announced it will once again bring this case before the Supreme Court, while at the same time requesting the ECtHR to render an interim measure in order to stop imprisonment on the grounds that Van Kouwenhoven (born 1942) would be unfit for prison because of his old age.

3 Christoph Burchard, 'Ancillary and Neutral Business Contributions to "Corporate: Political Core Crime": Initial Enquiries Concerning the Rome Statute', (2010) 8(3) *Journal of International Criminal Justice* 925.

4 Ibid.; Chrisje Brants, 'Gold Collar Crime', in Gilbert L. Geis and Henry N. Pontell (eds.), *International Handbook of White Collar Crime* (Springer 2007) 309–26.

5 Wim Huisman, *Business as Usual? Corporate Involvement in International Crimes* (Eleven International Publishing 2010) 11–12.

6 Wolfgang Kaleck and Miriam Saage-Maaß, 'Corporate Accountability for Human Rights Violations Amounting to International Crimes: The Status Quo and Its Challenges', (2010) 8(3) *Journal of International Criminal Justice* 721.

7 Wim Huisman and Elies van Sliedregt, 'Rogue traders, Dutch Businessmen, International Crimes and Corporate Complicity', (2010) 8(3) *Journal of International Criminal Justice* 826.

8 ICTY, *Prosecutor v. Momčilo Perišić*, Judgment, 6 September 2011, IT-04-81-T, para 37.

9 Ibid. paras 37–40.

10 Ibid. paras 71–2.

11 Eg, ICTY, *Prosecutor v. Šainović et al.*, Judgment, 23 January 2014, IT-05-87-A, paras 1649-50; ICTY, *Prosecutor v. Stanišić & Simatović Judgment*, 9 December 2015, IT-03-69-A, paras 104–8. See also ICTY, *Prosecutor v. Popović et al.*, Judgment, 30 January 2015, IT-05-88-A, paras 1758, 1764, 1783; Special Court for Sierra Leone (SCSL), *Prosecutor v. Charles Taylor*, Judgment, 26 September 2013, SCSL-03-01-A, paras 482–3, 480, 533.

12 Note that this specifically applies to case law of the ICTY. Art 25(3)(c) of the Rome Statute of the International Criminal Court (ICC Statute) stipulates a different – potentially higher – threshold for aiding.

13 Eg, ICTY, *Prosecutor v. Duško Tadić*, Sentencing Judgment, 7 May 1997, IT-94-1-T, para 229(iii)–(iv).

14 See, eg, Bundesgerichtshof 20 September 1999, *NStZ* 2000, 34; Bundesgerichtshof 1 August 2000, *BGHSt* 46, 107.

15 Wolfgang Joecks and Klaus Miebach, *Münchener Kommentar zum Strafgesetzbuch: StGB* (CH Beck 2017) § 27 Rn 58; Hans-Heinrich Jescheck and Thomas Weigend, *Lehrbuch des Strafrechts. Allgemeiner Teil* (Duncker & Humblot 1996) 695; Claus Roxin, *Strafrecht Algemeiner Teil. Band II. Besondere Erscheinungsformen der Straftat* (CH Beck 2003) § 26 Rn 218–24; Schönke/Schröder-Weißer/Heine, *Strafgesetzbuch: StGB: Kommentar* (29th edn, CH Beck 2014) § 27 Rn 10.

16 Joecks and Miebach (n 15) § 27 Rn 58, 77, and 86–7; Roxin (n 15) § 26 Rn 241–54; Schönke/Schröder-Weißer/Heine, (n 15) § 27 Rn 10; Bernd von Heintschel-Heinegg, *Strafgesetzbuch: StGB: Kommentar* (CH Beck 2017), 'A. Der Begriff der "neutralen" Handlung', Rn 15.

17 Huisman (n 5) reported on the neutralization techniques used to diffuse responsibility for corporate involvement in international crimes.

18 In analyzing cases of corporate involvement in international crimes, Huisman (n 5) found a strong correlation of such involvement with bribery. Because of this relation, Bantekas proposed qualifying corruption as a crime against humanity in these situations: Ilias Bantekas, 'Corruption as an International Crime and Crime against Humanity: An Outline of Supplementary Criminal Justice Policies', (2006) 4(3) *Journal of International Criminal Justice* 466.

19 Note that participation in apartheid is a crime against humanity under Art 7 of the ICC Statute.
20 Donna Katzin, 'Anatomy of a Boycott: The Royal Dutch/Shell Campaign in the US', in Richard Hengeveld and Jaap Rodenburg (eds.), *Embargo: Apartheid's Oil Secrets Revealed* (Amsterdam University Press 1995) 336.
21 Mark Bovens, *The Quest for Responsibility: Accountability and Citizenship in Complex Organisations* (Camdridge University Press 1998) 74–85; Mark J Hornman, *De strafrechtelijke aansprakelijkheid van leidinggevenden van ondernemingen. Een beschouwing vanuit multidimensionaal perspectief* (Boom juridisch 2016) 85–96, 163–91, 246–57.
22 Maurice Punch, *Dirty Business: Exploring Corporate Misconduct: Analysis and Cases* (Sage Publication 1996) 216: 'Some companies set out to break the law; some end up breaking the law; and some cannot manage the messes they get into.' Donald Palmer, *Normal Organizational Wrongdoing: A Critical Analysis of Theories of Misconduct in and by Organizations* (Oxford University Press 2012).
23 Wim Huisman, 'Criminogenic Organizational Properties and Dynamics', in Shanna Van Slyke, Michael Benson, and Francis T. Cullen (eds.), *The Oxford Handbook of White-Collar Crime* (Oxford University Press 2015).
24 See Bovens (n 21) and Hornman (n 21).
25 See Huisman (n 5) for some examples regarding joint ventures between Western companies and local State-owned or semi-private companies whose local officials may be more inclined to follow their own ambitions rather than complying with standards set by the Western mother company.
26 Bovens (n 21) 79.
27 DC The Hague, 23 December 2005, ECLI:NL:RBSGR:2005:AX6406.
28 That is the TDG.
29 CA The Hague (n 2).
30 SC 30 June 2009, ECLI:NL:HR:2009:BG4822, *NJ* 2009, 481.
31 *Van Anraat v the Netherlands* App no 65389/09 (ECtHR, 6 July 2010).
32 CA The Hague (n 2).
33 CA The Hague (n 2), paras 11.10 and 11.16.
34 Huisman and van Sliedregt (n 7) 823.
35 DC The Hague, 7 June 2006, ECLI:NL:RBSGR:2006:AX7098; CA The Hague, 10 March 2008, ECLI:NL:GHSGR:2008:BC7373; SC 20 April 2010, ECLI:NL:HR: 2010:BK8132, *NJ* 2011, 576.
36 CA 's-Hertogenbosch (n 2).
37 DC The Hague (n 35), para 6.
38 Larissa van den Herik, 'The Difficulties of Exercising Extraterritorial Criminal Jurisdiction: The Acquittal of a Dutch Businessman for Crimes Committed in Liberia', (2009) 9(1) *International Criminal Law Review* 223.
39 Ibid. 222.
40 CA 's-Hertogenbosch (n 2), para L.2.4.
41 Ibid. paras H.3 and J.6.1.
42 CA 's-Hertogenbosch (n 2).
43 Huisman and van Sliedregt (n 7) 820–1. Similarly, Norman Farrell, 'Attributing Criminal Liability to Corporate Actors: Some Lessons from the International Tribunals', (2010) 8(3) *Journal of International Criminal Justice* 880.
44 Hornman (n 21) 226 and 452.
45 Yet, at the same time, we should beware that where it concerns strategic decisions – such as the decision to invest in a country with poor human rights records – the top management may in fact be more closely involved. Sally S. Simpson, Nicole Leeper Piquero, and Raymond Paternoster, 'Rationality and Corporate Offending Decisions', in Alex R. Piquero and Stephen G. Tibbetts (eds.), *Rational Choice*

and Criminal Behavior: Recent Research and Future Challenges (Routledge 2012) 25–39.

46 Prakken d'Oliveira: Human Rights Lawyers, 'Aangifte tegen Rabobank Groep vanwege witwassen van winsten van Mexicaanse drugskartels' (2 February 2017) <www.prakkendoliveira.nl/nl/nieuws/2017/aangifte-tegen-rabobank-groep-vanwege-witwassen-van-winsten-van-mexicaanse-drugskartels> accessed 24 September 2019; NOS, 'Aangifte tegen Rabobank voor misdrijven tegen de menselijkheid' (2 February 2017) <http://nos.nl/artikel/2156175-aangifte-tegen-rabobank-voor-misdrijven-tegen-de-menselijkheid.html> accessed 24 September 2019; Marjolein van de Water, 'Aanklacht: Rabobank medeplichtig aan moord en misdaden drugskartels' (2 February 2017) <www.volkskrant.nl/binnenland/aanklacht-rabobank-medeplichtig-aan-moord-en-misdaden-drugskartels~a4456671/> accessed 24 September 2019.

47 Prakken d'Oliveira: Human Rights Lawyers (n 46). For more detail, see the full-text version of the criminal complaint at 8–9 <www.prakkendoliveira.nl/images/nieuws/2017/170202_aangifte_tegen_de_rabobank_groep_pers.pdf> accessed 24 September 2019.

48 See full text of the criminal complaint (n 47) 17–19.

49 Ibid. 19.

50 The United States Attorney's Office: Southern District of California, 'Bank Pleads Guilty, Pays Historic Penalty for Concealing Anti-Money Laundering Failures' (7 February 2018) <www.justice.gov/usao-sdca/pr/bank-pleads-guilty-pays-historic-penalty-concealing-anti-money-laundering-failures> accessed 24 September 2019.

51 Eg, SC 16 October 1990, ECLI:NL:HR:1990:AD1248, *NJ* 1991, 442, para 13.1; SC 10 July 2001, ECLI:NL:HR:2001:AD8636, *NJ* 2001, 687. See also Maria de Vries-Leemans, *Artikel 140 Wetboek van Strafrecht: een onderzoek naar de strafbaarstelling van deelneming aan misdaadorganisaties* (Gouda Quint 1995) 31–6; Jaap de Hullu, *Materieel strafrecht: over algemene leerstukken van strafrechtelijke aansprakelijkheid naar Nederlands recht* (Wolters Kluwer 2015).

52 Caroline M. Pelser, 'Preparations to Commit a Crime: The Dutch Approach to Inchoate Offences', (2008) 4(3) *Utrecht Law Review* 70.

53 CA The Hague, 30 April 2015, ECLI:NL:GHDHA:2015:1082, para 10.6.1.1.3.

54 Pelser (n 52). Even an online cooperation suffices (see CA The Hague, 18 January 2013, ECLI:NL:GHDHA:2013:BZ6496).

55 SC 2 February 2010, ECLI:NL:HR:2010:BK5175 and BK5193; Andries Kesteloo, *Deelneming aan een criminele organisatie. Een onderzoek naar de strafbaarstellingen in artikel 140 Sr* (Wolf Legal Publishers 2011) 37–8, 65.

56 SC (n 51) para 12.1.

57 Pelser (n 52).

58 de Hullu (n 51) 440; François Kristen, 'Maatschappelijk verantwoord ondernemen en strafrecht', in Jan Eijsbouts et al. (eds.), *Maatschappelijk verantwoord ondernemen* (Wolters Kluwer 2010) 153.

59 Harmen van der Wilt, 'Ontwikkeling van nieuwe deelnemingsvormen. Ben ik mijn broeders hoeder?', (2007) 37(2) *Delikt & Delinkwent* 138.

60 However, one can participate in – rather than perpetrate – the crime of Art 140 DPC from outside the organization. SC 3 July 2012, ECLI:NL:HR:2012:5132.

61 SC 29 January 1991, *DD* 91.168/169; SC 18 November 1997, ECLI:NL:HR:1997:ZD0858.

62 *Parliamentary Papers II* 2002/03, 28463, 10, 10.

63 SC 29 January 1991 (n 60); SC 18 November 1997 (n 60).

64 SC 10 February 2015, ECLI:NL:HR:2015:264.
65 SC 18 November 1997, *NJ* 1998, 225, para 5.3; SC, 8 October 2002, *NJ* 2003, 64; SC 5 September 2006, *NJ* 2007, 336.
66 Liesbeth Enneking et al., *Zorgplichten van Nederlandse ondernemingen inzake internationaal maatschappelijk verantwoord ondernemen: Een rechtsvergelijkend en empirisch onderzoek naar de stand van het Nederlandse recht in het licht van de UN Guiding Principles* (Boomjuridisch 2016) 227–8; Kristen (n 58) 146–51.
67 DC Rotterdam, 13 October 1995, *Milieu en Recht* 1996, 3; SC 5 July 2016, ECLI:NL:HR:2016:1393.
68 SC 14 March 2017, ECLI:NL:HR:2017:413, para 3.7; Conclusion Advocate General 20 December 2016, ECLI:PHR:2016:1510.
69 Prakken d'Oliveira: Human Rights Lawyers (n 46). For more detail, see the full-text of the criminal complaint (n 47) 29.
70 Ibid. See also Peter Reuter and Edwin M. Truman, *Chasing Dirty Money: The Fight Against Money Laundering* (Peterson Institute for International Economics 2004).
71 Enneking et al. (n 66) 227; Kristen (n 58) 146–51.
72 Conclusion Advocate General 8 April 2014, ECLI:NL:PHR:2014:1144.
73 Mark J. Hornman, 'Witwassen en deelname aan een criminele organisatie als vangnet voor indirecte betrokkenheid van ondernemingen bij mensenrechten-schendingen: Een analyse van de aangifte tegen de Rabobank', (2018) 5(1) *Tijdschrift voor Bijzonder Strafrecht & Handhaving* 4.
74 In The Netherlands, these violations are enforced through the Sanctions Act (*Sanctiewet*). For more information, see <www.government.nl/topics/international-peace-and-security/contents/compliance-with-international-sanctions/implementation-of-sanctions-in-the-netherlands>, <www.toezicht.dnb.nl/en/4/6/51-204700.jsp> and <www.coe.int/t/dlapil/cahdi/Source/un_sanctions/Netherlands%20UN%20Sanctions%202006%20E.pdf> accessed 24 September 2019. A well-known example of the application of this Act is the *Kouwenhoven* case, in which the accused was prosecuted not only as an aider of war crimes, but also for violating the Sanctions Act.
75 The latter is a well-known problem when it comes to investigating and prosecuting cross-border criminality, and was recently highlighted in the Netherlands by the Trafigura case concerning the dumping of toxic waste from the *Probo Koala* in the city of Abidjan in Ivory Coast. In this case, the investigation was severely hampered by the unwillingness of the Ivorian authorities to heed to the Dutch requests for legal assistance. See CA The Hague, 12 April 2011, ECLI:NL:GHSGR:2011:BQ1012.
76 See <www.fiu-nederland.nl/en> accessed 24 September 2019.
77 This obligation is an implementation of the Second Anti-Money Laundering Directive (Directive 2001/97/EC of the European Parliament and of the Council of 4 December 2001 amending Council Directive 91/308/EEC on prevention of the use of the financial system for the purpose of money laundering – Commission Declaration [2001] OJ L 344) and has been the norm throughout the EU ever since.
78 A politically exposed person is someone who, through his or her prominent position or influence, is more susceptible to being involved in bribery or corruption.
79 Prakken d'Oliveira: Human Rights Lawyers (n 46) 11–13 and 28–30.
80 With regard to the *Van Anraat* case, the Prevention Abuse of Chemicals Act (*Wet voorkoming misbruik chemicaliën*), which also applies to cases involving illicit substances, is worth mentioning as it imposes a number of notification requirements on so-called "operators as mentioned in Regulation (EC) No 273/2004 of the European Parliament and of the Council of 11 February 2004 on drug precursors".

81 David Nersessian, 'Comparative Approaches to Punishing Hate: The Intersection of Genocide and Crimes against Humanity', (2007) 43 *Stanford Journal of International Law* 255. See also Natalia Perova, 'Stretching the Joint Criminal Enterprise Doctrine to the Extreme: When Culpability and Liability Do Not Match', (2015) 16(5) *International Criminal Law Review* 761.

82 Nadia Bernaz, 'An Analysis of the ICC Office of the Prosecutor's Policy Paper on Case Selection and Prioritization from the Perspective of Business and Human Rights', (2017) 15(3) *Journal of International Criminal Justice* 527. According to the Special Representative on Business and Human Rights of the UNHRC, corporations have a "duty to respect human rights", but not a duty to protect them, as international law does not create binding human rights duties for non-State actors. This might change when current proposals to create a binding treaty on business obligations on human rights are successful. David Bilchitz, 'The Necessity for a Business and Human Rights Treaty', (2016) 1(2) *Business and Human Rights Journal* 203.

83 Surya Deva, *Regulating Corporate Human Rights Violations: Humanizing Business* (1st edn, Routledge 2012).

Bibliography

Bantekas I, 'Corruption as an International Crime and Crime against Humanity: An Outline of Supplementary Criminal Justice Policies', (2006) 4(3) *Journal of International Criminal Justice* 466.

Bernaz N, 'An Analysis of the ICC Office of the Prosecutor's Policy Paper on Case Selection and Prioritization from the Perspective of Business and Human Rights', (2017) 15(3) *Journal of International Criminal Justice* 527.

Bilchitz D, 'The Necessity for a Business and Human Rights Treaty', (2016) 1(2) *Business and Human Rights Journal* 203.

Bovens M, *The Quest for Responsibility: Accountability and Citizenship in Complex Organisations* (Camdridge University Press 1998).

Brants C, 'Gold Collar Crime', in Gilbert L. Geis and Henry N. Pontell (eds.), *International Handbook of White Collar Crime* (Springer 2007).

Burchard C, 'Ancillary and Neutral Business Contributions to "Corporate: Political Core Crime": Initial Enquiries Concerning the Rome Statute', (2010) 8(3) *Journal of International Criminal Justice* 925.

de Hullu J, *Materieel strafrecht: over algemene leerstukken van strafrechtelijke aansprakelijkheid naar Nederlands recht* (Wolters Kluwer 2015).

Deva S, *Regulating Corporate Human Rights Violations: Humanizing Business* (1st edn, Routledge 2012).

Enneking L et al., *Zorgplichten van Nederlandse ondernemingen inzake internationaal maatschappelijk verantwoord ondernemen: Een rechtsvergelijkend en empirisch onderzoek naar de stand van het Nederlandse recht in het licht van de UN Guiding Principles* (Boomjuridisch 2016).

Farrell N, 'Attributing Criminal Liability to Corporate Actors: Some Lessons from the International Tribunals', (2010) 8(3) *Journal of International Criminal Justice* 880.

Hornman MJ, *De strafrechtelijke aansprakelijkheid van leidinggevenden van ondernemingen. Een beschouwing vanuit multidimensionaal perspectief* (Boomjuridisch 2016).

———, 'Witwassen en deelname aan een criminele organisatie als vangnet voor indirecte betrokkenheid van ondernemingen bij mensenrechtenschendingen: Een analyse van de aangifte tegen de Rabobank', (2018) 5(1) *Tijdschrift voor Bijzonder Strafrecht & Handhaving* 4.

Huisman W, *Business as Usual? Corporate Involvement in International Crimes* (Eleven International Publishing 2010).

———, 'Criminogenic Organizational Properties and Dynamics', in Shanna Van Slyke, Michael Benson, and Francis T Cullen (eds.), *The Oxford Handbook of White-Collar Crime* (Oxford University Press 2015).

——— and van Sliedregt E,'Rogue Traders, Dutch Businessmen, International Crimes and Corporate Complicity', (2010) 8(3) *Journal of International Criminal Justice* 826.

Jescheck H-H and Weigend T, *Lehrbuch des Strafrechts. Allgemeiner Teil* (Duncker & Humblot 1996).

Joecks W and Miebach K, *Münchener Kommentar zum Strafgesetzbuch: StGB* (CH Beck 2017).

Kaleck W and Saage-Maaß M, 'Corporate Accountability for Human Rights Violations Amounting to International Crimes: The Status Quo and its Challenges', (2010) 8(3) *Journal of International Criminal Justice* 721.

Katzin D, 'Anatomy of a Boycott: The Royal Dutch/Shell Campaign in the US', in Richard Hengeveld and Jaap Rodenburg (eds.), *Embargo: Apartheid's Oil Secrets Revealed* (Amsterdam University Press 1995).

Kesteloo AN, *Deelneming aan een criminele organisatie. Een onderzoek naar de strafbaarstellingen in artikel 140 Sr* (Wolf Legal Publishers 2011).

Kristen FGH, 'Maatschappelijk verantwoord ondernemen en strafrecht', in AJAJ Eijsbouts et al. (eds.) *Maatschappelijk verantwoord ondernemen* (Wolters Kluwer 2010).

Nersessian D, 'Comparative Approaches to Punishing Hate: The Intersection of Genocide and Crimes against Humanity', (2007) 43 *Stanford Journal of International Law* 255.

Palmer D, *Normal Organizational Wrongdoing: A Critical Analysis of Theories of Misconduct in and by Organizations* (Oxford University Press 2012).

Pelser CM, 'Preparations to Commit a Crime: The Dutch Approach to Inchoate Offences', (2008) 4(3) *Utrecht Law Review* 70.

Perova N, 'Stretching the Joint Criminal Enterprise Doctrine to the Extreme: When Culpability and Liability Do Not Match', (2015) 16(5) *International Criminal Law Review* 761.

Punch M, *Dirty Business: Exploring Corporate Misconduct: Analysis and Cases* (Sage Publication 1996).

Reuter P and Truman EM, *Chasing Dirty Money: The Fight against Money Laundering* (Peterson Institute for International Economics 2004).

Roxin C, *Strafrecht Algemeiner Teil. Band II. Besondere Erscheinungsformen der Straftat* (CH Beck 2003).

Schönke/Schröder-Weißer/Heine, *Strafgesetzbuch: StGB: Kommentar* (29th edn, CH Beck 2014).

Simpson SS, Piquero NL, and Paternoster R, 'Rationality and Corporate Offending Decisions', in AR Piquero and SG Tibbetts (eds.), *Rational Choice and Criminal Behavior: Recent Research and Future Challenges* (Routledge 2012).

van den Herik L, 'The Difficulties of Exercising Extraterritorial Criminal Jurisdiction: The Acquittal of a Dutch Businessman for Crimes Committed in Liberia', (2009) 9(1) *International Criminal Law Review* 223.

van der Wilt H, 'Ontwikkeling van nieuwe deelnemingsvormen. Ben ik mijn broeders hoeder?', (2007) 37(2) *Delikt & Delinkwent* 138.
von Heintschel-Heinegg B, *Strafgesetzbuch: StGB: Kommentar* (CH Beck 2017).
Vries-Leemans MJHJ, *Artikel 140 Wetboek van Strafrecht: een onderzoek naar de strafbaarstelling van deelneming aan misdaadorganisaties* (Gouda Quint 1995).

10 Legally binding duties for corporations under domestic criminal law not to commit modern slavery

Anne-Jetske Schaap

10.1 Introduction

Given the important role of corporations in the globalized modern-day world, it is not surprising that the adverse effects of corporate activities on human rights within and across states have given rise to widespread concern. This concern has raised the question of how corporations can be held legally accountable for the adverse effects of their cross-border activities on people and the planet abroad. Hard law in the host countries in which the cross-border activities of these corporations are conducted does not always sufficiently address the negative impacts.[1] In addition, if hard law does exist, for many reasons the host state may be unwilling or unable to enforce it.[2] At the same time, hard law on this matter at an international level does not yet exist.[3] Therefore, the answer to the previous question is often sought in the domestic law of the corporations' home State, most notably in civil law.[4] Domestic criminal law is not often looked at, yet it can provide interesting possibilities in addressing corporate violations of human rights or environmental norms abroad.

This contribution addresses the potential of domestic criminal law to hold internationally operating corporations legally accountable for the adverse effects of their cross-border activities.[5] This is done by focusing on one particular human rights-related issue that has generated a great deal of debate among NGOs, policymakers, and scholars recently – that is, modern slavery. In addressing the potential of domestic criminal law to tackle the issue of modern slavery, the focus will be on Dutch and English law (that is, the law of England and Wales).[6] Accordingly, the question central to this chapter is whether, and to what extent, corporations have binding duties under Dutch and English criminal law not to commit modern slavery in their cross-border activities.

Modern slavery comprises various sorts of conduct. In the absence of a clear and commonly shared definition, various concepts are used to define and/or to differentiate among forms of modern slavery.[7] These include trafficking in human beings, slavery, servitude, forced labor, sexual and labor exploitation, the worst forms of child labor, and debt bondage.[8] These practices and institutions all pose a great threat to the human rights, labor rights, and the health of the workers involved. It is widely recognized that corporations often play a key role in the practices' occurrence, either directly or indirectly.[9] Nonetheless, holding corporations legally accountable for conduct that constitutes some form of modern slavery is not self-evident. This has been shown in recent debates, at both the national and the international level, on possibilities for legislative action, which have also left their marks in the Netherlands and England.[10]

The proposed detailed doctrinal study of the law as it currently stands in two jurisdictions with a focus on specific pieces of legislation will offer insight into the potential of domestic criminal law in the case of modern slavery. This external legal comparison is an example of the multidimensional research approach.[11] It will be particularly suited to highlight factors that are decisive for the potential of domestic criminal law in addressing modern slavery, especially when the results of the study of the two jurisdictions are compared. These insights are relevant not only for the two jurisdictions studied, but potentially also for other jurisdictions, and may provide inspiration for the criminalization of other violations of human rights as well.[12]

In order to answer this chapter's central question, it is necessary first to assess how modern slavery is currently criminalized under Dutch and English law. In both jurisdictions, multiple offenses criminalize conduct that may fall under the umbrella of modern slavery. Think of specific provisions of labor law, immigration law, sexual offenses, or – more generally – fraud offenses. However, in this chapter the focus is on those offenses that are perceived to be the "core offense" of modern slavery in the respective jurisdictions and that are used to implement the same core international obligations on this issue. These offenses are laid down in art 273f of the Dutch Criminal Code (DCC) and in Part 1 of the UK Modern Slavery Act 2015 (MSA).[13] The description of these offenses is limited to modern slavery in the form of labor exploitation.[14] Second, the question arises as to whether and how it is possible to hold corporations criminally liable for these offenses. Here, the focus is on corporations' own and direct criminal liability.[15] Since the focus of this chapter is on corporations' cross-border activities, the third question that needs to be addressed is when the home State can exercise jurisdiction over the corporations' conduct.

The answers to these three questions will be discussed in Section 10.2 for Dutch law and in Section 10.3 for English law. In Section 10.4, the findings for the two jurisdictions will be compared.[16] The chapter will close with a conclusion in Section 10.5.

10.2 Duties for corporations not to commit modern slavery in their cross-border activities under Dutch criminal law

10.2.1 The offense of modern slavery

In Dutch criminal law, the offense of modern slavery is laid down in the long and complex provision of art 273f DCC. Under influence of various international obligations, this provision has come to encompass many paragraphs and subparagraphs, several of which can be considered to be offenses on their own.[17] These "offenses" are aimed at criminalizing various forms and stages of modern slavery. For the present purposes – that is, for modern slavery in the form of labor exploitation – four of those "offenses" are relevant: (1) human trafficking, (2) child trafficking, (3) coercion or induction of a person into making her/himself available for work or services, and (4) profiting from the exploitation of a person.

The first two offenses are the so-called trafficking offenses. They concern the activity of human trafficking in art 273f (1)(1) and child trafficking in section (1)(2) DCC. The conduct criminalized in both offenses is the recruitment, transportation, transfer, harboring, and receipt of persons, including transferring or exchanging control over those persons. For human trafficking other than child trafficking, the conduct should be effected by one or more "impermissible means", for example by the use of force, coercion, or deception.[18] There should be a causal connection between the conduct and the means. For the offense of child trafficking, proof of the use of impermissible means is not required. At this point, just as in other parts of the provision, minors are especially protected.

Apart from the *actus reus*, a mental element (or *mens rea*) is also required. Clear from the provision is that both trafficking offenses should be carried out for the purpose of exploitation. According to Dutch law, this means that proof is required of direct or indirect intent with regard to exploitation.[19] Direct intent requires that the main aim of the offender's conduct (for example, of the recruitment) was the exploitation of that person. For indirect intent, it suffices that the offender realized that exploitation was a virtually certain consequence and thus accepted it as such. It does not necessarily need to have been the intended consequence.[20] It is important to note that although it is necessary for a conviction that the conduct has been engaged in for the purpose of exploitation, an actual situation of exploitation does not yet need to exist.

Implicitly, both provisions also require at least *dolus eventualis* on the conduct and on use of the means (if required). *Dolus eventualis* is a form of intent in Dutch criminal law. It requires that the offender knows of the existence of significant possibility and willfully accepts that significant possibility of the conduct occurring.[21] For example, it needs to be established that the offender was aware of the existence of a significant possibility that he or she would be recruiting a person by deception and that he or she accepted that possibility. Establishing *dolus eventualis* thus requires less than direct and indirect intent.

In short, through their focus on "trafficking", section 1(1) and 1(2) of art 273f DCC criminalize conduct preceding the actual exploitation of another person. However, it must be noted also that in the case actual labor exploitation is already taking place, criminal liability can be established via these provisions. After all, all the elements described (that is, the illegal conduct, the means, a causal connection between the two, and the required *mens rea*) can very well be present if a person is already being exploited.

The third offense can be found in art 273f (1)(4) DCC. It criminalizes conduct close to the actual exploitation of another person and the actual exploitation of another person, effected by the same impermissible means as in subsection 1 (the trafficking offense).[22] To be more precise, the provision criminalizes (1) coercing or inducing a person, or (2) acting in a way in which one knows or reasonably suspects that a person would be coerced or induced, by using one or more impermissible means, into making him-/herself available for work or services. The work or services should amount to exploitation if actually performed.[23]

As for *mens rea*, *dolus eventualis* for the conduct and for the use of the impermissible means suffices for the first variant. For the second variant, an additional *mens rea* element of at least negligence needs to be proven with regard to the victim making him-/herself available for the performance of work or services. Negligence in Dutch criminal law means "acting considerably and culpably imprudent".[24]

The fourth offense is set out in art 273f(1)(6) DCC and criminalizes "profiting from the exploitation of another person". This offense brings people who normally operate in the background, or several steps removed from the actual exploitation, within the scope of the criminal law.[25] Given that "profiting" is to be interpreted broadly, any real profit or benefit suffices.[26] This can be financial profit, but also "other" profit, and arguably even competitive advantage. For this offense, the existence of a situation of exploitation needs to be proven. However, that situation does not have to be created by the offender him-/herself. It suffices that an actual situation of exploitation exists.[27] That said, the profit does need to be the result of the exploitation; there must be a causal connection between the profit and the exploitation. Yet the profit does not have to follow directly from the exploitation. Indirect profit – for example, financial advantage several steps removed from the actual exploitation – suffices as well.[28]

As for *mens rea*, there needs to exist at least *dolus eventualis* on "profiting" *and* on the existence of exploitation. This means that the offender must consciously have accepted an actual significant possibility not only of profiting but also of the exploitation of another person.[29]

Considering (the interpretation of) all elements of this offense, it is already interesting to note that it may very well be possible to hold corporations criminally liable if they profit from exploitation that takes place somewhere in their supply chain, provided that the Netherlands has jurisdiction. The requirements for establishing corporate criminal liability and for jurisdiction are addressed in the following sections.

What falls under the concept of exploitation is specified in art 273f (2) DCC. This specification is relevant for all four offenses discussed. After all, the two "trafficking offenses" should be conducted for the purpose of exploitation. The third offense should amount to exploitation if actually performed, and, for the profiting offense, there should be an actual situation of exploitation. According to 273f (2) DCC, exploitation includes at least forced or compulsory labor or services, slavery, practices comparable to slavery, and servitude. For interpretation of these practices, the international instruments that have influenced the development of art 273f DCC and case law, at both national and international level, are important.[30]

However, art 273f DCC covers more forms of exploitation than those explicitly set out in paragraph 2.[31] Case law shows that in order to determine whether there is a situation of exploitation, various factors that may point to exploitation should be weighed.[32] An analysis of both national and international case law shows that these factors include: the kind of work, the duration, the working conditions, and, if applicable, the housing conditions, the restrictions that follow from the work, the received income, the economic profit for the offender, the age of the victim, and the level of involuntariness and unavoidability. For the latter, proof can come from the use of impermissible means. Dutch standards function as the benchmark in weighing all these factors. For example, reference can be made to the Dutch legal minimum wage.[33]

However, the question may be raised as to how exploitation can be established if it takes place abroad – for example, in the supply chain. After all, using Dutch standards as a benchmark in weighing the aforementioned "exploitation factors" in cases where exploitation does not take place in the Netherlands does not seem self-evident. So far, there is no case law on this issue. In my view, the same approach as that outlined previously (weighing the factors) can be used. Yet instead of using the Dutch standards as a benchmark in such cases, one should consider (1) international standards derived from broadly supported international instruments[34] and (2) local standards – to the extent available – if they offer more protection compared to international standards.[35] In short, the international standards provide the lower limit, but more protection is possible if provided for in the respective host state where the alleged labor exploitation takes place.

10.2.2 Corporate criminal liability

The next question is whether, and how, according to Dutch law, corporations can be held criminally liable for labor exploitation on the basis of the four modern slavery offenses. In art 51, the DCC provides a basis for corporate wrongdoing for – in principle – all offenses. This thus includes the four modern slavery offenses of art 273f DCC. Corporations under Dutch criminal law include all entities with legal personality according to Dutch civil law,[36] all entities summed up in art 51(3) DCC, and foreign corporations with legal personality in their own respective jurisdiction.[37] However, neither art 51 DCC itself nor its legislative history provide an answer to the question regarding the circumstances under which a corporation can be held criminally liable. This is a key question due to the uneasy fit of corporations with the criminal law, which makes establishing the *actus reus* and *mens rea* at the level of a legal person not self-evident. In the Netherlands, the task of answering this question has been left to the judiciary.[38]

In 2003, the Dutch Supreme Court (*Hoge Raad*) delivered a landmark decision in the *Drijfmest* case, in which it partly answered this question.[39] The Supreme Court held that *actus reus* can be established at the level of the corporation if the conduct can reasonably be attributed to the corporation. Whether it is reasonable to attribute conduct to a legal person depends on all of the circumstances of the case, including the nature of the conduct. The Dutch Supreme Court did not deem it desirable to formulate a general rule, but did state that an important factor to take into account is whether the conduct took place *within the sphere of the corporation*. If such is the case, it is in principle reasonable to attribute the conduct to the corporation.[40]

The Supreme Court concretized its "within the sphere of the corporation" criterion by identifying four non-cumulative and non-exhaustive guiding circumstances. The first is whether the conduct was performed by someone who worked for the corporation, either formally as an employee or on another basis.[41] Considering the nature of the conduct of the four modern slavery offenses of art 273f DCC discussed here, it is certainly not unlikely that people performing the *actus reus* of these offenses will work – either directly or indirectly – for the corporation.

The second circumstance is whether the relevant conduct was part of the normal course of business of the corporation. This concerns the act or omission abstracted from its illegal character.[42] In order to establish the normal course of business, the factual day-to-day operation is decisive.[43] It is not difficult to imagine this circumstance to be present in cases dealing with the offenses laid down in art 273f DCC, especially when there is a situation of actual exploitation and/or profiting from exploitation. After all, if one abstracts labor exploitation or profiting from such exploitation from its illegal character, this conduct will often be part of the normal course of business of corporations: corporations often make employees perform work and/or services or profit from the labor of these employees.

The third circumstance is whether the act or omission was beneficial for the corporation, for example if it has resulted in financial gain or benefited the corporation in another way.[44] If there is an actual situation of labor exploitation, it is easy to imagine it to be lucrative for the corporation – all the more so when the "profiting from exploitation" offense can be established.

The fourth circumstance centers first of all on the question of whether the corporation had a *de facto* "power of disposal" over the illegal conduct. This power of disposal needs to be established objectively: of relevance is whether the corporation had a real possibility to prevent the illegal conduct from occurring or to affect the illegal conduct.[45] If the corporation indeed had such power, the follow-up question is whether, judging by the factual circumstances of the case, the corporation accepted the conduct or was accustomed to accepting similar conduct. The Supreme Court has added that the question of whether the conduct or similar conduct was accepted can be answered in the affirmative if the corporation did not exercise the level of due care that could reasonably be expected of it in order to prevent the conduct from occurring.[46]

In relation to the four modern slavery offenses of art 273f DCC, this "duty of care" is an interesting factor. For example, if the corporation did not take the care that could reasonably be expected of it to prevent the profiting from the exploitation, the sphere criterion can be fulfilled, and it is in principle reasonable to attribute the conduct to the corporation. However, this raises a question regarding the meaning of these duties of care. What type and level of care is expected of corporations in preventing modern slavery? Dutch criminal law does not (yet) provide an answer. There is currently no legislative guidance, and case law does not provide much insight.

Meyer, Van Roomen, and Sikkema have suggested that the existence of adequate supervision and control is important for fulfilling this duty of care.[47] Whether this is the case may, according to them, be assessed by looking at statuary obligations, contractual obligations, the specific circumstances of the respective criminal offense, and even customary professional standards and self-regulatory instruments.[48] In this regard, it is interesting to consider what role international "soft-law" instruments relating to CSR and/or business and human rights and directed at corporations, such as the OECD Guidelines for Multinational Enterprises or the UNGPs, may play in this regard. I will come back to this in Section 10.2.4.

As already set out, each of the four *Drijfmest* circumstances, which can be used independently to fulfil the sphere criterion, offers potential in the case of modern slavery. Still, even if the sphere criterion is fulfilled, the question remains as to whether it is *reasonable* to attribute the conduct to the corporation. In practice, this means that in many cases, more than one of the circumstances needs to be present in order to reasonably attribute the act or omission to the corporation. This especially seems to be the case with the first (work) and third (lucrative) circumstance.[49] The question of the relative weight of the *Drijfmest* circumstances has so far not received a definitive answer through statutory or case law. According to literature, fulfilment of the sphere criterion on the basis of the second and/or the fourth circumstance (and thus also on the basis of the duty of care) is considered a powerful indication of reasonableness of the attribution.[50]

Another, more dogmatic, question that has been raised in Dutch literature is what the exact consequence of fulfilling one's duty of care should be for the establishment of corporate criminal liability, and, more specifically, whether conduct can still be attributed if the corporation has fulfilled its duty of care. However, no definitive answer has been provided so far.[51]

Apart from the *actus reus*, the corporation must also have the required *mens rea*. Dutch criminal law offers two alternative ways to establish the necessary mental elements at the level of the corporation. First, by attributing to the corporation the mental state of an individual or of aggregates of individuals involved in the illegal conduct. The tasks of the individual or individuals, their responsibilities, and the internal organization of the corporation are important factors in determining whether the mental element can be attributed to the corporation.[52] Second, *mens rea* can be established directly at the level of the corporation based on factors such as organizational politics, decision-making processes, and the daily business operations.[53]

The latter may provide interesting possibilities in establishing *mens rea* for modern slavery offenses by internationally operating corporations, for example for the profiting offense of art 273f (1)(6) DCC, which only requires *dolus eventualis*. As is clear from the preceding section, to establish this form of *mens rea* for the profiting offense, first an actual significant possibility of profiting from the exploitation of another person must have been present. For example, if the circumstances of the specific case show that a corporation operates in a sector in which there is a high risk of modern slavery occurring and the corporation buys underpriced products, this possibility can very well be present. Second, the corporation must be shown to have consciously accepted this significant possibility of buying products manufactured by means of exploitation. For example, this can be the case if it was confronted with issues of modern slavery before but continued to operate in the same way, and this becomes apparent from the corporation's organizational politics and daily business operations. Conditional intent can then be established directly at the level of the corporation. It should be noted that if the corporation acted in accordance with its duty of care, it is unlikely that it may be said to have consciously accepted the significant possibility of the conduct occurring. In that case, *dolus eventualis* cannot be attributed to the corporation.[54]

Direct and indirect intent as required for the trafficking offenses of art 273f (1) and (2) DCC may be more difficult to establish at the level of the corporation, but in order to establish these forms of intent, it can be important if, for example, the offense has systematically (or perhaps also frequently) been conducted within the sphere of the corporation.[55]

The previous shows that the dynamic framework of establishing corporate criminal liability, with regard to both the *actus reus* and the *mens rea*, offers potential in attributing the four offenses related to labor exploitation discussed here to the corporation. In particular, subsections 4 and 6 of art 273f(1) DCC offer potential in this respect, as they criminalize conduct of such a nature that it can be attributed to corporations fairly easy, and no direct intent or indirect intent needs to be established. Interestingly, the duty of care of a corporation can play a decisive role in this regard: failure to comply can contribute to the establishment of corporate criminal liability, whereas compliance may prevent it.

10.2.3 Jurisdiction

In order to establish corporate criminal liability for modern slavery, the relevant conduct needs to fall within the jurisdiction of the Dutch state. Whether a state exercises jurisdiction depends on legal-political choices made by the respective state itself, but the state's discretion is restricted by (customary) rules of international public law.[56] In Dutch criminal law, arts 2–8d of the DCC, in combination with the "Extraterritorial Jurisdiction (International Obligations) Decree" (hereinafter "the Decree")[57] and a number of provisions in specific acts provide the basis for jurisdiction.

In principle, the Dutch state may exercise jurisdiction over all acts committed within its territory and under the Dutch flag (art 2 DCC).[58] The *locus delicti* of an offense can be established at the location of the actual conduct, the location of the consequences of the offense, and potentially also the location where an instrument used by the offender to commit the crime "operates" (such as the internet).[59] Considering the different elements of the modern slavery offenses discussed herein, and the prevailing doctrine of the *locus delicti*, jurisdiction can be established for the four offenses as long as at least part of the conduct can be located in the Netherlands.

Furthermore, even when the *locus delicti* cannot be located on Dutch territory, the Netherlands may still have jurisdiction. Arts 3–8c DCC and the Decree provide a legal basis for this. Following international obligations, these provisions establish a special regime for art 273f DCC. This means that an art 273f DCC offense committed by a Dutch corporation falls within the scope of Dutch criminal law, including when the modern slavery takes place abroad and even when it is not criminalized in the respective state, as the requirement of "double criminality" does not apply.[60] Accordingly, a Dutch corporation can be held criminally liable in the Netherlands for exploitation, including conduct preceding the exploitation and profiting from the exploitation, wherever the offense has been committed.

However, in cases concerning a company without Dutch nationality and conduct that is not located in the Netherlands, corporate criminal liability can only be established for modern slavery if there is a Dutch victim.[61] When labor exploitation takes place abroad, this will seldom be the case.

10.2.4 Analysis

Do corporations have a binding duty under Dutch criminal law not to commit modern slavery in their cross-border activities, and, if so, to what extent? As is clear from the legal framework set out in the preceding sections, corporations do indeed have such a duty. For corporations with Dutch nationality, this duty extends to conduct preceding the exploitation, the actual exploitation, and profiting from the exploitation – that is, conduct criminalized in the four offenses of art 273f DCC – wherever committed. If the Dutch corporations do not comply with this duty, they can be held criminally liable. For foreign corporations, this duty only applies when the criminalized conduct takes place (at least partly) in The Netherlands.

With this in mind, it is interesting to take a closer look at this duty. What does it mean in practice? As a result of its broad scope, it offers significant potential to establish corporate criminal liability for modern slavery committed (at least partly) in the Netherlands or for modern slavery committed abroad by a Dutch corporation. However, when we consider modern slavery abroad, Dutch companies will usually not be directly involved in the exploitation. In most cases, it will be the foreign subsidiaries or the supply chain partners of Dutch companies that perform the conduct preceding the exploitation, or the exploitation itself. With respect to the conduct of these foreign companies, the Dutch State has – in principle – no jurisdiction. Thus, jurisdiction seems to constitute a barrier.

However, in this regard, one aspect of Dutch criminal law deserves special attention. This is the way in which the offense of profiting from the exploitation of another person of art 273f (1)(6) DCC is formulated. Contrary to the other three offenses, this offense criminalizes conduct that is further removed from the actual exploitation. After all, the conduct central to this offense is the *profiting* and not the exploitation itself. Clearly, there must be a situation of exploitation; however, this does not have to be created by the offending company itself, nor does the profiting have to follow directly from the situation of exploitation. Indirect profit – that is, profit that is a several steps removed from the actual exploitation – suffices.

Considering the Dutch regime on jurisdiction, this provision creates a legally binding duty for corporations not to profit in the Netherlands – or for Dutch corporations not to profit at any given place – from a situation of exploitation, no matter where the exploitation has taken place. This includes exploitation in the supply chain. For example, if a Dutch company financially profits, or even gains competitive advantage, from selling products acquired from a subcontractor that had the products manufactured by committing modern slavery, the company has profited from exploitation, violated its duty, and can be held criminally liable in the Netherlands. Of course, for criminal liability to arise the remaining elements of art 273f (1)(6) DCC also need to be proven – though, as already set out, this is not unthinkable.

Thus, the scope of the duty under Dutch criminal law not to commit modern slavery turns out to be quite extensive in practice. It offers the possibility to address modern slavery abroad, including modern slavery in the supply chain.

Another aspect that warrants closer attention is the way in which corporate criminal liability can be established under Dutch criminal law and, more specifically, the role and meaning of the duty of care in this regard. As seen before, failure to comply with these duties of care can establish corporate criminal liability. At the same time, compliance may prevent corporate criminal liability from arising.

However, the question remains as to what this duty of care of corporations not to commit modern slavery in their cross-border activities may entail. It is interesting to consider whether the duty may be shaped and further specified by soft-law instruments that are directed at corporations and address the potential adverse effects of their transnational activities, such as the UNGPs[62] and the OECD Guidelines.[63] Especially interesting in this regard are the due diligence requirements that both the UNGPs and the OECD Guidelines set out. Due diligence can be defined as "the process through which enterprises can identify, prevent, mitigate and account for how they address their actual and potential adverse impacts as an integral part of business decision making and risk management systems".[64] The process comprises several steps.[65] In order to assess what, exactly, is expected from corporations in each step of the process, several factors are important. These include the size of the enterprise, the context of its operations, the severity of its adverse impacts, and also specific recommendations provided for in, for example, the OECD Guidelines.[66]

Considering the fact that this due diligence framework sets out the conduct that is expected of corporations to prevent adverse human rights (and environmental) impacts, and the authoritative status and broad national and international support of these soft-law instruments,[67] they arguably provide a good starting point in determining the content of the corporate duty of care under Dutch criminal law not to commit modern slavery in cross-border activities. If the UNGPs and the OECD Guidelines can indeed shape the duty of care under Dutch criminal law, this would mean that (parts of) these soft-law instruments may thus become part of "hard law". However, this does raise the question of whether the fact that a corporation has indeed conducted its due diligence according to the provisions laid down in these frameworks would also mean that its duty of care under Dutch criminal law has been fulfilled. Potentially, depending on the specific circumstances of the case, other (legal) instruments, steps, and/or factors may also be of importance.

However, it is important to note here that even though the scope of the duties under Dutch criminal law not to commit modern slavery turns out to be extensive in practice and even extends to the supply chain, this does not automatically mean that these duties are also enforced as such. In the past six years, only three modern slavery-related cases with a corporation as a defendant have made it to court.[68] Only one conviction of a corporation for modern slavery still stands in the Netherlands.[69] The case concerned labor exploitation on a mushroom farm in the south of the Netherlands. Duties of care did not play a role in that judgement, as attribution was based on the normal course of business and the fact that it was beneficial for the corporation.[70] Moreover, due to the fact that the labor exploitation was committed by the corporation itself, and because the exploitation took place in the Netherlands rather than abroad, the case does not provide much guidance as to the way in which Dutch courts would interpret the law in cases relating to the indirect involvement of Dutch corporations in modern slavery in their international supply chains.

10.3 Duties for corporations not to commit modern slavery in their cross-border activities under English criminal law

10.3.1 Offenses of modern slavery

Under English law, modern slavery is criminalized in part 1 of the MSA.[71] The MSA criminalizes three offenses: (1) holding a person in slavery or servitude or requiring a person to perform forced or compulsory labor; (2) trafficking in human beings; and (3) the commission of any offense with the intention of trafficking in human beings.

Section 1 MSA criminalizes holding a person in slavery or servitude or requiring a person to perform forced or compulsory labor (that is, the actual exploitation). Slavery, servitude, and forced and compulsory labor should be interpreted in accordance with art 4 of the ECHR.[72] The upshot of this is that case law of the ECtHR on art 4 is relevant for the interpretation.[73] To determine whether someone has been kept in slavery or servitude or has been required to perform forced or compulsory labor, regard may be given to all the circumstances.[74] The MSA provides some examples, such as the age of the victim, but these are not exhaustive.[75]

For the required *mens rea*, section 1 demands that the offender knew or ought to have known that the *actus reus* was being conducted. To know means that there was a true belief that the relevant circumstance indeed existed.[76] It is important that the knowledge is correct.[77] "Ought to have known" is a form of constructive knowledge and therefore falls within the category of negligence.[78] Negligence does not require a certain state of mind to be established on the part of the offender. It concerns an objective analysis of a risk that can objectively be recognized by using the standard of the reasonable man: the question is whether the offender fell below the standard of the reasonable man.[79]

Section 2 MSA criminalizes arranging or facilitating the travel of another person with a view to that person being exploited. Arranging or facilitating includes recruiting, transporting, transferring, harboring, or receiving that person, or transferring or exchanging control over that person.[80] "Travel" is defined as arriving in, entering, departing, or travelling within any country.[81]

In order to constitute a crime, the arranging or facilitating needs to have been done with a view to the exploitation of the victim. "With a view to" normally constitutes a form of ulterior intent in English criminal law[82] – in other words, an intention to bring about a certain consequence beyond the illegal conduct. Intent in English criminal law includes direct intent (it was the offender's purpose) and oblique intent (it was a virtually certain consequence and the offender knew this).[83] However, subsection 2(4) specifies that for purposes of criminal liability under section 2 MSA, this *mens rea* requirement is considered to be met not only if the person *intends* to exploit the victim (in any part of the world) during or after the travel, but also if the person *knows or ought to know* that another person is likely to exploit the victim (in any part of the world) during or after the travel. "To know" and "ought to know" have the same meaning as under section 1 MSA.

Exploitation is explained in section 3 MSA as including at least slavery, servitude, and forced or compulsory labor, and similar behavior outside England and Wales. In other words, conduct falling under section 1 MSA. However, exploitation for trafficking is broader. Following section 3(5), exploitation includes "all other types of exploitation where a person is subject to force, threats or deception which is designed to induce him into providing a service of any kind, providing a person with benefits or enabling another to acquire benefits". Section 3(6) expands the scope of exploitation even more by including various situations in which someone attempts to use the person for one of the purposes described in section 3(5), without there being a need for any force, threats, or deception when it concerns a child or a vulnerable person.

In short, the offense of section 2 criminalizes conduct preceding the exploitation. However, actual exploitation can potentially also fall under the trafficking offense. After all, the prohibited conduct (such as harboring or transporting) can also be carried out when actual exploitation is already going on. The same is true for the other elements of the offense.

Section 4 constitutes the third offense: committing an offense – any offense under English criminal law – with the intention of committing the trafficking offense under section 2. This provision does not actually create an "independent" offense, but ensures that higher penalties are available.[84]

10.3.2 Corporate criminal liability

Again, the next question is whether, and how, corporations can be held criminally liable under English law for the offenses set out in the MSA. Under English law, where statutory offenses are concerned, the word "person" in the statutory provisions is taken to include a body of persons, corporate or unincorporate.[85] A corporate body of persons includes all corporations registered under the Companies Act 2006, such as public limited companies (plc), private limited companies (Ltd), and limited liability partnerships (LLP). Companies registered under one of the predecessors of the Companies Act 2006 and entities that are considered to be corporations based on similar legislation in other jurisdictions also qualify. Unincorporated bodies include other entities, such as clubs or partnerships.[86] In principle, all these entities can be held criminally liable in the UK for modern slavery, since the offense is punishable by fine and is explicitly nor implicitly excluded from corporate criminal liability.[87]

English criminal law currently has several models on the basis of which corporate criminal liability can be established.[88] For the modern slavery offenses, the identification doctrine is decisive.[89] The upshot of the applicability of this doctrine is that corporate criminal liability can be established if the offense is committed by an individual who is the "directing mind and will"[90] of the corporation and who, when acting in the company's business, is considered to be the "embodiment of the company".[91] This means that a so-called controlling officer must have committed the offense when acting within the scope of his or her authority.

However, the exact scope of the concept of "controlling officer" is not yet clear. Existing case law suggests that only senior managers and individuals who have explicitly been authorized by the Board to act on the company's behalf can – under certain circumstances – qualify as controlling officers.[92] However, a more lenient approach can be found in the Privy Council's case of *Meridan*. In this case, the identification of the for attribution relevant corporate officers was made dependent on the intention of the legislature as apparent from the specific statute involved.[93] Still, it is uncertain whether, and to what extent, this approach applies to English statutory law in general.[94]

However, what is certain is that the *actus reus* and *mens rea* need to be established at the level of one and the same individual; the identification doctrine does not allow the *mens rea* to be aggregated.[95] As a result, the possibilities for holding corporations criminally liable for the modern slavery offenses are rather limited under English law. After all, it is usually not the controlling officer him-/herself who commits the "slavery" or the "trafficking" offense, and thus fulfils both the *actus reus* and the *mens rea*. In addition, it can be difficult to identify the controlling officer and establish the necessary elements. The same is true for the offense of section 4 MSA.[96]

10.3.3 Jurisdiction

Traditionally, common law jurisdiction in England can only be established if the charged act or omission took place within the UK.[97] However, in recent decades, a growing number of statutes have created exceptions to this rule. The MSA is one of these statutes. According to section 2 MSA, human trafficking committed by a person – thus including a corporation[98] – of British nationality can be criminally liable independent of the location where the trafficking took place and regardless of whether it would amount to an offense in the respective country.[99] Put differently, this section creates extraterritorial jurisdiction in case the trafficking offense has been committed by a controlling officer of a British corporation and there is no requirement of double criminality. However, a controlling officer of a foreign corporation falls within the scope of the provision only if the conduct took place to, from, or within the UK.[100]

By contrast, section 1 MSA does not provide for a statutory exception. This means that the principle of territoriality does apply to the offense of holding a person in slavery or servitude or requiring a person to perform forced or compulsory labor. Decisive for establishing the *locus delicti* is whether there is a substantial connection between the offense and the territory of England and/or Wales. This can be the case when the conduct, a substantial part of the conduct, or the consequences described in the provision took place in the UK.[101]

10.3.4 Analysis

Do corporations have a binding duty under English criminal law not to commit modern slavery in their cross-border activities, and, if so, to what extent? As under Dutch criminal law, corporations do have such a statutory duty under English criminal law. All corporations are under the duty not to commit conduct preceding the exploitation and actual exploitation, whether on British territory or having a substantial connection with British territory. As regards corporate activities abroad, the duty not to commit modern slavery only extends to conduct falling under the trafficking offense of section 2 and when it concerns a British corporation.

Due to the identification model, these duties in practice only extend to the controlling officers of the corporations. Since controlling officers are not likely to commit the modern slavery offenses themselves, establishing corporate criminal liability for the modern slavery offenses laid down in the MSA is rather difficult, especially when it concerns large corporations. Considering the identification model and the applicable regime of jurisdiction, if modern slavery is committed overseas or in the supply chains of corporations, the options to establish corporate criminal liability are even more limited. This reflects broader, widespread criticism of the identification model: it does not successfully incorporate the reality of the internal structure of modern and large multinational corporations, and works inequitably with regard to small and large corporations.[102]

10.4 A comparative perspective on the duty not to commit modern slavery in corporations' cross-border activities

In both jurisdictions, corporations are under a statutory duty not to commit modern slavery in their transnational activities. However, the scope of these duties differs in various respects. In Sections 10.4.1–10.4.3, I assess how these legally binding duties differ, and the determinative factors in this regard, by comparing the answers provided in the previous sections. In Section 10.4.4, I examine what these results mean for the potential of domestic criminal law in addressing the adverse effects of corporations' cross-border activities.

10.4.1 The offenses

First and foremost, both Dutch and English law impose duties on corporations not to commit labor exploitation and not to commit conduct that precedes such exploitation. That said, these offenses differ on various points. An example can be found in the definition of exploitation. The English offense of section 1 MSA (holding a person in slavery or servitude or requiring a person to perform forced or compulsory labor) defines "exploitation" more restrictively (only the core forms of art 4 ECHR) compared to the Dutch definition of exploitation (weighing various factors, using the Dutch standards as a benchmark). Clearly, this difference influences the scope of the accompanying duty. Various other differences can be found in the *actus reus* and *mens rea* requirements in English and Dutch offenses, both in their "existence" and in their "definition", thus influencing – either restricting or expanding – the scope of the accompanying duty.[103]

For the purpose of this contribution, the most striking difference is that under Dutch criminal law, profiting from modern slavery constitutes an offense. This offense does not exist under English law. This means that under Dutch criminal law, corporations are under a legally binding duty to not only not commit modern slavery, but also to not profit from it, wherever the exploitation may have taken place, and by whomever it has been committed. At the offense level, this clearly increases the potential of domestic criminal law to hold corporations legally accountable for modern slavery.

The Dutch profiting offense has a purely national origin.[104] Yet, at a European level, several instruments encourage Member States to make it a crime to knowingly use services of victims of trafficking in human beings.[105] The profiting offense can be said to do exactly that for situations where "using services" results in a profit for the corporation. Since profiting can be interpreted in a broad manner, using services of labor exploitation will often result in profit.

In turn, section 4 of the MSA stipulates "committing an offence with intent to commit the trafficking offence". Dutch criminal law does not have a similar provision. However, since section 4 relies on other offenses in English criminal law, the provision itself does not directly create a new duty for the corporation, nor does it influence already existing duties. However, it is interesting that if a corporation were to be convicted for section 4, the offense would be labeled as "a modern slavery offense". Considering the potential reputational damage of such a label for a corporation, this offense offers potential with regard to the preventive function of criminal law.

The former thus shows that the way in which conduct falling under the rubric of modern slavery is criminalized in offenses, and the *actus reus* and *mens rea* requirements of these offenses, are determinative factors for the scope of the duty not to commit modern slavery under domestic criminal law.

10.4.2 *Corporate criminal liability*

The models on the basis of which corporate criminal liability can be established in the Netherlands and England differ to a great extent. Dutch criminal law imposes an extensive duty on the corporation not to commit modern slavery offenses. After all, the Dutch model based on attribution offers ample opportunities to establish corporate criminal liability for modern slavery offenses. However, attribution must always be reasonable. Especially interesting is the fact that Dutch criminal law does not just impose a duty on a corporation, but that this can be a duty of care. This duty of care can potentially turn broadly supported and authoritative soft-law instruments, such as the UNGPs and OECD Guidelines, into "hard law", thus providing a legally binding framework for the level of care expected of corporations to prevent, for example, modern slavery offenses. Compliance with due diligence requirements as set out in these instruments could then potentially provide a means to avoid corporate criminal liability.

The options to establish corporate criminal liability for modern slavery offenses under English law are more limited. In contrast to the Dutch model, under the English identification doctrine, it is a controlling officer acting within the scope of his or her duty who must have committed the offense. As such, it does not allow for establishment of the necessary elements of the crime at the level of the corporation directly, at the level of a number of individuals, or at the level of a lower employee. In practice, this means that under English law, the duty not to commit modern slavery offenses extends only to controlling officers, which makes it very unlikely that a corporation – other than a small corporation – can be held criminally liable for the offenses of the MSA. The identification model thus severely limits the extent of the duties.

At this point, it is interesting to note that in the past decade, three statutory instruments have been enacted in England that create a specific basis for corporate criminal liability: the Corporate Manslaughter and Corporate Homicide Act 2007, the Bribery Act 2010, and the Criminal Finances Act 2017. All of these instruments meet (at least partly) the well-known critique on the identification model with regard to its limited options to successfully prosecute (large) corporations. In these instruments, duties of care also play a role in establishing or exculpating corporate criminal liability. Yet the MSA, while enacted in 2015, does not include such a statutory basis and still relies on the common law principle of identification.

10.4.3 Jurisdiction

Both the Netherlands and England can exercise jurisdiction if modern slavery is committed on the respective territories. In addition, both systems feature a special, broader regime of jurisdiction for modern slavery. This is the result of the implementation of the same international obligations in both countries.[106] It must be noted that the mere existence of a special regime that provides for jurisdiction based on the nationality principle and without the requirement of double criminality is already very interesting with regard to existence of the duty, especially since, in absence of such a special regime, the territoriality principle would be decisive for England. In the Netherlands, the "standard regime of jurisdiction" is a little broader, with, for example, standard applicability of the nationality principle (with the requirement of double criminality) in art 7 DCC.

However, an important difference is that the Dutch regime covers all four offenses; in England, only the trafficking offense is covered. This can be explained by the fact that the international obligations only cover the trafficking offenses, and this has been implemented as such in the MSA. However, in the Netherlands, all four offenses are laid down in one provision, and this entire provision has been subjected to the special jurisdiction regime. The result is that in cases where modern slavery is committed abroad, Dutch corporations have a duty (of care) not to commit any of the four offenses. In England, controlling officers of English corporations are only under a duty not to commit the trafficking offenses. This illustrates that the applicable regime of jurisdiction also clearly determines the existence and scope of the duty.

10.4.4 The potential

It has become clear that under both Dutch and English law corporations have a legally binding duty not to commit modern slavery in their cross-border activities. This shows that domestic criminal law indeed offers potential when it comes to holding corporations criminally liable for modern slavery in their cross-border activities. Yet the way in which the undesirable conduct is criminalized, the way in which corporate criminal liability can be established for the offenses, and the applicable jurisdiction regime differ. These are all decisive factors in determining the scope of these duties, and thus also for the actual potential of domestic criminal law.

Comparing the duties shows that the potential under English criminal law is a lot more limited due to barriers imposed by these determining factors. In order to (at least partially) remove these barriers, it is of course possible to opt for a different method of shaping corporate criminal liability and – within the limits set by public international law – establish a broader regime of jurisdiction. That said, it is interesting to note that if England had an offense similar to the profiting offense of art 273f (1)(6) DCC, this would not only expand the scope of the duty but also make "the model" and "the regime of jurisdiction" less determinative factors. Put differently, the profiting offense has the ability to circumvent these barriers. After all, a controlling officer – also of a large corporation – is a lot more likely to commit the profiting offense than the offenses criminalized in the MSA. Moreover, the fact that extraterritorial jurisdiction can only be established for the trafficking offense would also no longer be a problem. Exploitation can very well take place abroad while controlling officers profit from it in England, and for offenses committed in England, England can exercise jurisdiction. Taking this into consideration, it becomes clear that the Dutch profiting offense could provide inspiration for future legislative action not only in England and in relation to modern slavery, but potentially also in other jurisdictions, and conceivably with regard to other corporate violations of human rights or environmental norms abroad.

Considering the duties, and especially the broad potential in the Netherlands, it is remarkable that so far, no case of corporate criminal liability for modern slavery abroad has made it to court, and only one conviction of corporate criminal liability for modern slavery in the Netherlands is still standing. However, this contribution only shows part of the picture. After all, there are additional factors that ultimately determine the potential of domestic criminal law in this context – for example, procedural-legal aspects, such as the investigative powers and the applicable law of evidence. Apart from legal factors, political factors, policy considerations, and practical matters need to be considered. For example, think of policies developed at the level of the public prosecutor's office with regard to prioritizing the investigation of specific offenses and/or the available means, time, knowledge, and skills at the investigational level.

10.5 Conclusion

The adverse effects of corporate activities on human (and other) rights within and across states have given rise to widespread concern in the globalized modern world. This concern has raised the question of how corporations can be held legally accountable for the adverse effects of their cross-border activities on people and the planet abroad. In the preceding sections, it has become clear that domestic criminal law can offer an answer to this question in the case of modern slavery, but potentially also with regard to other transgressions. It can put duties on corporations not to commit modern slavery in their cross-border activities; these duties may also take the form of duties of care, and domestic criminal law may even offer potential in addressing modern slavery in the supply chain. In this regard, the Dutch profiting offense could provide inspiration for future legislative action. Domestic criminal law can offer an interesting route to hold corporations legally accountable. After all, once corporate criminal liability is established and criminal sanctions imposed, the aims of criminal law that can be distinguished in many jurisdictions, such as retribution, deterrence, and even redress, can be served. However, in order to serve these aims, these possibilities must be taken up in practice. So far, this does not seem to be the case. This reveals an important task for policy makers, public prosecutors, legal practitioners, and other actors.

Notes

1 Various interpretations and definitions of "hard law" exist. However, in this contribution, Abbott and Snidal's definition is adhered to, where hard law is considered as "legally binding obligations that are precise (or that can be made precise through adjudication or the issuance of detailed regulations) and that delegate authority for interpreting and implementing the law". See Kenneth Abbott and Duncan Snidal, 'Hard and Soft Law in International Governance', (2000) 3 *International Organization* 421. See also Liesbeth Enneking et al., *Zorgplichten van Nederlandse ondernemingen inzake internationaal maatschappelijk verantwoord ondernemen* (Boom Juridisch 2016) 64.

2 See the contribution by Zerk in this volume on models of cross-border legal cooperation (Chapter 6).

3 See, for instance: Jernej Letnar Černič and Tara Van Ho, *Human Rights and Business: Direct Corporate Accountability for Human Rights* (Wolf Legal Publishers 2015) 3.

4 For example via so called "foreign direct liability cases". See Enneking (n 1) 77–83.

5 In this contribution, "company", "corporation", and "legal person" are used interchangeably. For their meaning in the respective jurisdictions, see sections on corporate criminal liability to follow.

6 Focusing on the Netherlands and England provides the opportunity not only to study interesting and varying legislative instruments on modern slavery, but also to examine two very different models of corporate criminal liability and different regimes of jurisdictions. At the same time, both countries have had to implement several of the same international instruments, which makes it possible to hold up a mirror in terms of legislation.

7 For examples of (differing) definitions, see: Marnix Alink and Just Wiarda, 'Materieelrechtelijke Aspecten van Mensenhandel', in Dajo de Prins et al. (eds.), *Vereniging voor de Vergelijkende Studie van het Recht van België en Nederland* (Preadviezen, Boom Juridische Uitgevers 2010) 176; Joel Quirk, 'Modern Slavery', in Trevor Burnard and Gad Heuman (eds.), *The Routledge History of Slavery* (Routledge 2011); Holly Cullen, 'Contemporary International Legal Norms on Slavery', in Jean Allain (ed.), *The Legal Understanding of Slavery: From the Historical to the Contemporary* (Oxford University Press 2012); Klara Skrivankova, *Between Decent Work and Forced Labour: Examining the Continuum of Exploitation* (Joseph Rowntree Foundation 2012).

8 It should be noted that these concepts are not always used in a consistent manner and can refer to different sorts of conduct. In addition, several of the practices can and often do overlap.

9 Nicola Jägers and Conny Rijken, 'Prevention of Human Trafficking for Labor Exploitation: The Role of Corporations', (2014) 12 *Northwestern Journal of Human Rights* 47, 52.

10 In England, this is evidenced by the enactment of the Modern Slavery Act 2015, with its famous transparency clause in s 6. In The Netherlands, at the time of writing, a bill imposing a duty of care on corporations to prevent the provision of products and services produced by the worst forms of child labor has been accepted by the House of Representatives. The bill is currently pending in the Senate. See *Proceedings II* 2016/17, 49. See also *Parliamentary Papers I* 2016/17, 34506, A. In addition, a motion has been filed by two members of parliament to request for enactment of legislation aimed at combatting modern slavery in supply chains of corporations. See *Parliamentary Papers II* 2016/17, 34506, 24.

11 See the introduction by Liesbeth Enneking et al. in this volume (Chapter 1).

12 In this regard, see, eg, Ivo Giesen and François Kristen, 'Editorial Liability, Responsibility and Accountability: Crossing Borders', (2014) 10 *Utrecht Law Review* 1, 4–5, 12–13.

13 The legislation is selected by use of the functional institutional method. See Marieke Oderkerk, 'The Need for a Methodological Framework for Comparative Legal Research: Sense and Nonsense of "Methodological Pluralism" in Comparative Law', (2015) 79 *Rabels Zeitschrift für ausländisches und internationales Privatrecht* 589.

14 Labor exploitation in this chapter is used as a functional concept (rather than a legal concept) to connote basically every conduct in the continuum of exploitation that relates to labor, ranging from the violation of labor standards to actual slavery. Whether it constitutes exploitation under criminal law depends on the legal definition at hand.

15 Complicity and inchoate offenses do not fall within the scope of this contribution.

16 It must be noted that this contribution does not aim to engage in a full comparison but rather a case study of the potential of specific legislation in two jurisdictions.

17 For a description of the legislative history, see Alink and Wiarda (n 7) 178–207. For more recent changes to the law, see the Law of 28 February 2013, *stb.* 2013, 84; Law of 6 November 2013, *stb.* 2013, 44.

18 The means are: threat or use of force or another hostile act, coercion, extortion, fraud, deception, abuse of power, abuse of a position of vulnerability, and the giving or receiving of payments or benefits to achieve the consent of a person having control over another person. For a discussion of these means and their interpretation, see Anne-Jetske Schaap, *De strafrechtelijke aansprakelijkheid van ondernemingen voor moderne slavernij* (Wolf Legal Publishers 2017) 14–32.

19 Supreme Court 27 October 2009, ECLI:NL:HR:2009:BI7099; Jaap de Hullu, *Materieel strafrecht. Over algemene leerstukken van strafrechtelijke aansprakelijkheid naar Nederlands recht* (6th edn, Wolters Kluwer 2015) 252–4; Alink and Wiarda (n 7) 218.

20 de Hullu (n 19), 252–4.

21 See, eg, de Hullu (n 19) 326, 238, 241; Constantijn Kelk and Ferry de Jong, *Studieboek materieel strafrecht* (5th edn, Wolters Kluwer 2013) 266–9. Considering the English terminology, *dolus eventualis* has features of both intent and recklessness.

22 See also Schaap (n 18) 38–42.

23 Supreme Court 20 December 2011, ECLI:NL:HR:2011:BR0448; Supreme Court 24 November 2015, ECLI:HR:NL:2015:3309; Supreme Court 5 April 2016, ECLI:NL:HR:2016:556.

24 de Hullu (n 19) 264–5.

25 *Parliamentary Papers II* 1996/97, 25437, 3, 9.

26 Schaap (n 18) 42–3.

27 Ibid. 44–6.

28 Ibid.

29 Supreme Court 8 September 2015, ECLI:NL:HR:2015:2467.

30 A more detailed discussion of all these forms of exploitation is beyond the scope of this contribution. For now, it suffices to state that their meaning can be obtained by considering, for example, the case law and guidance of the ECtHR on art 4 of the ECHR, which lays down the prohibition of slavery and forced labor. See also Schaap (n 18) 46–52.

31 As is apparent from the text of art 273f (2) DCC. See A-G Knigge in his conclusion of Supreme Court 27 October 2009, ELCLI:NL:HR:2009:BI7099; See also Schaap (n 18) 43–4.

32 Supreme Court 27 October 2009, ECLI:NL:HR:2009:BI7099.

33 For this analysis, see Schaap (n 18) 46–52.

34 With regard to living wage, see, eg, art 23(3) of the UDHR, and subsequently developed methods to estimating living wages (such as the so-called "Anker method", used for the SA8000 Standard of Social Accountability International, and the Asia Floor Wage, both of which are referred to by the Social Economic Council of the Netherlands as methods to determine the living wage). See SER Commissie Internationaal Maatschappelijk Verantwoord, 'Leefbaar Loon', (2015) 8 <www.energieakkoordser.nl/~/media/Files/Internet/Publicaties/Overige/2010_2019/2015/brochure-leefbaar-loon/brochure-leefbaar-loon.ashxx> accessed 24 September 2019.

35 Schaap (n 18) 46–52.

36 Following book 2 of the DCC. This includes entities such as "*naamloze vennootschap*" (NV) and "*besloten vennootschap*" (BV), which can be compared with (but are not necessarily similar to) plc and Ltd. See François Kristen, 'Maatschappelijk Verantwoord Ondernemen en Strafrecht', in Jan Eijsbouts et al. (eds.), *Maatschappelijk verantwoord ondernemen. Handelingen Nederlandse Juristen Vereniging 2010–1* (Wolters Kluwer 2010) 132–3.

37 Schaap (n 18) 58–9.

38 *Parliamentary Papers II* 1975/76, 13655, 5, 2; see also Supreme Court 21 October 2003, ECLI:NL:HR:2003:AF7938; de Hullu (n 19) 171.

39 Supreme Court 21 October 2003, ECLI:NL:HR:2003:AF7938.

40 For more information on the Dutch model of corporate criminal liability, see, eg, Berend Keulen and Erik Gritter, 'Corporate Criminal Liability in the Netherlands', in Mark Pieth and Radha Ivory (eds.), *Corporate Criminal Liability: Emergence, Convergence and Risk* (Springer 2011); Bram Meyer, Tessa van Roomen, and Eelke Sikkema, 'Corporate Criminal Liability for Corruption Offences and the Due Diligence Defence: A Comparison of the Dutch and English Legal Frameworks', (2014) 10 *Utrecht Law Review* 37.

41 Kristen (n 36) 134.

42 Supreme Court 29 March 2005, ECLI:N:HR:2005:AR7619; de Hullu (n 19) 172.

43 Richard van Elst, 'Daderschap van rechtspersonen na het Zijpe-arrest', in Tineke Cleiren et al. (eds.) *Jurisprudentie Strafrecht Select* (Sdu Uitgevers 2006) 488; Kristen (n 36) 134.

44 de Hullu (n 19) 172.

45 Erik Gritter, *Effectiviteit en aansprakelijkheid in het economisch ordeningsrecht* (Boom Uitgevers Den Haag 2003) 219; Kristen (n 36) 136; Kelk and de Jong (n 21) 499.

46 Supreme Court 21 October 2003, ECLI:NL:HR:2003:AF7938.

47 Meyer, van Roomen, and Sikkema (n 40) 47.

48 ibid with reference to Rechtbank Dordrecht 5 March 2008, ECLI:NL:RBDOR:2008:BC6022.

49 Kristen (n 36) 134–5; de Hullu (n 19) 172.

50 Mark Hornman, 'Concretisering van redelijke toerekening; invulling van de drijfmestcriteria in de feitenrechtspraak', (2010) 3(40) *Delikt en Delinkwent* 370.

51 See, eg, van Elst (n 43) 494; Erik Gritter, 'De Strafbaarheid van de rechtspersoon', in Bas van der Leij (ed.), *Plegen en deelnemen* (Deventer: Kluwer 2007) 64, 69; Eelke Sikkema, *De strafrechtelijke aansprakelijkheid van leidinggevenden in Nederland* (Wolf Legal Publishers 2010) 48–9; de Hullu (n 19) 174.

52 Supreme Court 24 April 2016, ECLI:NL:HR:2016:773 (s 3.4.2); De Hullu (n 19) 278–83; Kristen (n 36) 138–9.

53 Ibid.

54 Gritter (n 51) 66–70.

55 de Hullu (n 19) 279.

56 Malcolm Evans, *International Law* (3rd edn, Oxford University Press 2010) 321–6.
57 *Stb.* 2014, 47 in combination with a recent amendment of the Decree of 15 May 2015, *Stb.* 2015, 182.
58 These articles also apply to legal persons, as illustrated by parliamentary history. See *Parliamentary Papers I* 2004/05, 29291, C, 2.
59 Hein Wolswijk, *Locus delicti en rechtsmacht* (Gouda Quint 1998) 90–1; de Hullu (n 19) 198–200.
60 Art 4(4) of the Decree. The principle of nationality also applies to corporations. See Supreme Court 14 September 1981, NJ 1982/532. See also Wolswijk (n 59) 256. According to the literature, a corporation is considered to be Dutch for the purpose of criminal law if it has its factual domicile in the Netherlands. See Robert Mok and Rogier Duk, 'Toepassing van het Nederlandse strafrecht op buiten Nederland begane delicten', in *Handelingen 1980 der Nederlandse Juristen-Vereniging* (Tjeenk Willink 1980) 131; Wolswijk (n 59) 272. However, according to the Public Prosecutor's office, the formal domicile of the corporation is decisive. Since Dutch law seemingly also provides for extraterritorial jurisdiction for modern slavery in case a person resides in the Netherlands, it can be submitted that jurisdiction can also be established when a corporation has its factual domicile in the Netherlands. Allegedly, both options are possible. See Schaap 2017 (n 18) 85–8.
61 Arts 4(4) and 4(5) of the Decree.
62 Guiding Principles on Business and Human Rights: Implementing the United Nations "Protect, Respect and Remedy", Annex to UNHRC, Report of the Special Representative of the Secretary-General on the Issue of Human Rights and Transnational Corporations and Other Business Enterprises, John Ruggie (21 March 2011) UN Doc A/HRC/17/31.
63 OECD, *Guidelines for Multinational Enterprises* (OECD Publishing 2011).
64 Definition provided by the OECD Guidelines (n 63), ch II, commentary para 14.
65 These are: assessment, integration, taking action, tracking, and communication.
66 OECD Guidelines (n 63), ch II, commentary para 15 and more generally pt I. Examples of specific steps and more factors that can be of meaning in this regard can be found in the respective (and guiding) instruments. See, eg, UNGP (n 62) princ 17–21; OHCHR, 'The Corporate Responsibility to Respect Human Rights: An Interpretative Guide' (UN 2012) ch III B <www.ohchr.org/Documents/Publications/HR.PUB.12.2_En.pdf> accessed 24 September 2019; OECD Guidelines (n 63) pt I. See also Nicolas Bueno, 'Corporate Liability for Violations of the Human Right to Just Conditions of Work in Extraterritorial Operations', (2017) 21 *The International Journal of Human Rights* 565, 571–3.
67 The standards and principles are consistent with applicable laws and internationally recognized standards. See, eg, OECD Guidelines (n 63) preface. See also UNGP (n 62). In addition, the Dutch government has stated several times that it expects corporations to comply with the OECD Guidelines. See, eg, the following policy letter: 'Maatschappelijk verantwoord ondernemen loont' (28 June 2013) <www.rijksoverheid.nl/documenten/beleidsnota-s/2013/06/28/beleids brief-maatschappelijk-verantwoord-ondernemen-loont> accessed 24 September 2019https://www.rijksoverheid.nl/documenten/beleidsnota-s/2013/06/28/beleidsbrief-maatschappelijk-verantwoord-ondernemen-loont.
68 This assertion is based on an analysis of published case law from 1 January 2011 until 1 January 2017. It is therefore possible that there has been a conviction of a corporation that has not (yet) been published at the time of writing.
69 However, at the time of writing, this conviction is not yet final.
70 Rechtbank Limburg 10 November 2016, ECLI:NL:RBLIM:2016:9615.

71 Pt 6, s 54 creates the "well-known" transparency clause. However, this clause is not directly criminally enforceable and therefore does not fall within the scope of this chapter. See the contribution by Bueno in this volume on the Swiss Federal Initiative on Responsible Business (Chapter 12).

72 S 2(2). See also Explanatory Notes MSA 18. It should be noted that the Explanatory Notes are not part of the MSA, are not ratified by parliament, and have no official legal force. However, they are considered to be an important source of information for interpretation of the act.

73 However, it is also relevant how these ECHR terms are constructed in national case law. See, e.g., the interpretation in *Attorney General's Reference (Nos 2,3, 4, and 5 of 2013)*, [2013] EWCA Crim 324 on s 71 Coroners and Justice Act 2009, the predecessor of the MSA. Previous case law is considered to be relevant for interpretation of the MSA. See John Frederick Archbold, *Archbold: Criminal Pleading, Evidence and Practice* (Sweet & Maxwell 2016) ch 19, pt XV.

74 Sub-s 1(3). Sub-s 1(5) determines that it does not matter whether the victim consented to the conduct amounting to an offense under s 1.

75 Sub-s 1(4); Explanatory Notes 20–1.

76 Andrew Simester et al., *Simester and Sullivan's Criminal Law* (4th edn, Hart Publishing 2010).

77 *Regina v Montila and Others* [2004] I WLR 3141; *R v Saik* [2006] UKHL 18.

78 David Ormerod and Karl Laird, *Smith and Hogan's Criminal Law* (14th edn, Oxford University Press 2015) 125.

79 Simester et al. (n 76) 152.

80 S 2(3) MSA; Explanatory Notes MSA 26. Again, consent is irrelevant. See s 2(2).

81 S 2(5) MSA. See also *R v Ali and Ashraf* CA [2015] EWCA Crim 1279 on the geographical element in travel.

82 Simester et al. (n 76) 138, 159.

83 *R v Woollin* [1998] 4 All ER 103 (*Woollin* must be read in light of previous judgements, such as *R v Moloney* [1985] 1 AC 905, *R v Hancock and Shankland* [1986] AC 455 and *R v Nedrick* [1986] 3 All ER 1); see also *R v Matthews and Alleyne* [2003] 3 Cr App R 30.

84 Explanatory Notes MSA 36.

85 Interpretation Act 1978; s 1b Companies Act 2006; Archbold (n 73) ch 1, pt IV; Ormerod and Laird (n 78) 303.

86 Archbold (n 73), ch 1, pt IV.

87 For limits to corporate criminal liability, see Ormerod and Laird (n 78) 303ff.

88 Ibid. 290–320.

89 Schaap (n 18) 114–15. More generally, see Celia Wells, 'Corporate Criminal Liability: A Ten Year Review', (2014) 12 *Criminal Law Review* 97.

90 *Lennard's Carrying Co Ltd v Asiatic Petroleum Co Ltd* [1915] AC 705 per Viscount Haldane LC.

91 *Essendon Engineering Co Ltd V Maile* [1982] RTR 260, [1982] Crim LR 510. Ormerod and Laird (n 78) 294.

92 *COSA v Conway* [2012] EWHC 2930 (Admin). See also *Tesco Supermarkets Ltd v Nattrass* [1972] AC 153 at 171, 187, and 200. However, the exact test does not appear to be fixed or clear. See also Ormerod and Laird (n 78) 295–6.

93 *Meridian Global Funds Management Asia Ltd v Securities Commission* [1995] 2 AC 500.

94 Ormerod and Laird (n 78) 298.

95 *Attorney General's Reference (No 2 of 1999)* [2000] QB 796.

96 This may be different in cases of indirect liability, but this falls outside the scope of this chapter.

97 *Board of Trade v Owen* [1957] AC 602 per Lord Tucker at 625 and further; *Cox v Army Council* [1963] AC 48.

98 See s 3.2.
99 S 2(6) MSA.
100 Ss 2(6) and 2(7) MSA.
101 *R v Smith (Wallace Duncun)* (No 4) [2003] 3 WLR 299 per Lord Chief Justice Wolf.
102 Ormerod and Laird (n 78) 295.
103 For a detailed description and interesting similarities, see Schaap (n 18) ch 7.
104 See *Parliamentary Papers II* 1996/97, 25437, 3, 9.
105 Art 19 of the Council of Europe Convention on Action against Trafficking in Human Beings [2005] CETS 197. See also Explanatory Report to the Council of Europe Convention on Action against Trafficking in Human Beings [2005] CETS 197, points 229–36; art 18(4) of Directive 2011/36/EU of the European Parliament and of the Council of 5 April 2011 on Preventing and Combating Trafficking in Human Beings and Protecting Its Victims, and Replacing Council Framework Decision 2002/629/JHA [2011] OJ L 101/1. See also Yasmin van Damme and Gert Vermeulen, 'Criminalisation of Demand-Side Actors of Trafficking in Human Beings, Forced Labour and Labour Exploitation: Paving the Way for Assessing the Feasibility and Added Value of a Criminal Justice Response', in Marc Cools et al. (eds.), *Governance of Security Research Paper Series: European Criminal Justice and Policy* (vol. 7, Maklu 2012) 205ff.
106 Most notably, art 10 of Directive 2011/36/EU (n 105).

Bibliography

Abbott K and Snidal D, 'Hard and Soft Law in International Governance', (2000) 3 *International Organization* 421.

Alink M and Wiarda J, 'Materieelrechtelijke Aspecten van Mensenhandel', in Dajo de Prins et al. (eds.), *Vereniging voor de Vergelijkende Studie van het Recht van België en Nederland* (Preadviezen, Boom Juridische Uitgevers 2010).

Archbold JF, *Archbold: Criminal Pleading, Evidence and Practice* (Sweet & Maxwell 2016).

Bueno N, 'Corporate Liability for Violations of the Human Right to Just Conditions of Work in Extraterritorial Operations', (2017) 21 *The International Journal of Human Rights* 565.

Černič JL and Van Ho T, *Human Rights and Business: Direct Corporate Accountability for Human Rights* (Wolf Legal Publishers 2015).

Cullen H, 'Contemporary International Legal Norms on Slavery', in Jean Allain (ed.), *The Legal Understanding of Slavery: From the Historical to the Contemporary* (Oxford University Press 2012).

de Hullu J, *Materieel strafrecht. Over algemene leerstukken van strafrechtelijke aansprakelijkheid naar Nederlands recht* (6th edn, Wolters Kluwer 2015).

Enneking L et al., *Zorgplichten van Nederlandse ondernemingen inzake internationaal maatschappelijk verantwoord ondernemen* (Boom Juridisch 2016).

Evans M, *International Law* (3rd edn, Oxford University Press 2010).

Giesen I and Kristen F, 'Editorial Liability, Responsibility and Accountability: Crossing Borders', (2014) 10 *Utrecht Law Review* 1.

Gritter E, 'De Strafbaarheid van de rechtspersoon', in Bas van der Leij (ed.), *Plegen en deelnemen* (Deventer: Kluwer 2007).

———, *Effectiviteit en aansprakelijkheid in het economisch ordeningsrecht* (Boom Uitgevers Den Haag 2003).

Hornman M, 'Concretisering van redelijke toerekening; invulling van de drijfmestcriteria in de feitenrechtspraak', (2010) 3(40) *Delikt en Delinkwent* 370.

Jägers N and Rijken C, 'Prevention of Human Trafficking for Labor Exploitation: The Role of Corporations', (2014) 12 *Northwestern Journal of Human Rights* 47.

Kelk C and de Jong F, *Studieboek materieel strafrecht* (5th edn, Wolters Kluwer 2013).

Keulen B and Gritter E, 'Corporate Criminal Liability in the Netherlands', in Mark Pieth and Radha Ivory (eds.), *Corporate Criminal Liability: Emergence, Convergence and Risk* (Springer 2011).

Kristen F, 'Maatschappelijk Verantwoord Ondernemen en Strafrecht', in Jan Eijsbouts et al. (eds.), *Maatschappelijk verantwoord ondernemen. Handelingen Nederlandse Juristen Vereniging 2010–1* (Walters Kluwer 2010).

Meyer B, van Roomen T, and Sikkema E, 'Corporate Criminal Liability for Corruption Offences and the Due Diligence Defence: A Comparison of the Dutch and English Legal Frameworks', (2014) 10 *Utrecht Law Review* 37.

Mok R and Duk R, 'Toepassing van het Nederlandse strafrecht op buiten Nederland begane delicten', in *Handelingen 1980 der Nederlandse Juristen-Vereniging* (Tjeenk Willink 1980).

Oderkerk M, 'The Need for a Methodological Framework for Comparative Legal Research: Sense and Nonsense of 'Methodological Pluralism' in Comparative Law', (2015) 79 *Rabels Zeitschrift für ausländisches und internationales Privatrecht* 589.

Ormerod D and Laird K, *Smith and Hogan's Criminal Law* (14th edn, Oxford University Press 2015).

Quirk J, 'Modern Slavery', in Trevor Burnard and Gad Heuman (eds.), *The Routledge History of Slavery* (Routledge 2011).

Schaap A-J, *De strafrechtelijke aansprakelijkheid van ondernemingen voor moderne slavernij* (Wolf Legal Publishers 2017).

Sikkema E, *De strafrechtelijke aansprakelijkheid van leidinggevenden in Nederland* (Wolf Legal Publishers 2010).

Simester A et al., *Simester and Sullivan's Criminal Law* (4th edn, Hart Publishing 2010).

Skrivankova K, *Between Decent Work and Forced Labour: Examining the Continuum of Exploitation* (Joseph Rowntree Foundation 2012).

van Damme Y and Vermeulen G, 'Criminalisation of Demand-Side Actors of Trafficking in Human Beings, Forced Labour and Labour Exploitation: Paving the Way for Assessing the Feasibility and Added Value of a Criminal Justice Response', in Marc Cools et al. (eds.), *Governance of Security Research Paper Series: European Criminal Justice and Policy* (vol 7, Maklu 2012).

Wells C, 'Corporate Criminal Liability: A Ten Year Review', (2014) 12 *Criminal Law Review* 97.

Wolswijk H, *Locus delicti en rechtsmacht* (Gouda Quint 1998).

Part 4

Accountability through domestic private law mechanisms

11 Limited liability and separate corporate personality in multinational corporate groups

Conceptual flaws, accountability gaps, and the case for profit-risk liability

*Paul Dowling**

11.1 Introduction

The purpose of this chapter is to discuss, from a theoretical and practical perspective, some of the difficulties arising from the principles of limited liability (LL) and separate corporate personality (SCP), primarily in the context of corporate groups and multinational enterprises (MNEs). The way in which these company law principles operate has particular ramifications for those who wish to obtain civil redress in the home courts of multinational parent companies for harm arising from the activities of their overseas subsidiaries or joint ventures. The extent to which parent companies can be held liable for harm arising from the activities of subsidiaries has been the subject of a number of important recent decisions of the courts of England, Wales and elsewhere. While the principal focus of this chapter is on issues that arise or have arisen in an English/common law context, I also draw upon civil law concepts and jurisprudence as the potential basis for future development of the law in this area.

The chapter begins with a critical analysis of the historical development and theoretical foundation of the LL and SCP structure, followed by a consideration of some of the conceptual difficulties associated with the operation of these principles, focusing chiefly on the schizophrenic nature of the corporation as both a commodity and a social entity. I then turn to some of the practical implications of these theoretical problems, particularly the manner in which the LL and SCP structure can frustrate the pursuit of legal accountability for harm caused by dangerous activities associated with MNEs and thereby operate as a barrier to justice. I conclude with a discussion of the potential for reform of this area, including an examination of some existing proposals and the extent to which they address the conceptual and practical obstacles identified in the preceding sections of the chapter. Having considered these alternatives, the adoption of a profit risk/created risk liability regime is discussed. This proposal represents a shift away from the predominant control-based approach to one that instead focuses on the interface between profit and risk creation.

11.2 Limited liability and separate corporate personality: theoretical foundations and historical development

11.2.1 The principles

The principle of LL, by which shareholders' liability for a company's debts is limited to the amount they have paid, or have agreed to pay, to the company for its shares,[1] is a relatively recent invention in the context of the historical development of business organizations. Prior to the passage of the English Companies' Acts of 1844–62, the predominant form of business organization was the partnership, in which small groups of individuals "clubbed together" resources in pursuit of a business objective.

There is broad consensus that the professed policy reason behind the legalization of LL companies in England was to facilitate investment in business enterprises. This was to be achieved by shielding those who gave financial backing to the venture from potential personal ruin if the business failed. This externalization of risk and consequent permissive environment for investors was considered by English legislators to be a necessary catalyst for the capital-intensive projects that ultimately drove forward the industrial revolution, and has since been termed an "economic necessity", without which "full economic development was impossible".[2]

The mid-19th century legislator's ostensible intention in affirming the principle of LL was to afford greater investment opportunities so as to facilitate economic progress.[3] However, others have questioned the influence of, or need for, this company structure in the promotion of industrial development at that time,[4] in circumstances where the industrial revolution was already well underway[5] and unlimited liability partnerships had hitherto sufficed in stimulating the development of key industries associated with the period, such as iron and cotton.[6] The legalization of the LL form is also said to have appeased the desires of a bourgeoning middle- and upper-class *rentier* investor. Such individuals exercised increasing political influence and wished to share in the profits of rapidly growing industries, but had neither the requisite business experience nor the desire to have any close involvement in the operation of the firm. It is argued that this led to the gradual departure from partnership principles from 1840 onward, and the ultimate reconceptualization of a company share from a stake in the assets of the company to a right to profit.[7]

The entrenchment of the principle of LL gave rise to a new conceptual entity: the legal person, "capable of enjoying rights and of being subject to duties which are not the same as those enjoyed by its members".[8] This concept of SCP was enshrined in common law by virtue of the landmark case of *Salomon v Salomon*,[9] which cemented the position that a company is entirely separate from its members, even in situations where it is effectively a "one-person operation" financed and managed by a single individual.

Irrespective of the motives behind the legalization and subsequent universal embracement of the LL company and its partner doctrine of SCP, it is clear that a business enterprise constructed upon these principles generates an asymmetry of risk between the shareholders of the company and its creditors. While the shareholders are able to reap their full share of the benefits of an enterprise when the going is good, the financial risk that arises for them if the business fails is capped at the value of their investment, with the burden of that risk being shifted onto the company's creditors. If the company is insolvent, involuntary creditors such as tort victims are likely to be left without any means of economic redress. Even if the company is solvent, the only route to reparation may be by way of legal action against the corporation itself, which can pose particular difficulties associated with the corporation's separate personality, as discussed further in the following section.

11.2.2 The schizophrenia of the corporation

The doctrine of SCP gave rise to the idea of the corporation as a "person" with its own socio-legal identity. This novel construction inevitably led to the advancement of a number of theories as to how the legal person should be conceptualized both internally and in terms of its relationship with wider society.[10] This debate can broadly be polarized into a dichotomy between "nominalist" and "realist" understandings of corporate personhood. While realists understand the corporation as a "fully fledged organizational entity whose legal personality is no more than an external expression of its real personality in society",[11] nominalists see the corporate form as merely a contractual association of individual shareholders for the purposes of facilitating business transactions.[12] Katsuhitu Iwai attempted to close this seemingly endless debate by recognizing the corporation's dual role as both an item of property belonging to its shareholders, and a social entity endowed with rights and duties.[13] Indeed, it is this schizophrenic identity of the corporation that is of particular relevance to the issues explored in the following sections of this chapter.

11.2.3 The theoretical challenges of corporate personhood

At common law, the property conception of the corporate purpose has historically received strong judicial support. In this understanding, the furtherance of social needs or desires that underpin the existence of a corporation cannot supersede its overriding objective to generate profit for its shareholders.[14] The mid-20th century gave way to "managerial" theories of the corporation, which recognized a social obligation for corporations to act as a "good citizen . . . with a sense of social responsibility".[15] However, as we moved into the 1990s there was a generalized shift in common law jurisdictions, such as England, Wales and the US, back toward the property conception of corporate personhood, which led Canadian law professor Joel Bakan to conclude that "corporate social responsibility is thus illegal – at least when it is genuine".[16] On that analysis, incidental social costs associated with the firm's underlying economic imperative must be quantified and balanced against the economic benefits of the relevant activity. If the latter outweighs the former, the corporation is compelled to undertake to bear those social costs in furtherance of its economic goals.

Nevertheless, corporations have been duly bestowed with rights and responsibilities akin to those held by human beings. Since the US Supreme Court case of *Santa Clara County v Southern PacR Co*,[17] in the US, corporations are considered natural persons under the US Constitution with all the rights and protections granted to human beings by the Bill of Rights. US corporations have subsequently used their "human" right to lobby the legislature, not only to extend the human rights to free speech and privacy to corporations, but also to grant corporations additional "non-human" rights, such as perpetual existence and the right to own others of their own kind.[18] Equally, in Europe, Art 1 of Protocol 1 to the ECHR specifically grants the right to peaceful enjoyment of possessions to legal as well as natural persons. The ECHR has since extended the benefit of certain aspects of other human rights to corporations, notably the right to respect for private and family life under Art 8 and freedom of expression under Art 10.[19]

The corporation's schizophrenic identity as an item of property implanted with a market-driven imperative to generate wealth for its creators, but which is simultaneously capable of exercising "human" rights and forming social relationships, can give rise to perverse consequences. In particular, the realist conception of the corporation allows companies to prey on humans' inherent nature as social beings,[20] by adopting a persona that engages in and publicizes outwardly benevolent social activities, where to do so will enable the furtherance of the company's economic ends.[21] The ability of a corporation to manipulate public opinion in this way has the effect of ameliorating for the corporation the potential impacts of what Karl Polanyi described as the "double movement",[22] whereby a protective countermovement emerges to resist the negative impacts of the market economy on human beings and the natural environment. In this understanding, CSR activities carried out by modern corporations are merely a vehicle to legitimize the corporation's status as a social entity, as opposed to one that is driven exclusively by market considerations. The effect of this is to blunt the force of any resistance against the corporation's existence or the manner in which it conducts its business. The ability of a corporation to dampen social resistance to its role as an instrument of the market economy presents itself in particular ways in the context of overseas operations of MNEs; this issue will be considered in further detail in the sections to follow.

11.3 Limited liability, separate corporate personality, and the problem of multinational enterprises

11.3.1 The multinational enterprise

The economic rationale behind the development and proliferation of MNEs over the course of the last 150 years has been the subject of detailed analysis.[23] However, for the purposes of this chapter, it is sufficient to note the broadly recognized principle that firms invest overseas in order to extract higher profits from their existing competitive advantage, for instance in terms of reputation, capital, and knowhow.[24]

MNEs can take a variety of forms, "ranging from a highly integrated hierarchy of jointly held entities to a loose network of coordinated economic collaborators acting on behalf of a lead firm or as equal collaborators".[25] Controlling the presence and activities of foreign investors is in principle subject to the absolute discretion of the host State, but that discretion is in reality often fettered by international economic agreements to which the host State is signatory. Furthermore, economic pressures on host States to appease the interests of foreign investors, or the absence of sufficient host State resources, may give rise to a more relaxed regulatory environment than would apply in the foreign investor's home country. It has also been argued that where host States attempt to exercise influence over or control a MNE by enforcing an element of local participation in its activities, MNEs will continue to be responsible for major decision-making and host States remain reliant on the international framework of the MNE for the success of the venture.[26]

11.3.2 Limited liability, separate corporate personality, and the accountability deficit for multinational corporations

The principles of LL and SCP continue to apply within corporate groups, albeit the courts have arrived at this conclusion "without any deep consideration of the matter as an inevitable consequence of the doctrine of separate legal personality".[27] It has been argued that the extension of LL to corporate groups creates a situation whereby the risks associated with carrying out dangerous activities are shifted away from corporate shareholders who are best placed to bear those risks, onto involuntary creditors such as tort victims who are generally poorer risk bearers.[28] Subsidiary companies within corporate groups are also difficult to characterize as free and independent beings consistent with the doctrine of SCP, not least because of potential conflicts of interest that may arise between the parent and the subsidiary.[29]

The principles of LL and SCP are of particular significance in the context of tort liability associated with the negative effects of an MNE's overseas operations. As explained previously, the overarching purpose for an MNE in developing its business through an international corporate group structure is to take advantage of the economic benefits of operating in a foreign jurisdiction while simultaneously exploiting its existing competitive advantage. Such benefits might include a more relaxed regulatory enforcement or cheaper labor. However, we are concerned here with a particular incidental benefit that MNEs receive when operating overseas, which is the reduced ability of individuals harmed by their activities to seek redress for the damage they have suffered.

There are three key ways in which the application of LL and SCP to corporate groups can frustrate the pursuit of legal accountability for harm caused by their operations in host States:

(i) The use of foreign subsidiaries or joint ventures in partnership with host governments permits MNEs to present themselves as a national enterprise and thereby mask the reality of who is behind the operation.

(ii) Inadequate allocation or deliberate diversion of resources from foreign subsidiaries can ensure that they are unable to satisfy tort liabilities arising from their operations.
(iii) Limitations on access to justice in the countries where subsidiaries are domiciled can prevent victims from enforcing their legal rights.

First, the use of separate corporate persons for the purposes of engaging in business activities overseas (either through foreign registered subsidiaries or joint ventures), often with some element of participation by the host government, affords MNEs the benefit of a specific vehicle for ensuring that any Polanyian "double movement" in resistance to their activities is blunted. In particular, the use of a locally constituted separate corporate person allows the MNE to be "subsumed behind the local nationality of the joint venture, thereby reducing the risk of being identified as a 'foreign' corporation and being subject to discriminatory treatment".[30] This helps pave the way for the MNE to secure its "social license to operate" in the foreign jurisdiction.

An emblematic example of the operation of this technique in practice can be found in the case of *Pedro Emiro Florez Arroyo v Equion Energia Ltd*,[31] in which my firm acted on behalf of the claimants. This case concerned allegations of environmental damage caused by the construction of an oil pipeline in Colombia. The defendant, a former BP subsidiary, argued that it had no responsibility for construction of the pipeline, and said it was carried out exclusively by OCENSA, a joint venture vehicle constituted together with a group of other multinational oil companies alongside the Colombian State oil company, Ecopetrol. The English High Court held that BP had made "a strategic decision" that "for image and operative reasons" its employees "should be able to represent OCENSA and/or act as agents as such".[32] However, BP employees were not formally seconded to OCENSA, apparently for tax reasons. The court found this approach to be consistent with BP's written communication strategy to "project itself as the instrument of OCENSA and . . . seek to project the image of OCENSA and not its own image". The written strategy went on to state that "given that the desired image can be said to be in conflict with who owns, is building and will operate the line, further explanation may be needed".[33] While the claimants' claims ultimately failed chiefly on causation grounds, this evidence assisted the court in reaching its finding that BP had the necessary power of governance, direction, or control over the pipeline construction to establish primary liability under Colombian law.[34]

Florez provides a clear illustration of how MNEs can use the principle of SCP in an effort to conceal the reality of who owns and controls their foreign operations and use this as a basis to try to avoid civil liability. The use of SCP to disguise a foreign enterprise as a national initiative is likely to diminish resistance to the negative human and environmental impacts of its operations because the activity is thus perceived as a national venture carried out in pursuit of an overriding national interest. The use of the separate corporate person therefore permits the MNE to outsource the risks of its activities to the host State, while simultaneously manipulating public opinion so as to reduce local resistance to such risks. Indeed, the "politicization" of MNE activities in this way can be such that those who wish to resist or challenge such activities can find themselves isolated or at risk, particularly in volatile geopolitical environments where social activists and human rights defenders can be subject to persecution and excessive violence by private security, State, and paramilitary forces. Such episodes of violence have been the subject of legal proceedings in which my firm has acted on behalf of injured claimants.[35]

Second, it is common for a parent company to encourage a subsidiary to distribute the proceeds of a business as dividends so as to avoid tort liabilities.[36] This problem is perhaps less likely to arise in the context of MNEs and corporate groups, where the value of mass tort claims is generally unlikely to exceed the assets of the subsidiary, or, if it does, the liability is likely to be covered by an insurance policy.[37] However, it is by no means an irrelevant consideration. This issue has been addressed by the English Court of Appeal in *Dominic Liswaniso Lungowe &Ors v Vedanta Resources Plc& Anor*,[38] in which my firm is acting on behalf of a group of over 1,800 Zambian individuals who allege that their land and livelihood has been destroyed by pollution from a copper mine. The claim was issued against UK-domiciled parent company Vedanta Resources PLC and its Zambian subsidiary, Konkola Copper Mines (KCM). KCM disputed the English court's jurisdiction to hear the claim, but in its 2017 judgement the English Court of Appeal upheld the High Court's decision to assert jurisdiction over both defendants. One of the Court of Appeal's reasons for finding that it was reasonable for the Court to try the issue between the claimants and Vedanta was the fact that the claimants "have grounds to believe, and evidence to show, that KCM may be unable or unwilling to meet . . . a judgment".[39] This illustrates how MNEs can and do use inadequately financed foreign subsidiaries to perform dangerous activities overseas, and thereby expose victims of harm caused by such activities to the risk that tort liabilities toward them will not be fully satisfied.

A third common strategy employed by MNEs is to rely on the SCP of subsidiaries and locally incorporated joint venture vehicles in an effort to avoid being sued in the country where the MNE is headquartered or where its parent company is domiciled. This approach can restrict victims' ability to access justice in circumstances where a legal claim in the local jurisdiction of the subsidiary is not possible. This might be the case where there is a lack of available funding for legal costs and expenses in the local jurisdiction, or where the courts or lawyers in the local jurisdiction do not have the capacity to handle cases of such magnitude. There may also be a significant risk of injustice in local courts due to factors such as corruption or persecution of human rights defenders, including lawyers.

My firm is currently acting in a series of cases (including the *Vedanta* case, referred to previously) in which claims have been brought by groups of foreign individuals against UK-domiciled parent companies and their locally incorporated subsidiaries concerning alleged environmental damage and human rights abuses connected to the foreign subsidiary's operations.[40] The claimants in these cases have relied on the English Court of Appeal decision in *Chandler v Cape*

PLC[41] (another case in which my firm acted for the claimant), which held that a parent company can owe a duty of care toward employees of a subsidiary in certain circumstances. Such circumstances include a situation where the parent and the subsidiary's businesses are the same in a relevant respect and the subsidiary relied on the parent company's superior expertise in relation to a relevant aspect of health and safety.[42]

In the present line of cases in which my firm is acting, the foreign subsidiaries have disputed the jurisdiction of the English courts to hear the claims against them principally on the ground that there is no arguable case against the UK-domiciled parent company. The defendants contend that any claim against the subsidiary therefore pertains to the courts of the country in which the subsidiary is based. In all three of these cases, the MNEs essentially argue that the parent company does not exercise sufficient control over the relevant aspect of the subsidiary's business so as to give rise to a duty of care toward the claimants. In the language of the applicable common-law test, it is argued that there is no relationship of "proximity" between the claimants and the parent company.

In *Vedanta* (the first of the jurisdiction challenges to come before the Court of Appeal), the Court held that the first-instance judge was entitled to find that there was a serious issue to be tried between the claimants and the parent company. The court relied on a range of evidence regarding the degree of control exercised by the parent company, which was considered by the judge at first instance, including: (i) a Management and Shareholders agreement between Vedanta and KCM for the provision of various services by Vedanta to KCM; (ii) Vedanta's provision of environmental and health and safety training to KCM; (iii) Vedanta's financial support for KCM, including hundreds of millions of dollars' worth of loans; and (iv) evidence from a former KCM employee regarding the high level of control exercised by Vedanta over KCM.[43] The first-instance judge had also held (although it was ultimately not strictly relevant to the overall decision) that there was clear and cogent evidence that the claimants would not obtain access to justice in Zambia.[44] The factors that led to the court's conclusion on this latter point included the claimants' levels of poverty and the absence of available funding mechanisms in Zambia that would permit the prosecution of a complex environmental group action through to trial.[45] The defendants appealed these conclusions only to have their appeals rejected by the Court of Appeal, which found that there were no proper grounds to reopen the first-instance judge's conclusions on this issue.[46] At the time of writing, the defendants have sought permission to appeal to the Supreme Court. If granted, it remains conceivable that the Supreme Court could overturn the Court of Appeal's decision regarding the potential liability of the parent company, which in view of the lack of access to justice in Zambia would leave the claimants without a legal remedy.

Vedanta's litigation strategy has the apparent objective of diverting claims involving serious environmental contamination to the courts of one of the world's poorest countries, in circumstances where a court has found that the claimants would almost certainly not obtain justice there. This is a familiar tactic that has previously been used by MNEs even where there is no dispute that the claimant's case could not be tried in the local jurisdiction. For example, in *Connelly v RTZ Corporation Plc*,[47] another claim in which my firm acted for the claimant, the defendant disputed the jurisdiction of the English court to hear a claim brought against it by a miner who alleged to have contracted throat cancer during the course of his work in the defendant's Namibian subsidiary. This jurisdiction challenge was made despite the defendant having accepted that the costs associated with the action would be such that the claim could not be tried in Namibia.[48]

The second of the three recent jurisdiction challenges to be heard on appeal was the case of *Okpabi & Ors v Royal Dutch Shell PLC & Anor*,[49] which is a claim on behalf of Nigerian citizens with respect to alleged pollution and environmental damage caused by Shell's oil pipelines and other infrastructure in the Niger Delta. In this case, the Court of Appeal held by a majority of 2–1 that the evidence adduced by the claimants had not demonstrated a sufficient degree of control over the subsidiary's operations by the parent company so as to establish an arguable case on the issue of proximity. The court recognized the difficulty that claimants face in assembling evidence regarding the role of the parent company at this early stage of the litigation, but nevertheless found that the evidence presented was insufficient to found an arguable duty of care. Such evidence included, *inter alia*, mandatory and "quite specific" engineering standards issued by the parent in relation to matters of pipeline and facilities management, and witness evidence from ex-employees of the subsidiary regarding the close level of control and supervision exercised by the parent in health, safety, and environmental matters. The court nevertheless concluded that "the difficulty is that jurisdiction is founded on a properly arguable cause of action and not on what may (or may not) become a properly arguable cause of action".[50]

This case demonstrates the difficulties that claimants face in seeking to distinguish the roles of different corporate personalities in a corporate group in the context of a jurisdiction challenge before full disclosure of relevant documents by the defendants. As in *Vedanta*, the claimants contend that they would be unable to obtain justice in Nigeria. While the first-instance court expressed disagreement with the claimants on this issue, no formal ruling was made on the point.[51] Accordingly, there remains a risk that if this claim cannot go ahead in England the claimants will be left without access to a legal remedy.

The last of the three ongoing jurisdiction challenges in which my firm is currently acting is *AAA & Ors v Unilever plc & Anor*,[52] a claim concerning violent attacks on residents of a Unilever tea plantation during the 2007 Kenyan post-election violence. At first instance, the court found in the claimants' favor on the issue of proximity of the parent company, but concluded that the claim was bound to fail on other grounds. The claimants' appeal was heard at the end of April 2018. As in *Vedanta*, the first-instance court found that there was a substantial risk that the claimants would not obtain justice in Kenya. Accordingly, if the Court of Appeal finds that the case against the parent company is not arguable but there is a real issue vis-à-vis the subsidiary, the claimants may nevertheless be left without access to a legal remedy.

The legal strategy employed by the defendants in *Connelly*, *Vedanta*, *Shell*, and *Unilever* illustrates how MNEs exploit the principles of LL and SCP to delay and potentially frustrate the pursuit of justice by seeking to deflect litigation to the courts of countries where justice may not be achievable.

11.4 Limited liability and separate corporate personality: proposals for reform

11.4.1 Overview

While now widely accepted as foundational principles underpinning the modern market economy, the theoretical difficulties and practical injustices that arise from the operation of LL and SCP have given rise to various proposals for reform of this area.

1. Pro rata liability

A widely recognized critique is that of Hansmann and Kraakman, who advocated the replacement of LL vis-à-vis tort claimants with a system of pro rata liability,[53] which could be used to cover "any excess tort damages that the firm's estate fails to satisfy".[54] At the time this proposal was made, it sought to address the problem of a subsidiary's financial inability to satisfy tort judgments, but such an approach could also potentially help overcome the jurisdictional obstacles set out previously if parent companies could be sued directly in their home courts alongside the primary subsidiary company tortfeasor for their pro rata share of any liability. However, while this might work for classic MNE parent-company liabilities, the consequences could be problematic in more complex scenarios of companies with multiple minority international shareholders. If legal actions could be brought in the home courts of any such shareholders, this could lead to unacceptable forum shopping whereby genuinely passive, small minority shareholders are sued purely for the purposes of securing jurisdiction in a particular country.

It has also been contended that it would be too difficult and costly for victims to pursue legal action against large numbers of shareholders who each own a tiny fraction of the total shares.[55] Importantly, however, it is arguably inequitable to expose passive, small minority shareholders to litigation and potential legal liability for the actions of the companies in which they have invested. In particular, this type of investor has limited means of gaining a proper understanding of the risks associated with the activities of the corporation in which they have invested, and may have relied in good faith on information provided by the corporation assuring them of the safety and integrity of its operations.

2. Control-based liability

Another proposed alternative is a control-based approach, whereby a shareholder can be held liable for a subsidiary's activities on the basis of the control that it exercises either by virtue of its controlling equitable stake in the corporation or its de facto control over the subsidiary's operations by reason of that stake.[56] Such an approach militates against the difficulties associated with minority shareholder liability set out previously. Instead, it focuses on controlling shareholders who are best placed to influence the risky behavior of corporations, largely because their position affords them additional privileges that exceed the simple pro rata value of their equitable stake in the corporation.[57]

A further variation on this theme is the proposal for a rebuttable presumption of control, which would shift the burden onto parent companies to demonstrate that they do not exercise the requisite degree of control over their subsidiaries to found a duty of care with respect to the subsidiaries' activities.[58] Such an approach would to a degree alleviate the burden on claimants to adduce evidence of control at the jurisdiction stage when claimants may only have access to limited corporate documentation that is in the public domain. However, experience suggests that even if the onus is placed on MNEs to disprove control over their subsidiaries, MNEs can selectively use corporate literature to paint a compelling picture of parent and subsidiary companies operating entirely at arm's length, when the reality may be quite different. The true relationship between parent and subsidiary may only become apparent upon full disclosure of documents and cross-examination of relevant witnesses, which, at least in England, is not possible at the jurisdiction stage of proceedings.

3. Common-law duty of due diligence

The attachment of responsibility to those with the ability to control a subsidiary's activities is also captured by a proposal that advocates the judicial recognition of a common-law duty of care on parent companies to exercise due diligence with respect to the human rights impacts of the activities of all entities in the enterprise, including subsidiaries.[59] Under this proposal, parent companies would be under a common-law duty to use whatever leverage they have over a subsidiary in their exercise of due diligence.[60] This suggestion is in line with the groundbreaking law on duty of care that recently came into force in France.[61] This new law establishes an obligation of vigilance (*devoir de vigilance*) on large French companies to elaborate, disclose, and effectively implement a "vigilance plan" that assesses and addresses risks and serious harms throughout its business and supply chain.[62] The Swiss Popular Initiative on Responsible Business contains similar proposals, but at the time of writing, the relevant amendments to the Constitution of Switzerland have not yet been approved by Swiss citizens.[63]

The French law has potentially far-reaching consequences for French MNEs since the duty extends not just to the production of a vigilance plan, but also to its effective implementation. Such a duty potentially cuts across the separate personalities of parent, subsidiary, and supplier companies, giving rise to a positive legal duty on companies to control and influence the activities of separate legal persons.

It is argued that a common-law duty of due diligence "would not purport to pierce the corporate veil. Rather it would hold parent companies liable only for the foreseeable consequences of their own failures to exercise due diligence with regard to the enterprises over which they had effective leverage".[64] However, it is difficult to see how the imposition of such a duty would not trespass on the principle of SCP, at least in situations where the parent company has equity control over the subsidiary. The definition of "leverage" under the UNGPs (upon which the common-law duty proposal is based) is "the ability to effect change in the wrongful practices of an entity that causes that harm". In the case of a parent company with a significant controlling stake in a subsidiary, for practical purposes, the parent will have complete authority to control the subsidiary's corporate activity if it so wishes.[65] It follows that under this proposal parent companies with a significant controlling stake in a subsidiary would be legally compelled to exercise close supervision and control over matters of human rights in their exercise of due diligence. This would effectively prevent controlled subsidiaries from operating autonomously in relation to matters of human rights.

4. *Enterprise analysis*

Another approach to addressing difficulties associated with the operation of SCP within corporate groups is the use of enterprise analysis, which seeks to examine the "economic reality" of a group enterprise, rather than focusing on the individual corporate personalities within the group.[66] Enterprise liability has been subject to differing interpretations,[67] but, broadly speaking, the predominant concepts at the heart of enterprise analysis are "control" and "economic integration" if legal entities are under common control and economically integrated, they should be thought of together as one enterprise.[68]

Enterprise analysis has had limited impact in terms of tort liability so far. The Indian courts did introduce a form of strict enterprise liability through judicial development in the case of *Mehta v Union of India*.[69] However, it has been questioned whether subsequent application of the doctrine in a corporate group situation in fact conflated enterprise liability with veil piercing and direct parent company liability. The manner of operation of the doctrine was therefore left somewhat unclear.[70] Nevertheless, it has been argued that a statutory rule that attributes liability to the parent for negligent acts of the subsidiary on the basis of an enterprise liability principle would be a sensible way forward in eliminating the problems associated with tort liability in corporate group situations.[71]

5. *Evaluation*

Subject to concerns (discussed further in the remainder of this chapter) as to the applicable governing law in cases involving harm arising from overseas activities, the aforementioned proposals all represent a potential advancement on the status quo. The French duty of vigilance law should be singled out in particular as a legislative development that could have a potentially significant impact on corporate behavior as regards the activities of overseas subsidiaries and trading partners.

However, with the possible exception of a purely economic form of enterprise liability,[72] the proposals set out here remain rooted in the factual control that a corporation exercises or has failed to exercise with respect to its overseas activities. By maintaining an emphasis on control, such proposals fail to recognize the triumph (at least at common law) of the nominalist understanding of the corporation, which cements the corporation's status as an economic being whose primary duty is always to its shareholders. To expect or foist a duty upon a corporate shareholder to actively address negative human rights impacts caused by its subsidiaries' activities is to impose an artificial moralism on an entity that is pre-ordained to obey only economic motives.[73] Indeed, this tension may have the counterproductive effect of encouraging MNEs to decentralize their operations so as to avoid tort liabilities.[74] My professional experience certainly suggests that MNEs are increasingly careful to convey an image of foreign subsidiaries operating as independent decentralized entities. Furthermore, where the emphasis is on factual or economic control, those MNEs whose internal structure does not satisfy the required level of direction or economic integration with a foreign subsidiary, but whose investment nevertheless drives forward the performance of a dangerous activity, can continue to exploit the principles of LL and SCP so as to limit their accountability and legal liability for the harmful effects of the activity.

11.4.2 Profit-risk/created risk liability

The idea of connecting tort liability with the profit or benefit that is derived from risky activities is not alien to contemporary legal systems. The "risk theory" originated in France in the late 19th century and was constructed through jurisprudential development in the French courts. It advanced a new conception of civil liability based not on fault but rather on the performance of a risky activity. The purpose was to remove the element of subjectivity from civil liability by instead imposing fault automatically on anyone carrying out a dangerous activity.[75]

Drawing upon the Roman law principle of *ubi emolumentum ibi onus* (he who receives the benefit must likewise bear the burden), the risk theory has subsequently been developed to establish the profit risk theory, pursuant to which those who enjoy the benefit of a dangerous activity or thing must compensate any harm that is caused by the same.[76] This theory was extended by the created risk theory, under which all those who created the risk, irrespective of profit, would be liable for any resultant harm. Liability for dangerous activities is strict, such that defendants can only escape liability on the basis of *force majeure* or exclusive fault of the claimant.

In *Florez*,[77] the court held that the defendant was liable under the Colombian strict liability regime for dangerous activities. However, while the profit-risk and created risk theories have informed the development of civil liability for risky activities in Colombia, the test that was applied in *Florez* to determine who was liable for the harm caused was the guardianship theory, under which liability attaches to those who exercise "an independent power of direction, governance or control over the dangerous activity".[78] Therefore, while derived from a progressive theory based on the derivation of profit from inherently risky activities, the Colombian dangerous activities doctrine also applies a control-based approach when it comes to attribution of liability. However, the doctrine is considerably more generous to claimants compared to common-law negligence, in that it offers the benefit of strict liability while focusing on a *power* of direction, governance, or control, rather than *de facto* control over the relevant activity. It also contemplates a broader definition of control than that encapsulated by common law negligence liability.[79]

In Argentina, the concept of tort liability deriving from profit has been applied in a more radical way to directly impute liability upon a corporate shareholder based purely on its role as an investor. Art 1113 of the Argentinian Civil Code provides that "the obligation of the person who has caused harm extends to damage caused by his dependants or by those things from which he benefits, or which he has in his care".[80] In the case of *Arroyo, Ricardo Arturo c IRSA Inversiones y Representaciones*,[81] the Argentinean Court of Appeal, relying on the profit-risk/created risk theories, employed Art 1113 to impose liability on a shareholder, on the grounds that it was

> more than just a shareholder receiving dividends . . . but rather it promoted a "strategic union of companies" for the construction of a complex . . . and its subsequent economic exploitation . . . The purchase of shares in SAMAP was the procedure used to develop that activity for its own benefit.[82]

The court therefore founded liability on the defendant's use of a subsidiary corporation to promote a dangerous activity for the defendant's economic benefit.

By applying a profit-risk/created risk approach to the overseas activities of MNEs, parent companies that create environmental and human rights risks through their overseas investment could be strictly liable for harm that arises directly from that risk. The determination of whether liability should attach to a particular shareholder would be a fact-sensitive question that could be decided by reference to the extent to which the shareholder "created" the risk. The purpose of such an approach would be to identify and hold responsible those who are genuinely "behind" a risky activity.

The adoption of a profit-risk/created risk liability regime would address some of the difficulties associated with the proposals for legal reform that have been previously discussed. First, using the flexible concept of risk creation, genuine minority passive investors would escape liability on the grounds that they did not promote or create the risk and the level of profit they extract is insufficient to found liability on its own. Second, the imposition of primary liability under the created risk approach would require limited factual investigation into the nature of the shareholder's investment. That enquiry would be less onerous than establishing the requisite level of "economic integration" envisaged by the enterprise theory, thereby reducing the evidential burden for claimants.

The profit-risk approach would also help address the conceptual problem of applying control-based liability regimes to corporate shareholders. Such systems seek to impose standards of behavior based on subjective moral conceptions of fault that are inapposite for corporate shareholders as exclusively economic beings. Instead of a fault-based regime grounded in control, liability would be strict and premised purely on the creation of a risk through investment. These are economic factors that a corporation can readily analyze and quantify. By basing liability on risk creation rather than the imposition of duties with respect to subsidiaries, the profit/risk liability regime would not endanger the principle of SCP.

The profit-risk/created risk approach is presented here as a recommended general direction for development of the law as it applies to the negative human rights and environmental impacts of MNEs' overseas activities. It is recognized that procedural and political obstacles would need to be overcome in order to implement such an approach internationally. For example, the introduction of such a regime in the home country of an MNE would have limited effect where the law governing such disputes is the law of the country where the damage occurred.[83] Furthermore, it is recognized that any legal development that may be perceived as a challenge to the longstanding principles of LL and SCP is likely to be met with considerable political resistance by the business community. However, with France having led the way with its new *devoir de vigilance*, the development of more radical normative approaches to ensure international corporate accountability for human rights and environmental violations seems less daunting than it once did.

11.5 Conclusion

The principles of LL and SCP were established in the 19th century purportedly to encourage entrepreneurship and foster economic development. However, questions have been raised over the necessity of this corporate model to achieve these stated economic goals. The subsequent proliferation and empowerment of "corporate persons" has given rise to considerable social discordances, largely arising out of the corporation's schizophrenic identity as both an item of property and a social being, which allows shareholders to "externalize" risk by hiding behind the corporate form. Meanwhile, the burden of such risks is shifted onto involuntary creditors, such as tort victims. In the common-law world, the close of the 20th century witnessed the triumph of the nominalist understanding of the corporate form, such that the primacy of a corporation's underlying fiduciary duty to its shareholders is now incontrovertible.

Presentation of the corporation as a social being has nevertheless subsisted, for example through modern day "CSR" initiatives. However, the corporation's ability to present itself as a social entity while remaining duty-bound to obey the underlying economic imperative to generate wealth for its owners simply underlines the potential dangers of an artificial person that will go to any economically justifiable lengths to achieve its ends. In the context of MNEs and corporate groups, the corporate person's propensity to exploit its social status and privileges manifests in particular ways, notably use of the corporate form alongside partnerships with host governments to generate the image of a national enterprise operating in the overall national interest. Such techniques are employed to avoid discrimination against the foreign enterprise and generally to temper resistance against the MNE's activities.

The principles of LL and SCP can serve to frustrate the pursuit of corporate accountability for harm committed through foreign-registered subsidiaries and joint ventures, either through insufficient allocation of resources to the subsidiary to satisfy tort judgments, or by benefitting from social factors or systemic inadequacies that limit the availability of legal redress in the host State. The primary means by which victims have been able to overcome such difficulties is by bringing claims against parent companies in their home jurisdiction. However, such cases are complex, and in common-law jurisdictions, the law as it currently stands requires claimants to demonstrate that the parent exercises a certain degree of control over the activities of the subsidiary. Recent judicial developments in the UK have extended parent company liability to situations in which the subsidiary relied on the parent's superior expertise in relation to a relevant aspect of its business.

The control-based approach, grounded in traditional common-law tort principles, has resulted in some successes on behalf of foreign tort victims.[84] However, a profit-risk/created risk liability regime could represent a suitably flexible approach to the allocation of liability within corporate groups. The idea of "risk creation" as a basis for liability would seek to identify those who genuinely instigated, promoted, or developed a dangerous activity through their actions or investment. Such an approach would aim to attach strict joint and several liability to the "major players" behind a dangerous activity while exempting passive investors without a sufficient connection to the activity so as to qualify as risk creators. This would avoid the conceptual difficulties associated with imposing positive duties of care on economic corporate actors. Instead, shareholders' liability would be based purely on their role as risk creators, which would prevent MNEs from relying on the separate corporate personalities of subsidiaries in jurisdictional challenges that frustrate the pursuit of justice. This would ensure greater international accountability for violations of human rights and environmental standards.

Notes

* Associate Solicitor, Leigh Day, London. I am a legal practitioner specializing in civil claims on behalf of groups of individuals who claim to have suffered harm as a result of the overseas activities of British companies. My firm has acted in a number of the cases discussed in this chapter. The opinions expressed herein are my own.

1 Paul Davies and Sarah Worthington, *Gower & Davies' Principles of Modern Company Law* (9th edn, Sweet & Maxwell 2012) 207.

2 Paddy Ireland, 'Limited Liability, Shareholder Rights and the Problem of Corporate Irresponsibility', (2010) 34 *Cambridge Journal of Economics* 837.

3 Davies and Worthington (n 1) 208.

4 Ireland (n 2) 839.

5 Dan Plesch and Stephanie Blankenburg, *Corporate Rights and Responsibilities: Restoring Legal Accountability* (Royal Society for the Encouragement of Arts, Manufactures and Commerce 2007) 15.

6 Ireland (n 2) 839.

7 Ibid. 842.
8 Davies and Worthington (n 1) 35.
9 *Salomon v A Salomon & Co Ltd* [1896] UKHL 1, [1897] AC 22.
10 See, eg, Michael Jensen and William Meckling, 'Theory of the Firm: Managerial Behaviour, Agency Costs and Ownership Structure', (1976) 3 *Journal of Financial Economics* 305, 310; Katsuhito Iwai, 'Persons, Things and Corporations: The Corporate Personality Controversy and Comparative Corporate Governance', (1999) 47(4) *The American Journal of Comparative Law* 583; Sanford Grossman and Oliver Hart, 'The Costs and Benefits of Ownership: A Theory of Vertical and Lateral Integration', (1986) 94(4) *Journal of Political Economy* 691, 693; David Gindis, 'From Fictions and Aggregates to Real Entities in the Theory of the Firm', (2009) 5(1) *Journal of Institutional Economics* 25.
11 Iwai (n 10) 584.
12 Ibid.
13 Ibid 585.
14 *Dodge v Ford Motor Company*, 204 Mich 459, 170 NW 668 Note that this hard-core nominalist conception of corporate personhood is not widely accepted outside of the common law. In particular, jurisdictions based in whole or in part on civil law have incorporated more flexible ideas of "stakeholder capitalism" into their company law, which require the consideration of long-term objectives and third-party stakeholder interests in economic decision making. See, eg, Iwai (n 10), and Fabian Brandt and Konstantinos Georgiou, *Shareholders v Stakeholders Capitalism* (2016), Comparative Corporate Governance and Financial Regulation, Paper 10 <https://scholarship.law.upenn.edu/fisch_2016/10/> accessed 24 September 2019.
15 Ireland (n 2) 851–2; William Allen, 'Our Schizophrenic Conception of the Business Corporation', (1992) 14 *Cardozo Law Review* 261, 264–5, 279.
16 Joel Bakan, *The Corporation* (Constable 2005) 37. See also Meredith Dearborn, 'Enterprise Liability: Reviewing and Revitalizing Liability for Corporate Groups', (2009) 97 *California Law Review* 195, 249.
17 *Santa Clara County v. Southern Pacific Railroad Company* [1886] 118 US 394.
18 Plesch and Blankenburg (n 5) 8.
19 Marius Emberland, *The Human Rights of Companies* (Oxford University Press 2006).
20 See Karl Polanyi, *The Great Transformation: The Political and Economic Origins of Our Time* (2nd edn, Beacon 2001).
21 Bakan (n 16) 46–50.
22 Polanyi (n 20) 79.
23 For a helpful summary of relevant literature on this topic, see Peter Muchlinski, *Multinational Enterprises and the Law* (2nd edn, Oxford University Press 2007).
24 Ibid. 25–6.
25 Ibid. 33.
26 Ibid. 192.
27 Davies and Worthington (n 1) 210.
28 See Nina Mendelson, 'A Control-Based Approach to Shareholder Liability for Corporate Torts', (2002) 102(5) *Columbia Law Review* 1203.
29 For an elucidation of some potential conflicts, see Davies and Worthington (n 1) 244–5.
30 Muchlinski (n 23) 192.
31 *Pedro Emiro Florez Arroyo v Equion Energia Ltd* [2016] EWHC 1699 (TCC).
32 Ibid. 386.
33 Ibid.
34 Ibid. 476.

35 See, eg, *Kadie Kalma & Ors v African Minerals Ltd & Ors* [2018] EWHC 120 (QB).
36 Mendelson (n 29) 1251; *Dept of Envtl. Prot v Ventron Corp* 468 A.2d 150 (NJ 1983); *Walkovsky v Charlton* 223 N.E.2d 6 (New York 1966).
37 Peter Muchlinski, 'Limited Liability and Multinational Enterprises: A Case for Reform?', (2010) 34 *Cambridge Journal of Economics* 915, 925.
38 *Dominic Liswaniso Lungowe & Ors v Vedanta Resources Plc & Anor* [2017] EWCA Civ 1528, 96–7.
39 Ibid. 96.
40 *Vedanta* (n 39); *AAA & Ors v Unilever Plc & Anor* [2017] EWHC 371; *Okpabi & Ors v Royal Dutch Shell Plc & Anor* [2018] EWCA Civ 191.
41 *Chandler v Cape plc* [2012] EWCA Civ 525.
42 Ibid. 80.
43 *Vedanta* (n 38) 84.
44 *Lungowe & Ors v Vedanta Resources PLC & Anor* [2016] EWHC 975 (TCC) 169–98.
45 Ibid. 175–98.
46 *Vedanta* (n 38) 131–2.
47 *Connelly v RTZ Corporation Plc* [1997] UKHL 30, [1999] CLC 533.
48 Ibid. 31. I am grateful to Richard Meeran for drawing my attention to this point.
49 *Okpabi* (n 40).
50 ibid 122.
51 *Okpabi & Ors v RDS & Anor* [2017] EWHC 89 (TCC) 120–2.
52 *Unilever* (n 40).
53 Henry Hansmann and Reiner Kraakman, 'Toward unlimited Shareholder Liability for Corporate Torts', (1991) 100 *Yale Law Journal* 1879.
54 Ibid. 1896.
55 Mendelson (n 28) 1284.
56 Ibid.
57 Ibid. 1247–58.
58 Cees van Dam and Filip Gregor, 'Corporate Responsibility to Respect Human Rights vis a vis Legal Duty of Care', in Juan Jose Alvarez Rubio and Katerina Yiannibas (eds.), *Human Rights in Business: Removal of Barriers to Justice in the European Union* (Routledge 2007) 128.
59 Douglas Cassel, 'Outlining the Case for a Common Law Duty of Care of Business to Exercise Human Rights Due Diligence', (2016) 1 *Business and Human Rights Journal* 179, 202.
60 Ibid. 186.
61 Law no. 2017-399 of 27 March 2017 on the duty of vigilance for parent and instructing companies (*Loi no. 2017-399 du 27 Mars 2017 relative au devoir de vigilance des societies meres et des enterprises donneuses d'ordre*).
62 Sandra Cossart, Jerome Chaplier, and Tiphanie Beau de Lomenie, 'The French Law on Duty of Care: A Historic Step towards Making Globalization Work for All', (2017) 2 *Business and Human Rights Journal* 317, 320.
63 See the contribution by Bueno in this volume on the Swiss Popular Initiative on Responsible Business (Chapter 12).
64 Cassel (n 59) 181.
65 Mendelson (n 28) 1252.
66 Muchlinski (n 37) 919.
67 See Dearborn (n 16).
68 Kurt Strasser and Philip Blumberg, 'Legal Models and Business Realities of Enterprise Groups: Mismatch and Change' (2009) Comparative Research in Law & Political Economy Research Paper 18/2009 <https://papers.ssrn.com/sol3/papers.cfm?abstract_id=1440858> accessed 24 September 2019.

69 *M C Mehta v Union of India*, 1987 SCR (1) 819, 1086.
70 See Muchlinski (n 23) 314–15.
71 Muchlinski (n 37) 926–7; Dearborn (n 16).
72 See Dearborn (n 16) 252–4.
73 Ibid. 249.
74 Ibid. 249–50.
75 Franz Werro, 'Liability for Harm Caused by Things' (2010) Centre for the Study of European Contract Law Working Paper, 8 <https://papers.ssrn.com/sol3/papers.cfm?abstract_id=1639357> accessed 24 September 2019.
76 See, eg, Colombian Civil Chamber Decision of 15 November 1940 for how this concept has been interpreted in the Colombian jurisdiction.
77 *Florez* (n 31).
78 Art 1384(1) Code Civil of France; see also *Florez* (n 31) 476.
79 See, eg, Colombian Civil Chamber decision of 18 March 1976.
80 Art 1113 Civil Code of Argentina.
81 *Arroyo, Ricardo Arturo c IRSA Inversiones y Representaciones*, Exp 97114/97 CNCIV – SALA M – 10/07/2001.
82 Ibid. 2.
83 This can be the case, for example, in non-contractual disputes involving EU Member States under Art 4 of Regulation (EC) No 864/2007 of the European Parliament and of the Council of 11 July 2007 on the law applicable to non-contractual obligations (Rome II) [2007] OJ L 199.
84 For examples of successful cases in this area, see Richard Meeran, 'Tort Litigation against Multinational Corporations for Violation of Human Rights: On Overview of the Position Outside the United States', (2011) 3(1) *City University of Hong Kong Law Review* 1.

Bibliography

Allen W, 'Our Schizophrenic Conception of the Business Corporation', (1992–1993) 14 *Cardozo Law Review* 261.

Bakan J, *The Corporation* (Constable 2005).

Brandt F and Georgiou K, *Shareholders v Stakeholders Capitalism* (2016), Comparative Corporate Governance and Financial Regulation, Paper 10 <https://scholarship.law.upenn.edu/fisch_2016/10/>

Cassel D, 'Outlining the Case for a Common Law Duty of Care of Business to Exercise Human Rights Due Diligence', (2016) 1 *Business and Human Rights Journal* 179.

Cossart S, Chaplier J, and Beau de Lomenie T, 'The French Law on Duty of Care: A Historic Step Towards Making Globalization Work for All', (2017) 2 *Business and Human Rights Journal* 317.

Davies P and Worthington S, *Gower & Davies' Principles of Modern Company Law* (9th edn, Sweet & Maxwell 2012).

Dearborn M, 'Enterprise Liability: Reviewing and Revitalizing Liability for Corporate Groups', (2009) 97 *California Law Review* 195.

Gindis D, 'From Fictions and Aggregates to Real Entities in the Theory of the Firm', (2009) 5(1) *Journal of Institutional Economics* 25.

Grossman S and Hart O, 'The Costs and Benefits of Ownership: A Theory of Vertical and Lateral Integration', (1986) 94(4) *Journal of Political Economy* 691.

Hansmann H and Kraakman R, 'Toward unlimited Shareholder Liability for Corporate Torts', (1991) 100 *Yale Law Journal* 1879.

Ireland P, 'Limited Liability, Shareholder Rights and the Problem of Corporate Irresponsibility', (2010) 34 *Cambridge Journal of Economics* 837.

Iwai K, 'Persons, Things and Corporations: The Corporate Personality Controversy and Comparative Corporate Governance', (1999) 47(4) *The American Journal of Comparative Law* 583.

Jensen M and Meckling W, 'Theory of the Firm: Managerial Behaviour, Agency Costs and Ownership Structure', (1976) 3 *Journal of Financial Economics* 305.

Meeran R, 'Tort Litigation against Multinational Corporations for Violation of Human Rights: On overview of the Position outside the United States', (2011) 3(1) *City University of Hong Kong Law Review* 1.

Mendelson N, 'A Control-Based Approach to Shareholder Liability for Corporate Torts', (2002) 102(5) *Columbia Law Review* 1203.

Muchlinski P, 'Limited Liability and Multinational Enterprises: A Case for Reform?', (2010) 34 *Cambridge Journal of Economics* 915.

———, *Multinational Enterprises and the Law* (2nd edn, Oxford University Press 2007).

Plesch D and Blankenburg S, *Corporate Rights and Responsibilities: Restoring Legal Accountability* (Royal Society for the Encouragement of Arts, Manufactures and Commerce 2007).

Polanyi K, *The Great Transformation: The Political and Economic Origins of Our Time* (2nd edn, Beacon 2001).

Strasser K and Blumberg P, 'Legal Models and Business Realities of Enterprise Groups: Mismatch and Change' (2009) Comparative Research in Law & Political Economy Research Paper 18/2009 <https://papers.ssrn.com/sol3/papers.cfm?abstract_id=1440858>

van Dam C and Gregor F, 'Corporate Responsibility to Respect Human Rights vis a vis Legal Duty of Care', in Juan Jose Alvarez Rubio and Katerina Yiannibas (eds.), *Human Rights in Business: Removal of Barriers to Justice in the European Union* (Routledge 2007).

Werro F, 'Liability for Harm Caused by Things' (2010) Centre for the Study of European Contract Law Working Paper <https://papers.ssrn.com/sol3/papers.cfm?abstract_id=1639357>

12 The Swiss popular initiative on responsible business

From responsibility to liability

*Nicolas Bueno**

12.1 Introduction

Unless the Swiss Parliament adopts a new law on corporate due diligence, Swiss citizens will decide in 2020 whether to adopt or reject a partial revision of the Constitution of Switzerland that aims to introduce a specific provision on responsible business.[1] According to the proposal, companies that are based in Switzerland are required to carry out appropriate human rights and environmental due diligence in Switzerland and abroad. Furthermore, those companies shall be liable for human rights and environmental-related harm caused by (foreign) companies under their control unless they can prove that they took all due care to avoid the harm.

This contribution first presents the international corporate human rights due diligence framework, as defined by the UNGPs[2] and the OECD Guidelines for Multinational Enterprises ("OECD Guidelines").[3] In order to clarify the link between corporate due diligence and corporate liability, the first section focuses on the appropriate action that companies should take within this due diligence framework to prevent potential adverse impacts or to cease those that have occurred. The second section outlines the political background of the Swiss Popular Initiative on Responsible Business in light of the UNGPs and the OECD Guidelines, and then assesses this initiative.

The last section compares the Swiss popular initiative with other legislative developments that have occurred after the adoption of the UNGPs. It distinguishes between mandatory disclosure laws, mandatory due diligence laws, and laws clarifying the legal consequences of failing to comply with due diligence duties. In that third category, this contribution compares the Swiss popular initiative with the recently adopted French *loi relative au devoir de vigilance.* Both legislative initiatives clarify the corporate civil liability for human rights and environmental harm committed abroad, which should reduce, to some extent, the uncertainty related to outcomes of transnational litigation for corporate human rights and environment abuses.

12.2 Corporate human rights and environmental due diligence

The UNGPs and the OECD Guidelines are soft-law instruments and do not impose binding legal obligations upon states or companies. However, they have given rise to binding obligations regarding corporate human rights and environmental due diligence – for instance, in the French *loi relative au devoir de vigilance*. In any event, they provide a relatively clear standard of conduct for business enterprises.

With respect to other elements, both Guidelines define the due diligence that companies should apply regarding human rights.[4] Due diligence is the process through which enterprises can identify, prevent, mitigate, and account for how they address their actual and potential adverse impacts.[5] The OECD Guidelines define human rights due diligence in the same way.[6]

On the contrary, environmental issues are not specifically addressed in the UNGPs, which cover only human rights. Corporations are nevertheless expected to respect and conduct due diligence with regard to all internationally recognized human rights, including those that necessarily entail environmental aspects, such as the rights to health, water, or food, or the rights of indigenous peoples.[7] Additionally, Chapter VI of the OECD Guidelines defines the conduct that multinational enterprises should adopt to take due account of the need to protect the environment. This section focuses mainly on human rights and human rights-related environmental due diligence, as they are covered by both the UNGPs and the OECD Guidelines. Section 12.3 will present how the Swiss Popular Initiative defines human rights and environmental due diligence.

Both the UNGPs and the OECD Guidelines specify what is expected from business enterprises for each step of the due diligence process.[8] With a view to linking due diligence and corporate liability, this contribution focuses on the appropriate action that business enterprises should take to prevent potential adverse human rights impacts or cease actual ones (Section 12.2.1). Actual adverse impacts – those that have already occurred[9] – could also be subject to remediation. This section then discusses compensation through civil liability as one form of remedy (Section 12.2.2). Presenting this international standard of corporate conduct will aid assessment of the Swiss Popular Initiative on Responsible Business.

12.2.1 Corporate due diligence: taking appropriate action

Regarding the appropriate action that companies should take to prevent or cease adverse impact, Guiding Principle 19(b) of the UNGPs distinguishes between three scenarios. Each scenario has different implications for the nature of a business enterprise's responsibility.[10]

First, where a business enterprise *causes* or may cause an adverse impact, it should take the necessary steps to cease or prevent the impact.[11] This would apply, for example, in the case of a business enterprise being the main source of pollution in a community's drinking water supply due to chemical effluents from its production processes.[12] Second, where a business enterprise *contributes* or may contribute to an adverse impact, it should take the necessary steps to cease or prevent its contribution. According to the OECD Guidelines, contributing to an adverse impact should be interpreted as a substantial contribution, meaning an activity that causes, facilitates, or incentivizes another entity to cause an adverse impact.[13] The OHCHR gives the example of an enterprise changing product requirements for suppliers without adjusting production deadlines and prices, thus pushing suppliers to breach labor standards in order to deliver.[14] Although highly relevant in practice, it is not clear from the international framework to what extent failures to supervise or intervene in the harmful conduct of a business entity – such as a supplier – enter into the notion of contribution. However, in any event, the enterprise should use its leverage to mitigate impacts, in addition to ceasing or preventing its contribution.[15] Leverage is considered to exist where the enterprise has the ability to effect change in the wrongful practices of the entity that is causing or contributing to an adverse impact.[16]

In the two first scenarios, the business enterprise causes or contributes to adverse impacts through its own activities,[17] including its own activities in the supply chain.[18] An enterprise can finally be involved in an adverse impact when the impact is caused by an entity with which it has a business relationship and when the company is *directly linked* to that company's own operations, products, or services.[19] The OHCHR gives the example of a supplier acting contrary to the terms of its contract and using child or bonded labor to manufacture a product for the enterprise, without any intended or unintended pressure from the enterprise to do so.[20] Indeed, if the enterprise had pressured the supplier, it would have contributed to the adverse impact. The legal literature has provided other examples in which the notions of "contribution" and "directly linked" are sometimes understood in different ways.[21] In the third scenario, the appropriate measure to be taken depends on the leverage the enterprise has on the entity causing or contributing to the adverse impact. If the business enterprise has leverage to mitigate the adverse impact it should exercise this, as in the contribution scenario. If it lacks leverage, it should try to increase its leverage. Finally, when increasing leverage is impossible, it should consider terminating the relationship.[22]

In the two last scenarios, another entity is always involved. Thus, in both situations the appropriate actions to be taken vary according to the extent of an enterprise's leverage in addressing the impact.[23] The extent of leverage over another business entity is a factual question. Some factors help identify the extent of leverage, such as the degree of direct control by the enterprise over the entity; the terms of contract between the enterprise and the entity; the proportion of business the enterprise represents for the entity; or the ability of the enterprise to incentivize the other entity to improve human rights.[24]

12.2.2 *Human rights due diligence and corporate liability*

While the UNGPs recommend that states implement and enforce laws that are aimed at, or have the effect of requiring, business enterprises to respect human rights,[25] they do not entail specific recommendations about legal sanctions or corporate liability in the event that a business enterprise does not carry out human rights due diligence. However, they do provide guidance regarding remediation after an actual adverse impact has occurred, both to companies and to States.

Whenever enterprises identify that they have caused or contributed to adverse impacts – as in the first two scenarios – they are expected to provide for remediation through grievance mechanisms, which should conform to the effectiveness criteria of Guiding Principle 31 of the UNGPs.[26] As such, remediation is part of the corporate responsibility to respect human rights. States, on the other hand, are expected, among other elements, to take appropriate steps to ensure the effectiveness of domestic judicial mechanisms when addressing business-related human rights abuses, including considering ways to reduce legal, practical, and other relevant barriers that could lead to a denial of access to remedy.[27] Remedy may include apologies, restitution, rehabilitation, financial or non-financial compensation, and punitive sanctions, as well as the prevention of harm through, for example, injunctions or guarantees of non-repetition.[28]

Among legal barriers that could lead to a denial of access to remedy, the UNGPs mention the way in which legal responsibility is attributed among members of a corporate group under domestic laws. This should not facilitate the avoidance of appropriate accountability.[29] In this respect, the OHCHR adds that the corporate group structure does not make any difference regarding whether entities within the group have to respect human rights – it simply affects how they go about ensuring that rights are respected in practice. If human rights abuses do occur, it will be the national law in the relevant jurisdiction that determines where liability rests.[30] Other legal barriers also arise where claimants face a denial of justice in a host State and cannot access home State courts regardless of the merits of the claim.[31] The UNGPs finally note that many legal and practical barriers result from imbalances between the parties to business-related human rights claims, such as their financial resources, access to information, and expertise.[32]

The UNGPs are an important framework regarding corporate civil liability for human rights and human rights-related environmental abuses. However, they do not entail specific recommendations to States on how they should regulate issues of jurisdiction, applicable law, or the material conditions of parent or contracting company liability. These elements remain a matter of domestic law. They have given rise to much uncertainty in the emerging relevant transnational civil litigation, as is the case for material conditions of parent-company liability.

In the English case of *Chandler v Cape* of 2012, for example, the Court of Appeal developed four criteria to establish when law may impose on a parent company responsibility for the health and safety of its subsidiary's employees.[33] Concretely, it found the parent company Cape liable for asbestos-related injuries caused to an employee of a subsidiary. However, in *Thompson v The Renwick Group* of 2014, it found that the criteria were not met for a holding parent company carrying out any business at all apart from that of holding shares in other companies.[34] Similar questions of parent liability for the harm caused to employees of a subsidiary have been addressed in France in the cases of *Areva* and *Comilog*.[35] Finally, the *Dutch Shell Nigeria* case, which is, at the time of writing, pending, should shed light on the question of the duty of care owed by a parent company to third parties.[36]

So far, there has also been no court verdict on the merits of addressing the liability of a company for damage caused by a foreign supplier. In the case of Jabir et al. v. KiK, over 250 died in September 2012 in a fire at a factory in Pakistan that supplied the German textile corporation KiK. The plaintiffs filed a compensation claim against KiK alleging that it shared responsibility for the fire-safety deficiencies in the Pakistani factory.[37] Despite emerging case law, one lesson is the uncertainty for both plaintiffs and defendants about criteria to be used to determine a company's civil liability for the harm caused by a subsidiary or a supplier. The next section presents and assesses the Swiss Popular Initiative on Responsible Business in light of the UNGPs and the OECD Guidelines, and discusses the extent to which it will clarify the conditions of parent and contracting liability in transnational civil litigation.

12.3 The Swiss popular initiative on responsible business

12.3.1 Political background

1. The Position Paper on CSR and the National Action Plan

Three years after the endorsement of the UNGPs by the UNHRC in 2011, the Swiss government released a report in comparative law on the legal obligations of corporate directors to conduct due diligence with regard to business activities abroad.[38] In this comparative law report, the government identified potential measures that could be adopted in company law to increase the corporate responsibility to respect human rights. The proposed measures included the introduction of a specific duty for corporate directors to exercise human rights due diligence.[39] A failure to comply with their due diligence duties would trigger their liability.[40] In March 2015, however, the lower chamber of the Parliament rejected, with a narrow majority,[41] a motion requiring the government to take further steps with a view to implementing the measures identified in the comparative law report.[42]

In April 2015, the Swiss government also adopted the Position Paper on CSR (Position Paper 2015).[43] In this document, it presented four strategies for the period 2015–2019 regarding CSR. It set out plans to develop the definition of CSR within international fora, such as the UN and the OECD; support companies implementing their CSR; promote CSR in developing countries; and work for the improvement of corporate transparency.[44] Position Paper 2015 raised some criticism for not addressing the issue of corporate civil liability.[45] Indeed, the paper was not intended to introduce mandatory human rights due diligence provisions or clarify the conditions upon which corporations based in Switzerland could be held liable for human rights abuses committed abroad.

Finally, on 9 December 2016, the Swiss government released its National Action Plan (NAP) on implementation of the UNGPs, which should be read as a complement of equivalent value to Position Paper 2015.[46] In the NAP, the

Swiss government set out the expectation that corporations that are domiciled or active in Switzerland respect human rights in their activities in Switzerland and abroad.[47] However, like Position Paper 2015, the NAP did not introduce any mandatory human rights due diligence provisions in Swiss law, nor did it provide any clarification as to the conditions of liability of Switzerland-based companies for human rights or environmentally adverse impact abroad resulting from the operations of foreign subsidiaries, subcontractors, or suppliers.

Regarding mandatory due diligence, the NAP acknowledged that there is currently no legally binding provision in Swiss law requiring that corporations conduct human rights due diligence in their operations abroad.[48] In December 2016, when the NAP was released, the Swiss government outlined that no other country had adopted such legally binding provisions.[49] It concluded that any regulation that Switzerland would introduce in that regard should be broadly adopted internationally in order to avoid the Swiss economy being penalized.[50] Regarding access to remedy in Switzerland for victims of corporate abuses, the NAP focuses exclusively on private international law questions. It broadly states that for transnational tort claims there is always a forum in Switzerland when the defendant is a corporation domiciled in Switzerland, and that fundamental norms in Switzerland, such as human rights, are applicable regardless of the applicable law.[51] In September 2018, Switzerland released a specific report on Access to Remedy. Despite identified international developments, it did not recommend the adoption of regulatory measures introducing a mandatory due diligence provision in Swiss law.[52]

2. *Human rights due diligence and liability in specific sectors*

Beyond the political developments set out here, which cover companies in all economic sectors, the Swiss government has taken some measures in relation to specific sectors. A key example is the Swiss Federal Act on Private Security Services Provided Abroad 2013 recently entered into force. The Act expressly prohibits the provision, from Switzerland, of private security services for the purpose of direct participation in hostilities abroad, or of those that may be assumed to be utilized by the recipient or recipients in the commission of serious human rights violations.[53] These prohibitions apply expressly to parent and contracting companies based in Switzerland.[54]

Regarding liability, criminal sanctions are in place for individuals who infringe the prohibitions.[55] The Act does not cover corporate civil liability. However, it should be noted that article 6 of the Act sets out that where a company contracts out the provision of a security service to another company, it has to ensure that the subcontractor performs that service in keeping with the constraints to which the contracting company is itself subject. Interestingly, the civil liability of the contracting company for harm caused by the (foreign) subcontractor should be determined in accordance with the Swiss Code of Obligations.[56] The Act does not mention whether the Swiss Code of Obligations would also apply to determine the civil liability of a parent company for the harm caused by a foreign subsidiary. In any event, the Swiss Code of Obligations does not entail any specific provision on extracontractual liability of contracting companies for the harm caused to third parties by their subcontractors or subsidiaries, and no relevant case law currently exists in that regard.[57] Future case law will thus have to show how Swiss courts will solve the question of civil liability of Swiss-based providers of private security services abroad.

Finally, the Swiss government has set out two recommendations on the corporate responsibility to respect human rights for the commodities sector.[58] The first deals with the redaction of a guide on implementation of the UNGPs in the commodity sector; the second with mandatory due diligence provisions for corporations in that sector.[59] Regarding mandatory due diligence, the government is following international legislative developments on reporting and on mandatory due diligence in conflict minerals industries. It is following developments taking place in the EU[60] and has expressed the possibility of adopting similar provisions that are adapted to the Swiss context.[61] However, there is no recommendation to clarify the conditions of corporate liability of parent, subcontracting, or contracting companies in the commodity sector for human rights abuses.

12.3.2 The initiative text and its content

In parallel to the aforementioned political and legislative developments in Switzerland, the Swiss Coalition for Corporate Justice, representing over 80 NGOs in Switzerland, launched the popular constitutional initiative "Responsible Business: Protecting Human Rights and the Environment". The initiative collected the requisite threshold of 100,000 signatures and Swiss citizens will have to decide whether to adopt or reject this partial revision of the Swiss Constitution unless the Parliament adopts a satisfactory counter-proposal, which is in discussion.[62] In that case, the committee that launched the popular initiative could consider withdrawing the initiative.

Popular initiatives in Switzerland aim at revising the constitution; for example, that on responsible business aims to add article 101a, "Responsibility of Business", to the Swiss Constitution. Statistically, since the introduction of the popular initiative in 1891, 209 popular initiatives have led to a vote, 22 of which have been accepted. From 1848 to 2010, however, 47% of all popular initiatives triggered some kind of modification of the legislation.[63] Technically, if the constitutional initiative is adopted the constitutional rule will have to be implemented through a more detailed piece of sub-constitutional legislation, which would probably be included in the Swiss Code of Obligations.

1. The text of the initiative

The text of the proposed article 101a Constitution reads as follows:

1 The Confederation shall take measures to strengthen respect for human rights and the environment through business.

2 The law shall regulate the obligations of companies that have their registered office, central administration, or principal place of business in Switzerland according to the following principles:

- a Companies must respect internationally recognized human rights and international environmental standards, also abroad; they must ensure that human rights and environmental standards are also respected by companies under their control. Whether a company controls another is to be determined according to the factual circumstances. Control may also result through the exercise of power in a business relationship.
- b Companies are required to carry out appropriate due diligence. This means in particular that they must: identify real and potential impacts on internationally recognized human rights and the environment; take appropriate measures to prevent the violation of internationally recognized human rights and international environmental standards, cease existing violations, and account for the actions taken. These duties apply to controlled companies as well as to all business relationships. The scope of the due diligence to be carried out depends on the risks to the environment and human rights. In the process of regulating mandatory due diligence, the legislator is to take into account the needs of small and medium-sized companies that have limited risks of this kind.
- c Companies are also liable for damage caused by companies under their control where they have, in the course of business, committed violations of internationally recognized human rights or international environmental standards. They are not liable under this provision however if they can prove that they took all due care per paragraph b to avoid the loss or damage, or that the damage would have occurred even if all due care had been taken.
- d The provisions based on the principles of paragraphs a-c apply irrespective of the law applicable under private international law.[64]

2. *Mandatory due diligence, liability, and applicable law*

After setting the general goal of the initiative in Paragraph 1, the initiative text entails three elements to implement this goal in Paragraph 2. First, Article 101a(2)(b) introduces and defines the scope of a mandatory due diligence provision in the Swiss Constitution. Article 101a(2)(c) then addresses the liability of companies based in Switzerland, including their liability for harm caused by companies under their control. Finally, Article 101a(2)(d) aims to ensure that the introduced mandatory due diligence and liability provisions will apply even though the human rights or environmental-related harm typically occurs abroad. These three elements of mandatory due diligence, liability, and applicable law are discussed in turn.

First, the initiative requires that companies identify human rights and environmental impacts, take measures to prevent or cease adverse impacts, and account for how they address these impacts. In other terms, section (2)(b) introduces a mandatory due diligence provision. The scope of this due diligence covers human rights, as well as the environment. Regarding the environment, which the UNGPs do not cover explicitly,[65] the explanatory note of the initiative text expressly refers to the OECD Guidelines, which entails specific recommendations for multinational enterprises.[66]

Concretely, the introduction of a mandatory due diligence provision objectifies the expected conduct that Switzerland-based companies must apply with a view to preventing adverse human rights and environmental impacts in Switzerland and abroad. In this regard, the text of the initiative does not distinguish between the three scenarios presented here: causing an adverse impact, contributing to an adverse impact through the enterprise's own activities, and adverse impacts directly linked to the enterprise's operations by a business relationship.[67] It broadly states that due diligence "duties apply to controlled companies as well as to all business relationships".[68] However, according to the explanation of the initiative text, section (2)(b) introduces a mandatory due diligence provision based on the UNGPs and the OECD Guidelines.[69] Therefore, the international framework may provide guidance on how to interpret the text of the initiative. Although not expressly referenced in the text, this standard of conduct should help to identify whether a company has committed a fault and should be held liable *for its own actions and omissions* on the basis of the general tort of negligence.[70]

Second, section (2)(c) brings about a specific liability for the harm *caused by others*. "Others" means exclusively controlled companies, and thus not all business relationships to which due diligence duties apply. This liability for others has been modeled on the existing employer's liability in the Swiss Code of Obligations.[71] Accordingly, when a controlled company causes harm, the controlling company is liable unless it can prove that it took all due care to avoid the loss or damage, or that the damage would have occurred even if all due care had been taken. This liability provision addresses the practical difficulty that plaintiffs may face in bringing evidence about the conduct of controlling companies located abroad. As a result, it is not up to the plaintiff to prove that the controlling company acted negligently, but up to the company to prove that it took the required due care. For the rest, section (2)(c) does not reverse the burden of proof. It remains the plaintiff's responsibility to prove the harm, the causality, and the control relationship between the business entities.

The notion of "control" in section (2)(c) is not a UNGPs concept.[72] It is also not precisely defined in the initiative text, which states that control is to be determined according to the factual circumstances, and that control may also result through the exercise of power in a business relationship.[73] Thus, it is up to the legislative and the judiciary to clarify it in practice. However, according to the explanations of the initiative text, controlled companies are generally subsidiaries of parent companies. Nevertheless, in certain cases, a multinational company could also *de facto* control another company outside its strict legal structure through the exercise of economic control. For example, a relationship of control may exist if a Swiss company is the only purchaser from a supplier, even if the latter is not a direct subsidiary.[74] Therefore, control is narrower than the concept of leverage presented, as companies may have leverage over other entities without controlling them, according to the Swiss initiative.[75]

Finally, section (2)(d) ensures that the new standard of conduct for corporations and the conditions of liability for torts will apply in practice before Swiss courts. Under Swiss private international law, as in other countries, transnational claims in tort are generally governed by the law of the country in which the result occurred.[76] Thus, foreign tort law would generally apply to cases in which the result materializes abroad, which would render useless the mandatory due diligence and liability provisions Article 101a(2)(b) and (c) intend to introduce in Swiss law. Expressly making these provisions overriding mandatory provisions of Swiss law would ensure their application before Swiss courts in an international matter dealing with human rights or environmental due diligence.

12.4 The Swiss popular initiative in international comparison

12.4.1 Mandatory disclosure laws

An increasing number of laws require that companies disclose information regarding human rights. For example, the California Transparency in Supply Chains Act 2010 requires every retail seller and manufacturer doing business in California and having worldwide gross receipts that exceed US$100 million to disclose their efforts to eradicate slavery and human trafficking from their supply chains.[77] The Modern Slavery Act 2015 in the UK has a similar scope. It requires that commercial organizations prepare a slavery and human trafficking statement. Among other information, the statement must include information about parts of the organization's business and supply chains where a risk of slavery and human trafficking exists, and the steps it has taken to address that risk.[78]

The EU Directive 2014/95 on Disclosure of Non-Financial Information also enters into the category of mandatory disclosure laws. Large enterprises must include a non-financial statement containing information about the development, performance, position, and impact of their activity relating to environmental, social, and employee matters; respect for human rights; anti-corruption; and bribery matters.[79] Interestingly, the enterprise has to report the risks of adverse impact stemming not only from its own activities, but also from those linked to its operations, products, services, and business relationships, including its supply and subcontracting chains.[80] However, the company is not required to pursue policies in relation to those matters; in that case, it must only provide a clear and reasoned explanation for not doing so.[81]

The California Act, the Modern Slavery Act, and the EU Directive 2014/95 do not introduce a due diligence standard. They also do not clarify the conditions of liability for parent or contracting companies. Some suggest that even if the information that companies must disclose does not lead to any legal sanctions, companies may still seek to change their behavior if they believe that such information would lead to non-legal sanctions, such as reputational harm.[82] Although mandatory disclosure provisions have a preventive rather than remediation purpose, they may facilitate the establishment of corporate liability after harm has occurred. Indeed, mandatory disclosure requirements make it more difficult for a company to argue that it did not know, or could not have known, about adverse impacts. Therefore, these regulations may be an important step toward more accountability. However, in the end, since they do not clarify any due diligence standard and conditions of liability, they do not significantly reduce the uncertainty related to outcomes of transnational litigation for corporate abuses.[83]

12.4.2 Mandatory due diligence laws

With respect to specific issues, such as conflict minerals, some laws have introduced mandatory due diligence standards beyond disclosure requirements. For example, section 1502 of the Dodd–Frank Act on conflict minerals requires that some companies submit a report on the measures taken to exercise due diligence regarding the supply chain of conflict minerals.[84] In addition, the Final Rule for its implementation[85] does specify the standard for due diligence that must be exercised once a company has determined that it uses conflict minerals.[86] Accordingly, companies must follow a nationally or internationally recognized due diligence framework.[87] The Final Rule specifically states that the OECD's Due Diligence Guidance for Responsible Supply Chains of Minerals from Conflict-Affected and High-Risk Areas may be used as such a framework.[88] The EU has recently taken a similar approach by defining the due diligence that importers of some specific minerals originating from conflict-affected and high-risk areas must adopt beyond disclosure requirements.[89]

The introduction of a standard of conduct that companies should adopt would certainly help to assess corporate liability once harm occurs. The company's failure to meet the expected standard can be considered unlawful and result in the obligation to compensate the harm. However, like mandatory disclosure laws, mandatory due diligence laws do not mention or elaborate on corporate liability.

12.4.3 Human rights due diligence and liability provisions

A third category of laws includes those defining the standard of corporate due diligence and, in addition, specifying the legal consequences of failing to carry it out. Legal consequences can take the form of criminal liability or civil liability depending on who must enforce the due diligence standard – the public prosecutor or the victim. The Swiss popular initiative enters into that last category. Indeed, the text of the initiative entails a mandatory due diligence provision in section (2)(b) and clarifies the corporate liability for the harm, at least for the harm caused by controlled companies in section (2)(c). There are other examples of human rights due diligence laws accompanied by liability provisions.

The aforementioned Swiss Federal Act on Private Security Services Provided Abroad 2013,[90] for example, requires that companies that are based in

Switzerland and provide private security services abroad become signatories to the International Code of Conduct for Private Security Providers.[91] This code of conduct clarifies the due diligence that security service providers should carry out. Beyond defining the standard of due diligence, criminal liability provisions are in place to ensure that individuals within companies meet their due diligence obligations.[92] Another example is the Dutch Child Labour Due Diligence Proposal. The proposal entails a mandatory due diligence provision. In that regard, companies based in the Netherlands should act in accordance with the International Labour Organization Child Labour Guidance Tool for Business.[93] In addition, the proposal entails administrative and criminal fines for companies that do not submit a declaration that they have conducted due diligence, or that fail to conduct due diligence when required.[94] The legislative proposal was passed by the Dutch House of Representatives in February 2017 and was adopted and will enter into force in 2022.[95]

The French *loi relative au devoir de vigilance* also establishes a link between due diligence and civil corporate liability[96] – at least, both elements of due diligence and liability are mentioned in one single document. It requires that large companies based in France establish and implement a vigilance plan. In addition, it states that companies are liable and obliged to compensate for harm that due diligence would have permitted to avoid. After several back-and-forth exchanges between the two parliamentary chambers,[97] it reads as follows:

> Art. L. 225-102-4. Any company that at the end of two consecutive financial years, employs at least five thousand employees within the company and its direct and indirect subsidiaries, whose head office is located on French territory, or that has at least ten thousand employees in its service and in its direct or indirect subsidiaries, whose head office is located on French territory or abroad, must establish and implement an effective vigilance plan. . . .
>
> The plan shall include the reasonable vigilance measures to allow for risk identification and for the prevention of severe violations of human rights and fundamental freedoms, serious bodily injury or environmental damage or health risks resulting directly or indirectly from the operations of the company and of the companies it controls . . . as well as from the operations of the subcontractors or suppliers with whom it maintains an established commercial relationship, when such operations derive from this relationship.
>
> The plan shall be drafted in association with the company stakeholders involved, and where appropriate, within multiparty initiatives that exist in the subsidiaries or at territorial level. It shall include the following measures: 1. A mapping that identifies, analyses and ranks risks; 2. Procedures to regularly assess, in accordance with the risk mapping, the situation of subsidiaries, subcontractors or suppliers with whom the company maintains an established commercial relationship; 3. Appropriate action to mitigate risks or prevent serious violations; 4. An alert mechanism that collects reporting of existing or actual risks, developed in working partnership with the trade union organizations representatives of the company concerned; 5. A monitoring scheme to follow up on the measures implemented and assess their efficiency.

> The vigilance plan and its effective implementation report shall be publicly disclosed . . .
>
> Art. 225-102-5. – According to the conditions laid down in Articles 1240 and 1241 of the Civil Code, the author of any failure to comply with the duties specified in Article L. 225-102-4 of this code shall be liable and obliged to compensate for the harm that due diligence would have permitted to avoid.[98]

The French Law presents many similarities with the Swiss popular initiative. First, article L.225-102-4 introduces a mandatory human rights and environmental due diligence obligation. The law covers, more precisely than the Swiss initiative, severe violations of human rights and fundamental freedoms, serious bodily injury or environmental damage, and health risks. It lists five reasonable vigilance measures to adequately identify and prevent risks related to those matters.[99] As for the Swiss popular initiative, this due diligence process is based on the international human rights due diligence framework. Companies must identify risks, take appropriate actions to mitigate them, and account for the measures taken.

The French law also makes clear that these due diligence duties extend beyond the company's own operations. They additionally apply to operations of the companies it controls, and those of the subcontractors or suppliers with whom the company maintains an established commercial relationship. In comparison, due diligence duties in the Swiss initiative apply to "controlled companies and all business relationships".[100] It must be noted that the French law limits the scope of due diligence to the operations of subcontractors and suppliers "with whom the company maintains an established commercial relationship". In French law, an established commercial relationship is defined as a stable, regular commercial relationship, taking place with or without a contract, with a certain volume of business, and under a reasonable expectation that the relationship will last.[101] Whether this precision makes the scope of the due diligence narrower than the one in the Swiss initiative depends greatly on how "business relationships" will be translated and interpreted in the law implementing the Swiss initiative, if it is accepted.

However, there are at least four differences with the Swiss popular initiative. First, the French Law applies only to very large companies,[102] while the Swiss initiative only requires taking into account the needs of small and medium-sized companies. The second and third difference pertain to liability. Article L.225-102-5 expressly establishes a fault liability for the company's own actions and omissions on the basis of the general tort of negligence. It states that the author of any failure to comply with its due diligence duties shall be liable and obliged to compensate for the harm that due diligence would have permitted to avoid. This fault liability for the company's own conduct is only intended in the Swiss initiative.[103] In practice, however, fault liability should apply in a similar manner.

The third difference is that the French Law does not introduce specific ***liability for others***, while the Swiss initiative introduces liability for the harm caused by controlled companies. This does not mean that French parent or contracting companies cannot be liable for harm resulting from the operations of subsidiaries or suppliers at all, as presented in the previous paragraph. However, without specific liability for others, it remains for the plaintiff to prove that a French company failed to comply with its due diligence duties regarding the operations of these (foreign) companies,[104] which has implications for the plaintiffs. According to the Swiss initiative, it is instead up to the controlling company to prove that it conducted due diligence regarding its controlled companies.

Finally, the French law does not expressly make article L.225-102-4 and 5 mandatory overriding provisions of French law. Under EU Regulation 864/2007, the law applicable to non-contractual obligation arising out of a tort will generally be the law of the country in which the damage occurred.[105] Thus, it is questionable whether they will apply in practice in international matters concerning torts at all. A judge would first need to establish their mandatory character – however, regarding the *travaux préparatoires* and the purpose of article 225-102-4 and 5, this should be the case. It seems indeed unthinkable to adopt provisions aimed explicitly at ensuring that French companies respect human rights and the environment in France and abroad and not apply them when the situation requires it. Table 12.1 summarizes the findings of Section 12.4. It compares domestic legal instruments on business and human rights adopted and currently in discussion.

Table 12.1 Comparative overview legislative initiatives

Title (chronological order)	*Disclosure provisions*	*Due diligence provisions*	*Liability provisions (criminal/civil)*
California Transparency in Supply Chains Act 2010 (US)	X		
Dodd–Frank Act, sec 1502, 2010 (US)	X	X	
Federal Act on Private Security Services Provided Abroad 2013 (CH)		X	X
Directive 2014/95 on Disclosure of Non-Financial Information 2014 (EU)	X		
Modern Slavery Act 2015 (UK)	X		
Loi relative au devoir de vigilance 2017 (FR)	X	X	X
Regulation 2017/821 on Supply Chain Due Diligence Obligations for Importers of [Minerals] from Conflict-Affected and High-Risk Areas 2017 (EU)	X	X	
Modern Slavery Act 2018 (AU)	X		
Child Labour Due Diligence Law 2019	X	X	X
Popular Initiative on Responsible Business, currently in discussion (CH)	X	X	X

12.5 Conclusion

The Swiss Popular Initiative on Responsible Business aims to ensure that companies based in Switzerland respect human rights and the environment in Switzerland and abroad. It introduces mandatory due diligence and clarifies the legal consequence of a failure to conduct it. In particular, it introduces a specific liability provision for controlling companies. By clarifying the conditions under which companies may be held liable, the Swiss initiative goes beyond mandatory disclosure and due diligence laws.

Clarifying the conditions of liability for multinational enterprises could reduce the uncertainty related to outcomes of transnational civil litigation for corporate human rights and environmental abuses.[106] This is a smart move. What happens in jurisdictions hosting transnational corporations but having no such laws? The judiciary must rule on parent or contracting company liability based on unclear conditions of liability. This volume exemplifies this in the English cases of *Chandler v Cape* and *Thompson v The Renwick*, and the French cases of *Areva* and *Comilog*. This will happen again in the German case of *Jabir et al. v KiK* and the cases against Shell in the Netherlands. Why not simply clarify the conditions of liability?

Notes

* Postdoctoral researcher and senior lecturer at the University of Zurich Center for Human Rights Studies. Nicolas.Bueno@uzh.ch / Twitter @Nbueno_UZH

1 The official text of the initiative can be found in French, German, and Italian <www.bk.admin.ch/ch/f/pore/vi/vis462t.html> accessed 24 September 2019. The English translation presented below is available on the website of the Swiss Coalition for Corporate Justice <https://corporatejustice.ch> accessed 24 September 2019.

2 Guiding Principles on Business and Human Rights: Implementing the United Nations "Protect, Respect and Remedy", Annex to UNHRC, Report of the Special Representative of the Secretary-General on the Issue of Human Rights and Transnational Corporations and Other Business Enterprises, John Ruggie (21 March 2011) UN Doc A/HRC/17/31.

3 OECD, *OECD Guidelines for Multinational Enterprises* (OECD Publishing 2000).

4 UNGPs (n 2) Guiding Principles 17–21.

5 ibid Guiding Principle 17.

6 OECD Guidelines (n 3) ch II, commentary para 14 and ch IV, commentary para 15.

7 See for further comments, Mirina Grosz, 'Menschenrechte als Vehikel für ökologische Unternehmensverantwortung', (2017) *Pratique Juridique Actuelle* 982.

8 Nicolas Bueno, 'Corporate Liability for Violations of the Human Right to Just Conditions of Work in Extraterritorial Operations', (2017) 21 *The International Journal of Human Rights* 565, 571–3; Olga Martin-Ortega, 'Human Rights Due Diligence for Corporations: From Voluntary Standards to Hard Law at Last?', (2014) 32 *Netherlands Quarterly of Human Rights* 44, 55–7; Justine Nolan, 'The Corporate Responsibility to Respect Human Rights: Soft Law or not Law?', in Surya Deva and David Bilchitz (eds.), *Human Rights Obligations of Business: Beyond the Corporate Responsibility to Respect?* (Cambridge University Press 2013) 156–7.

9 UNGPs (n 2) Guiding Principle 19, commentary.
10 OHCHR, *The Corporate Responsibility to Respect Human Rights: An Interpretative Guide* (UN 2012) 15.
11 UNGPs (n 2) Guiding Principle 19, commentary.
12 OHCHR (n 10) 17.
13 OECD Guidelines (n 3) ch II, commentary para 14.
14 OHCHR (n 10) 19.
15 UNGPs (n 2) Guiding Principle 19, commentary.
16 Ibid.; OECD Guidelines (n 3) ch II, commentary para 19; OHCHR (n 10) 7.
17 UNGPs (n 2) Guiding Principle 13(a).
18 OECD Guidelines (n 3) ch II, commentary para 17.
19 UNGPs (n 2) Guiding Principle 19, commentary; OECD Guidelines (n 3) ch II, A 12.
20 OHCHR (n 10) 56. See also for other examples, Christine Kaufmann, 'Konzernverantwortungsinitiative: Grenzenlose Verantwortlichkeit?', (2016) *Swiss Review of Business and Financial Market Law* 45, 51; Nicolas Bueno, 'La responsabilité des entreprises de respecter les droits de l'Homme: État de la pratique suisse', (2017) *Pratique Juridique Actuelle* 1015, 1016.
21 Cf. Olivier de Schutter, 'Corporations and Economic, Social, and Cultural Rights', in Eibe Riedel, Gilles Giacca, and Christophe Golay (eds.), *Economic, Social, and Cultural Rights in International Law: Contemporary Issues and Challenges* (Oxford University Press 2014) 212–16; Martin-Ortega (n 8) 56; Christine Kaufmann et al., *Extraterritorialität im Bereich Wirtschaft und Menschenrechte* (Swiss Center of Expertise in Human Rights 2016).
22 UNGPs (n 2) Guiding Principle 19, commentary; OECD Guidelines (n 3) ch II, commentary para 22, for the steps to be taken before termination.
23 UNGPs (n 2) Guiding Principle 19(b)(ii).
24 OHCHR (n 10) 49, among other factors.
25 UNGPs (n 2) Guiding Principle 3(a).
26 OHCHR (n 10) 71, 75–80.
27 UNGPs (n 2) Guiding Principle 26, commentary.
28 Ibid. 25, commentary.
29 Ibid. See also for a comparative approach on the question of liability and the structure of the corporate group, Gwynne Skinner, Robert McCorquodale, and Olivier de Schutter, *The Third Pillar: Access to Judicial Remedies for Human Rights Violations by Transnational Business* (ICAR, CORE, ECCJ, 2013) 61.
30 OHCHR (n 10) 22.
31 UNGPs (n 2) Guiding Principle 26, commentary. The Council of Europe clarified the question of jurisdiction in Council of Europe, Recommendation CM/Rec(2016)3 of the Committee of Ministers to member States on human rights and business, 2 March 2016, paras 34–5.
32 UNGPs (n 2) Guiding Principle 26, commentary
33 *Chandler v Cape plc* (2012) EWCA Civ 525, para 80.
34 *Thompson v The Renwick Group plc* (2014) EWCA Civ 635, para 37. For details, see Bueno (n 8) 576.
35 Cour d'Appel de Paris, Arrêt du 24 octobre 2013, no 12/05650 (Areva); Cour d'Appel de Paris, Arrêt du 10 septembre 2015, nos 11/05955 and 11/0596 (Comilog). For more detail on the case of Comilog, see Liesbeth Enneking, 'Paying the Price for Socially Irresponsible Business Practices?', (2017) *Pratique Juridique Actuelle* 991 and on the case of Areva, see Bueno (n 8) 576–7.
36 Court of Appeal The Hague, 17 December 2015, ECLI:NL:GHDHA:2015:3586-7-8 (Oguru-Efanga/Shell), (Dooh/Shell), (Shell/Akpan). For more details, see Enneking (n 35) 992.

37 See Bueno (n 8) 579. However, in January 2019, a German court dismissed the case on the ground that the statute of limitation expired after one year under Pakistani law.

38 Swiss Federal Council, 'Rapport de droit comparé: Mécanismes de diligence en matière de droits humains et d'environnement en rapport avec les activités d'entreprises suisses à l'étranger' (2 May 2014) <www.ejpd.admin.ch/dam/data/bj/aktuell/news/2014/2014-05-28/ber-apk-nr-f.pdf> accessed 24 September 2019. See Annex I for the report of the Swiss Institute of Comparative Law.

39 Ibid. 9.

40 Ibid. 11.

41 The motion was first accepted by 91:90 before it was again submitted to vote and rejected by 95:86.

42 Swiss Parliament, 'Motion 14.3671: Mise en œuvre du rapport de droit comparé du Conseil fédéral sur la responsabilité des entreprises en matière de droits humains et d'environnement' (1 September 2014) <www.parlament.ch/fr/ratsbetrieb/suche-curia-vista/geschaeft?AffairId=20143671> accessed 24 September 2019.

43 Swiss Federal Council, 'La responsabilité sociétale des entreprises: Position et plan d'action du Conseil fédéral concernant la responsabilité des entreprises à l'égard de la société et de l'environnement' (1 April 2015) <www.news.admin.ch/NSBSubscriber/message/attachments/38882.pdf> accessed 24 September 2019.

44 Ibid. 13–17.

45 Rolf H. Weber, 'Auf dem Weg zu einem neuen Konzept der Unternehmensverantwortlichkeit?', (2016) 112 *Revue suisse de jurisprudence* 121, 123.

46 Swiss Federal Council, 'Rapport sur la stratégie de la Suisse visant à mettre en œuvre les Principes directeurs des Nations Unies relatifs aux entreprises et aux droits de l'homme' (9 December 2016) 12 <www.ohchr.org/Documents/Issues/Business/NationalPlans/Switzerland_NAP_FR.pdf> accessed 24 September 2019. The NAP follows the report.

47 Ibid 7–8, 12.

48 Ibid. 15.

49 Ibid.

50 Ibid.

51 Ibid. 39; Kaufmann et al. (n 21) 61–3; Christine Kaufmann et al., *Mise en oeuvre des droits humains en Suisse: Un état des lieux dans le domaine droits de l'homme et économie* (Swiss Center of Expertise in Human Rights 2013) 54–6, for private international law questions in Switzerland.

52 Swiss Federal Council, Entreprises et droits de l'homme: analyse comparée des mesures judiciaires et non judiciaires offrant un accès à la réparation, 14 September 2018.

53 Private Security Services Provided Abroad Act 2013 (CH), arts 8 and 9. Companies can also be subject to administrative sanctions defined in arts 25 and 26.

54 Ibid. arts 5 and 6.

55 Ibid. arts 21–4.

56 Ibid. art 6.

57 Nicolas Bueno and Sophie Scheidt, *Die Sorgfaltspflichten von Unternehmen im Hinblick auf die Einhaltung von Menschenrechten bei Auslandsaktivitäten* (Netzwerk Soziale Verantwortung 2015) 10.

58 Swiss Federal Council, '3e rapport concernant l'état d'avancement de la mise en œuvre des recommandations' (2 December 2016) 13–14 <www.newsd.admin.ch/newsd/message/attachments/46473.pdf> accessed 24 September 2019.

59 Ibid. 13.

60 Ibid. 14. In particular Regulation (EU) 2017/821 of the European Parliament and of the Council of 17 May 2017 laying down supply chain due diligence

obligations for Union importers of tin, tantalum and tungsten, their ores, and gold originating from conflict-affected and high-risk areas [2017] OJ L 130/1.
61 NAP (n 46) 29.
62 See Swiss National Council, Rapport complémentaire de la Commission des affaires juridiques du 18 mai 2018 sur les propositions de la commission en vue du dépôt d'un contre-projet indirect à l'initiative populaire "Entreprises responsables – pour protéger l'être humain et l'environnement" (18 May 2018) <www.parlament.ch/centers/kb/Documents/2016/Rapport_de_la_commission_CAJ-N_16.077_2018-05-18.pdf> accessed 24 September 2019. Bueno Nicolas, 'Diligence en matière de droits de l'homme et responsabilité de l'entreprise: Le point en droit suisse', (2019) 29(3) Swiss Review of International and European Law 345, 356–359.
63 Gabriela Rohner, *Die Wirksamkeit von Volksinitiativen im Bund 1848–2010* (Schulthess 2012) 115.
64 Swiss Coalition for Corporate Justice, 'The Initiative Text with Explanations' <https://corporatejustice.ch/wp-content/uploads//2018/06/KVI_Factsheet_5_E.pdf> accessed 24 September 2019.
65 See section 12.2.
66 Swiss Coalition for Corporate Justice (n 64).
67 See section 12.2.1.
68 Swiss Popular Initiative on Responsible Business, art 101a(2)(b).
69 Swiss Coalition for Corporate Justice (n 64).
70 In Switzerland, under art 41 Code des obligations. For more detail, see Gregor Geisser, 'Die Konzernverantwortungsinitiative: Darstellung, rechtliche Würdigung und mögliche Umsetzung', (2017) *Pratique Juridique Actuelle* 943, 948–9. Article 101a(2)(c) states that companies are *also* liable for damage caused by companies under their control, which means in addition to the liability for their own conduct.
71 Geisser (n 70) 954.
72 However, control is used in the OHCHR *Interpretative Guide* in relation to parent companies. OHCHR (n 10) 22, and in relation to leverage 48–9.
73 Swiss Initiative on Responsible Business, art 101a(2)(a).
74 Swiss Coalition for Corporate Justice (n 64).
75 See Swiss Initiative on Responsible Business and section 12.2.1.
76 Art 133(2) Swiss Private International Law Act.
77 California Transparency in Supply Chains Act 2010 (US), s 1714.43(a)(1). See for an overview, Benjamin T. Greer and Jeffrey Purvis, 'Corporate Supply Chain Transparency: California's Seminal Attempt to Discourage Forced Labour', (2016) 20 *The International Journal of Human Rights* 55.
78 Modern Slavery Act 2015 (UK), s 54(4)(a).
79 Directive 2014/95/EU of the European Parliament and of the Council of 22 October 2014 amending Directive 2013/34/EU as regards disclosure of non-financial and diversity information by certain large undertakings and groups [2014] OJ L 330/1, art 19a(1).
80 Ibid. art 19a(1)(d) and preamble, para 8.
81 ibid art 19a(1).
82 Stephen Park, 'Human Rights Reporting as Self-Interest: The Integrative and Expressive Dimensions of Corporate Disclosure', in Robert C. Bird, Daniel R. Cahoy, and Jamie D. Prenkert (eds.), *Law, Business and Human Rights: Bridging the Gap* (Edward Elgar Publishing 2014) 53.
83 Bueno (n 8) 580.
84 Dodd – Frank Wall Street Reform and Consumer Protection Act 2010 (US), s 1502(b)(p)(1)(a). See for reporting requirements, Park (n 82) 63.

85 Securities and Exchange Commission, 17 CFR pts 240 and 249b, Conflict Minerals, Final Rule, August 2012 (Sec 1502 Final Rule).
86 Martin-Ortega (n 8) 66.
87 Sec 1502 Final Rule (n 85) 205.
88 Ibid. 206; Martin-Ortega (n 8) 66.
89 Directive 2014/95/EU (n 79).
90 See n 53.
91 Private Security Services Provided Abroad Act 2013 (CH) (n 53) art 21–4.
92 Child Labour Due Diligence Law Proposal (NL), art 5(3).
93 Ibid. art 7(1).
94 Ibid. art 7(2). See also Christine Kaufmann, 'Menschen-und umweltrechtliche Sorgfaltsprüfung im internationalen Vergleich', (2017) *Pratique Juridique Actuelle* 974.
95 See Eerste Kamer der State-Generaal, 'Initiatiefvoorstel-Kuiken Wet zorgplicht kinderarbeid' <www.eerstekamer.nl/wetsvoorstel/34506_initiatiefvoorstel_kuiken> accessed 24 September 2019 and Eerste Kamer der State-Generaal, 'Debat Wet zorgplicht kinderarbeid aangehouden' <www.eerstekamer.nl/nieuws/20171219/debat_wet_zorgplicht_kinderarbeid> accessed 24 September 2019.
96 Loi no 2017-399 du 27 Mars 2017 relative au devoir de vigilance des sociétés mères et des entreprises donneuses d'ordre (FR).
97 See Sénat, 'Loi relative au devoir de vigilance des sociétés mères et des entreprises donneuses d'ordre' <www.senat.fr/dossier-legislatif/ppl14-376.html> accessed 24 September 2019, for the travaux préparatoires.
98 Non-official translation provided by the European Coalition for Corporate Justice and published on 14 December 2016 <https://business-humanrights.org/en/french-duty-of-vigilance-bill-english-translation> accessed 24 September 2019.
99 Sandra Cossart, Jérôme Chaplier, and Tiphaine Beau de Lomenie, 'The French Law on Duty of Care: A Historic Step Towards Making Globalization Work for All', (2017) 2 *Business and Human Rights Journal* 317, 320.
100 See Swiss Initiative on Responsible Business and section 12.3.2.
101 Cossart, Chaplier, and Beau de Lomenie (n 99) 320.
102 Code of Commerce (FR), art L. 225-102-4, I, para 1.
103 See Swiss Initiative on Responsible Business and section 12.3.2, in particular n 70.
104 Cossart, Chaplier, and Beau de Lomenie (n 99) 321.
105 Regulation (EC) No 864/2007 of the European Parliament and of the Council of 11 July 2007 on the law applicable to non-contractual obligations (Rome II) [2007] OJ L 199/40, art 4.
106 Bueno (n 8) 580.

Bibliography

Bueno N, 'Corporate Liability for Violations of the Human Right to Just Conditions of Work in Extraterritorial Operations', (2017) 21 *The International Journal of Human Rights* 565.

Bueno N, 'Diligence en matière de droits de l'homme et responsabilité de l'entreprise: Le point en droit suisse', (2019) 29(3) *Swiss Review of International and European Law* 345.

———, 'La responsabilité des entreprises de respecter les droits de l'Homme: État de la pratique suisse', (2017) *Pratique Juridique Actuelle* 1015.

——— and Scheidt S, *Die Sorgfaltspflichten von Unternehmen im Hinblick auf die Einhaltung von Menschenrechten bei Auslandsaktivitäten* (Netzwerk Soziale Verantwortung 2015).

Cossart S, Chaplier J, and Beau de Lomenie T, 'The French Law on Duty of Care: A Historic Step Towards Making Globalization Work for All', (2017) 2 *Business and Human Rights Journal* 317.

de Schutter O, 'Corporations and Economic, Social, and Cultural Rights', in Eibe Riedel, Gilles Giacca, and Christophe Golay (eds.), *Economic, Social, and Cultural Rights in International Law: Contemporary Issues and Challenges* (Oxford University Press 2014).

Enneking L, 'Paying the Price for Socially Irresponsible Business Practices?', (2017) *Pratique Juridique Actuelle* 991.

Geisser G, 'Die Konzernverantwortungsinitiative: Darstellung, rechtliche Würdigung und mögliche Umsetzung', (2017) *Pratique Juridique Actuelle* 943.

Greer BT and Purvis J, 'Corporate Supply Chain Transparency: California's Seminal Attempt to Discourage Forced Labour', (2016) 20 *The International Journal of Human Rights* 55.

Grosz M, 'Menschenrechte als Vehikel für ökologische Unternehmensverantwortung', (2017) *Pratique Juridique Actuelle* 982.

Kaufmann C, 'Konzernverantwortungsinitiative: Grenzenlose Verantwortlichkeit?', (2016) *Swiss Review of Business and Financial Market Law* 45.

———, 'Menschen-und umweltrechtliche Sorgfaltsprüfung im internationalen Vergleich', (2017) *Pratique Juridique Actuelle* 974.

——— et al., *Extraterritorialität im Bereich Wirtschaft und Menschenrechte* (Swiss Center of Expertise in Human Rights 2016).

——— et al., *Mise en oeuvre des droits humains en Suisse: Un état des lieux dans le domaine droits de l'homme et économie* (Swiss Center of Expertise in Human Rights 2013).

Martin-Ortega O, 'Human Rights Due Diligence for Corporations: From Voluntary Standards to Hard Law at Last?', (2014) 32 *Netherlands Quarterly of Human Rights* 44.

Nolan J, 'The Corporate Responsibility to Respect Human Rights: Soft Law or Not Law?', in Surya Deva and David Bilchitz (eds.), *Human Rights Obligations of Business: Beyond the Corporate Responsibility to Respect?* (Camdridge University Press 2013).

Park S, 'Human Rights Reporting as Self-Interest: The Integrative and Expressive Dimensions of Corporate Disclosure', in Robert C Bird, Daniel R Cahoy, and Jamie D Prenkert (eds.), *Law, Business and Human Rights: Bridging the Gap* (Edward Elgar Publishing 2014).

Rohner G, *Die Wirksamkeit von Volksinitiativen im Bund 1848–2010* (Schulthess 2012).

Skinner G, McCorquodale R, and de Schutter O, *The Third Pillar: Access to Judicial Remedies for Human Rights Violations by Transnational Business* (ICAR, CORE, ECCJ, 2013).

Weber RH, 'Auf dem Weg zu einem neuen Konzept der Unternehmensverantwortlichkeit?', (2016) 112 *Revue suisse de jurisprudence* 121.

13 The mismatch between human rights policies and contract law

Improving contractual mechanisms to advance human rights compliance in supply chains

*Martijn Scheltema**

13.1 Introduction

Trade has globalized in the last decades. This has resulted, among other things, in considerable internationalization of sourcing, and numerous and large supply chains. Globalization has been beneficial; for example, it has allowed companies to produce at lower cost and has resulted in a decrease in prices for Western consumers. However, the pressure on supply chains to produce in a timely and cost-effective manner also has its disadvantages. For example, human rights compliance by suppliers remains a challenge,[1] while the price reduction for the Global North connected with globalization has led to a shift in cost induced by negative externalities connected to production in the Global South.

Many globally operating companies recognize this issue, and several large and internationally operating ones in particular have implemented a CSR and/or business human rights (BHR) policy.[2] These policies often refer to (international) frameworks in this area, such as the UNGPs or the OECD Guidelines for Multinational Enterprises (OECD Guidelines), for example by prescribing human rights due diligence as required by these frameworks.[3] These policies often include suppliers and prescribe responsible business conduct throughout the company's supply chains.[4] Therefore, they frequently contain more issues than human and workers' rights. They refer to environmental rules, for example by prescribing on management systems, sustainability, corruption, and anti-trust issues.[5] Another feature in some policies connected with supply chains is procurement. These policies might render supplier human rights performance part of the procurement assessments.[6]

That said, contractual management of supply chains is often considered to be a subordinate feature in these policies. Moreover, contractual management is not even mentioned in them. Thus, a mismatch between policy and contract law seems to exist in the BHR field. Among other things, this may be caused by ineffective collaboration between the legal and CSR departments within companies. As contractual mechanisms might have the advantage of (better) enforcement than a human rights policy in itself,[7] they may contribute to improved human rights compliance by suppliers. Moreover, human rights policies in themselves are often considered by NGOs to be rather ineffective. It is conceivable that bridging the gap between human rights policies and contractual mechanisms through better aligning them may contribute to better human rights compliance by suppliers. Thus, contractual mechanisms should be considered an integral part of human rights policies, and those policies should elaborate on the utilization and shape of the contractual mechanisms to advance human rights compliance by suppliers.

Although companies' human rights policies often do not elaborate on the utilization and shape of contractual mechanisms, this does not mean that they are not deployed. Therefore, this contribution will describe the contractual mechanisms currently used to advance human and workers' rights in supply chains, and explain why they need to be improved. Subsequently, it will elaborate upon ways in which human rights policies could propose and advance (legal) approaches to improve supply chain contracts.

13.2 The current contractual arrangements

The implementation of supplier codes of conduct varies widely.[8] Some companies only publish them on their website, without implementing them through contractual mechanisms.[9] Another category of companies considers such codes of conduct to be a core element of their contracts with suppliers.[10] Some contractual mechanisms even create third-party rights to counter non-compliance of the code of conduct – for example, on behalf of employees of a supplier.[11] Other companies prescribe self-evaluation by suppliers in their code of conduct or require the completion of surveys, depending on the perceived risk.[12] However, such requirements are often only implemented through ancillary documents, such as general terms and conditions or umbrella agreements governing long-term business relationships between commercial parties.[13] Moreover, contracts do not always contain a reference to these terms and conditions. An example being that such reference might not be deemed necessary in specific instances.[14]

The content of a (supplier) code of conduct also varies significantly from company to company. Some provisions therein are relatively vague, implementing an obligation to "comply with all relevant local regulation", or use language such as "workers' conditions compliant with local regulation", "no use of child/forced labor", or "human rights-compliant production".[15] Some codes even allow suppliers to aim for these goals, yet (at this point) do not impose an obligation to reach them.[16] Other codes are much more specific as to supplier obligations. Furthermore, few codes include all relevant social standards in connection with human rights. For example, very few codes of conduct require Free Prior Informed Consent of third parties if a supplier uses land belonging to these third parties for its operations.[17]

Finally, monitoring compliance with and enforcement of (supplier) codes of conduct range from virtually no action by the buyer to strict monitoring and enforcement, sometimes even implementing third-party audits.[18] Some companies go beyond auditing and establish a dialogue with suppliers to discuss the situation and to improve compliance with the code of conduct or collaborate with (local) NGOs to audit compliance in dialogue with the supplier.[19] Audits by third parties (NGOs) might be more effective in instances where the company itself is not very well informed on the (complex) local conditions and the measures a supplier is able to implement in practice.[20] However, termination of a contract due to breach often does not solve the CSR/BHR issue. On the contrary, it might even cause the issue to worsen, since termination might force a supplier to contract other buyers who might be more lenient on these issues. For example, termination based on the use of child labor hardly improves the situation as long as families need child labor to secure their livelihood.[21] Furthermore, companies are reluctant to terminate contractual relationships with suppliers due to fears regarding replacement of the supplier. If the companies are unable to replace the supplier in question on short notice, they might try to improve the situation through dialogue instead.[22]

Still, even though the content, implementation, monitoring, and enforcement of codes of conduct varies, the majority of multinational enterprises who have implemented a CSR/BHR policy do utilize a contractual mechanism to enhance compliance with their code of conduct.[23]

13.3 The need for enhancing contractual mechanisms

13.3.1 Introduction

One might question the need to enhance contractual mechanisms, as the current supplier codes of conduct contribute to improvement of the human and labor rights conditions. One might also consider it an illusion to assume that drafting more thorough contractual provisions will solve human rights or labor-related issues in itself. As long as such provisions are not implemented in practice, or remain unenforced, their ability to achieve a shift in human or labor rights compliance might be rather dim.[24] Therefore, one may argue that including and prescribing contractual mechanisms in (BHR) policies is not very helpful, as these mechanisms hardly contribute to improvement.

That said, I feel that contractual mechanisms are important to address in human rights policies for two reasons. Although these mechanisms will not solve BHR issues in themselves, they may contribute to better human rights compliance – for example by suppliers – beside other measures. Next to this, and even more importantly, as explained before, contractual language on these issues is included in contractual mechanisms such as supply chain contracts to date, although it is often rather ineffective. Apparently, companies expect, or at least want to create the impression, that these mechanisms contribute to better human rights performance – otherwise it makes no sense to include language on these issues in contracts. From this starting point, it is important to assess, for example in human rights policies and evaluations, whether the current contractual mechanisms indeed contribute to human rights performance. As will be elaborated in the following sections, several issues can be identified as causing the current mechanisms to be rather ineffective in this respect.[25] From this, a need seems to emerge to improve them and thus to pay more attention to this aspect in BHR policies.

However, some have observed that the implementation of more thorough contractual provisions might create liability risks, as the buyer obviously assumes a more supervisory and controlling role.[26] That said, cases in which such liability has been established in practice are scarce, if any exist at all.[27] Furthermore, the risks of not assuming such a role might be considerably higher, including in financial terms. Human or labor rights-related issues might cause considerable reputational damage.[28] Furthermore, these issues may cause delay and high additional cost in projects, as well as expensive and time-consuming litigation.[29] Thus, the perceived liability issues should not be considered an impediment to enhance contractual mechanisms.

13.3.2 Legislative developments

Next to financial incentives, societal expectations toward business operations in connection with human rights (due diligence) and environmental compliance have changed. This is reflected in public regulation enacted mainly in Western countries.

For example, section 54 of the UK Modern Slavery Act[30] entails an obligation of governing companies selling goods or providing services above a certain financial threshold to report on the steps taken to prevent slavery in their business and supply chains in and outside of the UK. Alternatively, a company may confirm that it has refrained from implementing such measures. Section 1502 of the Dodd–Frank Act[31] implements an obligation of companies listed on the US Stock Exchange to report to the Securities Exchange Commission the processing of conflict minerals from the DRC or adjacent countries, as well as the measures taken to prevent human rights violations. Furthermore, an obligation to report on slavery, child labor, and human trafficking in supply chains is incorporated in Californian legislation.[32] Beyond that, France, for example, has adopted a statutory due diligence obligation in connection with human rights and labor conditions for larger companies (also for their activities abroad).[33] The Dutch Parliament has adopted a due diligence obligation to prevent the use of child labor in connection with goods sold or services provided by a Dutch company.[34] The EU has, like the US and UK, also implemented a non-financial reporting requirement. In order to comply with the requirement, corporations need to report on their CSR policy, on human rights violations that have occurred in their business, and on the measures taken to resolve the issue.[35] Furthermore, the EU has adopted legislation regarding conflict minerals that are imported into the EU which will come into force in 2021.[36]

13.3.3 International frameworks

Societal expectations are reflected not only in legislation, but also in authoritative instruments from the UN and the OECD, in particular the UNGPs and the

OECD Guidelines. Such instruments are to be found in specific industries as well, such as the Equator principles and the International Finance Corporation (IFC) Environmental and Social Performance Standards in the financial sector and the Voluntary Principles on Security and Human Rights in the extractive industry.[37] Although these frameworks are of a non-binding nature, they may serve as binding standards if they are implemented in contracts such as supply chain, project finance, lending, or export credit insurance agreements.[38] Some parties, for example in their supplier contracts, refer to these frameworks and require their suppliers to comply with the standards therein. Thus, these requirements become binding through contract. Furthermore, it is conceivable that these frameworks will permeate open norms in legislation or jurisprudence, such as the duty of care.[39]

However, if the obligations entailed in the UNGPs or the OECD Guidelines, such as the due diligence requirement, were to be transposed through contractual mechanisms in supply chains, it might still be unclear which specific obligations a supplier should meet. Thus, a contractual arrangement that only implements the obligation to meet specific requirements entailed in the UNGPs is too vague to be enforced in practice. Moreover, an obligation to exert leverage on others if a supplier is directly linked to a human rights violation might face even larger enforceability issues.[40]

The same goes for the contractual requirement to establish an operational-level grievance mechanism that meets Guiding Principle 31's requirements.[41] The quite frequent ineffectiveness of these mechanisms might be caused by the inability of companies to meaningfully engage with local communities. Often, skilled facilitators are necessary to perform this task.[42] Furthermore, operational-level grievance mechanisms only provide whistle-blower protection, only cover corruption and money-laundering issues, or only accept workers' complaints in many instances. Other stakeholders, such as local communities, often do not have the possibility to engage in these mechanisms.[43] If other stakeholders do not have access to the grievance mechanism, the external consequences of the company's operations may not be addressed and remedied. Thus, no access to remedy is available for those stakeholders, although Guiding Principle 31 requires such access.

13.3.4 Complexity of supply chains

Supply chains often include more suppliers than the first tier. In principle, a contract only covers the first tier; contracts take effect between parties and do in principle do not create obligations for others. Thus, if a buyer agrees on specific human rights clauses with its supplier this does not mean a second-tier supplier (or subcontractor) is bound by these clauses. In order to tackle this issue, one might implement a perpetuity clause.[44] This requires the first-tier supplier to pass the contractual requirements agreed upon between the buyer and the first-tier supplier to its (second-tier) supplier or subcontractor, and is often strengthened by a high penalty in case of non-compliance. However, it is questionable whether suppliers will always pass this obligation on to their suppliers or subcontractors, and whether the buyer is able to monitor this. Additionally, a company might impose requirements on the way in which a supplier has structured its procurement.[45] For example, it may prohibit subcontracting, limit the number of subcontractors, or require the supplier to provide information about its suppliers or subcontractors. Here also, it may be questionable whether (the buyer is able to monitor whether) the supplier complies with this obligation. Moreover, the question as to how many tiers of suppliers one should include remains unsolved, although the UNGPs and OECD Guidelines seem to include the full supply chain.

More generally speaking, the buyer often lacks (access to reliable) information on the human rights performance of a supplier, even if (third-party) audits are implemented. This may be due to the fact that audits only reflect performance at a specific moment in time, and may be evaded by the supplier, for example by subcontracting (part of) the work.[46] Furthermore, audit fatigue and duplication of audits may decrease the supplier's willingness to implement measures to improve its human rights performance. Thus, current contractual mechanisms implementing audits and monitoring of supplier performance may not provide the necessary information to the buyer to enable it to assess the actual human rights performance of the supplier.

13.3.5 Contractual arrangements as a contribution, not a solution, to human rights challenges

The aforementioned topics elucidate the need for improvement of contractual mechanisms governing and implementing supplier codes of conduct. Nevertheless, contractual arrangements are not the silver bullet to solve all human rights or labor-related issues, although they are part of the solution. Improving contractual mechanisms in connection with BHR issues is not simply a case of adapting contractual language and adding some clauses; BHR issues are highly complex and require sophisticated and integrated solutions, of which contractual mechanisms are part.

For example, even if a supplier were willing to meet the contractual requirements of the buyer, implementation in practice still poses a challenge. Thus, next to the contractual clause, training of and/or dialogue with the supplier may be necessary. Furthermore, others in the supplier's environment might consider these standards as Western interference, and therefore be reluctant to comply. This might decease the supplier's motivation to implement the standards. The same might be true if all contractual risks are geared toward the supplier. Thus, a more equal spread of contractual risks and profits might incentivize the supplier to implement the contractual requirements and to comply with labor and human rights standards.[47]

Broader collaboration within the company, as well as external collaboration, is necessary to solve human rights-related issues, for example by engaging in dialogue with suppliers or in local multi-stakeholder initiatives.[48] For example, if suppliers invest in more stable labor relations and achieve higher production as a result, they might be incentivized to continue, which also benefits the buyer in terms of uptake of human rights requirements.[49] More generally speaking, the more trust a supplier has in the buyer, the better the uptake of standards imposed by the buyer.[50] For example, if a supplier feels a buyer only aims at acquiring products at the lowest price, does not care about the interests of the supplier, and changes supplier after every order, the chances that this supplier is intrinsically motivated to comply with (onerous) human rights requirements of the buyer are dim, especially if it has options to evade monitoring by the buyer, or if the buyer does not monitor at all.

13.4 Ways to enhance contractual arrangements

13.4.1 Introduction

The previous sections elaborate on the need for contractual arrangements to enhance human rights performance in supply chains and the need to improve existing contractual instruments (and also elaborate on this issue in human rights policies). However, the proof of the pudding is in the eating. How, and to what extent, could existing mechanisms be improved through elaborating on this issue in human rights policies? I will try to answer this question by discussing several topics in connection with which more effective contractual approaches in human rights policies (that have not been developed to date) may be developed to, among other things, address these issues through (the improvement of) contractual clauses. However, as elaborated on before, these improvements do not solve human rights issues in themselves, but should be part of a broader, integrated solution.

Moreover, it may not be feasible in practice to implement all suggestions for improvement at once. For example, suppliers may not accept contracts including extensive paragraphs on human rights compliance and dispute resolution if their other buyers do not impose such requirements. Thus, the level playing field issue may hamper the implementation of highly sophisticated contractual arrangements overnight. A step-by-step approach, implementing one smaller change at the time, may be less effective but more practical. This may also enhance industry-wide acceptance of these (smaller) changes, especially if these improvements build on existing contractual clauses. In this regard, these smaller changes are preferably first implemented in the supply chains and in relation to the types of risk that pose the largest treat to human rights.[51] Therefore, it may be that of the suggestions provided in the remainder of this chapter, some could be implemented first in supply chains of specific industries, depending on the most salient human rights risks.

Beyond this, conducting human rights due diligence or implementing due diligence through contracts might pose a challenge for smaller companies (small and medium-sized enterprises) because of the required experience and costs. Smaller companies not able to monitor supply chains themselves may make use of multi-stakeholder initiatives, such as UTZ, Fairtrade, and Fairwear.[52] These initiatives implement certification schemes to, among other things, monitor human and labor rights compliance.[53] A company might then impose the contractual requirement to acquire a certificate from one of these multi-stakeholder initiatives.

In the following, I will provide suggestions for improvement of a different nature that may contribute to improving contractual mechanisms. Which suggestion it is most worthwhile to implement first will depend on the supply chain and the most salient human rights risks therein. Most suggestions are derived from my experience in practice, discussions with business, NGOs, and government representatives, as well as my work in the business and human rights project of the American Bar Association on the most salient issues in connection with human rights compliance in supply chains. The last suggestion builds on my work as a member of the arbitration and BHR working group.[54]

13.4.2 *Defining human rights*

If one desires to regulate human rights performance of suppliers through contractual mechanisms, a question might arise as to what human rights are. Human rights cover a broad spectrum.[55] One might, not exclusively, think of discrimination, women's rights, land tenure rights (for example, of indigenous peoples), security issues, sexual and gender-based violence, access to water and sanitation, restrictions on workers (for example through seizure of documents), debt bondage of workers, child labor, workers' health and safety, working hours, freedom of association, and living wages. The contractual arrangement should make clear what is expected from the supplier and which human rights the buyer is referring to.

For example, in connection with labor conditions, the contract could entail obligations on the right to unionize without any form of retaliation and the right to collective bargaining; a minimum wage that guarantees a decent living in the local circumstances (which might include remuneration for transportation costs or housing and is not, for example, based on bonuses that are connected to unrealistic or very high targets); a prohibition against requiring workers to engage in excessive or unpaid overtime (often connected with bonuses paid for achieving very high targets) or to work while they are ill (usually caused by a clause that reduces wages if a worker cannot work due to illness, or which provides a bonus for being at work all the time); provisions in connection with child and forced labor; the obligation to employ workers based on a contract that they receive, are informed of, and understand (also in connection with social security contributions and claims); and safe and healthy working conditions.[56]

13.4.3 *Assessing human rights performance of a supplier, and access to information*

A significant challenge arises in relation to measuring the human rights performance of a supplier. Often, information on supplier performance is unavailable or insufficient. Therefore, buyers need access to this information and a contractual provision implementing a supplier obligation to provide that information is helpful. This provision might entail an obligation to provide information on the supply chains of the supplier, as well as the most salient human rights risks in those supply chains.[57] Furthermore, it might entail an obligation to implement a thorough process to engage with subcontractors and provisions on cases in which subcontracting is permitted.[58] In connection with this, it might be worthwhile to impose human rights due diligence requirement on the supplier as well.[59] This creates an independent obligation for the (first-tier) supplier to conduct its own human rights due diligence and to deal with its suppliers, notwithstanding the need for the buyer to monitor whether this is actually done.

Moreover, implementing third-party audits, of which meaningful dialogue with local stakeholders is an important part, might prove beneficial. For example, if grounds belonging to local communities are needed for production and the ownership is unclear, it might be necessary to engage in a dialogue-based process involving the local community to map ownership, and include a grievance mechanism to resolve disputes over ownership.[60] However, this requires specific contractual measures and will thus not be suitable for all types of contractual arrangements, especially not for those intended to be used in many contractual relations with suppliers. It will thus depend on the salience of the risk, the leverage of the buyer, and the size of the order as to whether such an approach is feasible in practice.[61] Furthermore, third-party (NGO) audits might be more effective if the company itself is not well informed on the (complex) local conditions and the measures a supplier is able to implement in practice.[62] These audits are generally most effectively implemented at a point in the supply chain where only a few larger players are active.[63] Beyond that, to prevent audit fatigue, audits should be conducted where gaps in the information exist or the context is likely to have changed.[64] This also inhibits replication of existing audit systems.[65]

It is important to note that more general third-party audits seem to be focused on (highly) regulated topics, such as worker safety and labor conditions, and less on broader human rights-related issues. Audits involving a focus on human rights and engaging human rights specialists seem to perform better in revealing human rights-related risks. Globally operating companies that have adopted such a specific human rights audit have found human rights-related risks in 74% of their supply chains, whereas companies conducting a more general audit have found such risks in no more than 29% of their supply chains.[66] Interestingly, companies that have adopted a more specific human rights-oriented approach also appear to be more effective at monitoring whether agreed upon improvements with a supplier are actually implemented in practice.[67]

However, these audits focus on human rights compliance and do not assess the reliability of a supplier as such in terms of its true intentions to implement the contractual obligations, although this might be relevant for the efforts the supplier is willing to make to improve the human rights situation. Such reliability might be derived from thorough management systems of the supplier, including a responsible board representative and senior officer responsible for human rights compliance; human rights on the boardroom agenda; remuneration of the board connected to human rights performance; and mechanisms to direct human rights-related information to the responsible officers. Beyond that, the supplier might be incentivized to retrieve information from her suppliers. The larger the number of suppliers and the higher the volatility of the relationships, the more difficult it will be to control human rights-related risks.[68] Therefore, it might be feasible to contractually restrict the number of subcontractors or suppliers. Instead of these contractual arrangements, smaller companies may rely on multi-stakeholder initiatives and implement the obligation to participate in those initiatives.

Beyond this monitoring of the suppliers' performance, a contractual arrangement could include the obligation of the supplier to provide information. For example, this obligation could pertain to occupational hazards and environmental pollution. It may even be possible to implement the obligation to provide information on the working conditions; the impact of the supplier on local employment; land, water, and energy use; climate; and, if applicable, biodiversity and (sustainable) food supply.[69] Obviously, the contract may also include provisions on the use of (hazardous) chemicals, water use, and greenhouse gas emissions.[70] Another possibility is for the information to include payments made to the government. Obviously, the aforementioned obligation to share information should include the provision of said information in a timely and adequate manner.[71] Transparency might contribute to decreasing human rights-related risks, as the buyer would be better equipped to assess such risks and to adequately act upon them.[72] Finally, this obligation might necessitate the requirement to preserve documents in which the information is recorded for a certain period of time.[73] If the buyer is a smaller company or the supply chain is larger or more fragmented, it might be difficult to retrieve the aforementioned information from suppliers. Engaging in a multi-stakeholder initiative that gathers this information and uses it to monitor and improve supplier performance might be a viable alternative.

13.4.4 Building dialogue with a supplier

It is also important to establish a dialogue with suppliers, especially if they do not engage in multi-stakeholder initiatives, in order to explain why human rights compliance is pivotal. Furthermore, dialogue is necessary to discuss how human rights compliance can be achieved in the local conditions in which the supplier operates, and the challenges those conditions may pose to the supplier.[74] Top-down implementation of a code of conduct might not work when the supplier's motivation to comply is minimal or when it is difficult to implement a Western code of conduct in the supplier's daily practice. Furthermore, it is important for suppliers to engage in training on human rights-related topics organized by either the buyer or by local multi-stakeholder initiatives.[75] To this end, a contractual obligation to attend and facilitate such training might be beneficial. The advantage of an obligation to engage in local multi-stakeholder training is that the local challenges and possible means to overcome them might be more clear to local stakeholders than they are to a more remote buyer with suppliers in many other countries or regions. Additionally, such initiatives might be better equipped to verify compliance. Furthermore, an individual contractual arrangement between the buyer and the supplier may be more difficult if the buyer lacks leverage or uses contractual provisions intended for many supplier contracts.

Moreover, Western companies should realize that their contractual requirements outside the field of human rights (for example, timeliness requirements, possibilities for last-minute specification changes, and the price paid for products) might hamper the efforts of a supplier to improve the human rights conditions.[76] Therefore, contracts might also entail provisions to balance the powers of Western companies vis-à-vis those of suppliers, or at least contain a mechanism through which a supplier is enabled to complain about the buyer's behavior that allegedly impedes on compliance with human rights. This mechanism might also be of assistance in building a broader dialogue between the buyer and the supplier to enhance human rights compliance.

13.4.5 Enforcement

As mentioned before, audits may expose human rights violations. Obviously, the contractual arrangement should entail provisions to deal with such violations, as well as other types of non-compliance with the contractual provisions regarding human rights. Contractual arrangements usually contain a combination of liability, *force majeure*, termination, or penalty clauses to remedy these forms of non-compliance and to enhance compliance. Nevertheless, a major challenge in the business and human rights arena remains enforcement of these contractual provisions. Litigation in local courts might not prove to be a viable avenue for Western companies because of vague and time-consuming procedures, uncertainty over possible outcomes, corruption, and unfamiliarity with the local procedures, as well as lack of trust in local procedural laws. However, for the termination of a contract, litigation in local courts is not necessary.

That said, termination might be difficult because of operational considerations, and might not contribute – or could even be counterproductive – to the improvement of human rights conditions, as these issues often are quite complex. For example, if one terminates a contract with a supplier due to child labor issues, this does not necessarily mean that the children in question will go to school following the termination. As previously explained, the income these children earn might be crucial for their family's livelihood.[77] If they are fired by one supplier they might find a job with another where the labor conditions are even worse, or they might not be able to find a new job at all, with even more dramatic consequences. Even where a supplier agrees to paying these children wages, as well as allowing for their education (for example, work for half a day and go to school for half a day), this still might not solve the issue; for instance, parents might perceive this as an increase in income, and consequently desire the child to work the whole day to earn (even) more, or perceive the solution as an interference with their parental prerogative. Therefore, engagement with and training of parents might also be necessary to emphasize the benefits of education. Thus, a simple prohibition of child labor and termination of a contract based thereon is highly unlikely to solve the issue in complex environments.

Therefore, other means of enforcement should be implemented. Companies might want to improve local conditions through dialogue with the supplier or by engaging in a local multi-stakeholder initiative.[78] A probation period might also be agreed upon with the supplier to implement the improvements. If these improvements are not adequately implemented after this probation period, the supplier should be contractually bound to collaborate with the buyer in order to assess the causes of the inadequate implementation.[79] An obligation to compensate damages because of human rights violations may also be a beneficial part of the agreement.[80] Furthermore, an obligation could be included to upgrade faulty facilities to prevent future harm, or to strengthen management systems.[81]

Beyond that, enforcement in this context might not only imply the termination of contracts and fines, but could implement a more positive approach as well. For example, contractual advantages might be awarded if a supplier passes the thresholds of a continuous improvement approach to gradually improve the human rights and labor situation. This might also entail increasing orders or placing prospective orders.[82]

Furthermore, reports from NGOs may disclose alleged human rights violations. Unlike audits conducted on behalf of the buyer, these reports are public and therefore pose additional challenges of limiting reputational damage. In order to mitigate such damage, it is important that the buyer is enabled to prepare, direct, and supervise responses to these allegations. The contractual arrangement should entail provisions to empower the buyer to do so.

13.4.6 Implementing (non-judicial) dispute-resolution mechanisms

Furthermore, supply chain contracts should entail an obligation to establish or participate in effective local/operational level grievance mechanisms that meet Guiding Principle 31's requirements.[83] Such mechanisms should be trusted by their intended users. It is unlikely that trust will be generated when the grievance mechanisms are designed at the buyer's head office with the aim of global implementation of the same mechanisms without consulting the intended users; thus, the contracts should entail the design, establishment, and implementation of such mechanisms in collaboration with their intended users, preferably through local multi-stakeholder initiatives.[84] Meaningful involvement of the intended users is crucial in the process of establishing a trusted grievance mechanism. The contractual provision should allude to this inclusion.[85] It should also require sufficient measures to prevent harassment of or retaliation against human rights defenders, worker union representatives, or others who lodge a complaint themselves or incentivize others to make use of the grievance mechanism.

Beyond this, if an effective grievance mechanism is established, it is important to learn from processed grievances. Therefore, it is vital to implement a contractual obligation to forward aggregate information on the number and nature of grievances throughout the supply chain. Effective local grievance mechanisms are an important source of information.[86] Furthermore, a supplier should be contractually bound to implement the agreed-upon outcome of the grievance mechanism if necessary after consultation with the buyer who has imposed the obligations. Even an obligation to implement an outcome further down the supply chain might be part of the contractual arrangement.

Supply chain contracts might also entail, whether or not as an escalation mechanism to the aforementioned grievance mechanisms, an arbitral clause paving the way for arbitration as an escalation mechanism to solve human rights issues. This is not yet standing practice, but is proposed as a means to solve BHR disputes.[87] This escalation mechanism can be of assistance especially where non-judicial – for example, dialogue based – mechanisms have failed.[88] Arbitration has advantages compared to litigation in national courts.[89] Therefore, arbitration may improve enforcement of (contractual) arrangements in connection with human rights, and might enhance access to remedy if human rights violations occur.

13.5 Conclusion

I feel that neglected human rights issues should no longer be neglected in their respective supply chains. The obligation to respect human rights is not only incorporated in public legislation and authoritative guiding documents, but also stems from societal expectations that are closely connected to company reputation. An adverse reputation in the business and human rights arena may cause extensive (reputational) damage. Human rights issues in supply chains might also cause delays in the production of goods or the provision of services, which might prove costly. Therefore, many companies have implemented a human rights policy to prevent and mitigate human rights issues. Several of these companies have implemented contractual arrangements regarding the supplier's human rights performance, although these contractual mechanisms are hardly ever elaborated upon in these policies. Thus, I feel that companies have to recognize that contractual arrangements should be an integral part of human rights policies, and elaborated therein.

Bridging the existing mismatch between policies and contractual arrangements may improve human rights performance by suppliers. Implementing thorough language on the utilization and shape of contractual mechanisms in human rights policies might incentivize business to put more effective contractual mechanisms in place – for example, because of the aforementioned legal obligation to report on their human rights policies in the EU, UK, and California. As becomes clear from those reports, if no thorough contractual measures are implemented, NGOs and governments might question the effectiveness of their policy. Eventually, NGOs and governments might even expect these reports to be more specific on the types of contractual measures implemented; this may eventually be mandated by legislation, which might boost the effective use of contractual arrangements even further.

Although human rights policies often describe the utilization of contractual mechanisms in a superficial manner, contractual arrangements to enhance human rights performance are widely used in supply chains. That said, their effectiveness in terms of advancing human rights compliance by suppliers is definitely subject to improvement. Thus, strengthening these instruments through, among other things, addressing this need in human rights policies, is essential in order to improve human rights compliance in supply chains. Although these contractual arrangements do not provide the full solution to human rights issues, they do constitute a necessary element of the solution. Several ways to enhance improvement have been elaborated upon. These entail a clearer description of the human rights the buyer is referring to; enhancing measurement of supplier performance, including improved audits; building dialogue with suppliers; implementing effective grievance mechanisms with feedback loops to the buyer; enhancing supplier obligations to provide information; and increasing enforcement of contractual provisions, including arbitration as an escalation mechanism.

Notes

* Martijn Scheltema is Professor at Erasmus University Rotterdam and Partner at Pels Rijcken & Droogleever Fortuijn (a Dutch law firm).

1 See, eg, SOMO, ALR and LRDP, 'The Myanmar Dilemma: Can the Garment Industry Deliver Decent Jobs for Workers in Myanmar?' (August 2017) <www.somo.nl/the-myanmar-dilemma/> accessed 24 September 2019 and on tea production in India: Global Research (Hyderabad) & India Committee of the Netherlands (Utrecht), 'Certified Unilever Tea: A Cup Half Empty: Follow-Up Study on Working Conditions in Rainforest Alliance Certified Tea Plantations in India' (August 2016) <www.indianet.nl/pdf/CertifiedUnileverTea-ACupHalfEmpty.pdf> accessed 24 September 2019.

2 A total of 84% (340) of these large companies has implemented a CSR/BHR policy. See Shift, Oxfam and Global Compact Network Netherlands, 'Doing Business with Respect for Human Rights: A Guidance Tool for Companies' (2nd edn, 2016) <www.businessrespecthumanrights.org/image/2016/10/24/business_respect_human_rights_full.pdf> accessed 24 September 2019.

3 For these frameworks, see Guiding Principles on Business and Human Rights: Implementing the United Nations, "Protect, Respect and Remedy", Annex to UNHRC, Report of the Special Representative of the Secretary-General on the Issue of Human Rights and Transnational Corporations and Other Business Enterprises, John Ruggie (21 March 2011) UN Doc A/HRC/17/31 and OECD Guidelines for Multinational Enterprises (OECD Publishing 2011). Other topics might be addressed in these policies as well. For example, in the agricultural sector, these might include food safety, prevention of (the diffusion of) animal-related disease and animal welfare, etc. See OECD-FAO, 'Guidance for Responsible Agricultural Supply Chains' (16 February 2018) <www.oecd.org/daf/inv/investment-policy/rbc-agriculture-supply-chains.htm> accessed 24 September 2019.

4 A total of 51% of internationally operating companies utilize such a code of conduct (in which human rights are also specifically addressed). See The Legal 500, 'Human Rights: How Are New Human Rights Standards Changing the Way in House Counsel Operate?' (4 September 2016) 9 <www.legal500.com/assets/pages/client-insight/human-rights-insight.html> accessed 24 September 2019. Cf. Louise Vytopil, *Contractual Control in the Supply Chain: On Corporate Social Responsibility, Codes of Conduct, Contracts and (Avoiding) Liability* (Eleven International Publishing 2015) 137. For Unilever's supplier code of conduct (which prescribes continuous improvement of CSR/BHR performance), see

<www.unilever.com/Images/responsible-sourcing-policy-interactive-final_tcm244-504736_en.pdf> accessed 24 September 2019. For example, ABN AMRO and Total have not implemented a specific supplier code of conduct, instead they have implemented a general code of conduct for their own operations as well as those of suppliers. See for ABN AMRO <www.abnamro.com/en/images/Documents/010_About_ABN_AMRO/Compliance/ABN_AMRO_Code_of_Conduct.pdf> accessed 24 September 2019 and for Total <www.total.com/sites/default/files/atoms/files/total_code_of_conduct_va.pdf> accessed 5 November 2018.

5 Cf., in the agri-business, OECD-FAO Guidance (n 3) 65, 68.

6 A company might even require a supplier to participate in training in specific risk sectors before it is eligible to solicit for a contract.

7 However, the argument has been made that these policies in themselves (if published) have legal effects, for example in connection with the interpretation of contracts. See Anna Beckers, *Taking Corporate Codes Seriously: Towards Private Law Enforcement of Voluntary Corporate Social Responsibility Codes* (Maastricht University 2015) 50–93.

8 Ibid. 41 ff; Vytopil (n 4) 121 ff, who focuses on labour-related rights. On the way this issue is addressed in supply chains in Myanmar, see SOMO, ALR and LRDP, 'The Myanmar Dilemma' (n 1) 93–115.

9 Vytopil (n 4) 123, 124, 129, 135–8. Beckers (n 7) 50–71, who also discusses whether a public statement may be relevant in connection with the interpretation of a contract or become binding through other avenues.

10 Beckers (n 7) 41–3; Vytopil (n 4) 123, 129, 135, 136, 137. Sometimes a supplier has to confirm in writing the receipt of the code of conduct. See Vytopil (n 4) 137. Companies also refer to codes of conduct developed by third parties (such as NGOs), or to supporting documents such as ILO or OECD guidance (which raises the question of whether these documents become binding for the supplier). See Vytopil (n 4) 124, 136, 137.

11 Vytopil (n 4) 125, 126, 132, 138. However, third-party rights are explicitly rejected in other contracts. See ibid. 139.

12 See, eg, Ibid. 130, 132, 139. cf Caroline Rees, Shift; Business and Sustainable Development Commission, 'Business, Human Rights and the Sustainable Development Goals: Forging a Coherent Vision and Strategy' (November 2016) 56 <www.shiftproject.org/resources/publications/business-human-rights-sustainable-development-coherent-strategy/> accessed 24 September 2019.

13 Beckers (n 7) 45–50.

14 Vytopil (n 4) 123, 124, 129, 130, 136, 137.

15 Ibid. 123, 130, 135, 136. For the international normative framework, see Tim de Meyer, 'ILO Conventions Nos. 29 and 105(1)' (21 January 2014) 138, 182 <www.ilo.org/asia/info/WCMS_346426/lang-en/index.htm> accessed 24 September 2019.

16 Vytopil (n 4) 130.

17 Cf. for agri-business OECD-FAO Guidance (n 3) 80. On this issue in Myanmar, see also SOMO, ALR and LRDP, 'The Myanmar Dilemma' (n 1).

18 Vytopil (n 4) 128, 135, 139.

19 Rees (n 12) 74, 81.

20 Cf. Ibid. 85.

21 Ibid. 72, 73.

22 Vytopil (n 4) 126, 137, 139.

23 Overall, 77% of these companies use a contractual mechanism. In the extractive industry, this is as high as 100%, and in the energy sector 83%. See Norton Rose Fulbright, 'Business and Human Rights Due Diligence Project' (March 2015) 7 <www.nortonrosefulbright.com/en/knowledge/publications/0a6e811f/exploring-human-rights-due-diligence> accessed 24 September 2019.

24 Cf. SOMO, ALR and LRDP, 'The Myanmar Dilemma' (n 1) 11–15.
25 I will not discuss all types of contractual language that may be improved due to word count restrictions, but will provide several examples of avenues for improvement.
26 For example, authors have pointed at the good Samaritan liability doctrine in US law in connection with these risks. See, eg, Joe Philips and Suk-Jun Lim, 'Their Brothers' Keeper: Global Buyers and the Legal Duty to Protect Suppliers' Employees', (2009) 61(2) *Rutgers Law Review* 333, 351.
27 For example, this has been tried in the Walmart case, but unsuccessfully. See, eg, Beckers (n 7) 53.
28 However, this does not mean that the main objective of human rights due diligence is the prevention of such damage. Human rights due diligence focuses on the risks a company inflicts on third parties. See SOMO, ALR and LRDP, 'The Myanmar Dilemma' (n 1) 51.
29 For example, ibid. 14; Rees (n 12) 10, 11, 13.
30 See <www.legislation.gov.uk/ukpga/2015/30/contents/enacted> accessed 24 September 2019, which at s 54(5) entails reporting on a policy, due diligence conducted, supply chains in which issues have arisen, or measures being implemented. S 54(6)(a) requires approval by senior management (such as the board of directors). Furthermore, s 54(7) necessitates publication of the report on the company's website.
31 See supporting documents at <www.sec.gov/spotlight/dodd-frank/speccorpdisclosure.shtml> accessed 24 September 2019. On this see, eg, Global Witness, 'The Dood Frank Act's Section 1502 on Conflict Minerals' (Briefing Document, 10 August 2011) <www.globalwitness.org/en/archive/dodd-frank-acts-section-1502-conflict-minerals/> accessed 24 September 2019.
32 State of California Department of Justice, 'The California Transparency in Supply Chains Act 2010' <https://oag.ca.gov/SB657> accessed 24 September 2019. This obligation, which is implemented in s 1714.43 of the Civil Code, governs companies with a global turnover of US$100 million or more. S 1714.43(c) entails an obligation to report on the risk assessments conducted in connection with human trafficking and slavery, audits, the gathering of information from suppliers and proof thereof, enforcement, and training.
33 Article L 225-102-4 of the Trade and Industry Code provides that a company whose head office is located on French territory, or that has at least 10,000 employees in its service and in its direct or indirect subsidiaries, must establish and implement an effective vigilance (due diligence) plan for itself, as well as for the operations of all the subsidiaries or companies that it controls. The plan has to include reasonable due diligence measures for risk identification and for the prevention of severe violations of human rights and fundamental freedoms, serious bodily injury or environmental damage, or health risks resulting directly or indirectly from the operations of the company and of the companies it controls, as well as from the operations of subcontractors or suppliers with whom it maintains an established commercial relationship, when such operations derive from this relationship. Thus, the due diligence plan has to: (1) identify, analyze, and rank risks; (2) implement procedures to regularly assess, in accordance with the risk mapping, the performance of subsidiaries, subcontractors, or suppliers with whom the company maintains an established commercial relationship; (3) provide for appropriate actions to mitigate risks or prevent serious violations; (4) provide for a warning mechanism that builds on reports on existing or actual risks, developed in collaboration with the labor union representatives of the company; and (5) implement a monitoring scheme to assess the effectiveness of the measures implemented. For the French law, see <www.senat.fr/leg/ppl14-376.html> accessed 24 September 2019.
34 See arts 4 and 5 *Parliamentary Papers II* 2016/17, 34506, A.

35 Directive 2014/95/EU of the European Parliament and of the Council of 22 October 2014 amending Directive 2013/34/EU as regards disclosure of non-financial and diversity information by certain large undertakings and groups [2014] OJ L 330/1. For example, this directive is implemented through s 2:391(5) Civil Code (*Stb.* 2016, 352) in the Netherlands.

36 Regulation (EU) 2017/821 of the European Parliament and of the Council of 17 May 2017 laying down supply chain due diligence obligations for Union importers of tin, tantalum and tungsten, their ores, and gold originating from conflict-affected and high-risk areas [2017] OJ L 130/1. This legislation builds on OECD, *OECD Due Diligence Guidance for Responsible Supply Chains of Minerals from Conflict-Affected and High-Risk Areas* (3rd edn, OECD Publishing 2016).

37 See The Equator Principles Association, 'The Equator Principles' (June 2013) <http://equator-principles.com/> accessed 24 September 2019; IFC, 'IFC Performance Standards on Environmental and Social Sustainability' (1 January 2012) <www.ifc.org/wps/wcm/connect/topics_ext_content/ifc_external_corporate_site/sustainability-at-ifc/publications/publications_handbook_pps> accessed 24 September 2019; Voluntary Principles on Security and Human Rights <www.voluntaryprinciples.org> accessed 24 September 2019.

38 For example, the Dutch signatories of the agreement in the garment industry have committed themselves to implement due diligence as set forth by these frameworks, thus effectively rendering them binding in that regard. See the CSR agreement of the garment industry in the Netherlands, SER, 'Agreement on Sustainable Garment and Textile' paras 1.1, 41, 45–53 <www.indianet.nl/pdf/AgreementOnSustainableGarmentAndTextile.pdf> accessed 24 September 2019.

39 Private frameworks in other fields have already done so. For a Dutch example in connection with a privacy framework in the insurance sector, see Supreme Court 18 April 2014, NJ 2015/20 (Achmea/Rijnberg); Marie-Claire Menting, *Industry Codes of Conduct in a Multi-Layered Dutch Private Law* (Prisma Print 2016).

40 The leverage requirement is implemented through UNGP 19(b)(ii) and s IV(3) OECD Guidelines. What leverage entails is not exactly clear. On this and different ways to exert it, see Rees (n 12) 64–74; SHIFT, 'Using Leverage in Business Relationships to Reduce Human Rights Risks' (November 2013) <www.shiftproject.org/resources/publications/leverage-business-relationships-reduce-human-rights-risk/> accessed 24 September 2019.

41 In general, see, eg, Rees (n 12) 26, 109, 110, and for financial institutions SOMO, 'Access to Effective Remedy at International Financial Institutions?' (25 November 2014), <www.somo.nl/access-to-effective-remedy-at-international-financial-institutions/> accessed 24 September 2019. On OECD National Contact Points that provide a dispute-resolution system for alleged violations of the OECD Guidelines, see OECD Watch, 'Remedy Remains Rare' (June 2015) <www.oecdwatch.org/publications-en/Publication_4201> accessed 24 September 2019.

42 Rees (n 12) 43.

43 See Business and Human Rights Due Diligence Project (n 23) 5. cf The Legal 500 (n 4) 9.

44 These clauses are actually implemented in some supply chain contracts. See Rees (n 12) 27, 30; Vytopil (n 4) 124, 125, 131, 132, 138.

45 For example, does this supplier map its supply chain, does it organize training for its suppliers, and is human rights compliance secured through agreements with its subcontractors?

46 For example, SOMO, ALR and LRDP, 'The Myanmar Dilemma' (n 1) 72, refers to a company mentioning a Fair Wear Foundation audit being conducted and not being aware of human rights violations in a factory where the report revealed human rights issues.

47 Cf. cf in the agricultural sector OECD-FAO Guidance (n 3) 26, 52.
48 Ibid. 39.
49 Rees (n 12) 67.
50 Ibid. 81.
51 See UNGPs (n 3) 17(b) and 24 and OECD Guidelines (n 3) s IV(5).
52 See also the CSR agreement of the garment industry in the Netherlands, SER, 'Agreement on Sustainable Garment and Textile' (n 38) 17, 19, 26, para 3. See also OECD, *Responsible Supply Chains in the Garment and Footwear Sector* (OECD Publishing 2017) 25, 26, 55.
53 Certification is also used to prevent and mitigate human rights violations in supply chains in connection with minerals originating from conflict zones. For an elaborated framework, see OECD Due Diligence Guidance (n 36).
54 The documents produced by this working group are a working paper with a proposal on arbitration and human rights. Claes Cronstedt and Robert C. Thompson, 'An International Arbitration Tribunal on Business and Human Rights: Version Five' (14 April 2015) <https://business-humanrights.org/en/pdf-an-international-arbitration-tribunal-on-business-human-rights-version-five> accessed 24 September 2019; Working Group on International Arbitration of Business and Human Rights, 'International Arbitration of Business and Human Rights Disputes: Questions and Answers' (21 August 2017) <https://business-human-rights.org/en/qas-on-proposed-intl-arbitration-tribunal-to-resolve-business-human-rights-abuse-disputes> accessed 24 September 2019.
55 UNGP (n 3) 12 and the commentary thereto refer to the ICCPR, the ICESCR, and core ILO conventions, but emphasize that other UN human rights instruments might also be important, such as those regarding indigenous peoples or minorities.
56 Cf. in connection with existing issues on these rights and obligations in Myanmar SOMO, ALR and LRDP, 'The Myanmar Dilemma' (n 1) 11–15, 66–92. This could also include concluding global framework agreements. See OECD, 'Responsible Supply Chains in the Garment and Footwear Sector' (n 53) 26, 101–55. In connection with this, provisions should be implemented as to when, and under what conditions, engagement with third-party recruitment or employment agencies is permitted, and also regarding the use of homeworkers. cf OECD, 'Responsible Supply Chains in the Garment and Footwear Sector' (n 52) 38, 182–6.
57 This included information on the intent to subcontract, the selected subcontractor and its performance, and the size of contract allocation. See OECD, 'Responsible Supply Chains in the Garment and Footwear Sector' (n 52) 36, 60. cf for the agricultural sector OECD-FAO Guidance (n 3) 33, 34. Such a provision should also apply for buying agents engaged by a company. cf OECD, 'Responsible Supply Chains in the Garment and Footwear Sector' (n 52) 72.
58 For example, by analyzing the human rights performance of the subcontractor or only engaging with subcontractors on the buyer's list. See OECD, 'Responsible Supply Chains in the Garment and Footwear Sector' (n 52) 35 and 36.
59 See Rees (n 12) 29, 58. One might even implement a continuous improvement model in which human rights impact assessments are conducted and guided first by the buyer, then by the supplier, and eventually by (for example) local communities, or in collaboration with these stakeholders.
60 Ibid. 57.
61 That said, this role may also assumed by (local) multi-stakeholder initiatives to which a contractual provision may refer.
62 Cf. Rees (n 12) 85.
63 Cf. in the agricultural sector OECD-FAO Guidance (n 3) 38; see also OECD, 'Responsible Supply Chains in the Garment and Footwear Sector' (n 52) 57.
64 OECD, 'Responsible Supply Chains in the Garment and Footwear Sector' (n 52) 53, 82.

65 Cf. in the agricultural sector OECD-FAO Guidance (n 3) 38; see also OECD, 'Responsible Supply Chains in the Garment and Footwear Sector' (n 52) 25.

66 See Business and Human Rights Due Diligence Project (n 23) 4. Furthermore, in these more generic audits fewer references were included to the ICCPR and ILO core conventions, compared to in the UNGPs. See ibid. 5. Beyond that, 93 per cent of the companies adopting a specific human rights audit engaged with human rights experts, as opposed to 24 per cent of the companies implementing more generic audits. See ibid. 6. Finally, companies that have adopted a more specific human rights audit refer to the UNGPs in 81 per cent of the audits. See ibid. 4.

67 A total of 74 per cent of the companies that have implemented a specific human rights audit monitor implementation in practice, as opposed to 34 per cent of the companies that have not done so. See ibid 4.

68 See also OECD, 'Responsible Supply Chains in the Garment and Footwear Sector' (n 52) 46, 71.

69 Cf. for the agricultural sector OECD-FAO Guidance (n 3) 60, 61, and 66; see also OECD, 'Responsible Supply Chains in the Garment and Footwear Sector' (n 52) 80 and 81. In connection with worker conditions, clauses requiring the provision of information may pertain to the percentage of migrant workers whose passports have been confiscated, or to hours worked.

70 OECD, 'Responsible Supply Chains in the Garment and Footwear Sector' (n 52) 155–81.

71 Cf. for the agricultural sector OECD-FAO Guidance (n 3) 66.

72 Cf. for the agricultural sector ibid. 49. This of course implicates the buyer is prepared to comply with human rights obligations and does not use the contract to evade its obligations and shift them to the supplier.

73 Cf. for the agricultural sector ibid. 32.

74 Cf. Rees (n 12) 30.

75 Cf. for the agricultural sector OECD-FAO Guidance (n 3) 58.

76 Cf. OECD, 'Responsible Supply Chains in the Garment and Footwear Sector' (n 52) 70.

77 Rees (n 12) 72, 73. On this issue in Myanmar, see SOMO, ALR and LRDP, 'The Myanmar Dilemma' (n 1) 80–4.

78 Cf. Vytopil (n 4) 126, 137, 139.

79 See for the agricultural sector OECD-FAO Guidance (n 3) 37.

80 Cf. for the agricultural sector ibid. 36.

81 OECD, 'Responsible Supply Chains in the Garment and Footwear Sector' (n 52) 67.

82 Ibid. 72.

83 Cf. Rees (n 12) 96–9, 107, 109. cf especially for the agricultural sector OECD-FAO Guidance (n 3) 53, 54; see also OECD, 'Responsible Supply Chains in the Garment and Footwear Sector' (n 52) 26.

84 Rees (n 12) 108. See also OECD, 'Responsible Supply Chains in the Garment and Footwear Sector' (n 52) 23, 92, 94. In connection with child labor and sexual assault, specific mechanisms might be necessary. See OECD, 'Responsible Supply Chains in the Garment and Footwear Sector' (n 52) 109.

85 For example, local assistance in reporting a grievance might be necessary. See OECD, 'Responsible Supply Chains in the Garment and Footwear Sector' (n 52) 92.

86 Cf. Rees (n 12) 104, 107, explains what different outcomes of the grievance mechanism might say about the human rights situation.

87 See the documents referred to in n 60.

88 The Bangladesh Accord agreed upon in the aftermath of the Rahna Plaza disaster entails such an arbitration mechanism. Many major global brands are signatories to this accord. See IndustriAll Global Union and UNI Global Union, 'Accord on Fire and Building Safety in Bangladesh' (13 May 2013) s 5 <http://bangladeshaccord.org/wp-content/uploads/2013/10/the_accord.pdf> accessed 24 September

2019. A comparable escalation mechanism is entailed in the Dutch garment industry accord, SER, 'Agreement on Sustainable Garment and Textile' (n 38).

89 See especially Working Group on International Arbitration of Business and Human Rights (n 54).

Bibliography

Beckers A, *Taking Corporate Codes Seriously: Towards Private Law Enforcement of Voluntary Corporate Social Responsibility Codes* (Maastricht University 2014).

Philips J and Lim S-J, 'Their Brothers' Keeper: Global Buyers and the Legal Duty to Protect Suppliers' Employees', (2009) 61(2) *Rutgers Law Review* 333.

Vytopil L, *Contractual Control in the Supply Chain: On Corporate Social Responsibility, Codes of Conduct, Contracts and (Avoiding) Liability* (Eleven International Publishing 2015).

Part 5

Conclusion

14 Accountability, international business operations, and the law

The way forward

Cedric Ryngaert, Ivo Giesen, Lucas Roorda, Liesbeth Enneking, François Kristen, and Anne-Jetske Schaap

14.1 Introduction

In an era of economic globalization, corporations have expanded their business operations internationally. This process could potentially be a win-win situation for corporations and home State consumers, as well as for host States and their citizens as it decreases production costs for corporations, allowing them to sell products to home State consumers at lower prices. Globalization may also benefit host States of foreign production and extraction activities, as it may create additional employment and bring in resources that could be used for the provision of public services. Unfortunately, these benefits do not always materialize. Autocrats may claim resources for themselves and spend lavishly on personal luxuries and prestige projects without being accountable to their citizens.[1] Multinational corporations, in their quest to maximize profits ("shareholder value"),[2] may have little or no concern for human rights and the environment in the host States where those profits are generated – typically weak governance States in the Global South that have limited enforcement capacity or corrupt regimes. These externalities of international business operations have informed calls for increased corporate accountability, not least by the UN through international soft law instruments like the UNGPs.[3]

Accountability – that is, requiring an actor to answer for his/her activities – is obviously a multifaceted notion, as evidenced by Larry Backer's efforts in this volume to "unpack" (and subsequently "repack") the concept.[4] This volume has mainly focused on the legal/liability dimension of accountability, both in the sense of prosecution and punishment under the first pillar of the UNGPs, and as an aspect of the right of access to remedy, which is addressed in the third pillar of the UNGPs.

The UNGPs' drafters have called on states to "protect against human rights abuse within their territory and/or jurisdiction by third parties, including business enterprises", to "take appropriate steps to prevent, investigate, punish and redress such abuse",[5] and, "[a]s part of their duty to protect against business-related human rights abuse", to "take appropriate steps to ensure, through judicial, administrative, legislative or other appropriate means, that when such abuses occur within their territory and/or jurisdiction those affected have access to effective remedy".[6] However, they have refrained from fleshing out how states could and should hold corporations liable and what constitutes an effective legal remedy in this respect. In essence, they have considered these issues to be governed by domestic law and have called on States to "take appropriate steps to ensure the effectiveness of domestic judicial mechanisms when addressing business-related human rights abuses, including considering ways to reduce legal, practical and other relevant barriers that could lead to a denial of access to remedy."[7]

In other words, the UNGPs lay the groundwork for further legal and policy developments, but leave their actual implementation to States. It is the ambition of this volume to pick up where the UNGPs left off and to more clearly draw the boundaries of the legal/liability aspect of accountability, including the identification and/or reform of mechanisms that can contribute to realizing it. We have examined the conditions under which a corporation (or corporate officers) conducting international business operations can be held liable in law for the adverse effects of the operations on human rights, including labor rights (such as violations of health and safety standards, child or slave labor), and the environment (for example, pollution as a result of extractive activities)[8] in host States, and how procedural and substantive remedies could be shaped.[9]

A wide variety of legal accountability mechanisms have been discussed, ranging from private law (including contract and company law) to public law (including criminal law) to international law (including international arbitration and international criminal law) mechanisms. In addition, a number of tailor-made statutory instruments relating to corporate accountability in the business and human rights context have been passed in review. Some of these instruments, like the 2017 French *Loi relative au devoir de vigilance*[10] and the Swiss Responsible Business Initiative,[11] refer explicitly to the legal/liability aspect of accountability as they seek to impose – in different ways – legal liability for a corporation's failure to conduct adequate human rights (and/or environmental) due diligence.[12] Other instruments, notably those imposing reporting and disclosure requirements, primarily aim to create "market accountability" (that is, influencing consumers' and investors' economic choices) and may not explicitly mention legal liability. However, they could still inform a finding of liability, for instance under general principles of securities law,[13] criminal law, and/or tort law.[14]

Taken together, these examples show that corporate accountability mechanisms from different fields of law may be interrelated, complementary, and/or mutually reinforcing.[15] Ultimately, only a "smart mix" of such measures is likely bring about proper accountability and, by extension, the prospect of changes in corporate practices that are deemed desirable in order to enhance corporate accountability for human rights violations in global value chains.

14.2 Making the most of the existing law

The contributions to this volume demonstrate – perhaps surprisingly – that, to a large extent, legal accountability for corporate human rights abuse could be established by means of **existing legal mechanisms, techniques, and doctrines**. This means that a more or less complete overhaul of the legal system does not need to be the first priority for governments and NGOs. Instead, better and more creative use of existing tools may go a long way toward a tighter (for some: better) liability regime. Obviously, this does not exclude the possibility that a more fundamental reform of the law, insofar as is politically and institutionally feasible, may deliver additional accountability dividends.[16]

This section offers a critical appreciation of the opportunities offered by existing private, criminal, and international law instruments to bring about corporate accountability for human rights abuses. It addresses both the procedural and substantive dimension of the remedies sought by the victims. Attention is paid to questions of *access* to remedy (in particular, access to an adequate jurisdictional mechanism), and to questions of *substantive law* (particularly concerning due diligence-based liability with respect to abuses committed in the corporate supply chain), bearing in mind that the harm done to the victim can only be adequately remedied if both dimensions are realized.[17]

Private law, which mainly consists of contract and tort law, is the bread and butter of many a domestic legal practitioner, who may never come across a business and human rights case. However, contributors to this volume have highlighted how, for instance, tort litigation and contractual arrangements may hold major promise to dispense corporate accountability for human rights abuses. With regard to contracts, Scheltema has pointed out that a large number of MEs *already* enhance compliance with human rights codes of conduct by enshrining human rights obligations in contracts concluded with suppliers.[18] The risk of losing contractual opportunities with major purchasers may force suppliers to improve their human rights record. However, the issue remains that contractual human rights clauses are not always effective. This is mainly because of a mismatch between lofty corporate human rights policy declarations and actual enforcement of contracts in case of non-compliance. Scheltema offers some useful prescriptions to close this gap between policy and practice.[19]

Bueno has discussed provisions of tort liability in specific legislative initiatives on business and human rights, such as the aforementioned French law on *devoir de vigilance* and, more specifically, the Swiss Responsible Business Initiative.[20] As recent judicial practice shows, "extraterritorial" tort cases are possible, but face significant barriers.[21] Home State courts may establish their jurisdiction over parent corporations under the domicile principle, possibly over foreign subsidiaries under the "connected claims" doctrine, and even potentially over any foreign corporation under the "forum of necessity" doctrine in case victims were to face a denial of justice in the host State.[22] However, one of the major challenges in these cases is establishing that the parent company was under a duty of care in respect of third parties, particularly host country workers, neighbors, and communities that are detrimentally affected by the activities of the local subsidiaries, suppliers, and/or business partners of those parent companies. At the time of writing, interesting developments are taking place in relation to this issue of parent company liability, as discussed by Dowling.[23]

Arguably, legal certainty regarding the requisite standard of care could be improved by reliance on broadly accepted international corporate due diligence guidance. This issue is addressed at greater length in the following analysis, but for now we emphasize that duty of care-based reasoning in transnational corporate tort cases can enhance victims' access to a remedy, because this creates an additional "defendant" and thus a forum to go to. However, victims do need to establish supervisory failures by controlling corporate entities to be successful and success will also strongly depend on the applicable law. Under the host State's provisions on non-contractual liability, which according to the rules of private international law will ordinarily be the law that is applicable, corporate duties of care may not be fully developed. This problem could be remedied by inserting a specific provision in new business and human rights legislation that considers home State tort law, particularly the duty of care as identified by the home State, as the applicable law. As Bueno shows, the Swiss Responsible Business Initiative provides an example of what such a provision may look like.[24]

An even more fundamental obstacle is that, to the extent that it cannot be established that a corporation closely supervised and/or controlled another entity, the former cannot be held liable in respect of the latter's violations, as the principles of separate legal personality and limited liability oppose holding one legal (corporate) person liable for the liabilities of another. Dowling has denounced this classic corporate-law-based limitation as a major accountability loophole, and has instead suggested a "profit risk" or "created risk" approach to liability (which he borrowed from some Latin American legal systems).[25] Pursuant to this approach, the liability for abuses could be engaged of "those who genuinely instigated, promoted or developed a dangerous activity through their actions or investment", and even those who just "profited from" production or extraction activities down the supply chain involving abuses. The separate legal personality of the various corporate persons participating in the supply chain would then no longer be an obstacle for this economically more realistic, enterprise-liability model.

With regard to the **criminal law**, the contributors to this volume have brought to the fore a panoply of provisions in domestic criminal codes that could be productively applied to hold corporations and corporate officers accountable for their involvement in foreign human rights abuses. Thus, the issue here does thus not seem to be a lack of legal rules. However, harnessing the power of the criminal law is crucially dependent on prosecutorial willingness and capacity, which may explain why, in the real world – at least in most places – very few criminal cases relating to irresponsible business conduct in global value chains have been prosecuted.

Despite its current underuse, domestic criminal law may constitute a particularly potent tool to create accountability for corporate abuses, as – to a greater degree than tort litigation, in which the state is largely a "recipient" of cases rather than a proactive enforcer – it expresses a society's indignation and moral condemnation of particular abusive activities and practices. For instance, Schaap shows how the domestic criminalization of modern slavery and child labor may also capture labor rights violations committed in global supply chains.[26] She notably praises the Dutch model of criminalizing those who benefit domestically from slavery, labor exploitation, and human trafficking abroad, as a potential corporate accountability tool in respect of foreign human rights abuses.[27] Dutch law does not require that the predicate offense (the actual abuse) occurs in the Netherlands: it suffices that a Dutch corporation benefits from the abuse; for example, by purchasing a product assembled abroad in the (constructive) knowledge of an exploitative production process.[28] As under tort law, a company's failure to discharge its duty of care in relation to the impacts of its activities on human rights and/or the environment elsewhere may result in liability. Relatedly, a corporation's criminal liability may also be engaged by its failure to comply with mandatory due diligence provisions enshrined in domestic legislation that specifically addresses corporate human rights abuses in global supply chains, such as the recently adopted Dutch Child Labour Due Diligence Act.[29]

Cupido *et al.*, for their part, discuss the promises held by (Dutch) common criminal law provisions that were initially not designed or applied to create corporate accountability in respect of foreign abuses, but could be used to do just that.[30] They argue that, notably, money laundering and participation in a criminal organization – both criminalized by Dutch domestic law – lend themselves to prosecute Dutch(-based) corporations for their involvement in rights violations committed overseas. Just like profiting from labor exploitation, these crimes do not require that the predicate offense – the rights violation – occur on Dutch territory. It suffices that the illegal proceeds of the crime were laundered in the Netherlands, or that a corporation participated from the Netherlands in criminal schemes.

To successfully prosecute corporations for these offenses, as in tort litigation, jurisdiction may not be the main obstacle. Instead, prosecutors will have to establish sufficient causal and motivational proximity of the corporation to the foreign crime, including a failure to discharge the duty of care (that is, a failure to take adequate due diligence measures). The Swiss *Argor-Heraeus* case – discussed by Dam-de Jong in her contribution to this volume[31] – shows that this is a tall order indeed. A Swiss prosecutor discontinued money-laundering and pillage-based criminal proceedings against this Swiss gold refiner on the grounds that the company apparently did not know that the gold was sourced from an area in the Democratic Republic of the Congo (DRC) that was rife with conflict and rights violations committed by armed groups.[32] Still, it is not impossible for a corporation or a businessperson to be sufficiently proximate to the foreign crime for its/his liability to be engaged.[33] Even then, as Cupido *et al.* point out, one may wonder whether reliance on the rather technical domestic criminalization of money laundering or participation in a criminal organization adequately expresses a society's condemnation of the predicate human rights abuses.

Next to these domestic legal instruments, **international law** criminalizes the most shocking rights violations (war crimes, crimes against humanity, genocide), including complicity in such violations. In this respect, it is well known that the ICC has no jurisdiction over corporations.[34] Somewhat paradoxically perhaps, this does not mean that the ICC cannot prosecute corporate abuses. After all, it has jurisdiction over corporate officers. In fact, in a 2016 policy paper, the ICC Office of the Prosecutor announced that it would henceforth "give particular consideration to prosecuting Rome Statute crimes that are committed by means of, or that result in, *inter alia* . . . the illegal exploitation of natural resources",[35] crimes that may well involve (multinational) corporations. In addition, in States that know the concept of corporate criminal liability, domestic courts may well hold corporations as such accountable for violations of international criminal law. In particular, Dam-de Jong has highlighted the potential of prosecuting corporations for the war crime of pillage with regard to their irresponsible sourcing of various metals and minerals in conflict-affected areas.[36]

Accountability solutions under international law do not only need to have a criminal law dimension. As Yiannibas suggests in her contribution, the traditional dispute settlement mechanism of international arbitration could be relied on to settle disputes between corporations and victims of human rights abuses resulting from corporate activity (abroad), provided that several reforms to the classic principles governing arbitration are implemented to comply with the UNGPs.[37] This proposal again shows that making smart use of existing accountability mechanisms, and reforming them only to the extent needed, may be the way forward.[38] Zerk seems to have reached a similar conclusion in her contribution on models of cross-border legal cooperation in complex corporate cases.[39] She points out that better operational-level cooperation and communication between States is likely to be much more effective in addressing cases of business-related human rights abuse than the pursuit of fundamental reforms of an international legal system that is necessarily flawed when it comes to the regulation of transnational business actors and activities.

14.3 Finding new ways to operate: due diligence

What unites the various contributions on the domestic private law, domestic criminal law, and international law mechanisms for business and human rights accountability is that, from a substantive liability perspective, they all seem to underline, to some extent, the salience of mandatory due diligence. The consequence of a legal obligation to conduct human rights due diligence could be that a corporate actor could be held liable if, on the basis of a reasonable due diligence inquiry into its supply chain, it could have known that it contributed to human rights abuses and could have reasonably been expected to do more to prevent such abuses. As Bjorn Fasterling explains, this notion of human rights due diligence is already to be found in the UNGPs, where it grounds the responsibility of transnational corporations to respect human rights, albeit without any legal liability consequences having been attached by the UNGPs' drafters to non-compliance.[40]

However, we are currently witnessing a "legalization" of the concept, in the sense of an increase in its binding force, as failures to live up to "soft" due diligence standards may increasingly provide grounds for "hard" corporate liability in civil, criminal, or international law. One of the ways in which this development is taking place is through the use of open-ended criminal or tort law duties of care, the specification of which is informed by international and transnational soft-law due diligence guidance. For instance, Dam-de Jong argues that the *mens rea* of the classic war crime of pillage could be triggered if a corporate officer deliberately chose to "remain ignorant with respect to the origin of their natural resources procurements", in violation of, for example, the (in itself non-binding) OECD Due Diligence Guidance on responsible sourcing of conflict minerals, thus inducing liability of the corporate officer involved.[41] Alternatively, issue-specific legislation may enshrine due diligence as a standard for corporate liability in respect of human rights abuses, as is the case with the aforementioned French law on *devoir de vigilance* and the Swiss Responsible Business Initiative, or as a standard regarding disclosure about or importation of goods produced abroad.

The migration of the concept of due diligence, first from the field of business law to the business and human rights field and then to the field of legal liability, is a concrete manifestation of normative regime interaction that enhances corporate accountability. However, it is not without problems. Fasterling, for one, argues – taking the French law on *devoir de vigilance* as an example – that States may tend to impose due diligence obligations only on parent corporations rather than on the entire enterprise.[42] Inspired by the UNGPs' requirement to integrate due diligence findings, he instead draws attention to the responsibility of persons throughout the organization and down the supply chain to report and address human rights risks. Bueno, for another, while supporting first movers such as Switzerland, notes that due-diligence-based liability should not be introduced unilaterally, but should instead be broadly adopted internationally, to level the playing field for internationally active corporations.[43]

Even more fundamentally, despite specific sectoral international guidance instruments developed by the industry, States, or international organizations like the OECD,[44] the practical meaning of due diligence may remain elusive. In light of the principle of legal certainty, clarity about when a corporation discharges its due diligence obligations (allowing it to escape liability) and when it does not (leading to liability) is essential. In this respect, one may also ask whether corporate due diligence failures (should) *ipso facto* lead to liability, whether liability should only result from more serious failures, or whether liability should be limited to larger corporations that have the resources to conduct elaborate due diligence throughout the supply chain.[45]

Furthermore, an actual finding of liability for due diligence failures will crucially depend on *who* has to establish the failure. If, as is the case under the French law, it is incumbent on the victim/plaintiff to discharge that burden of proof, in line with what the "normal" rules on burden of proof would ask in most systems, the informational deficit from which he or she normally suffers, may let the corporation off the hook.[46] One must add to that the similar evidential difficulties that the victim/plaintiff is likely to experience in proving a causal link between the absence of a proper due diligence plan and the loss that he or she actually suffered. By contrast, if the corporation itself must prove compliance with due diligence requirements, as would be the case under the Swiss Responsible Business Initiative, the threat of liability may be much more serious.[47]

The latter model, which is based on a presumption of a corporate due care violation, is attractive from an accountability perspective in that it may unmask corporate window-dressing and blue-washing strategies. Nevertheless, casting the liability net too wide could have negative repercussions not only for corporations acting in good faith – which, hopefully, is the majority of them – but also for producers and suppliers abroad. Widespread corporate divestment from certain sectors, locations, or activities out of fear for liability could have serious welfare effects in the Global South. Perversely, then, relatively strict liability rules may actually aggravate the human rights risks that they were supposed to address.[48] For instance, commentators have warned that the US Dodd–Frank Act's imposition of stringent due diligence requirements regarding the sourcing of minerals in the DRC may lead corporations to no longer source from the DRC, which would plunge the DRC into even more abject poverty and entrench violations of economic and social rights.[49]

14.4 Practical challenges

Even if, in due course, (due diligence-based) liability standards with respect to corporate human rights violations in global value chains were to be enacted and/or clarified, there is still no guarantee that victims of corporate abuses would have access to a remedy. As highlighted previously, some of these problems of access may be jurisdictional or evidentiary in nature. Still, recent developments in extraterritorial tort cases in this context before English and Dutch courts suggest that existing jurisdictional doctrines under public and private international law may go some way toward accommodating victims' quest for a forum that is competent to hear complaints regarding "extraterritorial" abuses. However, practical challenges regarding access may be less easily surmountable. Various authors have identified such challenges and have suggested ways to overcome them. For instance, Jennifer Zerk points out that lawsuits and prosecutions regarding corporate abuses tend to be complex given the transnational character of corporate activities, especially as far as the taking of geographically dispersed evidence is concerned. For cases against corporations to be successful, cross-border legal cooperation will be required.[50]

Lawyers and law-enforcement agencies dealing with business and human rights abuses need not reinvent the wheel. Instead, as Zerk suggests, they could build on international cooperation arrangements that are already in place, such as joint investigative teams (JITs), a tool developed in the EU to boost cooperation between national investigative agencies addressing cross-border crime.[51] Such JITs could allow prosecutions for transnational corporate abuses to be more successfully mounted. Still, it will also be key to involve the State on whose territory the abuse has actually occurred, typically a non-EU Member State, even if such a State may well lack the resources to be a full partner in these investigations.

More generally, whereas it is often stated that host States lack the capacity to legally address corporate abuses in the business and human rights context – often due to poor judicial infrastructure – home States may also face major capacity problems. Home State police officers and prosecutors may not have the knowledge, time, or resources at their disposal to seriously investigate transnational corporate crime, even more so if and when their superiors decide to prioritize domestic crime for national political reasons.[52] In addition, victims may be reluctant to file tort claims for financial reasons. This situation can only be remedied by expanding victims' entitlements to financial assistance, or by law firms and NGOs taking up the case on a *pro bono* basis.

Suppliers, for their part, may face practical and financial difficulties to comply with strict human rights standards required by buyers, a problem that Scheltema argues can only be remedied if the buyer provides training and/or dialogue to enable the supplier to actually comply with contractual human rights clauses.[53] Also, buyers themselves, especially if they are small or medium-sized, may face problems in complying with statutory due diligence obligations. This challenge may be addressed by excluding such corporations from the scope of application of the law, by easing due diligence and/or burden of proof requirements, or by encouraging them to participate in multi-stakeholder initiatives that may be better able to monitor compliance. That it is not a pipedream to hope for increased capacity and resources is demonstrated by Buhmann's example of the Dutch OECD National Contact Point (NCP). That institution received substantial funds enabling it to travel and meet complainants in the DRC, and was able to bring about a form of accountability for extraterritorial corporate abuses.[54]

14.5 An integrated approach

The contributions in this volume also point to the inherent interconnectedness of many of the issues that exist when it comes to providing justice for corporate human rights violations in global value chains, and what this says about corporate accountability for human rights abuses as a field of study, and, by extension, business and human rights as a field of law. This interconnectedness can be observed, for instance, in the way in which particular legal concepts manifest themselves across legal domains. They migrate between different fields of law and transcend the boundaries between the domestic and the international, remaining only marginally connected to their doctrinal roots. Human rights due diligence, which is now rapidly evolving from an international soft-law guideline to a standard of conduct that informs enforceable obligations from both domestic and international law, is just one such concept.[55] Another example is the much-discussed "corporate veil", which is addressed in detail by Dowling,[56] but also plays a role in one way or another in most other contributions. While it is, at its core, a company law concept meant to encourage investment, it is now at the heart of the societal and legal debate relating to the governance and accountability of transnational corporate groups when it comes to preventing human rights abuses in their global value chains.

As the contributions to this book have highlighted, this migration and uprooting means that neither the study of accountability, international business operations and the law, nor the search for effective measures in this context, can take place from the within the confines of separate legal fields, domains, or disciplines. It cannot be conducted without paying regard to the fading divisions between the international and the domestic, between the public and the private, and between the substantive and the procedural. In this respect, business and human rights are at the forefront of a change in how we look at the study and reform of international law. Together with the role of the law in combating climate change or the role of the law in the digital era, business and human rights demonstrates a turn toward a more functionalist approach to law,[57] in the sense of a growing tendency to assess the law on its ability to perform particular societal functions. As the contributions to this book have shown, the law is currently not optimally shaped and/or utilized to adequately fulfill its function of ensuring accountability of transnational corporations in the business and human rights context.

Therefore, what is needed is an integrated approach that connects different fields of law to engage with the broader question of accountability – a holistic view of accountability, if you will. Rather than looking at corporate accountability from the perspective of changes within each legal field individually, we should take a broader view of how mechanisms that are present in different fields of law, and also those from outside the legal domain, may complement one another, if we are to promote accountability for corporate human rights violations in global value chains. That requires an increased and deepened collaboration across the boundaries between doctrines and disciplines: it requires a broader research and policy horizon. Hopefully, this book and its constituent contributions have provided a glimpse of that horizon, and what lies beyond.

14.6 Summing up: an agenda for future research

Some questions regarding accountability and liability for corporate human rights abuses in global value chains could only be addressed superficially in this volume. Other researchers are invited to discuss these issues in more depth, as we will do so ourselves in our continuous efforts to realize true justice for all involved in the field of international business and human rights. Most notably, mention could be made of the *effectiveness* and *legitimacy* of accountability initiatives. Productive scholarly inquiries could be made regarding the impact of enhanced liability "on the ground", in the corporate supply chain and for potential victims of abuse. Buhmann, for instance, suggests a future research agenda on the impact of the process of OECD National Contact points in ensuring substantive remedies for victims, and in generating longer-term change in corporate conduct.[58]

In any event, the impact of corporate accountability mechanisms in this context should not be taken for granted. For instance, Scheltema cautions, with respect to human rights clauses in buyer–supplier contracts, that termination of contracts on grounds of human rights abuses may "force a supplier to contract other buyers who might be more lenient on these issues", thereby worsening rather than improving matters.[59] However, even the underlying assumption that buyers are serious about providing accountability in the supply chain should by no means be seen as self-evident. There is, more generally, no guarantee that public or private actors supervising corporate compliance with human rights will adequately discharge their supervisory duties. Even worse, a supervisory agency, even if required by statute or regulation, may not even materialize.[60] Surely, unlike what Glaucon, one of Socrates' interlocutors in the *Republic*, stated, "it would [not] be absurd that a guardian should need a guard."[61] Analyzing how supervisory agencies can and should monitor corporate compliance, and how they themselves can be held to account, is another productive field of future inquiry in this context.

Ultimately, analyzing what works and what does not seems more important than legalistic hairsplitting in the heaven of legal concepts.[62] However, the fact that something "works" from an empirical perspective cannot and should not be the end of the scholarly enquiry.[63] Otherwise, one risks lapsing into reductionist scientism, pursuant to which only what can be measured is real and justified.[64] Put differently, what is effective is not necessarily fair and legitimate. The effectiveness of corporate accountability mechanisms may well be increased in the near future, but one may be left to wonder whether due diligence standards may not become too strict (see Section 14.3). Also, these mechanisms are in large part Western constructs, which elicits the question of whether they are sufficiently responsive to the expectations and interests of the envisaged beneficiaries: the individuals, workers, and communities in the Global South who tend to be the victims of corporate human rights abuse in global value chains. Future research could empirically examine the extent to which Western corporate accountability mechanisms are considered as invasive, imperialistic, or culturally inappropriate in and by non-Western host States. A distinction will then have to be made between elites, which tend to benefit from foreign corporate activity, and the masses that are at risk of human rights abuses and are most in need of true (access to) justice.

Notes

1 Leif Wenar, *Blood Oil: Tyrants, Violence and the Rules that Run the World* (Oxford University Press 2016).

2 As Dowling points out in this volume (Chapter 11), it is the underlying legal imperative of all corporations to act in the service of its shareholders, as a result of which CSR may even be "illegal".

3 Guiding Principles on Business and Human Rights: Implementing the United Nations "Protect, Respect and Remedy", Annex to UNHRC, Report of the Special Representative of the Secretary-General on the Issue of Human Rights and Transnational Corporations and Other Business Enterprises, John Ruggie (21 March 2011) UN Doc A/HRC/17/31.

4 See Chapter 4. See also, for instance: Mark Bovens, 'Two Concepts of Accountability: Accountability as a Virtue and as a Mechanism', (2010) 33 *West European Politics* 946; Deirdre Curtin and André Nollkaemper, 'Conceptualising Accountability in International and European Law', (2006) *Netherlands Yearbook of International Law* 3.

5 UNGPs (n 3) Guiding Principle 1.

6 Ibid. 25.

7 Ibid. 26.

8 Just like the UNGPs, this volume has not specifically focused on the environment as such, unlike, for instance, Chapter VI of the OECD Guidelines for Multinational Enterprises, see OECD, *OECD Guidelines for Multinational Enterprises* (OECD Publishing 2011). However, environmental abuses may have a human rights dimension, and may therefore be captured by corporate human rights obligations. This is not to deny that transnational corporate activities could have adverse impacts on local or global environmental goods without these impacts being reducible to human rights abuses.

9 The centrality of remedies explains why the volume features a contribution on OECD National Contact Points (NCP). Admittedly, the NCPs may not hold corporations liable in law. Thus, they are not a strictly legal mechanism. Nevertheless, as Buhmann points out in this volume (Chapter 3), they can hold corporations accountable via final statements on whether or not they have complied with OECD Guidelines, and thereby "facilitate agreements between parties, which may include reparations", thus contributing to the provision of a substantive remedy.

10 Loi no 2017-399 du 27 Mars 2017 relative au devoir de vigilance des sociétés mères et des entreprises donneuses d'ordre (FR). For more on the Swiss initiative, see the contribution by Bueno in this volume.

11 The official text of the initiative can be found in French, German, and Italian <www.bk.admin.ch/ch/f/pore/vi/vis462t.html> accessed 22 August 2019; the English translation is available on the website of the Swiss Coalition for Corporate Justice <https://corporatejustice.ch> accessed 22 August 2019. For more on this initiative, see Bueno (Chapter 12 in this volume).

12 For a discussion and comparison of both initiatives, see Bueno (Chapter 12 in this volume).

13 Under US securities law, fraudulent misstatements or omissions in reporting to the US Securities and Exchange Commission (SEC) could lead to liability (Securities Act, Section 12(a)(1)). This means that misstatements or omissions in reports submitted by corporations to the SEC under Section 1502 of the US Dodd–Frank Act (2010) could lead to liability. This section requires corporations (US issuers) to report whether or not their products contain "conflict minerals", by conducting due diligence.

14 For example, Robert Chambers and Anil Yilmaz-Vastardis, 'The New EU Rules on Non-Financial Reporting: Potential Impacts on Access to Remedy?', (2016) 10 *Human Rights and International Legal Discourse* 1, 18–40 (arguing that, by requiring parent companies to report on human rights impacts, Directive 2014/95/EU of the European Parliament and of the Council of 22 October 2014 amending Directive 2013/34/EU as regards disclosure of non-financial and diversity information by certain large undertakings and groups [2014] OJ L 330/1 "could be mandating companies to acquire knowledge of and involvement in the business of their subsidiaries and show this in their annual reports, which may result in them assuming a duty of care to employees (and others) affected by the actions of their subsidiaries").

15 See also supply chain contracts on human rights compliance, as discussed in this volume by Scheltema (Chapter 13), which may feature an arbitral clause providing for arbitration in case internal corporate grievance mechanisms fail to deliver results.

16 Such reform may possibly be addressed by the new business and human rights treaty that is being prepared by the Intergovernmental Working Group on transnational corporations and other business enterprises with respect to human rights, established by the UN. A first draft was released in July 2018, a revised draft in July 2019. For more information and further references, see <www.business-humanrights.org/en/about-us/blog/debate-the-treaty> accessed 22 August 2019.

17 See also Buhmann's observation in this volume that (merely) having access to remedy is no guarantee that harm done will be cured (Chapter 3).

18 See Chapter 13.
19 Scheltema advocates the following measures: "clearer description of the human rights the buyer is referring to; enhancing measurement of supplier performance, including improved audits; building dialogue with suppliers; implementing effective grievance mechanisms with feedback loops to the buyer; enhancing supplier obligations to provide information; and increasing enforcement of contractual provisions, including arbitration as an escalation mechanism" (Chapter 13).
20 See Chapter 12.
21 See, for example, Juan José Alvarez Rubio and Katerina Yiannibas (eds.), *Human Rights in Business: Removal of Barriers to Access to Justice in the European Union* (Routledge 2017).
22 See, for example, Liesbeth Enneking, 'Transnational Human Rights and Environmental Litigation: A Study of Case Law Relating to Shell in Nigeria', in Isabel Feichtner et al. (eds.), *Human Rights in the Extractive Industries: Transparency, Participation, Resistance* (Springer 2019) 511–51; Lucas Roorda and Cedric Ryngaert, 'Business and Human Rights Litigation in Europe and Canada: The Promises of Forum of Necessity Jurisdiction', (2016) 80(4) *Rabels Zeitschrift für internationales und ausländisches Privatrecht* 783.
23 See Chapter 11. See also Enneking (n 22).
24 See, e.g., para. 2(d) of the text of the Swiss Initiative ("[t]he provisions based on the principles of paragraphs a–c apply irrespective of the law applicable under private international law"), as discussed by Bueno in Chapter 12.
25 See Chapter 11.
26 See Chapter 10.
27 Dutch Penal Code, Article 273f.
28 Schaap also discusses the UK Modern Slavery Act 2015, s 54(4)(a), which requires, *inter alia*, that commercial organizations prepare a slavery and human trafficking statement that must include information about parts of the organization's business and supply chains that contain a risk of slavery and human trafficking, and the steps it has taken to address that risk. However, she also notes that this Act, unlike the Dutch provision, does not criminalize domestic profiting from extraterritorial abuses, which means it is no real substitute for the Dutch provision as a working model.
29 Voorstel van wet van het lid Van Laar houdende de invoering van een zorgplicht ter voorkoming van de levering van goederen en diensten die met behulp van kinderarbeid tot stand zijn gekomen (Wet zorgplicht kinderarbeid), *Kamerstukken I*, 2016/17, 34 506 <zoek.officielebekendmakingen.nl/kst-34506-A.html> accessed 22 August 2019. Article 9 provides for criminal sanctions on (officers of) companies that repeatedly fail to comply with the due diligence and reporting obligations set out in the Act.
30 See Chapter 9.
31 See Chapter 7.
32 Schweizerisches Bundesanwaltschaft, Dismissal of proceedings against Argor-Heraeus, Case Number SV.13-MUA, Bern, 10 March 2015.
33 This is evidenced by the Dutch convictions of individual businessmen Van Anraat and Kouwenhoven, discussed in this volume by Cupido et al.: both were held liable, on the basis of accomplice liability, for facilitating war crimes committed in Iraq and Liberia in the context of their delivering chemicals and arms to a party to the armed conflict.
34 Article 25 of the Rome Statute of the International Criminal Court limits its jurisdiction to natural persons.
35 ICC, Office of the Prosecutor, 'Policy Paper on Case Selection and Prioritisation', 15 September 2016, para. 41.
36 See Chapter 7.

37 See Chapter 5. Yiannibas reviews the mechanism of international arbitration in light of the requirements with which mechanisms offering a remedy should comply, according to General Principle 31 of the UNGPs, and makes a number of recommendations in order to make the mechanism of international arbitration more compatible with/effective in the business and human rights context.
38 See also Scheltema's emphasis on incremental reform, where, regarding contractual clauses on business and human rights compliance, he points out that "smaller changes are preferably first implemented in the supply chains and in relation to the types of risk that pose the largest treat to human rights" (Chapter 13).
39 See Chapter 6.
40 See Chapter 2. See also UNGPs (n 3) General Principles 17–21. General Principle 17 defines due diligence as the process through which enterprises can identify, prevent, mitigate, and account for how they address their actual and potential adverse impacts.
41 See Chapter 7.
42 See Chapter 2.
43 See Chapter 12.
44 See generally, regarding the OECD and due diligence: OECD (n 8) ch II, commentary para. 14 and ch IV, commentary para. 15. Under OECD auspices, various sectoral due diligence guidances have been developed, e.g., OECD Due Diligence Guidance for Responsible Supply Chains of Minerals from Conflict-Affected and High-Risk Areas, OECD Due Diligence Guidance for Responsible Supply Chains in the Garment and Footwear Sector.
45 Cf. Section 2b of the Swiss Initiative, which instructs the legislator to take into account the needs of small and medium-sized companies.
46 Regarding the French law, Fasterling observes: "As long as the parent company draws up a state-of-the-art risk map and due diligence plan, and is able to show that it implements and regularly follows up on the plan, the defendant is on the safe side".
47 The presumption of liability was already mooted by Steven Ratner, 'Corporations and Human Rights: A Theory of Legal Responsibility', (2001) 111 *The Yale Law Journal* 443, 520.
48 The assumption here would be that a decrease in welfare will lead to more human rights abuses, proof of which is not easy to obtain. However, this assumption can also be seen as the inverse of the much reported effect that an increase in welfare has on human rights compliance.
49 See, for instance, Christiana Ochoa and Patrick Keenan, 'Regulating Information Flows, Regulating Conflict: An Analysis of United States Conflict Minerals Legislation', (2011) 3(1) *Goettingen Journal of International Law* 129, 148. See also Annika van Baar, 'Conflict, Minerals and Reporting Obligations for Multinational Business Operations (what Did Dodd-Frank 1502 Do?)', Conference Paper UCALL Conference 2017 Accountability and International Business Operations: Providing Justice for Corporate Violations of Human Rights, Labor and Environmental Standards (Utrecht, the Netherlands), on file with the editors.
50 See Chapter 6.
51 Council Resolution on a Model Agreement for setting up a Joint Investigation Team (JIT) [2017] OJ C 18/1.
52 This issue is also highlighted by Schaap in respect of prosecutions for modern slavery involving corporate actors (Chapter 10).
53 See Chapter 13. Scheltema notes that Western buyers' behaviour may sometimes impede their suppliers' compliance with human rights, and suggests setting up mechanisms for suppliers to complain about this.
54 See Chapter 3. Nevertheless, Buhmann harbors doubts about the availability of resources for proactive instead of reactive accountability efforts by NCPs.

55 Compare how the normative force of due diligence can inform not just duties of care, but also standards of international criminal law, as discussed by Dam-de Jong (Chapter 7). It is a substantive concept that can fill the gaps in open norms with regard to corporate behavior.
56 See Chapter 11.
57 As noted by Michaels, "functionalism" in law, especially in comparative law, has a plethora of meanings that are often confused, but the interpretation here is that of instrumentalism as a functionalist approach. See Ralph Michaels, 'The Functional Method of Comparative Law', in Mathias Reimann and Reinhard Zimmerman (eds.), *The Oxford Handbook of Comparative Law* (Oxford University Press 2007), 351–2.
58 See Chapter 3.
59 See Chapter 13.
60 At the time of writing, it was still unclear what Dutch agency would supervise compliance with the EU Conflict Minerals Regulation (Regulation (EU) 2017/821 of the European Parliament and of the Council of 17 May 2017 laying down supply chain due diligence obligations for Union importers of tin, tantalum and tungsten, their ores, and gold originating from conflict-affected and high-risk areas [2017] OJ L 130/1), which requires that EU importers of a number of minerals comply with due diligence obligations.
61 Plato, 'The Republic', in Paul Shorey (ed. and trans.), *Plato: The Republic: Books I–V* (Loeb Classical Library Putnam 1930) Book III, XII, 403E, 265. The Roman author Juvenal is credited with posing the question 'who is guarding the guardians?' for the first time. Juvenal, *Satire* 6: 346–8 ('quis custodiet ipsos custodes?').
62 Cf. Rudolf von Jhering, 'Im Juristische Begriffshimmel', in *Scherz und Ernst in der Jurisprudenz* (Breitkopf und Härtel 1912) 245; translated in English as 'In the Heaven for Legal Concepts: A Fantasy', (1985) 58 *Temple Law Quarterly* 799.
63 Cf. Ivo Giesen, 'The Use and Incorporation of Extralegal Insights in Legal Reasoning', (2015) 11(1) *Utrecht Law Review* 1, 15–6.
64 Cf. Thomas Sorell, *Scientism: Philosophy and the Infatuation with Science* (Routledge 1994).

Bibliography

Alvarez Rubio JJ and Yiannibas K (eds.), *Human Rights in Business: Removal of Barriers to Access to Justice in the European Union* (Routledge 2017).

Bovens M, 'Two Concepts of Accountability: Accountability as a Virtue and as a Mechanism', (2010) 33 *West European Politics* 946.

Chambers R and Yilmaz-Vastardis A, 'The New EU Rules on Non-Financial Reporting: Potential Impacts on Access to Remedy?', (2016) 10 *Human Rights and International Legal Discourse* 1.

Curtin D and Nollkaemper A, 'Conceptualising Accountability in International and European Law', (2006) *Netherlands Yearbook of International Law* 3.

Enneking L, 'Transnational Human Rights and Environmental Litigation: A Study of Case Law Relating to Shell in Nigeria', in Isabel Feichtner et al. (eds.), *Human Rights in the Extractive Industries: Transparency, Participation, Resistance* (Springer 2019).

Giesen I, 'The Use and Incorporation of Extralegal Insights in Legal Reasoning', (2015) 11(1) *Utrecht Law Review* 1.

Michaels R, 'The Functional Method of Comparative Law', in Mathias Reimann and Reinhard Zimmerman (eds.), *The Oxford Handbook of Comparative Law* (Oxford University Press 2007).

Ochoa C and Keenan P, 'Regulating Information Flows, Regulating Conflict: An Analysis of United States Conflict Minerals Legislation', (2011) 3(1) *Goettingen Journal of International Law* 129.

OECD, *OECD Guidelines for Multinational Enterprises* (OECD Publishing 2011).

Ratner S, 'Corporations and Human Rights: A Theory of Legal Responsibility', (2001) 111 *The Yale Law Journal* 443.

Roorda L and Ryngaert C, 'Business and Human Rights Litigation in Europe and Canada: The Promises of Forum of Necessity Jurisdiction', (2016) 80(4) *Rabels Zeitschrift für internationales und ausländisches Privatrecht* 783.

Sorell T, *Scientism: Philosophy and the Infatuation with Science* (Routledge 1994).

van Baar A, 'Conflict, Minerals and Reporting Obligations for Multinational Business Operations (what Did Dodd-Frank 1502 Do?)', Conference Paper UCALL Conference 2017, Utrecht, the Netherlands: Accountability and International Business Operations: Providing Justice for Corporate Violations of Human Rights, Labor and Environmental Standards.

von Jhering R, 'Im Juristische Begriffshimmel', in *Scherz und Ernst in der Jurisprudenz* (Breitkopf und Härtel 1912) 245; translated in English as 'In the Heaven for Legal Concepts: A Fantasy', (1985) 58 *Temple Law Quarterly* 799.

Wenar L, *Blood Oil: Tyrants, Violence and the Rules that Run the World* (Oxford University Press 2016).

Index

Page numbers in bold indicate tables on the corresponding pages.

Printed in the United States
by Baker & Taylor Publisher Services